Contents

Sunshine Cobb salad 18
Low-sugar granola.. 18
Chicken & basil meatballs 19
Buckwheat & spring lamb stew 20
Barley & bulgur chopped herb salad.. 21
Cajun prawn pizza 22
Silvana's Mediterranean & basil pasta 23
Apple crunch 24
Egg & avocado open sandwich 24
Simple spicy fish stew.. 25
Harissa chicken & squash traybake 26
Roast chicken with lemon & rosemary roots 26
Home-style pork curry with cauliflower rice 27
Porcini loaf with summer greens 28
Feta frittatas with carrot & celery salad 30
Spicy Moroccan eggs 31
Pitta pocket... 32
Chicken fattoush... 32
Spinach soup 33
One-pot chicken with quinoa 34
Healthy pancakes.. 35
Healthy tikka masala 35
Healthy shakshuka 36
Healthy pasta primavera 37
Healthy porridge bowl.. 38
Healthy bolognese 39

Healthy Easter bunny pancakes	39
Healthy chicken katsu curry	41
Healthy Easter lamb	43
Healthy Halloween stuffed peppers	44
Healthy veg patch hummus	45
Healthy roast turkey crown	45
Healthy Halloween nachos	47
Healthy Halloween pizzas	48
Healthy Easter boiled eggs	49
Healthy gravy	50
Healthy full English	50
Healthy chilli	51
Healthy stuffing balls	52
Healthy pumpkin pancakes	53
Healthy Turkish meatloaf	54
Healthy egg & chips	55
Healthy banana bread	56
Healthy spiced rice pudding	57
Healthy tuna lettuce wraps	57
Healthy carrot soup	58
Healthy chocolate milk	59
Healthy turkey meatballs	59
Healthy banana & peanut butter ice cream	60
Hearty lentil one pot	61
Ham & potato hash with baked beans & healthy 'fried' eggs	62
Healthier veggie carbonara	63
Healthy fish & chips with tartare sauce	64
Hearty pasta soup	65

Healthy salad Niçoise	65
Healthy coleslaw	66
Saag aloo	67
Chinese chicken curry	68
Chicken jalfrezi	68
Ratatouille	70
Spiced lentil & butternut squash soup	72
Celery soup	73
Rosemary balsamic lamb with vegetable mash	73
Chicken madras	74
Healthier chicken balti	75
Double bean & roasted pepper chilli	77
Curried cod	78
Easy Singapore noodles	78
Curried chicken pie	79
Nutty chicken satay strips	80
Lentil salad with tahini dressing	81
Healthier flapjacks	82
Broccoli pesto & pancetta pasta	83
Meatball & tomato soup	83
Sweetcorn fritters with eggs & black bean salsa	84
Mexican penne with avocado	85
Tarragon roast chicken with summer greens	86
Pasta arrabbiata with aubergine	87
Roasted carrots	88
Chipotle chicken & slaw	89
Orzo & tomato soup	89
Corn & split pea chowder	90

- Breakfast egg wraps 91
- Chunky Bolognese soup with penne 92
- Sausage & white bean casserole 93
- Veggie yaki udon 94
- Lemony prawn & courgette tagliatelle 94
- Prawn & harissa spaghetti 95
- Smoky spiced veggie rice 96
- Chorizo, orzo & sweetcorn summer stew 97
- Moroccan chickpea, squash & cavolo nero stew 98
- Bombay potato frittata 99
- Prawn & salmon burgers with spicy mayo 100
- Spicy fish stew 101
- Black bean tortilla with salsa 102
- Peanut butter & date oat pots 103
- Spiced halloumi & pineapple burger with zingy slaw 104
- Winter warmer hearty risotto 105
- Spinach kedgeree with spiced salmon 106
- Roasted roots & sage soup 107
- Coconut & squash dhansak 108
- Curried spinach, eggs & chickpeas 109
- Healthier Victoria sandwich 110
- Vegan ragu 111
- **Brown butter chargrilled prawns** 112
- **Spiced pork chop schnitzel with pear and fennel slaw** 113
- **Pepper salmon escalopes with dill pesto** 113
- **Healthy pumpkin, lentil and mushroom curry** 114
- **Roasted alla Norma with rigatoni** 115
- **Christine Manfield's** 116

Spelt margherita pizza 117

Matt Moran's grilled Hervey Bay scallops with togarashi & chilli syrup dressing 118

Beetroot, fennel and rhubarb salad 119

Pear and coconut crumble with double-thick cream 119

Spiced crunchy salad 120

Kelp noodles with poached chicken and miso 121

Matt Moran's grilled sardines on toast 122

Healthy broccolini, pea and asparagus breakfast gratin 123

Vegan quinoa bircher with almond milk 124

Baked ocean trout with smashed cucumber salad 125

Herb-baked blue-eye on saffron and tomato potatoes 126

Roasted fennel and pine nut polpette 126

Couscous with chickpeas, dried apricots, pistachios and marinated feta 128

Chicken kiev with cabbage slaw 128

Chicken broth with kale, quinoa and preserved lemon 130

Seared tuna bruschetta 131

Pan-fried whiting with broccoli pesto 132

Farro, lentil and goat's cheese salad with avocado dressing 132

Lasagne for spring 133

Steak, corn and red bean salad 135

Moroccan lamb with chickpea salad 135

Cinnamon porridge 136

Blackened salmon with papaya mojo 137

Grilled chicken salad with parmesan dressing 138

Flat-roast chicken with lemon and herbs 139

Herb-roasted turkey breast 140

Spicy kingfish with caramelised onion couscous 141

Cajun chicken with avocado, lime and chilli salsa 142

Indian-spiced chicken with cucumber salad 142

Chargrilled swordfish with grape, almond & barley salad 143

Roasted sweet potatoes with chilli and seeds 144

Barbecued cuttlefish, fennel and soppressata salad 145

Ocean perch with broad bean and cucumber salad 146

Roast chicken panzanella 147

Sticky pork and crispy noodle salad 147

Double mint potato salad 148

Matt Moran's grilled avocado with radish, cucumber and herb salad 149

Bean, pea and lentil salad 150

Mint, bean and feta salad 150

Radish and tuna salad with wasabi dressing 151

Sticky barbecued prawn salad 152

New nicoise salad 153

Barbecue beef salad with beer vinaigrette 154

BAKED CHICKEN WITH PEACHES 155

SUMMER CORN SALAD 156

HONEY WHEAT BREAD 156

CREAMY ITALIAN WHITE BEAN SOUP 157

TURKEY CARCASS SOUPS 158

LOWER FAT BANANA BREAD 159

SLOW COOKER CHICKEN CREOLE 160

GRANOLA BARS 161

OATMEAL WHOLE WHEAT QUICK BREAD 162

OAT APPLESAUCE MUFFINS 162

FRESH TOMATO MARINARA SAUCE 163

CHICKEN BROCCOLI CA - UNIENG'S STYLE 164

SPICY TUNA FISH CAKES 165

TEXAS CAVIAR	166
FRESH STRAWBERRY PIE	166
MANDARIN CHICKEN PASTA SALAD	167
SPINACH LENTIL SOUP	168
RASPBERRY SAUCE	169
SPICY BLACK BEAN CAKES	170
ALFREDO LIGHT	171
AUNT JEWEL'S CHICKEN DRESSING CASSEROLE	172
BLACK BEAN CHILI	172
DELICIOUS APPLE SAUCE	173
OVEN FRIES	174
SWISS CHARD WITH GARBANZO BEANS AND FRESH TOMATOES	174
DEVIL'S STEAK SAUCE	175
BUTTERNUT SQUASH FRIES	176
CAJUN PASTA FRESCA	176
SUPERFAST ASPARAGUS	177
RANCH CRISPY CHICKEN	177
ROSEMARY TURKEY MEATLOAF	178
QUINOA WITH CHICKPEAS AND TOMATOES	179
PENNE WITH SHRIMP	179
'CHINESE BUFFET' GREEN BEANS	180
HONEY WHEAT BREAD	181
JAMIE'S SWEET AND EASY CORN ON THE COB	181
CAJUN STYLE BAKED SWEET POTATO	182
SLOW COOKER OATS	182
ROASTED ASPARAGUS AND MUSHROOMS	183
BAKED FRENCH FRIES	184
SPICED SLOW COOKER APPLESAUCE	184

LEMON CHICKEN ORZO SOUP 185

Asian eggs 186

Leek, almond and bruised tomato galette 187

Sesame butter radishes with lemon 188

Egg noodles with Sichuan pepper chicken and cucumber 188

Quick chicken roast 190

Eggplant kasundi warm rice salad 190

Taleggio sourdough salad with simple salsa verde 192

Prawn and spinach angel hair pasta with prawn oil 193

Orecchiette with hot-smoked salmon, peas and beurre blanc sauce 194

Valli Little's Cajun ocean trout with pineapple salad 195

Chopped chilli chicken stir fry 196

Minty lamb with beetroot and charred broccoli 197

Sardines stuffed with kale, pine nuts and raisins 198

Raw pad Thai 199

Seared tuna with Fijian-Style potato curry 200

Thai red fish curry with noodles 201

Char siu beef with broccolini 202

Broad bean and pecorino bruschetta 203

Mixed mushroom noodles with tea-marbled eggs 204

Valli Little's rolled rice noodles with crispy chilli tofu 205

Quick and easy chicken cacciatore 206

Garlic and spinach gnocchi with lemon and pecorino 207

Fish tacos with avocado salsa 208

Chicken quesadillas with chipotle relish and mango salsa 209

Zucchini carpaccio 210

Shannon Bennett's Welsh rarebit 210

Rigatoni with a spicy sausage sauce 211

Mexican eggs with potato hash ... 212

Ricotta dumplings with orecchiette, peas and prosciutto ... 213

Miso salmon with eggplant ... 214

Fish bread with quick pickled vegetables ... 215

Thai fish and pumpkin soup ... 216

Satay beef fillet with watercress and cucumber ... 217

Sri Lankan salmon curry ... 218

Pumpkin and goat's cheese bruschetta with sage burnt butter ... 219

Harissa lamb with roast carrots and quinoa pilaf ... 220

Cheat's blinis with jamon and figs ... 221

Hawker-style stir-fried noodles ... 221

Spiced coconut eggs ... 222

Korean barbecue chicken fried rice ... 223

Quick tomato and salami pizzas ... 224

Black pepper prawns ... 225

Gwyneth Paltrow's seared scallops with watercress and asparagus ... 226

Gwyneth Paltrow's Singapore rice noodles ... 227

Floating market fish soup ... 228

Korean fish stir-fry ... 229

Moroccan swordfish ... 230

Kingfish skewers with chargrilled tomatoes and chillies ... 230

Baked ocean trout with tahini and herb salad ... 231

Healthy turmeric and coconut fish curry ... 232

Cured kingfish with pickled baby beetroot ... 233

Quick filo fish pie ... 234

15-minute jacket sweet potatoes ... 235

Chermoula kingfish with moroccan beans ... 235

Fish with yoghurt tartar sauce and grain salad ... 237

Chargrilled swordfish with grape, almond & barley salad 238

Whole baked snapper with ginger and chilli 239

Spiced pork chop schnitzel with pear and fennel slaw 239

Aubergine & chickpea stew 240

Lamb jalfrezi with cumin rice 241

Chicken & sweetcorn tacos 242

Red pepper, squash & harissa soup 244

Roast chicken traybake 244

Lemon dressed salmon with leek & broad bean purée 245

Healthier potato salad 246

Cabbage soup 247

Red cabbage, cauliflower & coconut dhal 248

Swedish meatballs 249

Linguine with avocado, tomato & lime 250

Blackberry & apple oat bake 250

Salmon pesto traybake with baby roast potatoes 251

Easy butter chicken 252

Curried chicken & new potato traybake 253

Italian borlotti bean, pumpkin & farro soup 254

Chana masala with pomegranate raita 255

Leek, pea & watercress soup 256

Saucy bean baked eggs 257

Crunchy oat clusters with peach & yogurt 257

Overnight oats 258

Moroccan chicken with fennel & olives 259

Beetroot, cumin & coriander soup with yogurt and hazelnut dukkah 260

Caesar pitta 261

Peanut butter overnight oats 261

Herb & ricotta chicken with mushroom rice..262

Indian chickpeas with poached eggs 263

Ricotta, broccoli, & new potato frittata...264

Steaks with goulash sauce & sweet potato fries 265

Hake & seafood cataplana..266

Paneer jalfrezi with cumin rice 267

Sweet & sour tofu...268

Herby fish fingers with Chinese-style rice...269

Winter vegetable & lentil soup 270

Spiced salmon & tomato traybake 270

Courgette, leek & goat's cheese soup 271

Salmon salad with sesame dressing 272

Cod with cucumber, avocado & mango salsa salad...273

Butternut biryani with cucumber raita 274

Smoky chickpeas on toast 275

Chicken & lemon skewers 275

Greek-style roast fish 276

Chickpea tagine soup 277

Toddler recipe: Sweetcorn & spinach fritters 278

Cumin roast veg with tahini dressing...279

Cumin roast veg with tahini dressing...280

Leek, kale & potato soup topped with shoestring fries..281

Miso salmon with ginger noodles 282

Slow-cooker Bolognese 283

Butter bean, mushroom & bacon pot pies..284

Spaghetti puttanesca with red beans & spinach 285

Raspberry chia jam...285

Asparagus & lemon spaghetti with peas 286

Mexican-style bean soup with shredded chicken & lime 287

Quick chicken hummus bowl 288

Swedish meatballs with beetroot & apple salad 288

Vegan pumpkin soup 290

Mint & basil griddled peach salad 291

Punchy spaghetti 291

Burrito bowl with chipotle black beans 292

Mushroom hash with poached eggs 293

Hearty lamb stew 294

Avocado & black bean eggs 295

Ginger chicken & green bean noodles 295

Goan-style vegetable curry with kitchari 296

Chicken, sweet potato & pea curry 298

Feta & kale loaded sweet potato 298

Hearty lamb & barley soup 299

Cocoa & cherry oat bake 300

Easy vegan tacos 300

Smashed chicken with corn slaw 302

Pork souvlaki with Greek salad & rice 303

Sausage, mustard & apple hash 304

Mushroom & potato soup 305

Quinoa salad with avocado mayo 305

Guacamole & mango salad with black beans 306

Egyptian courgettes with dukkah sprinkle 307

Spanish chicken stew 308

Mexican beans & avocado on toast 308

Caponata bake 309

Prosciutto, kale & butter bean stew 310

Chicken bhuna 311

Veggie tahini lentils 312

Green minestrone with tortellini 313

Khatti dhal 313

Roasted new potato, kale & feta salad with avocado..314

Baked banana porridge...315

All-in–one chicken with wilted spinach..316

Miso beansprout rolls 317

Leek & butter bean soup with crispy kale & bacon..318

Herb omelette with fried tomatoes..319

Curried mango & chickpea pot 319

Triangular bread thins 320

Spiced chicken, spinach & sweet potato stew...321

Leek, tomato & barley risotto with pan-cooked cod..322

Miso mushroom & tofu noodle soup 323

Green chowder with prawns..323

Little spicy veggie pies..324

Sesame salmon, purple sprouting broccoli & sweet potato mash..325

Slow cooker pork fillet with apples 326

Easy chicken stew 327

One-pan egg & veg brunch 328

Sesame chicken & prawn skewers 329

Clementine & vanilla porridge with citrus salsa...329

Oat pancakes 330

Mushroom brunch 331

Cumin-spiced halloumi with corn & tomato slaw 332

Carrot & ginger soup...333

Veggie okonomiyaki 334

Tuna, avocado & quinoa salad 335

Chilli chicken & peanut pies 335

Curried chicken & baked dhal 337

Broccoli & pea soup with minty ricotta 337

Caponata with cheesy polenta 338

Cauliflower & squash fritters with mint & feta dip 339

Lighter chicken cacciatore 340

Red cabbage with apples 341

Indian bean, broccoli & carrot salad 342

Wild salmon veggie bowl 343

Grilled salmon tacos with chipotle lime yogurt 343

Smoked paprika prawn skewers 344

The ultimate makeover: Moussaka 345

Cherry tomato, kale, ricotta & pesto pasta 347

Cod with bacon, lettuce & peas 348

Creamy veggie korma 348

Soy salmon & broccoli traybake 350

BBQ chicken pizza 350

Prawn & lime noodles 352

Simple roast radishes 352

Moroccan tomato & chickpea soup with couscous 353

Salmon noodle soup 354

Quinoa stew with squash, prunes & pomegranate 354

Greek salad omelette 355

Pan-fried scallops with lime & coriander 356

Baked potato with cheesy mince 357

Pea & mint soup with crispy prosciutto strips 357

Red lentil & sweet potato pâté 358

Lemon cod with basil bean mash 359

Spicy cauliflower pilau 360

Indian chickpea & vegetable soup 360

Mixed bean goulash 361

Raid-the-cupboard tuna sweetcorn cakes 361

Oven-baked fish & chips 362

Kale & salmon kedgeree 363

Lemony prawn & chorizo rice pot 364

Lemon spaghetti with tuna & broccoli 364

Pineapple, beef & ginger stir-fry 365

Curry coconut fish parcels 366

Miso chicken & rice soup 367

Roasted carrot, spelt, fennel & blood orange salad 367

Sweet potato salad 368

Superhealthy Singapore noodles 369

Blueberry & lemon pancakes 370

Moroccan lamb with apricots, almonds & mint 371

Charred spring onions 372

Chipotle black bean soup with lime-pickled onions 372

Courgette & quinoa-stuffed peppers 373

Tangy trout 374

Vegetable & bean chilli 374

Pea hummus 375

Beef & bean chilli bowl with chipotle yogurt 376

Courgette tortilla with toppings 377

Spinach & sweet potato tortilla 377

Stuffed butternut squash with quinoa 378

Quinoa, pea & avocado salad 379

Chicken, edamame & ginger pilaf	380
Tomatillo salsa	381
Barley couscous & prawn tabbouleh	381
Turkey tortilla pie	382
Feta-stuffed mushrooms with mustard slaw	383
Roast chicken thighs with brown rice & salsa verde	384
Herby lamb fillet with caponata	385
Potato salad with anchovy & quail's eggs	386
Chicken with mustard lentils	386
Lighter lemon drizzle cake	387
Lemon pollock with sweet potato chips & broccoli mash	389
Chinese poached chicken & rice	390
Masala chicken pie	391
Thai red duck with sticky pineapple rice	392
Zesty salmon with roasted beets & spinach	393
Masala omelette muffins	394
Easy ratatouille	395
Lemon & garlic roast chicken with charred broccoli & sweet potato mash	396
Tropical overnight oats	397
Summer vegetable curry	398
Prawn & tomato stew with gremolata topping	398
Tomato & courgette stew	399
Turkey & coriander burgers with guacamole	400
Courgette & couscous salad with tahini dressing	401
Quinoa, squash & broccoli salad	401
Wild garlic & nettle soup	402
Pastry-less pork pie	403
Courgette & tomato soup	404

Instant berry banana slush ... 405

Sesame chicken salad ... 405

Fruit & nut breakfast bowl ... 406

Strawberry & banana almond smoothie ... 407

Sticky baked meatloaf with avocado & black bean salsa ... 407

Raspberry coconut porridge ... 409

Speedy soy spinach ... 409

Mumsy's vegetable soup ... 410

Asparagus & lentil salad with cranberries & crumbled feta ... 411

Spicy mushroom & broccoli noodles ... 411

Roasted summer vegetable casserole ... 412

Beetroot & lentil tabbouleh ... 413

Sweet mustard potato salad ... 414

Burnt leeks on toast with romesco ... 414

Corn cups with prawns, mango & chillies ... 415

Poor man's vongole rosso ... 416

Butternut squash & sage soup ... 417

Sushi burrito ... 418

Seared tuna & anchovy runner beans ... 419

Green breakfast smoothie ... 419

Courgette, pea & pesto soup ... 420

Baba ganoush & crudités ... 421

Smoky paprika seafood rice ... 422

Three-grain porridge ... 423

Sardines & tomatoes on toast ... 423

Sunshine Cobb salad

Prep: 20 mins **Cook:** 10 mins

Serves 2

Ingredients

- 1 large egg
- 400g can black beans , drained and rinsed
- 1 red, orange or yellow pepper , deseeded and diced
- thumb-sized piece cucumber , diced
- 8 cherry tomatoes , halved
- 198g can sweetcorn , drained
- 150g pack cooked prawns
- handful of watercress

For the chilli-lime dressing

- 1 red chilli , deseeded and finely chopped
- zest and juice 1 lime
- 1 tbsp white wine vinegar
- 2 tsp clear honey
- 1 tbsp extra virgin olive oil or rapeseed oil

Method

STEP 1

Bring a small pan of water to the boil. Add the egg and cook for 8 mins. Drain, then run under cold water to cool.

STEP 2

To assemble the salad, arrange the remaining ingredients in 2 containers. When the egg is cool, peel and quarter it and divide between the containers too.

STEP 3

Mix together the dressing ingredients in a small bowl and transfer to 2 mini jars or containers to take with the salads to work. Dress and toss together just before eating.

Low-sugar granola

Prep: 10 mins **Cook:** 30 mins - 35 mins

Makes 500g

Ingredients

- 200g rolled oats
- 150g bag mixed nuts
- 150g mixed seeds
- 1 orange , zested
- 2 tsp mixed spice
- 2 tsp cinnamon
- 2 tbsp cold pressed rapeseed oil
- 1½ tbsp maple syrup

Method

STEP 1

Heat oven to 160C/140C fan/gas 4. Mix all the ingredients in a bowl with a pinch of salt, then spread out on a baking tray.

STEP 2

Roast for 30-35 mins until golden, pulling the tray out of the oven twice while cooking to give everything a good stir – this will help the granola toast evenly. Leave to cool. Will keep in an airtight container for one month.

Chicken & basil meatballs

Prep: 20 mins **Cook:** 20 mins

24 (12 of each flavour)

Ingredients

- 1 shallot
- 250g chicken breast
- 25g seeded bread

For the Thai chicken chicory bites

- 12 chicory leaves , red or green
- sriracha or Thai sweet chilli sauce, to serve

For the roasted pepper sticks

- 2 roasted red peppers , cut into 24 chunks
- 24 fresh basil leaves

- ⅓ pack fresh basil leaves
- 1 clove garlic
- rapeseed oil , for frying

- 1 spring onion , cut lengthways and shredded into fine strips
- 25g salted peanuts , finely chopped

You will need

- 24 cocktail sticks

Method

STEP 1

Put the shallot into a food processor and pulse briefly to chop. Add all the remaining meatball ingredients, except for the oil, and blitz to make a soft purée. Shape into 24 mini meatballs with wet hands.

STEP 2

Heat a drizzle of the oil in a large non-stick frying pan. Add half the meatballs and fry for 5 mins, moving them around the pan to evenly colour them. Remove from the pan and cook the remaining meatballs. Keep chilled until ready to serve. Will keep in the fridge for up to one day.

STEP 3

To serve, warm the meatballs, if you like, at 180C/160C fan/gas 4 for 10 mins, then arrange half in the chicory leaves, top with some chilli sauce and sprinkle with the onion and peanuts.

STEP 4

For the pepper version, thread the meatballs onto 12 cocktail sticks with the 2 chunks of pepper and 2 fresh basil leaves either side.

Buckwheat & spring lamb stew

Prep: 25 mins **Cook:** 3 hrs and 15 mins

Serves 4

Ingredients

- 2 tbsp cold pressed rapeseed oil
- 400g stewing lamb , excess fat trimmed
- 1 onion , finely chopped
- 3 leeks , cut into 1 cm rounds
- 250g baby chantenay carrots
- 3 garlic cloves , finely chopped
- 2 tbsp plain flour
- 3 lemon thyme sprigs

- 1 bay leaf
- 150ml white wine
- 600ml low-salt veg stock
- 80g buckwheat
- 1 large unwaxed lemon, zested
- 1 small bunch parsley, leaves finely chopped

Method

STEP 1

Heat 1 tbsp oil in a casserole dish over a high heat. Fry the lamb in two batches for 5 mins each until evenly browned. Remove from the pan and set aside.

STEP 2

Heat the remaining oil in the same pan and fry the onion and leeks over a medium heat for 7 mins. Tip in the carrots and two-thirds of the garlic, then fry for 1 min. Stir the meat into the pan along with the plain flour and fry for another 2 mins. Add the thyme and bay leaf, then the wine and bring to a bubble before pouring in the stock. Mix everything together well. Put a lid on the pan and cook over a low heat for 2½-3 hrs or until the meat is tender. Add the buckwheat for the last 20 mins of cooking time.

STEP 3

Mix the remaining garlic with the lemon zest and parsley. Serve the stew in bowls, scattered with the parsley and lemon mixture.

Barley & bulgur chopped herb salad

Prep: 20 mins **Cook:** 25 mins plus 1 hr chilling

Serves 6

Ingredients

- 150g pearl barley
- 150g bulgur wheat
- 3 tbsp olive oil
- 3 white onions, halved and sliced
- 4 garlic cloves, crushed
- ¼ tsp ground cloves
- small bunch of parsley
- small bunch of dill
- small bunch of mint
- ½ cucumber, finely chopped
- 4 tomatoes, finely chopped
- 2 lemons, juiced

Method

STEP 1

Bring a pan of water to the boil and add the barley. Cover and cook for 25 mins, or until tender. Meanwhile, pour boiling water over the bulgur wheat to just cover, and set aside.

STEP 2

Heat 2 tbsp oil in a large frying pan and add the onions. Cook for 20-25 mins, stirring regularly, until golden and caramelised. Stir in the garlic and cloves for 30 secs.

STEP 3

Drain the barley and bulgur well and tip into a bowl. Add the remaining oil, the onions, and plenty of seasoning. Mix well and chill until you're ready to serve (up to 24 hrs ahead is fine, or at least 1 hr). Remove from the fridge 30 mins before you want to serve.

STEP 4

Toss through the remaining ingredients and serve on a large platter or in a bowl.

Cajun prawn pizza

Prep: 10 mins **Cook:** 20 mins

Serves 2

Ingredients

For the base

- 200g wholemeal flour , plus a little for kneading if necessary
- 1 tsp instant yeast
- pinch of salt
- 2 tsp rapeseed oil , plus extra greasing

For the topping

- 1 tbsp rapeseed oil , plus extra for greasing
- 2 large sticks celery , finely chopped
- 1 yellow pepper or green pepper, de-seeded and diced
- 225g can chopped tomatoes
- 1 tsp smoked paprika
- 165g pack raw, peeled king prawns
- 2-3 tbsp chopped coriander
- ½ - 1 tsp Cajun spice mix
- 2 handfuls rocket , optional

Method

STEP 1

Heat oven to 220C/200C fan/gas 7. Tip the flour into a mixer with a dough hook, or a bowl. Add the yeast, salt, oil and 150ml warm water then mix well to a soft dough. Knead in the food mixer for about 5 mins, but if making this by hand, tip onto a work surface and knead for about 10 mins. The dough is sticky, but try not to add too much extra flour. Leave in the bowl and cover with a tea towel while you make the topping. There is no need to prove the dough for a specific time, just let it sit while you get on with the next step.

STEP 2

For the topping: heat the oil in a non-stick pan or wok. Add the celery and pepper and fry for 8 mins, stirring frequently, until softened. Tip in the tomatoes and paprika then cook for 2 mins more. Set aside to cool a little then stir in the prawns.

STEP 3

With an oiled knife, cut the dough in half and shape each piece into a 25cm round with lightly oiled hands on oiled baking sheets. Don't knead the dough first otherwise it will be too elastic and will shrink back. Spread each with half of the tomato and prawn mix then scatter with the coriander and sprinkle with the Cajun spice. Bake for 10 mins until golden. Serve with a green salad.

Silvana's Mediterranean & basil pasta

Prep: 5 mins **Cook:** 30 mins

Serves 4

Ingredients

- 2 red peppers , seeded and cut into chunks
- 2 red onions , cut into wedges
- 2 mild red chillies , seeded and diced
- 3 garlic cloves , coarsley chopped
- 1 tsp golden caster sugar
- 2 tbsp olive oil , plus extra to serve
- 1kg small ripe tomatoes , quartered
- 350g dried pasta
- a handful of fresh basil leaves and 2 tbsp grated parmesan (or vegetarian alternative), to serve

Method

STEP 1

To roast the veg, preheat the oven to 200C/gas 6/fan 180C. Scatter the peppers, red onions, chillies and garlic in a large roasting tin. Sprinkle with sugar, drizzle over the oil and season well with salt and pepper. Roast for 15 minutes, toss in the tomatoes and roast for another 15 minutes until everything is starting to soften and look golden.

STEP 2

While the vegetables are roasting, cook the pasta in a large pan of salted boiling water according to packet instructions, until tender but still with a bit of bite. Drain well.

STEP 3

Remove the vegetables from the oven, tip in the pasta and toss lightly together. Tear the basil leaves on top and sprinkle with Parmesan to serve. If you have any leftovers it makes a great cold pasta salad – just moisten with extra olive oil if needed.

Apple crunch

Prep: 1 min **Serves 1**

Ingredients

- 1 small eating apple
- 1 tbsp organic unsalted crunchy peanut butter

Method

- Cut the apple in half and spread with the peanut butter.

Egg & avocado open sandwich

Prep: 10 mins **Cook:** 10 mins

Serves 1

Ingredients

- 2 medium eggs
- 1 ripe avocado

- juice 1 lime
- 2 slices rye bread
- 2 tsp hot chilli sauce - we used sriracha
- handful cress , to serve

Method

STEP 1

Bring a medium pan of water to the boil. Add the eggs and cook for 8-9 mins until hard-boiled. Meanwhile, halve the avocado and scoop the flesh into a bowl. Add the lime juice, season well and mash with a fork.

STEP 2

When the eggs are cooked, run under cold water for 2 mins before removing the shells. Spread the avocado on the rye bread. Slice the eggs into thin rounds and place on top of the avocado. Drizzle some chilli sauce over the eggs, scatter the cress on top and add a good grinding of black pepper.

Simple spicy fish stew

Prep: 5 mins **Cook:** 15 mins

Serves 4

Ingredients

- 1 tbsp olive oil
- 2 garlic cloves , crushed
- 1 tsp ground cumin
- ½ tsp paprika
- 200g can chopped tomato
- 1 red pepper , deseeded, cut into chunks
- 450g white fish fillets, cut into chunks
- handful coriander , roughly chopped
- 1 lemon , cut into wedges

Method

STEP 1

Heat oil in a saucepan. Tip in the garlic, cumin and paprika and cook for 1 min. Add 100ml water and the tomatoes. Bring to the boil, then turn down the heat. Add the pepper, simmer for 5 mins. Add the fish, simmer for 5 mins. Serve with coriander and a wedge of lemon.

Harissa chicken & squash traybake

Prep: 15 mins **Cook:** 35 mins

Serves 4

Ingredients

- 3 tbsp harissa
- ½ x 500g pot low-fat natural yogurt
- 4 skinless chicken breasts, slashed
- 1 small butternut squash, peeled, deseeded and cut into long wedges
- 2 red onions, cut into wedges

Method

STEP 1

Heat oven to 200C/180C fan/ gas 6. Mix 2 tbsp of the harissa with 3 tbsp of the yogurt. Rub all over the chicken breasts and set aside to marinate while you start the veg.

STEP 2

Toss the squash and the onions with remaining harissa, mixed with 2 tbsp oil (sunflower, vegetable or olive is fine), and some seasoning in a large roasting tin. Roast for 10 mins.

STEP 3

Remove veg from the oven, add the chicken to the tin, then roast for a further 20-25 mins until the chicken and veg are cooked through. Serve with the remaining yogurt on the side, and a big bowl of couscous or rice.

Roast chicken with lemon & rosemary roots

Prep: 20 mins **Cook:** 1 hr and 30 mins

Serves 4

Ingredients

- 4 large carrots (about 400g), cut into big chunks
- 1 celeriac (about 575g peeled weight), cut into roastie-sized chunks
- 1 large swede (550g unpeeled), quartered and cut into thick slices
- 2 red onions , cut into wedges
- 1 garlic bulb

- 2 tbsp rapeseed oil
- 2 tsp sprigs rosemary leaves and woody stalks separated
- 1 lemon
- 1 medium chicken (about 1.4kg)
- 2 x 200g bags curly kale

Method

STEP 1

Heat oven to 200C/180C fan/gas 6. Tip the carrots, celeriac, swede, onions and garlic into a large roasting tin with the oil, rosemary leaves and a grinding of black pepper. Toss well and roast for 5-10 mins while you get the chicken ready.

STEP 2

Grate the zest and squeeze the juice from the lemon, set aside and put the lemon shells and the woody stalks from the rosemary inside the chicken. Stir the veg, scatter over the lemon zest and drizzle over the juice, then sit the chicken on top of the veg and roast for 1-1 1/4 hrs until the chicken is tender but still moist. Take the chicken from the oven and leave to rest for 10 mins. Keep the veg in the oven and steam one of the bags of kale (if you're eating this over two days for the Healthy Diet Plan, otherwise steam both).

STEP 3

Squeeze the garlic from the skins, carve the chicken and serve with the vegetables.

Home-style pork curry with cauliflower rice

Prep: 15 mins **Cook:** 1 hr

Serves 4

Ingredients

For the curry

- 425g lean pork fillet (tenderloin), cubed
- 2 tbsp Madras curry powder
- 2 tbsp red wine vinegar
- 1 tbsp rapeseed oil
- 1 large onion , finely chopped
- 2 tbsp finely shredded ginger

- 1 tsp fennel, toasted in a pan then crushed
- 1 tsp cumin, toasted in a pan then crushed

For the cauliflower rice

- 1 medium cauliflower
- good handful coriander, chopped

- 400g can chopped tomatoes
- 2 tbsp red lentils
- 350g pack baby aubergine, quartered
- 1 reduced-salt vegetable stock cube

- cumin seeds, toasted (optional)

Method

STEP 1

Tip the pork into a bowl and stir in the curry powder and vinegar. Set aside. Heat the oil in a heavy-based pan and fry the onion and ginger for 10 mins, stirring frequently, until golden. Tip in the pork mixture and fry for a few mins more. Remove the pork and set aside. Stir in the toasted spices, then tip in the tomatoes, lentils and aubergine, and crumble in the stock cube. Cover and leave to simmer for 40 mins, stirring frequently, until the aubergine is almost cooked. If it starts to look dry, add a splash of water. Return the pork to the pan and cook for a further 10-20 mins until the pork is cooked and tender.

STEP 2

Just before serving, cut the hard core and stalks from the cauliflower and pulse the rest in a food processor to make grains the size of rice. Tip into a heatproof bowl, cover with cling film, then pierce and microwave for 7 mins on High – there is no need to add any water. Stir in the coriander and serve with the curry. For spicier rice, add some toasted cumin seeds.

Porcini loaf with summer greens

Prep: 20 mins **Cook:** 50 mins

Serves 4

Ingredients

For the vegetables

- 450g salad potatoes, halved
- 2 tsp cold-pressed rapeseed oil, plus extra for the tin

- 1 lemon, zested and juiced (you'll need 2 tbsp lemon juice)
- 1 tsp vegetable bouillon powder

- 2 leeks, cut into rings
- 350g asparagus (250g pack and 100g pack), ends trimmed, cut crosswise into quarters
- 320g frozen peas
- 260g bag young leaf spinach
- 2 tbsp bio Greek yogurt
- 1 tbsp chopped tarragon leaves

For the loaf

- 410g can jackfruit, drained
- 1 tbsp chopped tarragon leaves
- 1 garlic clove, finely grated
- ½ tsp smoked paprika
- 3 eggs
- 40g dried porcini mushrooms
- 200g pack chestnut purée
- 40g roasted unsalted cashews

Method

STEP 1

Heat the oven to 190C/170C fan/gas 5. Oil and line a 500g loaf tin with two strips of baking parchment so it's fully lined, with an overhang at the top that could be folded over. Toss the potatoes with the oil and put in a small roasting tin.

STEP 2

To make the loaf, weigh out 125g jackfruit, choosing the pieces that have the most 'open' texture, then thinly slice. Tip into a bowl and stir in the tarragon, garlic and paprika.

STEP 3

Tip the rest of the jackfruit into a bowl with the eggs and dried mushrooms and blitz with a stick blender until very smooth. Add the chestnut purée, then blitz again until well mixed. Stir 150g of the mushroom mix with the sliced jackfruit. Spoon half of the remaining dried mushroom mix into the tin, then add the mushroom and sliced jackfruit mix, and cover with the rest of the dried mushroom mix. Press down and scatter over the cashews. Fold over the baking parchment and bake alongside the potatoes for 45 mins, or until firm.

STEP 4

Toss the lemon zest with the potatoes. Cover the loaf and leave it to rest while you cook the veg.

STEP 5

Tip 150ml water into a pan with the bouillon and leeks. Cover and cook over a medium heat for 2 mins. Add the asparagus and peas, then cover and cook for 2 mins more. Finally, add the spinach and stir to wilt. Add the lemon juice and the yogurt to the veg mix and stir well. If you're following our Healthy Diet Plan, serve half the veg with four slices of the loaf, reserving the remaining four slices and the rest of the veg for another night. Will keep for up to three days, covered, in the fridge. To serve on the second night, reheat the leftovers in the microwave until piping hot.

Feta frittatas with carrot & celery salad

Prep: 15 mins **Cook:** 25 mins

Serves 2

Ingredients

For the frittatas

- 2 tsp rapeseed oil , plus a drizzle for the salad (optional)
- 1 large leek , well washed and thinly sliced
- 25g baby spinach
- 3 large eggs
- ⅓ pack dill , stalks removed, fronds chopped
- 2 tbsp natural bio-yogurt
- 50g feta , crumbled
- 1 garlic clove , finely grated

For the salad

- 2 tsp balsamic vinegar
- 2 tsp tahini
- 2 celery sticks , sliced
- 2 carrots , peeled into ribbons
- 1 very small red onion , thinly sliced
- 2 romaine lettuces leaves, torn into pieces
- 6 pitted black Kalamata olive , rinsed and halved

Method

STEP 1

Heat oven to 220C/200C fan/gas 7 with a muffin tin inside. Heat the oil in a frying pan and fry the leek for about 4 mins, stirring regularly, over a medium-high heat to soften it. Stir in the spinach and cook for 1 min until wilted down, then set aside to cool slightly.

STEP 2

Beat the eggs, dill, yogurt and feta together in a jug with black pepper and the garlic. Add the leeks and spinach, and stir well. Take the muffin tin out of the oven and drop in four muffin cases, add the egg mixture and bake for 15-18 mins until set and golden.

STEP 3

Meanwhile, mix the balsamic vinegar with the tahini and 1-2 tbsp water in a bowl to make a dressing, then toss with the vegetables and olives. Pile onto plates, carefully remove the paper cases from the frittatas and serve.

Spicy Moroccan eggs

Prep: 10 mins **Cook:** 15 mins - 20 mins

Serves 4

Ingredients

- 2 tsp rapeseed oil
- 1 large onion , halved and thinly sliced
- 3 garlic cloves , sliced
- 1 tbsp rose harissa
- 1 tsp ground coriander
- 150ml vegetable stock
- 400g can chickpea
- 2 x 400g cans cherry tomatoes
- 2 courgettes , finely diced
- 200g bag baby spinach
- 4 tbsp chopped coriander
- 4 large eggs

Method

STEP 1

Heat the oil in a large, deep frying pan, and fry the onion and garlic for about 8 mins, stirring every now and then, until starting to turn golden. Add the harissa and ground coriander, stir well, then pour in the stock and chickpeas with their liquid. Cover and simmer for 5 mins, then mash about one-third of the chickpeas to thicken the stock a little.

STEP 2

Tip the tomatoes and courgettes into the pan, and cook gently for 10 mins until the courgettes are tender. Fold in the spinach so that it wilts into the pan.

STEP 3

Stir in the chopped coriander, then make 4 hollows in the mixture and break in the eggs. Cover and cook for 2 mins, then take off the heat and allow to settle for 2 mins before serving.

Pitta pocket

Prep: 2 mins **Serves** 1

Ingredients

- ½ wholemeal pitta bread
- 25g cooked skinless chicken breast
- ¼ cucumber, cut into chunks
- 4 cherry tomatoes, halved

Method

STEP 1

Fill the pitta half with the chicken breast, cucumber and cherry tomatoes.

Chicken fattoush

Prep: 15 mins No cook

Serves 4

Ingredients

- juice 2 lemons
- 2 tbsp olive oil
- 1 Cos lettuce, chopped
- 2 tomatoes, chopped into chunks
- small pack flat-leaf parsley, chopped
- ½ cucumber, chopped into chunks
- 200g pack cooked chicken pieces (or leftover cooked chicken)
- 2 spring onions, sliced
- 2 pitta breads
- 1-2 tsp ground sumac

Method

STEP 1

Pour the lemon juice into a large bowl and whisk while you slowly add the oil. When all the oil has been added and the mixture starts to thicken, season.

STEP 2

Add the lettuce, tomatoes, parsley, cucumber, chicken pieces and spring onions, and stir well to coat the salad in the dressing.

STEP 3

Put the pitta breads in the toaster until crisp and golden, then chop into chunks. Scatter the toasted pitta pieces over the salad and sprinkle over the sumac. Serve straight away.

Spinach soup

Prep: 10 mins **Cook:** 25 mins

Serves 4

Ingredients

- 25g butter
- 1 bunch spring onions, chopped
- 1 leek (about 120g), sliced
- 2 small sticks celery (about 85g), sliced
- 1 small potato (about 200g), peeled and diced
- ½ tsp ground black pepper
- 1l stock (made with two chicken or vegetable stock cubes)
- 2 x 200-235g bags spinach
- 150g half-fat crème fraîche

Method

STEP 1

Heat the butter in a large saucepan. Add the spring onions, leek, celery and potato. Stir and put on the lid. Sweat for 10 minutes, stirring a couple of times.

STEP 2

Pour in the stock and cook for 10 – 15 minutes until the potato is soft.

STEP 3

Add the spinach and cook for a couple of minutes until wilted. Use a hand blender to blitz to a smooth soup.

STEP 4

Stir in the crème fraîche. Reheat and serve.

One-pot chicken with quinoa

Prep: 5 mins **Cook:** 30 mins

Serves 2

Ingredients

- 1 tbsp cold-pressed rapeseed oil
- 2 skinless chicken breasts (about 300g/11oz)
- 1 medium onion, sliced into 12 wedges
- 1 red pepper, deseeded and sliced
- 2 garlic cloves, finely chopped
- 100g green beans, trimmed and cut in half
- 1/4-1/2 tsp chilli flakes, according to taste
- 2 tsp ground cumin
- 2 tsp ground coriander
- 100g uncooked quinoa
- 85g frozen sweetcorn
- 75g kale, thickly shredded

Method

STEP 1

Heat the oil in a large, deep frying pan or sauté pan. Season the chicken and fry over a medium-high heat for 2-3 mins each side or until golden. Transfer to a plate. Add the onion and pepper to the pan and cook for 3 mins, stirring, until softened and lightly browned.

STEP 2

Tip in the garlic and beans, and stir-fry for 2 mins. Add the chilli and spices, then stir in the quinoa and sweetcorn. Pour in 700ml just-boiled water with 1/2 tsp flaked sea salt and bring to the boil.

STEP 3

Return the chicken to the pan, reduce the heat to a simmer and cook for 12 mins, stirring regularly and turning the chicken occasionally. Add the kale and cook for a further 3 mins or until the quinoa and chicken are cooked through.

Healthy pancakes

Prep: 15 mins **Cook:** 30 mins

Makes 10-12

Ingredients

- 50g self-raising flour
- 50g wholemeal or wholegrain flour
- 2 small eggs, separated
- 150ml skimmed milk
- berries and low-fat yogurt or fromage frais to serve

Method

STEP 1

Sift the flours into a bowl or wide jug and tip any bits in the sieve back into the bowl. Add the egg yolks and a splash of milk then stir to a thick paste. Add the remaining milk a little at a time so you don't make lumps in the batter.

STEP 2

Whisk the egg whites until they stand up in stiff peaks, then fold them carefully into the batter – try not to squash out all the air.

STEP 3

Heat a non-stick pan over a medium heat and pour in enough batter to make a pancake about 10 cm across. Cook for just under a minute until bubbles begin to pop on the surface and the edges are looking a little dry. Carefully turn the pancake over. If it is a bit wet on top, it may squirt out a little batter as you do so. In that case, leave it on the other side a little longer. Keep warm while you make the remaining pancakes. Serve with your favourite healthy toppings.

Healthy tikka masala

Prep: 10 mins **Cook:** 55 mins

Serves 4

Ingredients

- 1 large onion, chopped
- 4 large garlic cloves
- thumb-sized piece of ginger
- 2 tbsp rapeseed oil
- 4 small skinless chicken breasts, cut into chunks
- 2 tbsp tikka spice powder
- 1 tsp cayenne pepper
- 400g can chopped tomatoes
- 40g ground almonds
- 200g spinach
- 3 tbsp fat-free natural yogurt
- ½ small bunch of coriander, chopped
- brown basmati rice, to serve

Method

STEP 1

Put the onion, garlic and ginger in a food processor and whizz to a smooth paste.

STEP 2

Heat 1 tbsp of the oil in a flameproof casserole dish over a medium heat. Add the onion mixture and fry for 15 mins. Tip into a bowl and wipe out the pan.

STEP 3

Add the remaining oil and the chicken and fry for 5-7 mins, or until lightly brown. Stir in the tikka spice and cayenne and fry for a further minute. Tip the onion mixture back into the pan, along with the tomatoes and 1 can full of water. Bring to the boil, then reduce to a simmer and cook, uncovered, for 15 mins. Stir in the almonds and spinach and cook for a further 10 mins. Season, then stir though the yogurt and coriander. Serve with brown rice.

Healthy shakshuka

Prep:10 mins **Cook:**30 mins

Serves 2

Ingredients

- 1 tbsp cold pressed rapeseed oil
- 1 red onion, cut into thin wedges
- 1 red pepper, finely sliced
- 1 yellow pepper, finely sliced
- 3 large garlic cloves, crushed
- 1 tsp cumin seeds
- 1 tsp coriander seeds, crushed
- 1 heaped tsp sweet smoked paprika
- 400g can cherry tomatoes
- 115g baby spinach
- 4 medium eggs

- ½ small bunch coriander, roughly chopped
- ½ small bunch dill, roughly chopped

Method

STEP 1

Heat the oil in a large, non-stick frying pan. Add the onion and peppers and fry over a medium heat for 8-10 mins until the veg is beginning to soften. Add the garlic, cumin, coriander and paprika and fry for 1 min more. Tip in the tomatoes, spinach and 100ml water and bubble until the spinach has wilted, then lower to a simmer and cook, uncovered, for 10 mins. Season to taste.

STEP 2

Make four indentations in the tomato mixture and gently crack an egg into each one. Cover with a lid or foil and cook over a gentle heat for 8-10 mins, or until the eggs are just set. Uncover, scatter with the fresh herbs and serve.

Healthy pasta primavera

Prep: 10 mins **Cook:** 20 mins

Serves 4

Ingredients

- 75g young broad beans (use frozen if you can't get fresh)
- 2 x 100g pack asparagus tips
- 170g peas (use frozen if you can't get fresh)
- 350g spaghetti or tagliatelle
- 175g pack baby leeks, trimmed and sliced
- 1 tbsp olive oil, plus extra to serve
- 1 tbsp butter
- 200ml tub fromage frais or creme fraiche
- handful fresh chopped herbs (we used mint, parsley and chives)
- parmesan (or vegetarian alternative), shaved, to serve

Method

STEP 1

Bring a pan of salted water to the boil and put a steamer (or colander) over the water. Steam the beans, asparagus and peas until just tender, then set aside. Boil the pasta following pack instructions.

STEP 2

Meanwhile, fry the leeks gently in the oil and butter for 5 mins or until soft. Add the fromage frais to the leeks and very gently warm through, stirring constantly to ensure it doesn't split. Add the herbs and steamed vegetables with a splash of pasta water to loosen.

STEP 3

Drain the pasta and stir into the sauce. Adjust the seasoning, then serve scattered with the cheese and drizzled with a little extra olive oil.

Healthy porridge bowl

Prep: 10 mins **Cook:** 5 mins

Serves 2

Ingredients

- 100g frozen raspberries
- 1 orange, 1/2 sliced and 1/2 juiced
- 150g porridge oats
- 100ml milk
- ½ banana, sliced
- 2 tbsp smooth almond butter
- 1 tbsp goji berries
- 1 tbsp chia seeds

Method

STEP 1

Tip half the raspberries and all of the orange juice in a pan. Simmer until the raspberries soften, about 5 mins.

STEP 2

Meanwhile stir the oats, milk and 450ml water in a pan over a low heat until creamy. Top with the raspberry compote, remaining raspberries, orange slices, banana, almond butter, goji berries and chia seeds.

Healthy bolognese

Prep: 5 mins **Cook:** 20 mins

2 generously, 4 as a snack

Ingredients

- 100g wholewheat linguine
- 2 tsp rapeseed oil
- 1 fennel bulb , finely chopped
- 2 garlic cloves , sliced
- 200g pork mince with less than 5% fat
- 200g whole cherry tomatoes
- 1 tbsp balsamic vinegar
- 1 tsp vegetable bouillon powder
- generous handful chopped basil

Method

STEP 1

Bring a large pan of water to the boil, then cook the linguine following pack instructions, about 10 mins.

STEP 2

Meanwhile, heat the oil in a non-stick wok or wide pan. Add the fennel and garlic and cook, stirring every now and then, until tender, about 10 mins.

STEP 3

Tip in the pork and stir-fry until it changes colour, breaking it up as you go so there are no large clumps. Add the tomatoes, vinegar and bouillon, then cover the pan and cook for 10 mins over a low heat until the tomatoes burst and the pork is cooked and tender. Add the linguine and basil and plenty of pepper, and toss well before serving.

Healthy Easter bunny pancakes

Prep: 15 mins **Cook:** 30 mins

Serves 4-6

Ingredients

- 50g self-raising flour
- 50g wholemeal flour

- 2 small eggs, separated
- 150ml skimmed milk
- oil, for frying
- a few raisins for bunny paws, to serve (optional)
- 30g banana, sliced into rounds for the tails
- extra chopped fruit, to serve

Method

STEP 1

Put both the flours into a large bowl and whisk to break up any lumps. Add the egg yolks and a little of the milk, whisking to a thick paste. Add the remaining milk, a splash at a time, to loosen the batter. (Use whole or semi-skimmed milk if cooking for under fives, dependent on age.)

STEP 2

In a separate bowl and using a clean whisk, whisk the egg whites until they hold stiff peaks. Gently fold the egg whites into the batter with a spatula, trying to keep in as much air as possible.

STEP 3

Heat a large non-stick pan over a medium heat and carefully wipe it with some oiled kitchen paper. Using a large spoon, add a generous dollop of batter to the pan in a round, for the bunny body. Add a smaller round for the head, two small ovals for feet, and two long thin strips for ears. Fit all the bunny components into the pan, or cook them in batches.

STEP 4

Flip the pancakes after a minute or two, once the edges are set, the base is golden brown and bubbles start to pop on the surface. Cook for another min until golden brown.

STEP 5

Put the bunny body in the middle of the plate, position the head, ears and feet just overlapping to look like the back of a bunny. Add a banana slice for the tail, and raisins (if using) for the feet pads.

STEP 6

Repeat with the remaining batter. Decorate with extra chopped fruit, if you like.

Healthy chicken katsu curry

Prep:20 mins **Cook:**35 mins

Serves 2

Ingredients

- 25g flaked almonds
- 1 tsp cold-pressed rapeseed oil
- 2 boneless, skinless chicken breasts (about 300g/11oz total)
- lime wedges, for squeezing over

For the sauce

- 2 tsp cold-pressed rapeseed oil
- 1 medium onion, roughly chopped
- 2 garlic cloves, finely chopped
- thumb-sized piece ginger, peeled and finely chopped
- 2 tsp medium curry powder
- 1 star anise
- ¼ tsp ground turmeric
- 1 tbsp plain wholemeal flour

For the rice

- 100g long-grain brown rice
- 2 spring onions, finely sliced (include the green part)

For the salad

- 1 medium carrot, peeled into long strips with a vegetable peeler
- ⅓ cucumber, peeled into long strips with a vegetable peeler
- 1 small red chilli, finely chopped (deseeded if you don't like it too hot)
- juice ½ lime
- small handful mint leaves
- small handful coriander leaves

Method

STEP 1

Heat oven to 220C/200C fan/gas 7. Cook the brown rice in plenty of boiling water for 35 mins or until very tender.

STEP 2

Crush the almonds using a pestle and mortar, or blitz in a food processor until finely chopped, then sprinkle over a plate. Grease a small baking tray with a little of the oil. Brush the chicken on both sides with the remaining oil and season well. Coat the chicken with the nuts and place on the tray. Press any remaining nuts from the plate onto each breast. Bake for 20 mins or until browned and cooked through. Rest for 4-5 mins on the tray, then slice thickly.

STEP 3

Meanwhile, make the sauce. Heat the oil in a medium non-stick saucepan and add the onion, garlic and ginger. Loosely cover the pan and fry gently for 8 mins or until softened and lightly browned, stirring occasionally. Remove the lid for the final 2 mins, and don't let the garlic burn.

STEP 4

Stir in the curry powder, star anise, turmeric and a good grinding of black pepper. Cook for a few secs more, stirring. Sprinkle over the flour and stir well. Gradually add 400ml water to the pan, stirring constantly.

STEP 5

Bring the sauce to a simmer and cook for 10 mins, stirring occasionally. If it begins to splutter, cover loosely with a lid. Remove the pan from the heat and blitz the sauce with a stick blender until very smooth. Adjust the seasoning to taste. Keep warm.

STEP 6

Once the rice is tender, add the spring onions and cook for 1 min more. Drain well, then leave to stand for a few mins while you make the salad. Toss the carrot and cucumber with the chilli, lime juice and herbs.

STEP 7

Divide the sliced chicken between two plates, pour over the sauce and serve with the rice, salad and lime wedges for squeezing over.

Healthy Easter lamb

Prep:30 mins **Cook:**55 mins

Serves 8 -10

Ingredients

- 2 onions , peeled and thickly sliced
- 2 large carrots , thickly sliced
- boneless leg of lamb (around 1.5kg), trimmed of excess fat

- 4 garlic cloves , sliced
- 3 rosemary sprigs , leaves picked
- 2 tbsp olive oil

For the veg

- 800g baby carrots , peeled
- 500g frozen broad beans
- 600g frozen peas

- small bunch mint , finely chopped
- small bunch parsley , finely chopped
- 1 lemon , zested and juiced

Method

STEP 1

Heat the oven to 200C/180C fan/gas 6. Put the onions and sliced carrots in a large roasting tray. Remove any string from the lamb and put it on top of the veg, skin-side up. Pierce the lamb with the tip of a knife to make small pockets in the meat, add garlic slices and a few rosemary leaves to the holes. Rub the lamb with 1 tbsp olive oil and season. Pour 100ml water into the tray.

STEP 2

Roast uncovered for 45 minutes at the top of the oven. Check the internal temperature, it should read 60C for medium (pink). Cook for another 15 minutes for well done. Rest the meat under foil for 10 mins while you cook the veg.

STEP 3

Bring a large pan of salted water to the boil. Add the carrots, and cook for 8 minutes until tender, adding the peas and beans for the last 2 minutes. Drain the veg and toss with 1 tbsp oil, chopped herbs, lemon zest and juice. Season to taste.

STEP 4

Carve the lamb into thin slices. Spread the veg onto a large warmed serving platter and arrange the meat in the middle.

Healthy Halloween stuffed peppers

Prep: 25 mins **Cook:** 35 mins

Serves 4

Ingredients

- 4 small peppers (a mix of orange, red and yellow looks nice)
- 25g pine nuts
- 1 tbsp olive or rapeseed oil
- 1 red onion , chopped
- 2 fat garlic cloves , crushed
- 1 small aubergine , chopped into small pieces
- 200g pouch mixed grains (we used bulghur wheat and quinoa)
- 2 tbsp sundried tomato paste
- zest of 1 lemon
- bunch basil , chopped

Method

STEP 1

Cut the tops off the peppers (keeping the tops to one side) and remove the seeds and any white flesh from inside. Use a small sharp knife to carve spooky Halloween faces into the sides. Chop any offcuts into small pieces and set aside.

STEP 2

Toast the pine nuts in a dry pan for a few mins until golden, and set aside. Heat the oil in the pan, and heat the oven to 200C/180C fan/gas 6. Cook the onion in the oil for 8-10 mins until softened. Stir in the garlic, pepper offcuts and aubergine and cook for another 10 mins, until the veggies are soft. Add a splash of water if the pan looks dry. Season.

STEP 3

Squeeze the pouch of grains to break them up, then tip into the pan with the tomato paste. Stir for a minute or two to warm through, then remove from the heat and add the lemon zest, basil and pine nuts.

STEP 4

Fill each pepper with the grain mixture. Replace the lids, using cocktail sticks to secure them in place, and put the peppers in a deep roasting tin with the carved faces facing upwards. Cover with foil and bake for 35 mins, uncovered for the final 10. The peppers should be soft and the filling piping hot.

Healthy veg patch hummus

Prep: 20 mins **Serves 6**

Ingredients

- 1 x 400g can chickpeas, drained and rinsed
- ½ lemon, juiced
- 1 garlic clove, crushed
- 2 tbsp olive oil
- 2 tbsp tahini
- 250g baby carrots
- 1 pot of parsley

Method

STEP 1

Put the chickpeas, lemon juice, garlic, olive oil and tahini into a food processor and blitz to a smooth consistency. Loosen with 1–2 tbsp water if it seems a little thick.

STEP 2

Make a hole in the top of each carrot with a skewer or by cutting a small hole with the tip of a sharp knife. Dab a small amount of hummus into the hole and push in a small sprig of parsley.

STEP 3

Spoon the hummus into thoroughly cleaned small, plant pots or bowls and push in the carrots. Let the children dunk into the hummus with the carrots.

Healthy roast turkey crown

Prep: 25 mins **Cook:** 1 hr and 30 mins

Serves 4-6

Ingredients

- 2kg turkey crown on the bone
- 3 oranges, 1 cut into wedges, ½ sliced, 1 ½ juiced
- 1 tbsp runny honey, plus extra for drizzling
- handful thyme sprigs, leaves picked from one, two left whole, plus sprigs to serve (optional)
- 1 tsp soy sauce
- 2 bay leaves
- 500g carrots, peeled and cut into long batons
- 500g parsnips, peeled and cut into long batons

Method

STEP 1

Take your turkey crown out of the fridge 1-2 hrs before you want to cook it. Heat oven to 200C/180C fan/gas 6. Cut 4 slices from one of the oranges. Juice the rest of it along with another of the oranges. In a small bowl, stir the orange juice together with the honey and the picked thyme leaves, the soy sauce and a good grinding of black pepper.

STEP 2

Loosen the skin over the turkey breast. Place two slices of orange, a bay leaf and thyme sprig under the skin, on both sides of the breast, then spoon in some of the juice mix and smooth the skin back over. Tip the orange wedges into a roomy roasting tin with the carrots and parsnips. Nestle the crown amongst the vegetables and oranges. Drizzle over about a third of the remaining orange juice mix and roast everything in the oven for 30 mins. Remove, give the veg a stir and drizzle over another third of the juice mix, then return to the oven and do that again one more time, roasting the turkey for a total of 1hr 30 mins (covering with foil halfway through if it begins to colour too much).

STEP 3

Remove the turkey from the roasting tin and place on a board covered with foil, then turn the oven up to 220C/200C fan/gas 8. Toss the veg in a drizzle of honey and put the tin back in the oven to caramelise the veg for 25-30 mins, leaving the turkey crown to rest. Serve the crown on a platter surrounded by the glazed roots, orange wedges and extra thyme sprigs, if you like. Remove the sticky skin from the breast before carving the meat to serve as a side.

Healthy Halloween nachos

Prep:40 mins **Cook:**5 mins

Serves 4 - 6

Ingredients

For the guacamole

- 2 limes , juiced
- 2 small avocados , peeled and chopped
- 1 bunch coriander , finely chopped

For the sweetcorn salsa

- ½ a 160g can sweetcorn
- 200g cherry tomatoes , quartered
- 1 red pepper , finely chopped
- 2 spring onions , thinly sliced
- 3 sundried tomatoes , finely chopped
- 400g can black beans
- ½ tsp cumin
- ½ tsp coriander
- ½ tsp smoked paprika

For the bat-shaped nachos

- 4 wholewheat tortillas
- 1 ½ tsp oil
- 4 purple carrots , cut into sticks

Method

STEP 1

Start by making the guacamole. Pour the lime juice into a bowl and add the avocado. Mash well with a potato masher or the back of a fork until it's the consistency you like – we served ours fairly chunky. Add half of the chopped coriander, season to taste and spoon into a shallow bowl or serving dish.

STEP 2

Now mix all of the salsa ingredients together, along with the remaining chopped coriander. Season with salt and pepper. Arrange clumps of the salsa on top of the guacamole – this will allow guests to get a bit of everything with each scoop. Cover and chill for up to 30 mins while you make the bat nachos.

STEP 3

Lay a tortilla wrap out on your chopping board and brush with a little of the oil. Cut out bats (or other spooky shapes) using a cookie cutter, scissors or both. Cut them as close together as possible to minimise waste. You should be able to get about 8-10 from each wrap, depending on the size of your cutter.

STEP 4

Heat oven to 200C/180C fan/gas 6. Put all the tortilla shapes on 2 or 3 large baking sheets and bake for about 4-5 mins or until golden and crisp, then serve with the carrot sticks, guacamole and salsa plate.

Healthy Halloween pizzas

Prep: 20 mins **Cook:** 10 mins

Serves 4

Ingredients

- 200g strong white flour
- 200g strong wholewheat flour
- 1 tsp or 7g sachet easy-blend dried yeast
- 250ml warm water

For the topping

- 300g passata
- 1 garlic clove , crushed
- 1 tbsp olive or rapeseed oil
- 75g grated mozzarella
- 10 black olives
- handful cherry tomatoes , halved
- handful basil leaves , to serve

Method

STEP 1

Mix the flours and yeast with a pinch of salt in a food processor fitted with a dough blade, or combine in a bowl. Pour in the water and mix to a soft dough, then work for 1 min in a processor or 5 mins by hand. Remove the dough, divide into 4 pieces and roll out on a lightly floured surface to rounds about 15cm across. Lift onto heavily oiled baking sheets.

STEP 2

Mix the passata with the garlic, oil and a little seasoning. Spread over the dough to within 2cm of the edges. Scatter with the mozzarella. Halve the olives and tomatoes. Place an olive in the centre of each pizza to make the spider's body. Cut the rest into little legs and arrange them around the spider bodies. Dot the tomatoes here and there. Leave to rise for 20 mins. Heat oven to 240C/ fan 220C/gas 9 or the highest setting.

STEP 3

Bake the pizza for 10-12 mins until crisp and golden around the edges. Scatter with the basil to serve.

Healthy Easter boiled eggs

Prep: 20 mins **Cook:** 10 mins

Serves 4-6

Ingredients

- 6 medium eggs
- 1 tbsp currants
- 1 small carrot , peeled and cut in to small triangles
- 80g cherry tomatoes
- 80g sliced cucumber
- 30g rocket
- A few sprigs of rosemary , to serve
- Mini carrots , to serve

Method

STEP 1

Bring a large pan of water to the boil. Add the eggs and simmer for 10 mins. Drain the eggs and plunge into ice water to cool down, gently peel off the shells and discard.

STEP 2

Cut some of the eggs in half and decorate with currants for eyes and a small triangle of carrot for a beak to create egg chicks (as per picture). Slice the remaining eggs to create bunny shapes (as per picture) quartering some for ears and halving some lengthways for the body. Create a round tail by slicing the top off one of the eggs.

STEP 3

Decorate the plate/board with sprigs of rosemary and miniature carrots, if you like. Serve with the cucumber, cherry tomatoes and rocket.

Healthy gravy

Prep: 5 mins **Cook:** 25 mins

Serves 8

Ingredients

- 1 tsp sunflower oil
- 1 large onion , chopped
- 3 large carrots , chopped
- 1 tbsp ketchup
- handful dried porcini mushrooms
- 3 tbsp balsamic vinegar
- 1l low-salt vegetable stock , or chicken stock if not making it vegetarian
- 1 tbsp cornflour

Method

STEP 1

Heat the oil in a saucepan then add the vegetables and cook them over a medium-high heat for 10-15 mins to brown – if they burn at the edges, then all the better. Stir in the ketchup and dried mushrooms and cook together until everything becomes sticky, then splash in the vinegar. Stir in the stock and season with a pinch of salt, if you like. Bring to the boil, then simmer gently for 20 mins.

STEP 2

Using a hand blender, blitz to create a thin soup-like consistency, then pass through a sieve into another saucepan and bring to the simmer. Slake the cornflour with a splash of water, then pour into the liquid and continue to cook until thickened. Serve straightaway, chill, or freeze for reheating at a later date. Can be frozen for up to three months in an airtight container.

Healthy full English

Prep: 10 mins **Cook:** 30 mins

Serves 4

Ingredients

- 2 tbsp rapeseed oil
- 1 small onion , finely sliced
- 3 garlic cloves , 1 crushed, 2 whole
- 1 heaped tsp sweet smoked paprika

- 400g can cannellini beans, drained and rinsed
- ½ x 400g can chopped tomatoes with herbs
- 1 tbsp reduced-salt brown sauce
- 300g Portobellini or chestnut mushrooms, halved
- 3 thyme sprigs, plus extra to serve
- 400g cherry tomatoes on the vine
- 8 chipolatas
- 4 medium eggs

Method

STEP 1

Heat oven to 200C/180C fan/gas 6 and heat 1 tbsp of the oil in a small saucepan. Add the onion and fry over a medium heat for 8-10 mins, or until softened and starting to turn golden brown. Add the crushed garlic and paprika and cook for 1 min more, then add the beans, chopped tomatoes and brown sauce and bring to the boil. Lower to a simmer and cook for 10-12 mins, stirring occasionally. Cover to keep warm and set aside.

STEP 2

Meanwhile, toss the mushrooms, thyme and cherry tomatoes in a roasting tin with the remaining garlic and oil. Roast for 12 mins until the mushrooms and tomatoes are soft, then remove from the oven and cover to keep warm. Turn the grill to its highest setting. Put the chipolatas on a foil-lined baking sheet and grill for 4-5 mins on each side, or until golden brown and cooked through.

STEP 3

Crack the eggs into a small bowl. Bring a pan of lightly salted water to the boil and swirl vigorously with a wooden spoon to create a whirlpool. Once the whirlpool has almost subsided, tip in one egg, then lower the heat and gently cook for 3 mins. Scoop out with a slotted spoon, transfer to a plate and repeat with the remaining eggs. Serve the roasted veg with the sausages, eggs and beans, season and scatter with thyme leaves.

Healthy chilli

Prep: 5 mins **Cook:** 2 hrs and 15 mins

Serves 4

Ingredients

- 1-2 tbsp olive oil, plus extra if needed
- 400g diced stewing beef
- 1 onion, finely chopped
- 2 garlic cloves, finely chopped
- 1 ½ tsp ground cumin
- 1-2 tbsp chipotle paste (or gluten-free alternative), depending on how spicy you like it
- 400g can kidney bean in chilli sauce
- 400g can chopped tomato
- 1 lime, zested and cut into wedges
- ¼ small pack coriander, leaves only
- cooked rice, to serve (optional)

Method

STEP 1

Heat the oil in a large pan and cook the beef pieces for a few mins on each side until browned all over. Remove from the pan with a slotted spoon and set aside.

STEP 2

Add the onion to the pan, with extra oil if needed, and cook until softened. Stir in the garlic, cumin and chipotle paste, and cook for 1 min. Sieve the kidney beans, reserving the sauce. Add this sauce, along with the chopped tomatoes and a can full of water, to the pan. Stir well, then return the meat to the pan. Bring to a simmer, then cook, covered, for 2 hrs or until the beef is tender (or bake in the oven for 3 hrs at 160C/140C fan/gas 3).

STEP 3

Add the reserved kidney beans and lime zest, season and warm through. Serve with a scattering of coriander leaves, the lime wedges to squeeze over, and rice, if you like.

Healthy stuffing balls

Prep: 20 mins **Cook:** 45 mins

Serves 8, makes about 12

Ingredients

- 1 tbsp olive oil
- 1 large onion , finely chopped
- 2 sticks celery , stringed and finely chopped
- 2 garlic cloves , finely chopped

- 15g dried apricots , roughly chopped
- 75g peeled chestnuts
- 75g almonds
- 100g wholemeal bread , crusts removed and roughly torn (about 6 slices)
- large bunch parsley , chopped
- large pinch dried sage
- 1 egg

Method

STEP 1

Heat oven to 200C/180C fan/gas 6. Gently heat the oil in a shallow saucepan then add the onion, celery and garlic. Keep everything sizzling on a medium heat for 15 mins until soft. Tip into a food processor with the rest of the ingredients, except the egg, plus a small pinch of salt, if you like. Pulse until everything is chopped, then add the egg and pulse until combined. Use wet hands to roll the mixture into walnut-sized balls, then place on a baking sheet lined with baking parchment.

STEP 2

Bake in the oven for 25-30 mins until golden and hot through. Will freeze for up to three months; defrost fully before reheating.

Healthy pumpkin pancakes

Prep: 10 mins **Cook:** 30 mins

Makes 9 large or 27 mini pancakes

Ingredients

- 200g plain flour
- ½ tsp baking powder
- 200ml milk
- 100g cooked butternut squash or pumpkin, mashed
- 1 egg , separated

Method

STEP 1

Tip the flour into a bowl and add the baking powder. Measure the milk into a jug and stir in the butternut squash, followed by the egg yolk.

STEP 2

Make a well in the centre of the flour and gradually add the milk mixture until you have a lump-free batter. Alternatively, tip everything into a blender and whizz it.

STEP 3

Whisk the egg white until stiff, then fold it into the batter.

STEP 4

Heat a non-stick pan and cook 1 large or 3 small pancakes at a time (if making small pancakes, use 1 tbsp for each). Wait until lots of bubbles have risen to the top and the surface has begun to dry out before turning them over, but keep an eye on the base to make sure it doesn't get too brown. Repeat with the remaining mixture.

Healthy Turkish meatloaf

Prep: 15 mins **Cook:** 1 hr and 30 mins

Serves 6

Ingredients

- a little rapeseed oil for the tin
- 1 onion, finely chopped
- 1 large aubergine, cut into slices lengthways then finely diced (about 320g)
- 250g pouch cooked brown rice
- 3 tbsp tomato purée
- 1 tsp vegetable bouillon powder
- ½ pack dill, chopped, plus extra to serve (optional)
- 2 tsp each ground cinnamon and allspice
- 250g lamb mince (10% fat)
- 2 large eggs
- 227g can chopped tomatoes

For the salad

- 1 pack of three peppers, deseeded and roughly chopped
- 2 large courgettes (about 500g), halved and sliced
- 2 large red onions, sliced
- 1 tbsp rapeseed oil
- 1 tbsp cider vinegar
- 1 garlic clove, finely grated
- handful chopped mint

Method

STEP 1

Heat oven to 180C/160C fan/gas 4. Line a 900g loaf tin with baking parchment and lightly oil it.

STEP 2

Put the onion and aubergine in a large bowl with the rice, tomato purée, bouillon, dill, spices and lamb. Mix and squash together with your hands then add the egg and mix again. Tip the can of tomatoes into the base of the loaf tin then pack the mince mixture on top and press down lightly to compact it. Cover the tin with foil and bake in the oven for 1 hr 40 mins, taking off the foil for the last 15 mins.

STEP 3

Once the meatloaf has been cooking for 1 hr, tip the peppers, courgettes and red onion into a roasting tin and toss with the oil. Roast in the oven with the meatloaf for 40 mins until the vegetables are tender and a little charred.

STEP 4

Take the meatloaf and roasted veg from the oven, leave the loaf to settle for 5 mins, then tip out onto a platter or board, remove the baking parchment and scatter with dill if using. Toss the roasted veg with the vinegar, garlic and mint and serve them with the meat loaf.

Healthy egg & chips

Prep: 10 mins **Cook:** 1 hr

Serves 4

Ingredients

- 500g potatoes , diced
- 2 shallots , sliced
- 1 tbsp olive oil
- 2 tsp dried crushed oregano or 1 tsp fresh leaves
- 200g small mushroom
- 4 eggs

Method

STEP 1

Heat oven to 200C/fan 180C/gas 6. Tip the potatoes and shallots into a large, non-stick roasting tin, drizzle with the oil, sprinkle over the oregano, then mix everything together well. Bake for 40-45 mins (or until starting to go brown), add the mushrooms, then cook for a further 10 mins until the potatoes are browned and tender.

STEP 2

Make four gaps in the vegetables and crack an egg into each space. Return to the oven for 3-4 mins or until the eggs are cooked to your liking.

Healthy banana bread

Prep: 20 mins **Cook:** 1 hr and 15 mins

Cuts into 10 slices

Ingredients

- low-fat spread, for the tin, plus extra to serve
- 140g wholemeal flour
- 100g self-raising flour
- 1 tsp bicarbonate of soda
- 1 tsp baking powder
- 300g mashed banana from overripe black bananas
- 4 tbsp agave syrup
- 3 large eggs, beaten with a fork
- 150ml pot low-fat natural yogurt
- 25g chopped pecan or walnuts (optional)

Method

STEP 1

Heat oven to 160C/140C fan/gas 3. Grease and line a 2lb loaf tin with baking parchment (allow it to come 2cm above top of tin). Mix the flours, bicarb, baking powder and a pinch of salt in a large bowl.

STEP 2

Mix the bananas, syrup, eggs and yogurt. Quickly stir into dry ingredients, then gently scrape into the tin and scatter with nuts, if using. Bake for 1 hr 10 mins-1 hr 15 mins or until a skewer comes out clean.

STEP 3

Cool in tin on a wire rack. Eat warm or at room temperature, with low-fat spread.

Healthy spiced rice pudding

Prep: 45 mins **Cook:** 4 hrs

Serves 6

Ingredients

- 1 tsp butter
- 1l semi-skimmed milk + 100ml
- 200g wholegrain rice
- 1 orange , finely zested
- 1 tsp mixed spice
- 1 tsp cinnamon
- A grating of nutmeg
- 1 tbsp orange segments
- honey and raisins, to serve

Method

STEP 1

Butter the slow cooker all over the base and half way up the sides. Heat the milk to a simmer. Mix the pudding rice and the milk and pour into the slow cooker. Add the orange zest, and spices. Cook for 4 hours on low and stir once or twice if you can. If after 3 hours the rice pudding is beginning to stick to the base of the cook, add a splash of water. The rice will be tender when cooked. Add 100ml milk to loosen the pudding, if necessary.

STEP 2

Serve topped with orange segments and honey, fruit and raisins, if you like.

Healthy tuna lettuce wraps

Prep: 15 mins **Cook:** 2 mins

Serves 2

Ingredients

- 2 drops rapeseed oil , for brushing
- 2 x 140g fresh tuna fillets, defrosted
- 1 ripe avocado
- ½ tsp English mustard powder
- 1 tsp cider vinegar
- 1 tbsp capers
- 8 romaine lettuce leaves
- 16 cherry tomatoes , preferably on the vine, halved

Method

STEP 1

Brush the tuna with a little oil. Heat a non-stick pan, add the tuna and cook for 1 min each side, or a min or so longer for a thicker fillet. Transfer to a plate to rest.

STEP 2

Halve and stone the avocado and scoop the flesh into a small bowl. Add the mustard powder and vinegar, then mash well so that the mixture is smooth like mayonnaise. Stir in the capers. Spoon into two small dishes and put on serving plates with the lettuce leaves, and tomatoes.

STEP 3

Slice the tuna (it should be slightly pink inside) and arrange on the plates. Spoon some 'mayo' on the lettuce leaves and top with tuna and cherry tomatoes and a few extra capers. To eat, roll up into little wraps.

Healthy carrot soup

Prep: 5 mins **Cook:** 5 mins

Serves 1

Ingredients

- 3 large carrots
- 1 tbsp grated ginger
- 1 tsp turmeric
- a pinch of cayenne pepper , plus extra to serve
- 20g wholemeal bread
- 1 tbsp soured cream , plus extra to serve
- 200ml vegetable stock

Method

STEP 1

Peel and chop the carrots and put in a blender with the ginger, turmeric, cayenne pepper, wholemeal bread, soured cream and vegetable stock. Blitz until smooth. Heat until piping hot. Swirl through some extra soured cream, or a sprinkling of cayenne, if you like.

Healthy chocolate milk

Prep: 5 mins No cook

Serves 1

Ingredients

- 200ml unsweetened soya milk
- 170g fat-free Greek yogurt (we used Total)
- 25g cooked quinoa
- 3 tsp cocoa powder
- ½ tsp vanilla bean paste
- ½ tsp cinnamon
- 3-4 cubes frozen spinach

Method

STEP 1

Whiz all the ingredients together in a blender until smooth, pour into a tall glass and serve.

Healthy turkey meatballs

Prep: 25 mins **Cook:** 40 mins

Serves 4

Ingredients

For the sauce

- 1 tbsp rapeseed oil
- 1 onion , finely chopped
- 2 carrots , finely diced
- 2 celery sticks, finely diced
- 2 garlic cloves , thinly sliced
- 1 fennel bulb , halved and thinly sliced, fronds reserved
- 500g carton tomato passata
- 500ml reduced-salt chicken stock
- 2 tbsp chopped parsley
- broccoli and potatoes or pasta and salad , to serve

For the meatballs

- 400g pack lean turkey breast mince
- 4 tbsp porridge oat
- 1 tsp fennel seed , crushed
- 1 garlic clove , crushed
- spray of oil

Method

STEP 1

Heat the oil in a large non-stick frying pan with a lid, then tip in the onion, carrots, celery, garlic and fennel, and stir well. Cover the pan and cook over a medium heat for 8 mins, stirring every now and then. Pour in the passata and stock, cover and leave to simmer for 20 mins.

STEP 2

Meanwhile, tip the mince into a large bowl. Add the oats, fennel seeds and leaves, the garlic and plenty of black pepper, and mix in with your hands. Lightly shape into 25 meatballs about the size of a walnut. Spray or rub a non-stick pan with a little oil and gently cook the meatballs until they take on a little colour. Give the sauce a stir, then add the meatballs and parsley. Cover and cook for 10 mins until they are cooked through and the veg in the sauce is tender. Serve with broccoli and baby potatoes in their skins, or pasta and salad.

Healthy banana & peanut butter ice cream

Prep: 10 mins plus 1 hr freezing

Serves 4

Ingredients

- 4 ripe bananas , chopped into 3cm chunks, then frozen
- 2 tbsp almond milk
- 1 tbsp organic peanut butter
- 1 tsp ground cinnamon
- 1 tbsp dark chocolate , grated
- 1 tbsp flaked almonds

Method

STEP 1

Tip the frozen bananas and almond milk into a blender. Blend together to create a smooth consistency. Add the peanut butter and cinnamon, and blend again. Taste and add more cinnamon, if you like.

STEP 2

Transfer to a freezer-proof container and freeze for 1 hr.

STEP 3

Take out of the freezer and serve with grated chocolate and flaked almonds sprinkled over.

Hearty lentil one pot

Prep: 10 mins **Cook:** 1 hr

Serves 4

Ingredients

- 40g dried porcini mushrooms, roughly chopped
- 200g dried brown lentils
- 1 ½ tbsp chopped rosemary
- 3 tbsp rapeseed oil
- 2 large onions, roughly chopped
- 150g chestnut baby button mushrooms
- 4 garlic cloves, finely grated
- 2 tbsp vegetable bouillon powder
- 2 large carrots (350g), cut into chunks
- 3 celery sticks (165g), chopped
- 500g potatoes, cut into chunks
- 200g cavolo nero, shredded

Method

STEP 1

Cover the mushrooms in boiling water and leave to soak for 10 mins. Boil the lentils in a pan with plenty of water for 10 mins. Drain and rinse, then tip into a pan with the dried mushrooms and soaking water (don't add the last bit of the liquid as it can contain some grit), rosemary and 2 litres water. Season, cover and simmer for 20 mins.

STEP 2

Meanwhile, heat the oil in a large pan and fry the onions for 5 mins. Stir in the fresh mushrooms and garlic and fry for 5 mins more. Stir in the lentil mixture and bouillon powder, then add the carrots, celery and potatoes. Cover and cook for 20 mins, stirring often, until the veg and lentils are tender, topping up the water level if needed.

STEP 3

Remove any tough stalks from the cavolo nero, then add to the pan and cover and cook for 5 mins more. If you're following our Healthy Diet Plan, serve half in bowls, then chill the rest to eat another day. Will keep in the fridge for two to three days. Reheat in a pan until hot.

Ham & potato hash with baked beans & healthy 'fried' eggs

Prep: 10 mins **Cook:** 25 mins - 30 mins

Serves 4

Ingredients

- 600g potato , diced
- 1 Cal cooking spray , for frying
- 2 leeks , trimmed, washed and sliced
- 175g lean ham , weighed after trimming and discarding any fat, chopped
- 2 tbsp wholegrain mustard
- 5 eggs
- 2 x 415g cans reduced sugar & salt baked beans

Method

STEP 1

Bring a large pan of salted water to the boil. Add the potatoes and boil for 5 mins until just tender. Drain well and leave in the colander to steam-dry.

STEP 2

Meanwhile, spray an ovenproof pan with cooking spray. Add the leeks with a splash of water and fry until very soft and squishy. Add a few more sprays of the oil, tip in the potatoes along with the ham, and fry to crisp up a little. Heat oven to 200C/180C fan/gas 6.

STEP 3

Stir in the mustard, 1 egg and a good amount of seasoning with a fork – break up some of the potatoes roughly as you do. Flatten down the mixture, spray the top with oil, and bake in the oven for 15-20 mins until the top is crisp.

STEP 4

When the hash is nearly ready, heat 200ml water in a non-stick frying pan with a lid (or use a baking sheet as a lid). When it is steaming (but before it simmers), crack in the remaining 4 eggs and cover with a lid. Cook for 2-4 mins until the eggs are done to your liking. Meanwhile, heat the beans.

STEP 5

Lift an egg onto each plate, add a big scoop of hash and spoon on some beans.

Healthier veggie carbonara

Prep: 20 mins **Cook:** 10 mins

Serves 4

Ingredients

- 4 medium courgettes (use a mix of yellow and green if you can get them)
- 300g spaghetti
- 3 large egg yolks
- 160g vegetarian parmesan-style cheese
- 1 tbsp olive oil
- small bunch fresh lemon thyme or thyme, leaves picked
- 200g chestnut mushrooms, roughly chopped
- 4 garlic cloves, crushed
- small bunch flat-leaf parsley, chopped (optional)
- ½ lemon, zested and juiced

Method

STEP 1

Put a large pan of salted water on to boil. Halve the courgettes lengthways and scoop out and discard the core, then slice the courgettes at an angle into small diagonal pieces. Put the spaghetti in the pan of boiling water and cook following pack instructions.

STEP 2

To make the creamy carbonara sauce, put the egg yolks in a bowl, add half of the grated cheese, and mix with a fork. Add up to 3 tbsp water to make the sauce less thick. Season and set aside.

STEP 3

Heat a large frying pan on a medium to high heat and pour in a little olive oil. Fry the courgette slices and thyme leaves with a good grinding of black pepper for a minute or two until the courgette starts to soften, then add the mushrooms. Fry for 2-3 mins until golden and slightly softened. For the last minute of the cooking, add the garlic.

STEP 4

Working quickly, drain the pasta, reserving a little of the cooking water. Toss the pasta in the pan with the courgettes and mushrooms, then remove from the heat and add a ladleful of the reserved cooking water and the egg and cheese sauce. Add the fresh parsley, if using, and the lemon zest and juice, then sprinkle over most of the remaining cheese. Stir everything together quickly to coat the pasta. The egg will cook if the pasta is still hot. If you're worried about it, put back on the heat for 1 min.

STEP 5

Pour in a little more of the cooking water, if needed. You should have a silky and shiny sauce. Season to taste, then sprinkle with a little more cheese to serve. Eat straight away, as the sauce can become thick and stodgy if left for too long.

Healthy fish & chips with tartare sauce

Prep: 5 mins **Cook:** 40 mins Ready in 40-45 mins

Serves 2

Ingredients

- 450g potatoes, peeled and cut into chips
- 1 tbsp olive oil, plus a little extra for brushing
- 2 white fish fillets about 140g/5oz each
- grated zest and juice 1 lemon
- small handful of parsley leaves, chopped
- 1 tbsp capers, chopped
- 2 heaped tbsp 0% Greek yogurt
- lemon wedge, to serve

Method

STEP 1

Heat oven to 200C/fan 180C/gas 6. Toss chips in oil. Spread over a baking sheet in an even layer, bake for 40 mins until browned and crisp. Put the fish in a shallow dish, brush lightly with oil, salt and pepper. Sprinkle with half the lemon juice, bake for 12-15 mins. After 10 mins sprinkle over a little parsley and lemon zest to finish cooking.

STEP 2

Meanwhile, mix the capers, yogurt, remaining parsley and lemon juice together, set aside and season if you wish. To serve, divide the chips between plates, lift the fish onto the plates and serve with a spoonful of yogurt mix.

Hearty pasta soup

Prep: 5 mins **Cook:** 25 mins

Serves 4

Ingredients

- 1 tbsp olive oil
- 2 carrots, chopped
- 1 large onion, finely chopped
- 1l vegetable stock
- 400g can chopped tomato
- 200g frozen mixed peas and beans
- 250g pack fresh filled tortellini (we used spinach and ricotta)
- handful of basil leaves (optional)
- grated parmesan (or vegetarian alternative), to serve

Method

STEP 1

Heat oil in a pan. Fry the carrots and onion for 5 mins until starting to soften. Add the stock and tomatoes, then simmer for 10 mins. Add the peas and beans with 5 mins to go.

STEP 2

Once veg is tender, stir in the pasta. Return to the boil and simmer for 2 mins until the pasta is just cooked. Stir in the basil, if using. Season, then serve in bowls topped with a sprinkling of Parmesan and slices of garlic bread.

Healthy salad Niçoise

Prep: 15 mins **Cook:** 10 mins

Serves 2

Ingredients

- 200g new potato, thickly sliced
- 2 medium eggs
- 100g green bean, trimmed

- 1 romaine lettuce heart, leaves separated and washed
- 8 cherry tomatoes, halved
- 6 anchovies in olive oil, drained well
- 197g can tuna steak in spring water, drained
- 2 tbsp reduced-fat mayonnaise

Method

STEP 1

Bring a large pan of water to the boil. Add the potatoes and the eggs, and cook for 7 mins. Scoop the eggs out of the pan, tip in the green beans and cook for a further 4 mins. Drain the potatoes, beans and eggs in a colander under cold running water until cool. Leave to dry.

STEP 2

Peel the eggs and cut into quarters. Arrange the lettuce leaves in 2 shallow bowls. Scatter over the beans, potatoes,tomatoes and egg quarters. Pat the anchovies with kitchen paper to absorb the excess oil and place on top.

STEP 3

Flake the tuna into chunks and scatter over the salad. Mix the mayonnaise and 1 tbsp cold water in a bowl until smooth. Drizzle over the salad and serve.

Healthy coleslaw

Prep: 10 mins No cook

Serves 6

Ingredients

- 6 tbsp plain yogurt
- ½ tsp Dijon mustard
- 2 tbsp mayonnaise
- ½ white cabbage
- 2 carrots
- ½ onion

Method

STEP 1

Mix the yogurt, mustard and mayonnaise together in a bowl. Then, use a grater attachment on a food processor, or a box grater, to grate the cabbage and carrots. Either grate the onion or chop as finely as you can. Tip all of the vegetables into the bowl and stir through the dressing.

STEP 2

Will keep in the fridge for up to 3 days.

Saag aloo

Prep: 10 mins **Cook:** 15 mins

Serves 4 as a side dish

Ingredients

- 2 tbsp sunflower oil
- 1 onion, finely chopped
- 2 garlic cloves, sliced
- 1 tbsp chopped ginger
- 500g potato, cut into 2cm (¾in) chunks
- 1 large red chilli, halved, deseeded and finely sliced
- ½ tsp each black mustard seeds, cumin seeds, turmeric
- 250g spinach leaves

Method

STEP 1

Heat 2 tbsp sunflower oil in a large pan, add 1 finely chopped onion, 2 sliced garlic cloves and 1 tbsp chopped ginger, and fry for about 3 mins.

STEP 2

Stir in 500g potatoes, cut into 2cm chunks, 1 halved, deseeded and finely sliced red chilli, ½ tsp black mustard seeds, ½ tsp cumin seeds, ½ tsp turmeric and ½ tsp salt and continue cooking and stirring for 5 mins more.

STEP 3

Add a splash of water, cover, and cook for 8-10 mins.

STEP 4

Check the potatoes are ready by spearing with the point of a knife, and if they are, add 250g spinach leaves and let it wilt into the pan. Take off the heat and serve.

Chinese chicken curry

Prep: 15 mins **Cook:** 40 mins

Serves 4

Ingredients

- 4 skinless chicken breasts, cut into chunks (or use thighs or drumsticks)
- 2 tsp cornflour
- 1 onion, diced
- 2 tbsp rapeseed oil
- 1 garlic clove, crushed
- 2 tsp curry powder
- 1 tsp turmeric
- ½ tsp ground ginger
- pinch sugar
- 400ml chicken stock
- 1 tsp soy sauce
- handful frozen peas
- rice to serve

Method

STEP 1

Toss the chicken pieces in the cornflour and season well. Set them aside.

STEP 2

Fry the onion in half of the oil in a wok on a low to medium heat, until it softens – about 5-6 minutes – then add the garlic and cook for a minute. Stir in the spices and sugar and cook for another minute, then add the stock and soy sauce, bring to a simmer and cook for 20 minutes. Tip everything into a blender and blitz until smooth.

STEP 3

Wipe out the pan and fry the chicken in the remaining oil until it is browned all over. Tip the sauce back into the pan and bring everything to a simmer, stir in the peas and cook for 5 minutes. Add a little water if you need to thin the sauce. Serve with rice.

Chicken jalfrezi

Prep: 10 mins **Cook:** 1 hr

Serves 4

Ingredients

For the sauce

- ½ large onion, roughly chopped
- 2 garlic cloves, chopped
- 1 green chilli, finely chopped
- vegetable oil, for frying
- 400g can plum tomatoes
- 1 tbsp ground coriander
- 1 tbsp ground cumin
- 1 tsp turmeric

For the meat & veg

- 2-3 chicken breasts, diced
- 1 tsp ground cumin
- 1 tsp ground coriander
- 1 tsp turmeric
- ½ large onion, sliced
- 1 red pepper, chopped
- 2 red chillies, finely chopped (optional)
- 2 tsp garam masala
- handful of fresh, chopped coriander leaves
- cooked basmati rice or naan bread to serve

Method

STEP 1

Take 2-3 diced chicken breasts and coat in 1 tsp cumin, 1 tsp coriander and 1 tsp turmeric then leave it to marinate in the fridge while you make the sauce.

STEP 2

To make the sauce, fry ½ roughly chopped large onion, 2 chopped garlic cloves and 1 finely chopped green chilli in a large pan with a little vegetable oil, for around 5 mins, until browned.

STEP 3

Add 300ml water to the onion mixture and simmer for around 20 minutes.

STEP 4

Meanwhile, put a 400g can plum tomatoes in a food processor and give it a good whizz (aim for a smooth consistency).

STEP 5

Heat another large pan and gently fry 1 tbsp coriander, 1 tbsp cumin and 1 tsp turmeric in a splash of oil for about a minute. Add the tomatoes to this pan and simmer for around 10 minutes.

STEP 6

Next, whizz your onion mixture in the food processor and add it to the spiced tomato sauce. Season generously, stir, then simmer for 20 minutes. You can make large batches of this sauce and freeze it for later use.

STEP 7

Fry the marinated chicken in vegetable oil and stir continuously. After a few minutes, turn down the heat and add the remaining ½ sliced onion, 1 chopped red pepper and 2 finely chopped red chillies. Stir until the onions and pepper soften.

STEP 8

Add the sauce you prepared earlier to the cooked chicken and simmer for around 10-20 minutes, adding a splash of water if it gets too thick.

STEP 9

Just before you dish it up, stir in 2 tsp garam masala and handful of chopped coriander leaves. Serve with basmati rice or naan bread.

Ratatouille

Prep: 15 mins **Cook:** 35 mins

Serves 4

Ingredients

- 2 large aubergines
- 4 small courgettes
- 2 red or yellow peppers
- 4 large ripe tomatoes
- 5 tbsp olive oil
- supermarket pack or small bunch basil
- 1 medium onion, peeled and thinly sliced
- 3 garlic cloves, peeled and crushed
- 1 tbsp red wine vinegar
- 1 tsp sugar (any kind)

Method

STEP 1

Cut 2 large aubergines in half lengthways. Place them on the board, cut side down, slice in half lengthways again and then across into 1.5cm chunks. Cut the ends off 4 small courgettes, then across into 1.5cm slices.

STEP 2

Peel 2 red or yellow peppers from stalk to bottom. Hold upright, cut around the stalk, then cut into 3 pieces. Cut away any membrane, then chop into bite-size chunks.

STEP 3

Score a small cross on the base of each of 4 large ripe tomatoes, then put them into a heatproof bowl. Pour boiling water over, leave for 20 secs, then remove. Pour the water away, replace the tomatoes and cover with cold water. Leave to cool, then peel the skin away.

STEP 4

Quarter the tomatoes, scrape away the seeds with a spoon, then roughly chop the flesh.

STEP 5

Set a sauté pan over medium heat and when hot, pour in 2 tbsp olive oil. Brown the aubergines for 5 mins on each side until the pieces are soft. Set them aside.

STEP 6

Fry the courgettes in another tbsp oil for 5 mins, until golden on both sides. Repeat with the peppers. Don't overcook the vegetables at this stage.

STEP 7

Tear up the leaves from the bunch of basil and set aside. Cook 1 thinly sliced medium onion in the pan for 5 minutes. Add 3 crushed garlic cloves and fry for a further minute. Stir in 1 tbsp red wine vinegar and 1 tsp sugar, then tip in the tomatoes and half the basil.

STEP 8

Return the vegetables to the pan with some salt and pepper and cook for 5 mins. Serve with basil.

Spiced lentil & butternut squash soup

Prep: 10 mins **Cook:** 40 mins

Serves 4-6

Ingredients

- 2 tbsp olive oil
- 2 onions, finely chopped
- 2 garlic cloves, crushed
- ¼ tsp hot chilli powder
- 1 tbsp ras el hanout
- 1 butternut squash, peeled and cut into 2cm pieces
- 100g red lentils
- 1l hot vegetable stock
- 1 small bunch coriander, leaves chopped, plus extra to serve
- dukkah (see tip) and natural yogurt, to serve

Method

STEP 1

Heat the oil in a large flameproof casserole dish or saucepan over a medium-high heat. Fry the onions with a pinch of salt for 7 mins, or until softened and just caramelised. Add the garlic, chilli and ras el hanout, and cook for 1 min more.

STEP 2

Stir in the squash and lentils. Pour over the stock and season to taste. Bring to the boil, then reduce the heat to a simmer and cook, covered, for 25 mins or until the squash is soft. Blitz the soup with a stick blender until smooth, then season to taste. To freeze, leave to cool completely and transfer to large freezerproof bags.

STEP 3

Stir in the coriander leaves and ladle the soup into bowls. Serve topped with the dukkah, yogurt and extra coriander leaves.

Celery soup

Prep: 15 mins **Cook:** 40 mins

Serves 3 - 4

Ingredients

- 2 tbsp olive oil
- 300g celery, sliced, with tough strings removed
- 1 garlic clove, peeled
- 200g potatoes, peeled and cut into chunks
- 500ml vegetable stock
- 100ml milk
- crusty bread, to serve

Method

STEP 1

Heat the oil in a large saucepan over a medium heat, tip in the celery, garlic and potatoes and coat in the oil. Add a splash of water and a big pinch of salt and cook, stirring regularly for 15 mins, adding a little more water if the veg begins to stick.

STEP 2

Pour in the vegetable stock and bring to the boil, then turn the heat down and simmer for 20 mins further, until the potatoes are falling apart and the celery is soft. Use a stick blender to purée the soup, then pour in the milk and blitz again. Season to taste. Serve with crusty bread.

Rosemary balsamic lamb with vegetable mash

Prep: 15 mins **Cook:** 35 mins

Serves 4

Ingredients

- 320g celeriac, peeled and diced
- 320g swede, peeled and diced
- 320g potato, peeled and diced
- 1 tbsp rapeseed oil
- 3 red onions, thinly sliced
- 550g lean, trimmed lamb steak, diced
- 1 tsp finely chopped rosemary
- 1 tbsp vegetable bouillon powder

- 2 tbsp balsamic vinegar
- 1 tbsp chopped parsley
- 320g spinach, to serve
- 320g frozen peas, to serve

Method

STEP 1

Put the celeriac, swede and potato in a large steamer, then steam for 25 mins until softened.

STEP 2

Meanwhile, heat the oil in a large non-stick frying pan and fry the onions for 10 mins until softened and golden. Push to the side of the pan, then add the lamb and rosemary and stir-fry over the heat until browned, but still a little pink in the middle – try not to overcook it as it will become tough and will need a longer cook to become tender again. Add the bouillon and balsamic vinegar with 200ml boiling water. Stir to make a sauce.

STEP 3

Mash the steamed veg and spoon half into the centre of two plates. Top with half the lamb and gravy, scatter with the parsley and serve with the spinach and peas. Chill the remaining lamb and veg to reheat and serve on another evening.

Chicken madras

Prep: 20 mins **Cook:** 35 mins

Serves 3 - 4

Ingredients

- 1 onion, peeled and quartered
- 2 garlic cloves
- thumb-sized chunk of ginger, peeled
- ½ red chilli
- 1 tbsp vegetable oil
- ½ tsp turmeric
- 1 tsp ground cumin
- 1 tsp ground coriander
- 1-2 tsp hot chilli powder (depending on how spicy you like your curry)
- 4 chicken breasts, cut into chunks
- 400g can chopped tomatoes
- small pack coriander, chopped
- rice, naan and mango chutney, to serve

Method

STEP 1

Blitz 1 quartered onion, 2 garlic cloves, a thumb-sized chunk of ginger and ½ red chilli together in a food processor until it becomes a coarse paste.

STEP 2

Heat 1 tbsp vegetable oil in a large saucepan and add the paste, fry for 5 mins, until softened. If it starts to stick to the pan at all, add a splash of water.

STEP 3

Tip in ½ tsp turmeric, 1 tsp ground cumin, 1 tsp ground coriander and 1-2 tsp hot chilli powder and stir well, cook for a couple of mins to toast them a bit, then add 4 chicken breasts, cut into chunks. Stir and make sure everything is covered in the spice mix.

STEP 4

Cook until the chicken begins to turn pale, adding a small splash of water if it sticks to the base of the pan at all.

STEP 5

Pour in 400g can chopped tomatoes, along with a big pinch of salt, cover and cook on a low heat for 30 mins, until the chicken is tender.

STEP 6

Stir through small pack of coriander and serve with rice, naan and a big dollop of mango chutney.

Healthier chicken balti

Prep: 25 mins **Cook:** 30 mins Plus marinating

Serves 4

Ingredients

- 450g skinless, boneless chicken breast, cut into bite-sized pieces
- 1 tbsp lime juice
- 1 tsp paprika
- ¼ tsp hot chilli powder
- 1½ tbsp sunflower or groundnut oil
- 1 cinnamon stick
- 3 cardamom pods, split
- 1 small to medium green chilli
- ½ tsp cumin seed

- 1 medium onion, coarsely grated
- 2 garlic cloves, very finely chopped
- 2½ cm-piece ginger, grated
- ½ tsp turmeric
- 1 tsp ground cumin
- 1 tsp ground coriander
- 1 tsp garam masala
- 250ml organic passata
- 1 red pepper, deseeded, cut into small chunks
- 1 medium tomato, chopped
- 85g baby spinach leaves
- handful fresh coriander, chopped
- chapatis or basmati rice, to serve (optional)

Method

STEP 1

Put the chicken in a medium bowl. Mix in the lime juice, paprika, chilli powder and a grinding of black pepper (step 1), then leave to marinate for at least 15 mins, preferably a bit longer.

STEP 2

Heat 1 tbsp of the oil in a large non-stick wok or sauté pan. Tip in the cinnamon stick, cardamom pods, whole chilli and cumin seeds, and stir-fry briefly just to colour and release their fragrance (step 2). Stir in the onion, garlic and ginger and fry over a medium-high heat for 3-4 mins until the onion starts to turn brown. Add the remaining oil, then drop in the chicken and stir-fry for 2-3 mins or until it no longer looks raw. Mix the turmeric, cumin, ground coriander and garam masala together. Tip into the pan, lower the heat to medium and cook for 2 mins (step 3). Pour in the passata and 150ml water, then drop in the chunks of pepper. When starting to bubble, lower the heat and simmer for 15-20 mins or until the chicken is tender.

STEP 3

Stir in the tomato, simmer for 2-3 mins, then add the spinach and turn it over in the pan to just wilt. Season with a little salt. If you want to thin down the sauce, splash in a little more water. Remove the cinnamon stick, chilli and cardamom pods, if you wish, before serving. Scatter with fresh coriander and serve with warm chapatis or basmati rice, if you like.

Double bean & roasted pepper chilli

Prep: 30 mins **Cook:** 1 hr and 15 mins

Serves 8

Ingredients

- 2 onions, chopped
- 2 celery sticks, finely chopped
- 2 yellow or orange peppers, finely chopped
- 2 tbsp sunflower oil or rapeseed oil
- 2 x 460g jars roasted red peppers
- 2 tsp chipotle paste
- 2 tbsp red wine vinegar
- 1 tbsp cocoa powder
- 1 tbsp dried oregano
- 1 tbsp sweet smoked paprika
- 2 tbsp ground cumin
- 1 tsp ground cinnamon
- 2 x 400g cans chopped tomatoes
- 400g can refried beans
- 3 x 400g cans kidney beans, drained and rinsed
- 2 x 400g cans black beans, drained and rinsed

Method

STEP 1

Put the onions, celery and chopped peppers with the oil in your largest flameproof casserole dish or heavy-based saucepan, and fry gently over a low heat until soft but not coloured.

STEP 2

Drain both jars of peppers over a bowl to catch the juices. Put a quarter of the peppers into a food processor with the chipotle paste, vinegar, cocoa, dried spices and herbs. Whizz to a purée, then stir into the softened veg and cook for a few mins.

STEP 3

Add the tomatoes and refried beans with 1 can water and the reserved pepper juice. Simmer for 1 hr until thickened, smoky and the tomato chunks have broken down to a smoother sauce.

STEP 4

At this stage you can cool and chill the sauce if making ahead. Otherwise add the kidney and black beans, and the remaining roasted peppers, cut into bite-sized pieces, then reheat. (This makes a large batch, so once the sauce is ready it might be easier to split it between two pans when you add the beans and peppers.) Once bubbling and the beans are hot, season to taste and serve.

Curried cod

Prep: 10 mins **Cook:** 25 mins

Serves 4

Ingredients

- 1 tbsp oil
- 1 onion, chopped
- 2 tbsp medium curry powder
- thumb-sized piece ginger, peeled and finely grated
- 3 garlic cloves, crushed
- 2 x 400g cans chopped tomatoes
- 400g can chickpeas
- 4 cod fillets (about 125-150g each)
- zest 1 lemon, then cut into wedges
- handful coriander, roughly chopped

Method

STEP 1

Heat the oil in a large, lidded frying pan. Cook the onion over a high heat for a few mins, then stir in the curry powder, ginger and garlic. Cook for another 1-2 mins until fragrant, then stir in the tomatoes, chickpeas and some seasoning.

STEP 2

Cook for 8-10 mins until thickened slightly, then top with the cod. Cover and cook for another 5-10 mins until the fish is cooked through. Scatter over the lemon zest and coriander, then serve with the lemon wedges to squeeze over.

Easy Singapore noodles

Prep: 15 mins **Cook:** 15 mins

Serves 4

Ingredients

- 200g vermicelli rice noodles
- 1 tbsp mild curry powder

- ¼ tsp turmeric
- 1 tsp caster sugar
- 1 tbsp sesame oil
- 2½ tbsp low-salt soy sauce
- 1 tbsp sunflower or vegetable oil
- 1 onion, sliced
- 1 pepper, sliced (we used ½ green and ½ orange)
- 200g beansprouts
- 1 red chilli, sliced (optional)

Method

STEP 1

Boil the kettle and put the noodles in a large pan or bowl. Pour over enough boiled water to cover, pushing the noodles under the water to help them soften evenly. Set aside for 5-10 mins, until the noodles are completely soft. Mix the curry powder, turmeric, sugar, sesame oil, soy sauce and 1 tbsp water in a bowl.

STEP 2

Heat the wok until very hot. Add the sunflower oil, onion and pepper. Stir-fry for 3-4 mins until softened and starting to brown in places. Drain the noodles and add to the pan, along with the sauce mixture and beansprouts. Stir-fry for a further 3-4 mins, tossing everything through the sauce, until hot. Adjust the seasoning with a little more soy or sugar, if you like, and scatter over the chilli, if you like more spice.

Curried chicken pie

Prep: 20 mins **Cook:** 25 mins

Serves 4

Ingredients

- 2 tbsp cold pressed rapeseed oil
- 500g chicken breasts, cut into chunks
- 4 spring onions, sliced
- 3 garlic cloves, grated
- thumb-sized piece ginger, grated
- 1 tbsp curry powder
- 1 large head broccoli, cut into florets, top of stalk thinly sliced
- 1 tsp soy sauce
- 250ml low-fat coconut milk, plus a splash
- 250ml chicken stock
- 1 heaped tsp cornflour mixed with 1 tbsp hot water
- 4 large handfuls kale
- 4 sheets filo pastry
- ½ tbsp nigella seeds

Method

STEP 1

Heat oven to 220C/200C fan/gas 7. Pour 1 tbsp oil into a flameproof casserole dish. Add the chicken, season and fry for 4-5 mins on a medium heat, turning, until lightly browned. Remove with tongs and set aside.

STEP 2

Pour another ½ tbsp oil into the casserole dish and add the spring onions. Fry gently for a couple of mins, then stir in the garlic, ginger and curry powder. Cook for 1 min, then tip the chicken back into the pan, along with the broccoli, soy sauce, coconut milk, chicken stock and cornflour mixture. Bring to the boil, then stir in the kale. Once the kale has wilted, take the dish off the heat.

STEP 3

Mix the remaining oil with the splash of coconut milk. Unravel the pastry. Brush each sheet lightly with the oil mixture, then scrunch up and sit on top of the pie mixture. Scatter over the nigella seeds, then cook in the oven for 12 mins, or until the pastry is a deep golden brown. Leave to stand for a couple of mins before serving.

Nutty chicken satay strips

Prep: 10 mins **Cook:** 8 mins - 10 mins

Serves 2

Ingredients

- 2 tbsp chunky peanut butter (without palm oil or sugar)
- 1 garlic clove, finely grated
- 1 tsp Madras curry powder
- few shakes soy sauce
- 2 tsp lime juice
- 2 skinless, chicken breast fillets (about 300g) cut into thick strips
- about 10cm cucumber, cut into fingers
- sweet chilli sauce, to serve

Method

STEP 1

Heat oven to 200C/ 180C fan/ gas 4 and line a baking tray with non-stick paper.

STEP 2

Mix 2 tbsp chunky peanut butter with 1 finely grated garlic clove, 1 tsp Madras curry powder, a few shakes of soy sauce and 2 tsp lime juice in a bowl. Some nut butters are thicker than others, so if necessary, add a dash of boiling water to get a coating consistency.

STEP 3

Add 2 skinless chicken breast fillets, cut into strips, and mix well. Arrange on the baking sheet, spaced apart, and bake in the oven for 8-10 mins until cooked, but still juicy.

STEP 4

Eat warm with roughly 10cm cucumber, cut into fingers, and sweet chilli sauce. Alternatively, leave to cool and keep in the fridge for up to 2 days.

Lentil salad with tahini dressing

Prep: 15 mins **Cook:** 20 mins

Serves 4

Ingredients

- 2 tbsp cold-pressed rapeseed oil
- 320g sweet potatoes , cut into cubes
- 2 large carrots , cut into thin sticks (320g)
- 2 large courgettes , (375g) cut into chunks
- 2 medium red onions , halved and sliced
- 1 tsp cumin seeds
- 2 tbsp finely chopped ginger
- 2 tbsp pumpkin seeds
- 2 x 390g cans green lentils , drained
- 2 tsp vegetable bouillon powder
- 1 lemon , zested
- good handful of mint , roughly chopped
- handful of parsley , roughly chopped
- 2.5-3 tbsp tahini
- 1 garlic clove , finely grated
- 2 x 120g pot bio yogurt
- a little smoked paprika , to serve

Method

STEP 1

Heat the oil in a large non-stick wok. Add the sweet potato and fry for 5 mins, stirring frequently until it starts to soften. If it starts to brown too quickly, put a lid on the pan. Add the carrot, courgette, onion, cumin and ginger, then cook over a high heat, stirring frequently, until the veg is tender and a little charred. Stir in the seeds towards the end so they cook for a couple of mins. Remove from the heat and add the lentils, bouillon powder, lemon zest, mint and parsley.

STEP 2

Meanwhile, stir the tahini with the garlic, yogurt and 1 tbsp water to make a dressing. Spoon the lentil salad into bowls and top with the dressing and paprika, if using. If you're following our Healthy Diet Plan, save two portions stored in containers and chill until ready to eat.

Healthier flapjacks

Prep: 10 mins **Cook:** 20 mins

Makes 12

Ingredients

- 150g ready-to-eat stoned dates
- 100g low-fat spread
- 3 generous tbsp agave syrup
- 50g ready-to-eat stoned dried apricots, finely chopped
- 50g chopped toasted hazelnuts
- 3 tbsp mixed seeds
- 50g raisins
- 150g porridge oats

Method

STEP 1

Heat the oven to 190C/170C fan/gas 5. Line an 18cm square tin with baking parchment. Put the dates into a food processor and blitz until they are finely chopped and sticking together in clumps.

STEP 2

Put the low-fat spread, agave syrup and dates into a saucepan and heat gently. Stir until the low-fat spread has melted and the dates are blended in. Add all the remaining ingredients to the pan and stir until well mixed. Spoon the mixture into the tin and spread level.

STEP 3

Bake in the oven for 15-20 mins until golden brown. Remove and cut into 12 pieces. Leave in the tin until cold. Store in an airtight container.

Broccoli pesto & pancetta pasta

Prep: 10 mins **Cook:** 15 mins

Serves 4

Ingredients

- 300g head broccoli , broken into florets
- 300g pasta (we used orecchiette)
- 1 tbsp pine nuts
- 1 large bunch of basil
- 1 large garlic clove
- 2 tbsp parmesan , finely grated
- 1 tbsp olive oil
- 50g smoked pancetta , diced
- 200g cherry tomatoes , halved

Method

STEP 1

Bring a pan of lightly salted water to the boil. Add the broccoli and boil for 5 mins. Scoop out with a slotted spoon and set aside.

STEP 2

Put the pasta in the same pan and cook following pack instructions. Meanwhile, tip the broccoli into a food processor with the pine nuts, basil, garlic, parmesan and oil, and blitz until smooth. Season with black pepper and a little salt (the pancetta is very salty).

STEP 3

Set a frying pan over a medium heat and cook the pancetta for 2 mins. Add the tomatoes and cook for 3 mins, or until softened. Toss the pasta with the broccoli pesto, tomatoes and pancetta, and loosen with a splash of pasta water, if needed. Spoon into bowls and serve.

Meatball & tomato soup

Prep: 5 mins **Cook:** 15 mins

Serves 4

Ingredients

- 1½ tbsp rapeseed oil
- 1 onion, finely chopped
- 2 red peppers, deseeded and sliced
- 1 garlic clove, crushed
- ½ tsp chilli flakes
- 2 x 400g cans chopped tomatoes
- 100g giant couscous
- 500ml hot vegetable stock
- 12 pork meatballs
- 150g baby spinach
- ½ small bunch of basil
- grated parmesan, to serve (optional)

Method

STEP 1

Heat the oil in a saucepan. Fry the onion and peppers for 7 mins, then stir through the garlic and chilli flakes and cook for 1 min. Add the tomatoes, giant couscous and veg stock and bring to a simmer.

STEP 2

Season to taste, then add the meatballs and spinach. Simmer for 5-7 mins or until cooked through. Ladle into bowls and top with the basil and some parmesan, if you like.

Sweetcorn fritters with eggs & black bean salsa

Prep: 10 mins **Cook:** 20 mins

Serves 4

Ingredients

For the fritters & eggs

- 1 tsp rapeseed oil
- 1 small red onion (85g), finely chopped
- 1 red pepper, deseeded and finely diced
- 100g wholemeal self-raising flour
- 1 tsp smoked paprika
- 1 tsp ground coriander
- 1 tsp baking powder
- 325g can sweetcorn, drained
- 6 large eggs

For the salsa

- 1 small red onion (85g), finely chopped
- 4 tomatoes (320g), chopped
- 2 x 400g cans black beans, drained
- 1 lime, zested and juiced

- ½ x 30g pack coriander, chopped

Method

STEP 1

Heat the oven to 200C/180C fan/gas 6 and line a large baking tray with baking parchment.

STEP 2

Heat the oil in a small pan and fry the onion and pepper for 5 mins until softened. Meanwhile, mix the flour, spices and baking powder in a bowl. Add the onions, pepper, corn and 2 of the eggs, then mix together well.

STEP 3

Spoon eight mounds of the mixture onto the baking tray, well spaced apart, then flatten slightly with the back of the spoon. Bake for 20 mins until set and golden.

STEP 4

Meanwhile, mix together the salsa ingredients and poach 2 of the remaining eggs to your liking. If you're following our Healthy Diet Plan, serve four fritters on the day you make them, topped with half the salsa and the poached eggs. Chill the remaining fritters for another day. Reheat them in a pan or microwave and serve with 2 more poached eggs and the remaining salsa.

Mexican penne with avocado

Prep: 10 mins **Cook:** 20 mins

Serves 2

Ingredients

- 100g wholemeal penne
- 1 tsp rapeseed oil
- 1 large onion, sliced, plus 1 tbsp finely chopped
- 1 orange pepper, deseeded and cut into chunks
- 2 garlic cloves, grated
- 2 tsp mild chilli powder
- 1 tsp ground coriander
- ½ tsp cumin seeds
- 400g can chopped tomatoes
- 196g can sweetcorn in water
- 1 tsp vegetable bouillon powder
- 1 avocado, stoned and chopped

- 1/2 lime, zest and juice
- handful coriander, chopped, plus extra to serve

Method

STEP 1

Cook the pasta in salted water for 10-12 mins until al dente. Meanwhile, heat the oil in a medium pan. Add the sliced onion and pepper and fry, stirring frequently for 10 mins until golden. Stir in the garlic and spices, then tip in the tomatoes, half a can of water, the corn and bouillon. Cover and simmer for 15 mins.

STEP 2

Meanwhile, toss the avocado with the lime juice and zest, and the finely chopped onion.

STEP 3

Drain the penne and toss into the sauce with the coriander. Spoon the pasta into bowls, top with the avocado and scatter over the coriander leaves.

Tarragon roast chicken with summer greens

Prep: 20 mins **Cook:** 1 hr and 40 mins

Serves 4

Ingredients

- 1 lemon
- large woody sprig of tarragon
- 1 medium chicken (about 1.4kg)
- 450g baby potatoes, halved
- 2 tsp cold pressed rapeseed oil (about 1.4kg)

For the summer greens

- 1 tsp vegetable bouillon powder
- 2 leeks, cut into rings (about 300g)
- 350g asparagus (250g pack plus 100g pack) ends trimmed, each cut into 4
- 320g frozen peas
- 260g bag of young leaf spinach
- 2 tbsp bio Greek yogurt
- 1 tbsp tarragon leaves, chopped

Method

STEP 1

Heat the oven to 190C/170C fan/gas 5. Finely grate the zest and squeeze the juice from the lemon, then set aside, keeping them separate from each other. Put the squeezed-out lemon and the tarragon sprig in the chicken cavity. Tip the potatoes into a large roasting tin and toss with the oil and a grinding of black pepper. Sit the chicken in the middle, but not on top of the potatoes and roast for 1¼-1½ hrs until the chicken is cooked but still moist, and the potatoes are tender and golden. Remove the tin from the oven, pour off any juices into a jug and set aside. Toss the lemon zest through the potatoes and leave the chicken to rest, covered, while you cook the greens.

STEP 2

Pour 150ml water into a pan and add the bouillon. Drop in the leeks, cover and cook for 2 mins, then add the asparagus and peas. Cover again and cook for 2 mins more. Finally, stir through the spinach to wilt it. Pour the roasting juices into the veg with 2 tbsp lemon juice, the yogurt and tarragon leaves, and stir well. If you're following our Healthy Diet Plan, serve half the veg with the meat from a skinless chicken leg and breast. Eat the other breast and leg with the remaining veg on another day. Will keep for up to three days, covered, in the fridge. To serve, reheat on plates in the microwave. Reserve any meat left on the carcass for our healthy quinoa salad.

Pasta arrabbiata with aubergine

Prep: 8 mins **Cook:** 35 mins

Serves 2

Ingredients

- 1 tbsp cold-pressed rapeseed oil
- 1 large onion, finely chopped (160g)
- 2 large garlic cloves, finely grated
- 1 tsp chilli flakes
- 1 tsp smoked paprika
- 400g can chopped tomatoes
- 1 tsp vegetable bouillon powder
- 1 aubergine, chopped
- 150g wholemeal penne or fusilli
- large handful of basil, plus extra to serve
- 25g parmesan or vegetarian Italian-style hard cheese, finely grated

Method

STEP 1

Heat the oil in a large non-stick pan, add the onions, cover and cook for 5 mins. Remove the lid and cook for 5 mins more, stirring frequently until softened. Add the garlic, chilli flakes and paprika, stir briefly, then tip in the tomatoes and a can of water. Stir in the bouillon and aubergine, then bring to a simmer, cover and cook for 20 mins.

STEP 2

Cook the penne in a pan of boiling water for 12 mins until al dente. Drain, reserving 60ml of the cooking water. Add the cooked penne to the sauce, and toss well with the basil and a little of the reserved water, if needed. Spoon into two shallow bowls, and serve topped with the cheese and some extra basil, if you like.

Roasted carrots

Prep: 10 mins **Cook:** 45 mins

Serves 8

Ingredients

- 2kg carrots, halved or quartered lengthways
- 4 tbsp olive oil
- 4 tbsp honey
- 2 tbsp red wine or cider vinegar

Method

STEP 1

Heat the oven to 200C/180C fan/gas 6. Bring a large pan of water to the boil. Add the carrots, bring back up to the boil and cook for 5 mins.

STEP 2

Drain and leave in a colander to steam dry for a few minutes, and then toss in a large roasting tin with the olive oil, honey, vinegar and seasoning. Roast for 30-40 mins.

Chipotle chicken & slaw

Prep: 25 mins **Cook:** 40 mins

Serves 4

Ingredients

- 1 tbsp rapeseed oil
- 2 tbsp chipotle paste
- 1½ tbsp honey
- 8 chicken drumsticks
- 1 lime, zested and juiced
- 1 small avocado, stoned
- 2 tbsp fat-free Greek yogurt
- 125g each red and white cabbage, both shredded
- 1 large carrot, cut into matchsticks
- 3 spring onions, sliced
- 4 corn on the cobs, steamed, to serve (optional)

Method

STEP 1

Heat the oven to 200C/180C fan/gas 6. Whisk the oil, chipotle paste and honey together in a large bowl. Add the chicken and toss to coat, then spread out on a non-stick baking tray. Roast for 30 mins, turning halfway through.

STEP 2

Put the lime zest and juice, avocado flesh, yogurt and a good pinch of salt into a blender and blitz until completely smooth. Put the sauce in a large bowl with the cabbage, carrot and spring onion and toss to combine.

STEP 3

Serve the drumsticks with the slaw and steamed corn, if you like.

Orzo & tomato soup

Prep: 5 mins **Cook:** 25 mins

Serves 4

Ingredients

- 2 tbsp olive oil
- 1 onion, chopped
- 2 celery sticks, chopped
- 2 garlic cloves, crushed
- 1 tbsp tomato purée
- 400g can chopped tomatoes
- 400g can chickpeas
- 150g orzo pasta
- 700ml vegetable stock
- 2 tbsp basil pesto
- crusty bread, to serve

Method

STEP 1

Heat 1 tbsp olive oil in a large saucepan. Add the onion and celery and fry for 10-15 mins, or until starting to soften, then add the garlic and cook for 1 min more. Stir in all the other ingredients, except for the pesto and remaining oil, and bring to the boil.

STEP 2

Reduce the heat and leave to simmer for 6-8 mins, or until the orzo is tender. Season to taste, then ladle into bowls.

STEP 3

Stir the remaining oil with the pesto, then drizzle over the soup. Serve with chunks of crusty bread.

Corn & split pea chowder

Prep: 10 mins **Cook:** 50 mins

Serves 4

Ingredients

- 200g dried yellow split peas
- 3 celery sticks (about 160g), sliced
- 1 thyme sprig, plus 1 tbsp thyme leaves
- 2 onions (350g), halved and sliced
- 1 tbsp rapeseed oil
- 50g ginger, finely grated
- 2 red chillies, deseeded and sliced
- 3 large garlic cloves, chopped
- 1 large green pepper, chopped into small pieces
- 1 large potato (about 215g), unpeeled, cut into 1-2cm pieces
- 2 tbsp vegetable bouillon powder
- 320g frozen sweetcorn
- 150g dairy-free coconut yogurt

Method

STEP 1

Tip the split peas, celery and thyme sprig into a medium pan with 1 litre of boiling water, bring back to the boil and simmer, covered, for 25 mins.

STEP 2

Meanwhile, fry the onion in the oil in a large pan for 10 mins. Stir in the ginger, chilli and garlic. Tip in the pepper and potato, and pour in ½ litre boiling water with the bouillon and remaining thyme. Tip in the split pea mixture and corn, bring to the boil, then cover and simmer for 30-35 mins until the veg is tender.

STEP 3

Remove the thyme sprig. Take out a third of the veg, then purée the rest in the pan with a hand blender (or use a potato masher). Return the veg to the pan with the yogurt, and stir well. If you're following our Healthy Diet Plan, eat two portions now, and cool then chill the rest for another day. Will keep in the fridge for three days.

Breakfast egg wraps

Prep: 5 mins **Cook:** 7 mins

Serves 4

Ingredients

- 500g pack closed cup mushrooms
- 4 tsp cold pressed rapeseed oil , plus 2 drops
- 320g cherry tomatoes , halved, or 8 tomatoes, cut into wedges
- 2 generous handfuls parsley , finely chopped
- 8 tbsp porridge oats (40g)
- 10 eggs
- 4 tsp English mustard powder made up with water

Method

STEP 1

Thickly slice half the pack of mushrooms. Heat 2 tsp rapeseed oil in a non-stick pan. Add the mushrooms, stir briefly then fry with the lid on the pan for 6-8 mins. Stir in half the tomatoes then cook 1-2 mins more with the lid off until softened.

STEP 2

Beat together the eggs really well with the parsley and oats. Heat a drop of oil in a large non-stick frying pan. Pour in a ¼ of the egg mix and fry for 1 min until almost set, flip over as if making a pancake. Tip from the pan, spread with a quarter of the mustard, spoon a ¼ the filling down the centre and roll up. Now make a second wrap using another ¼ of the egg mix and filling. If you're following our Healthy Diet Plan, save the rest for the following day.

Chunky Bolognese soup with penne

Prep: 10 mins **Cook:** 35 mins

Serves 4

Ingredients

- 2 tsp rapeseed oil
- 3 onions , finely chopped
- 3 large carrots , finely diced
- 2 celery sticks , finely diced
- 3 garlic cloves , finely chopped
- 250g pack 5% fat steak mince
- 500g carton passata
- 1 tbsp vegetable bouillon powder
- 1 tsp smoked paprika
- 4 sprigs fresh thyme
- 100g wholemeal penne
- 45g finely grated parmesan , plus extra to serve

Method

STEP 1

Heat the oil in a large non-stick pan and fry the onions for a few mins. Add the carrots, celery and garlic, then fry for 5 mins, stirring until the vegetables start to soften.

STEP 2

Add the meat and stir well so it breaks down as it cooks. Once it's turned brown, add the passata and bouillon along with 1.3 litres of boiling water. Add the paprika, thyme and some black pepper. Cover the pan and simmer for 15 mins.

STEP 3

Tip in the penne and cook for 12-15 mins until tender. Stir through the cheese, then ladle into bowls. Sprinkle over extra cheese, if you like.

STEP 4

If you're following our Healthy Diet Plan, serve two portions on the first day. Cool the remaining soup, remove the thyme and chill. Will keep for up to seven days. Reheat in a pan, adding some water if it's thickened.

Sausage & white bean casserole

Prep: 20 mins **Cook:** 1 hr and 5 mins

Serves 4

Ingredients

- 1 red or yellow pepper, deseeded and cut into chunks
- 2 carrots, cut into thick slices
- 2 red onions, cut into wedges
- 8 chipolatas, cut into thirds
- 400g can peeled cherry tomatoes
- 400g can white beans, drained
- 200ml low-salt chicken stock
- 2 tsp Dijon mustard
- 100g frozen peas
- potatoes, pasta or rice, to serve

Method

STEP 1

Heat oven to 220C/200C fan/gas 7. Roast the pepper, carrots and onion in a deep baking dish for 15 mins. Add the sausages and roast for a further 10 mins.

STEP 2

Reduce oven to 200C/180C fan/gas 6, tip in the tomatoes and beans, then stir in the stock. Cook for another 35 mins. Stir in the mustard and peas and return to the oven for 5 mins. Rest for 10 mins, then serve with potatoes, pasta or rice.

Veggie yaki udon

Prep: 10 mins **Cook:** 15 mins

Serves 2

Ingredients

- 1½ tbsp sesame oil
- 1 red onion , cut into thin wedges
- 160g mangetout
- 70g baby corn , halved
- 2 baby pak choi , quartered
- 3 spring onions , sliced
- 1 large garlic clove , crushed
- ½ tbsp mild curry powder
- 4 tsp low-salt soy sauce
- 300g ready-to-cook udon noodles
- 1 tbsp pickled sushi ginger , chopped, plus 2 tbsp of the brine

Method

STEP 1

Heat the oil in a non-stick frying pan or wok over a high heat. Add the onion and fry for 5 mins. Stir in the mangetout, corn, pak choi and spring onions and cook for 5 mins more. Add the garlic, curry powder and soy sauce, and cook for another minute.

STEP 2

Add the udon noodles along with the ginger and reserved brine, and stir in 2-3 tbsp hot water until the noodles are heated through. Divide between bowls and serve.

Lemony prawn & courgette tagliatelle

Prep: 10 mins **Cook:** 10 mins

Serves 2

Ingredients

- 2 tbsp olive oil
- 2 courgettes (about 500g), trimmed and coarsely grated
- 1 large garlic clove , finely grated
- 1 small red chilli , finely chopped
- 180g tagliatelle
- 150g raw king prawns , peeled and deveined

- 1 lemon, zested and juiced
- ½ small bunch of parsley, finely chopped

Method

STEP 1

Heat the oil in a frying pan and fry the courgette for 4-5 mins, then stir through the garlic and chilli.

STEP 2

Cook the tagliatelle following pack instructions. Drain, reserving some of the cooking water.

STEP 3

Add the prawns to the courgette mixture, and cook for 2 mins until pink. Toss through the tagliatelle, the lemon zest and juice, parsley, some seasoning and a splash of the reserved cooking water. Divide between bowls and serve.

Prawn & harissa spaghetti

Prep: 5 mins **Cook:** 15 mins

Serves 2

Ingredients

- 100g long-stem broccoli, cut into thirds
- 180g dried spaghetti
- 2 tbsp olive oil
- 1 large garlic clove, lightly bashed
- 150g cherry tomatoes, halved
- 150g raw king prawns
- 1 heaped tbsp rose harissa paste
- 1 lemon, finely zested

Method

STEP 1

Bring a pan of lightly salted water to the boil. Add the broccoli and boil for 1 min 30 secs, or until tender. Drain and set aside. Cook the pasta following pack instructions, then drain, reserving a ladleful of cooking water.

STEP 2

Heat the oil in a large frying pan, add the garlic clove and fry over a low heat for 2 mins. Remove with a slotted spoon and discard, leaving the flavoured oil.

STEP 3

Add the tomatoes to the pan and fry over a medium heat for 5 mins, or until beginning to soften and turn juicy. Stir through the prawns and cook for 2 mins, or until turning pink. Add the harissa and lemon zest, stirring to coat.

STEP 4

Toss the cooked spaghetti and pasta water through the prawns and harissa, season to taste and serve.

Smoky spiced veggie rice

Prep:15 mins **Cook:**1 hr

Serves 6

Ingredients

- 25g cashews
- 4 tbsp olive oil
- 1 corn cob
- 250g rainbow baby carrots , halved lengthways
- 2 red onions , finely chopped
- 2 celery sticks , finely chopped
- 2 large red peppers , finely sliced
- 3 garlic cloves , crushed
- 2 tbsp Cajun seasoning
- 1½ tbsp smoked paprika
- 1 tsp chipotle paste
- 2 tbsp tomato purée
- 200g heirloom cherry tomatoes , halved
- 400g can kidney beans , drained and rinsed
- 400g can cherry tomatoes
- 300g long-grain rice , washed
- 400ml vegetable or vegan stock
- 1 tbsp red wine vinegar (vegan varieties are readily available)
- 2 tbsp caster sugar
- 2 spring onions , finely sliced

Method

STEP 1

Dry-fry the cashews in a large saucepan or casserole dish over a medium heat until golden brown. Remove from the heat, leave to cool, then roughly chop. Heat 1 tbsp oil in the same pan over a high heat, then fry the corn on each side for 20 seconds to char. Remove from the pan, set aside, then tip in the carrots and fry for 5 mins. Remove from the pan and set aside.

STEP 2

Heat the rest of the oil in the same pan over a medium heat and fry the onions and celery for 10 mins until soft and slightly coloured. Tip in the peppers and garlic, then fry for another 5 mins before adding the Cajun seasoning, smoked paprika, chipotle paste and tomato purée. Fry for 1 min until the spices are fragrant, then add the cherry tomatoes and fry for another 2 mins.

STEP 3

Stir in the kidney beans, canned tomatoes, rice, stock, vinegar and sugar, then stir until everything is combined. Bring to the boil, then cover with a lid and simmer with a lid on for 35-40 mins on a medium-low heat, stirring halfway through, until the rice is cooked and liquid absorbed.

STEP 4

Slice the corn off the cob and mix it through the rice along with the carrots. Season and garnish with the spring onions and cashews.

Chorizo, orzo & sweetcorn summer stew

Prep: 10 mins **Cook:** 25 mins

Serves 2

Ingredients

- 1 tsp olive oil
- bunch of spring onions , sliced, green and white parts separated
- 1 red pepper , cut into small cubes
- 50g chorizo , cut into small cubes
- 1 garlic clove , crushed
- 75g orzo
- ½ tsp smoked paprika
- 200g can sweetcorn , drained
- 1 large tomato , chopped
- 350ml low-salt chicken or vegetable stock
- ½ small bunch of parsley , chopped
- ½ lemon , zested and juiced

Method

STEP 1

Heat the oil in a deep frying pan and fry the white parts of the spring onions, the peppers and chorizo for 8 mins, until the peppers are soft and the chorizo is just golden.

STEP 2

Stir in the garlic, orzo, paprika, sweetcorn and tomato, and fry for 2-3 mins more. Pour in the stock. Bring to a simmer and cook for 8-10 mins, stirring often, until the orzo is tender. Stir in the parsley, the green parts of the spring onions, and the lemon juice and zest.

Moroccan chickpea, squash & cavolo nero stew

Prep: 35 mins **Cook:** 50 mins

Serves 4

Ingredients

- 4 tomatoes, halved
- 5 tbsp olive oil
- 250g butternut squash, peeled and chopped into large chunks
- 1 tbsp thyme leaves
- 1 garlic clove, crushed
- 1 onion, sliced
- 2 x 400g cans chickpeas, drained
- 1 bay leaf
- 1 tbsp ground cumin
- 1 tsp ground cinnamon
- ½ tsp turmeric
- 1 tbsp harissa
- 1l vegetable stock
- 100g feta, crumbled
- 1 lemon, zested, then cut into wedges
- 2 tsp fennel seeds
- 1 tsp ground coriander
- 200g cavolo nero, shredded
- handful fresh coriander leaves, to serve

Method

STEP 1

Heat oven to 200C/180C fan/gas 6. Put the tomatoes on a baking sheet lined with baking parchment, drizzle over 2 tbsp olive oil, season and roast in the oven for 20 mins or until soft. Set aside.

STEP 2

Meanwhile, pour 2 tbsp oil into a large saucepan and add the squash, thyme, garlic and onion. Season generously and cook on a low heat for 15 mins or until the vegetables begin to soften (but not brown).

STEP 3

Add the tomatoes, chickpeas, bay, ground spices and harissa. Season to taste and pour in the stock. Bring to the boil, then reduce the heat and simmer for 30-35 mins until the liquid has reduced.

STEP 4

Put the feta in a small bowl and add the remaining olive oil and the lemon zest. Mix well and set aside.

STEP 5

Toast the fennel seeds in a frying pan for 1 min, then lightly crush with a pestle and mortar, or in a bowl with the back of a rolling pin.

STEP 6

Add the ground coriander and cavolo nero to the stew and cook for 2 mins. Put the stew in a bowl and top with a scoop of feta, a sprinkling of coriander leaves and fennel seeds, and some seasoning. Serve with lemon wedges on the side.

Bombay potato frittata

Prep: 15 mins **Cook:** 35 mins

Serves 2

Ingredients

- 4 new potatoes, sliced into 5mm rounds
- 100g baby spinach, chopped
- 1 tbsp rapeseed oil
- 1 onion, halved and sliced
- 1 large garlic clove, finely grated
- ½ tsp ground coriander
- ½ tsp ground cumin
- ¼ tsp black mustard seeds
- ¼ tsp turmeric
- 3 tomatoes, roughly chopped
- 2 large eggs
- ½ green chilli, deseeded and finely chopped
- 1 small bunch of coriander, finely chopped
- 1 tbsp mango chutney
- 3 tbsp fat-free Greek yogurt

Method

STEP 1

Cook the potatoes in a pan of boiling water for 6 mins, or until tender. Drain and leave to steam-dry. Meanwhile, put the spinach in a heatproof bowl with 1 tbsp water. Cover and microwave for 3 mins on high, or until wilted.

STEP 2

Heat the rapeseed oil in a medium non-stick frying pan. Add the onion and cook over a medium heat for 10 mins until golden and sticky. Stir in the garlic, ground coriander, ground cumin, mustard seeds and turmeric, and cook for 1 min more. Add the tomatoes and wilted spinach and cook for another 3 mins, then add the potatoes.

STEP 3

Heat the grill to medium. Lightly beat the eggs with the chilli and most of the fresh coriander and pour over the potato mixture. Grill for 4-5 mins, or until golden and just set, with a very slight wobble in the middle.

STEP 4

Leave to cool, then slice into wedges. Mix the mango chutney, yogurt and remaining fresh coriander together. Serve with the frittata wedges.

Prawn & salmon burgers with spicy mayo

Prep:15 mins **Cook:**10 mins

Serves 4

Ingredients

- 180g pack peeled raw prawns , roughly chopped
- 4 skinless salmon fillets, chopped into small chunks
- 3 spring onions , roughly chopped
- 1 lemon , zested and juiced
- small pack coriander
- 60g mayonnaise or Greek yogurt
- 4 tsp chilli sauce (we used sriracha)
- 2 Little Gem lettuces , shredded
- 1 cucumber , peeled into ribbons
- 1 tbsp olive oil
- 4 seeded burger buns , toasted, to serve

Method

STEP 1

Briefly blitz half the prawns, half the salmon, the spring onions, lemon zest and half the coriander in a food processor until it forms a coarse paste. Tip into a bowl, stir in the rest of the prawns and salmon, season well and shape into four burgers. Chill for 10 mins.

STEP 2

Mix the mayo and chilli sauce together in a small bowl, season and add some lemon juice to taste. Mix the lettuce with the cucumber, dress with a little of the remaining lemon juice and 1 tsp olive oil, then set aside.

STEP 3

Heat the remaining oil in a large frying pan and fry the burgers for 3-4 mins each side or until they have a nice crust and the fish is cooked through. Serve with the salad on the side or in toasted burger buns, if you like, with a good dollop of the spicy mayo.

Spicy fish stew

Prep: 10 mins **Cook:** 40 mins

Serves 4

Ingredients

- 1 tbsp rapeseed oil
- 2 onions , thinly sliced
- 3 spring onions , chopped
- 3 garlic cloves , chopped
- 1 red chilli , seeded and thinly sliced
- few thyme sprigs
- 2 x 400g cans chopped tomatoes
- 400ml vegetable bouillon made with 2 tsp vegetable bouillon powder
- 2 green peppers , seeded and cut into pieces
- 160g brown basmati rice
- 400g can and 210g can red kidney beans , drained
- handful fresh coriander , chopped, plus a few sprigs extra
- handful flat-leaf parsley , chopped
- 550g pack frozen wild salmon , skinned and cut into large pieces
- 1 lime , zested

Method

STEP 1

Heat the oil in a large non-stick pan and fry the onions for 8-10 mins until softened and golden. Add the spring onions, garlic, chilli and thyme. Cook, stirring, for 1 min. Pour in the tomatoes and bouillon, then stir in the peppers. Cover and leave to simmer for 15 mins.

STEP 2

Meanwhile, cook the rice according to pack instructions. Stir in the beans with the coriander and parsley, then leave to cook gently for another 10 mins until the peppers are tender. Add the salmon and lime zest and cook for 4-5 mins until cooked through.

STEP 3

Ladle half of the stew into two bowls and scatter with the coriander sprigs. Cool the remaining stew, then cover and chill to eat on another night. Gently reheat in a saucepan until bubbling.

Black bean tortilla with salsa

Prep: 10 mins **Cook:** 20 mins

Serves 4

Ingredients

For the salsa

- 400g can chopped tomatoes
- 1 onion , finely chopped
- 1 red chilli , halved, deseeded and finely chopped
- 2 tsp smoked paprika
- 15g (1/2 pack) coriander , finely chopped
- 6 Kalamata olives , thinly sliced
- ½ lemon or lime, juiced

For the omelette

- 2 x 400g can black beans , drained
- 3 garlic cloves , finely grated
- 2 tsp ground cumin
- 2 tsp ground coriander
- 6 large eggs
- 1 tbsp rapeseed oil
- 4 generous handfuls of rocket

Method

STEP 1

Tip the tomatoes into a pan and stir in the onion, ½ the chilli and the smoked paprika. Cook over a low heat for 10 mins. Tip ¾ into a bowl, then stir in 2 tbsp of the coriander and the olives and lemon juice.

STEP 2

Meanwhile, heat the grill. Tip the beans into a bowl and stir in the remaining chilli, the garlic, cumin and coriander. Beat in the eggs, then add the reserved ¼ of the salsa and the remaining fresh coriander with a little salt to taste. Blitz a little using a hand blender or mash some of the beans with a potato masher.

STEP 3

Heat a 24cm non-stick pan with the oil. Pour in the bean mixture and leave to cook gently for 5-7 mins until the base is set, then grill for 5 mins. Tip out and cut into 4 wedges. If you're following our Healthy Diet Plan, serve two wedges with half of the remaining salsa and the rocket. Chill the rest for the following day.

Peanut butter & date oat pots

Prep: 10 mins No cook

Serves 6

Ingredients

- 180g porridge oats
- 75g 100% crunchy peanut butter
- 40g stoned medjool dates, chopped
- 2 tsp vanilla extract
- 5 x 120g pots plain bio yogurt (or 600g from a large pot)
- ground cinnamon, for dusting

Method

STEP 1

Tip the oats into a large bowl and pour over 600ml boiling water. Add the peanut butter, dates and vanilla and stir well. Cool, then stir through 240g of the yogurt. Dilute with a small amount of water if the consistency is a little stiff.

STEP 2

Spoon into six glasses, then top with the remaining yogurt and dust with cinnamon. Cover each glass and keep in the fridge until ready to eat. Will keep well for up to five days.

Spiced halloumi & pineapple burger with zingy slaw

Prep: 20 mins **Cook:** 5 mins

Serves 2

Ingredients

- ½ red cabbage, grated
- 2 carrots, grated
- 100g radishes, sliced
- 1 small pack coriander, chopped
- 2 limes, juiced
- 1 tbsp cold-pressed rapeseed oil
- big pinch of chilli flakes
- 1 tbsp chipotle paste
- 60g halloumi, cut into 4 slices
- 2 small slices of fresh pineapple
- 1 Little Gem lettuce, divided into 4 lettuce cups, or 2 small seeded burger buns, cut in half, to serve (optional)

Method

STEP 1

Heat the barbecue. Put the cabbage, carrot, radish and coriander in a bowl. Pour over the lime juice, add ½ tbsp oil and the chilli flakes, then season with salt and pepper. Give everything a good mix with your hands. This can be done a few hours before and kept in the fridge.

STEP 2

Mix the remaining oil with the chipotle paste then coat the halloumi slices in the mixture. Put the halloumi slices on a sheet of foil and put on the barbecue with the pineapple (or use a searing hot griddle pan if cooking inside). Cook for 2 mins on each side until the cheese is golden, and the pineapple is beginning to caramelise. Brush the buns with the remaining chipotle oil, then put your burger buns, if using, cut-side down, on the barbecue for the last 30 seconds of cooking to toast.

STEP 3

Assemble your burgers with the lettuce or buns. Start with a handful of the slaw, then add halloumi and pineapple. Serve with the remaining slaw.

Winter warmer hearty risotto

Prep: 10 mins **Cook:** 50 mins

Serves 4

Ingredients

- 1 medium butternut squash
- 2 tbsp olive oil
- pinch of nutmeg , or pinch of cinnamon
- 1 red onion , finely chopped
- 1 vegetable stock cube
- 2 garlic cloves , crushed
- 500g risotto rice (we used arborio)
- 100g frozen peas
- 320g sweetcorn , drained
- 2 tbsp grated parmesan (or vegetarian alternative)
- handful chopped mixed herbs of your choice

Method

STEP 1

Heat oven to 200C/180C fan/gas 6. Peel the butternut squash, slice it in half, then scoop out and discard the seeds.

STEP 2

Cut the flesh of the butternut squash into small cubes and put in a mixing bowl. Drizzle 1 tbsp olive oil over the squash, and season with black pepper, and nutmeg or cinnamon. Transfer the squash to a roasting tin and roast in the oven for about 25 mins until cooked through, then set aside.

STEP 3

Heat the remaining oil in a large saucepan over a low heat. Add the onion and cover the pan with a tight-fitting lid. Allow the onion to cook without colouring for 5-10 mins, stirring occasionally.

STEP 4

In a measuring jug, make up 1.5 litres of stock from boiling water and the stock cube. Stir well until the stock cube has dissolved. When the onion is soft, remove the lid and add the garlic to the onion pan. Leave it to cook for 1 min more.

STEP 5

Rinse the rice under cold water. Turn up the heat on the pan and add the rice to the onion and garlic, stirring well for 1 min. Pour a little of the hot stock into the pan and stir in until the liquid is absorbed by the rice.

STEP 6

Gradually add the rest of the stock to the pan, a little at a time, stirring constantly, waiting until each addition of stock is absorbed before adding more. Do this until the rice is cooked through and creamy – you may not need all the stock. This should take 15-20 mins. Take the roasting tin out of the oven – the squash should be soft and cooked.

STEP 7

Add the squash, peas and sweetcorn to the risotto and gently stir it in. Season to taste. Take the risotto pan off the heat and stir in the Parmesan and herbs. Put the lid back on the pan and let the risotto stand for 2-3 mins before serving.

Spinach kedgeree with spiced salmon

Prep: 15 mins **Cook:** 45 mins

Serves 2

Ingredients

- 2 tsp rapeseed oil
- 1 large onion , halved and sliced
- thumb-sized piece of ginger , finely chopped
- ½ tsp cumin seeds
- ½ tsp ground cinnamon
- 6-8 cardamom pods , seeds crushed
- 1½ tsp ground turmeric
- 1½ tsp ground coriander

- 1 red chilli , deseeded and sliced
- 1 garlic clove , finely chopped
- 1 large red pepper , deseeded and roughly chopped
- 70g brown basmati rice
- 375ml vegetable stock , made with 2 tsp bouillon powder
- 160g baby spinach leaves , roughly chopped

For the salmon

- 3 tbsp fat-free natural yogurt
- 1 tbsp finely chopped mint or coriander

- 2 skinless wild salmon fillets
- 1 tbsp toasted almonds , to serve

Method

STEP 1

Heat the oil in a large frying pan and fry the onion and ginger for 5 mins or until soft. Add the cumin, cinnamon, crushed cardamom seeds, and 1 tsp each of the turmeric and coriander. Cook for 30 secs until fragrant. Add the chilli, garlic, pepper and rice, stir briefly, then pour in the stock. Cover and simmer for 35 mins or until the rice is tender and the stock has been absorbed. If the rice is cooked but some liquid remains, remove the lid and simmer uncovered to allow the liquid to evaporate. Add the spinach, cover and cook for 3 mins to wilt.

STEP 2

Meanwhile, prepare the salmon. Heat the grill to medium and line a baking sheet with foil. Mix the yogurt with the mint or coriander and the remaining turmeric and ground coriander. Spread the yogurt mixture over the salmon, then transfer to the prepared baking sheet and grill for 8-10 mins until the fish can be flaked easily with a fork. Top the kedgeree with the salmon fillets or flake the fish into it, and scatter over the almonds to serve.

Roasted roots & sage soup

Prep: 15 mins **Cook:** 45 mins

Serves 2

Ingredients

- 1 parsnip, peeled and chopped
- 2 carrots, peeled and chopped
- 300g turnip, swede or celeriac, chopped
- 4 garlic cloves, skin left on
- 1 tbsp rapeseed oil, plus ½ tsp
- 1 tsp maple syrup
- ¼ small bunch of sage, leaves picked, 4 whole, the rest finely chopped
- 750ml vegetable stock
- grating of nutmeg
- 1½ tbsp fat-free yogurt

Method

STEP 1

Heat the oven to 200C/180C fan/gas 6. Toss the root vegetables and garlic with 1 tbsp oil and season. Tip onto a baking tray and roast for 30 mins until tender. Toss with the maple syrup and the chopped sage, then roast for another 10 mins until golden and glazed. Brush the whole sage leaves with ½ tsp oil and add to the baking tray in the last 3-4 mins to crisp up, then remove and set aside.

STEP 2

Scrape the vegetables into a pan, squeeze the garlic out of the skins, discarding the papery shells, and add with the stock, then blend with a stick blender until very smooth and creamy. Bring to a simmer and season with salt, pepper and nutmeg.

STEP 3

Divide between bowls. Serve with a swirl of yogurt and the crispy sage leaves.

Coconut & squash dhansak

Prep: 5 mins **Cook:** 15 mins

Serves 4

Ingredients

- 1 tbsp vegetable oil
- 500g butternut squash (about 1 small squash), peeled and chopped into bite-sized chunks (or buy a pack of ready-prepared to save time), see tip, below left
- 100g frozen chopped onions
- 4 heaped tbsp mild curry paste (we used korma)
- 400g can chopped tomatoes
- 400g can light coconut milk
- mini naan bread, to serve
- 400g can lentils, drained
- 200g bag baby spinach
- 150ml coconut yogurt (we used Rachel's Organic), plus extra to serve

Method

STEP 1

Heat the oil in a large pan. Put the squash in a bowl with a splash of water. Cover with cling film and microwave on High for 10 mins or until tender. Meanwhile, add the onions to the hot oil and cook for a few mins until soft. Add the curry paste, tomatoes and coconut milk, and simmer for 10 mins until thickened to a rich sauce.

STEP 2

Warm the naan breads in a low oven or in the toaster. Drain any liquid from the squash, then add to the sauce with the lentils, spinach and some seasoning. Simmer for a further 2-3 mins to wilt the spinach, then stir in the coconut yogurt. Serve with the warm naan and a dollop of extra yogurt.

Curried spinach, eggs & chickpeas

Prep: 15 mins **Cook:** 35 mins

Serves 2

Ingredients

- 1 tbsp rapeseed oil
- 1 onion , thinly sliced
- 1 garlic clove , crushed
- 3cm piece ginger , peeled and grated
- 1 tsp ground turmeric
- 1 tsp ground coriander
- 1 tsp garam masala
- 1 tbsp ground cumin
- 450g tomatoes , chopped
- 400g can chickpeas , drained
- 1 tsp sugar
- 200g spinach
- 2 large eggs
- 3 tbsp natural yogurt
- 1 red chilli , finely sliced
- ½ small bunch of coriander , torn

Method

STEP 1

Heat the oil in a large frying pan or flameproof casserole pot over a medium heat, and fry the onion for 10 mins until golden and sticky. Add the garlic, ginger, turmeric, ground coriander, garam masala, cumin and tomatoes, and fry for 2 mins more. Add the chickpeas, 100ml water and the sugar and bring to a simmer. Stir in the spinach, then cover and cook for 20-25 mins. Season to taste.

STEP 2

Cook the eggs in a pan of boiling water for 7 mins, then rinse under cold running water to cool. Drain, peel and halve. Swirl the yogurt into the curry, then top with the eggs, chilli and coriander. Season.

Healthier Victoria sandwich

Prep: 25 mins **Cook:** 20 mins

Cuts into 8 slices

Ingredients

- 2 tbsp rapeseed oil , plus extra for the tin
- 175g self-raising flour
- 1 ½ tsp baking powder
- 140g golden caster sugar
- 25g ground almond
- 2 large eggs
- 175g natural yogurt
- 2-3 drops vanilla extract
- 25g butter , melted
- 4 tbsp raspberry conserve
- ½ tsp icing sugar , to decorate

Method

STEP 1

Heat oven to 180C/160C fan/gas 4. Lightly oil 2 x 18cm sandwich cake tins (preferably loose-bottomed) and line the bases with baking parchment. Tip the flour, baking powder, caster sugar and ground almonds into a large mixing bowl, then make a well in the centre. Beat the eggs in a bowl, then stir in the yogurt and vanilla. Pour this mixture, along with the melted butter and oil, into the dry mixture (step 1) and stir briefly together with a large metal spoon until well combined.

STEP 2

Divide the mixture evenly between the 2 tins (step 2) and level the tops. Bake both cakes, side by side, for 20 mins until risen and beginning to come away slightly from the edges of the tins.

STEP 3

Remove the cakes from the oven and loosen the sides with a round-bladed knife. Let the cakes cool briefly in the tins, then turn them out. If the tins are loose-bottomed, an easy way is to sit the tin on an upturned jam jar and let the outer ring of the tin drop down (step 3). Peel off the lining paper and sit the cakes on a wire rack. Leave until completely cold.

STEP 4

Put one of the cakes on a serving plate and spread over the conserve (step 4). Put the other cake on top and sift over the icing sugar, or make a pattern (see tip below).

Vegan ragu

Prep: 20 mins **Cook:** 1 hr

Serves 6

Ingredients

- 30g dried porcini mushrooms
- 3 tbsp olive oil
- 1 onion, finely chopped
- 2 carrots, finely chopped
- 2 celery sticks, finely chopped
- 4 garlic cloves, sliced
- few thyme sprigs
- 1 tsp tomato purée
- 100ml vegan red wine (optional)
- 250g dried green lentils
- 2 x 400g cans plum tomatoes
- 250g pack chestnut mushrooms, sliced
- 250g pack portobello mushrooms, sliced
- 1 tsp soy sauce
- 1 tsp Marmite

Method

STEP 1

Pour 800ml boiling water over the dried porcini and set aside for 10 mins. Meanwhile, pour 1½ tbsp oil into a large pan and gently cook the onion, carrot, celery and a pinch of salt, stirring for 10 mins, until soft. Remove the porcini and roughly chop. Set aside with the liquid.

STEP 2

Add the garlic and thyme. Cook for 1 min, then stir in the purée and cook for 1 min. Pour in the wine. Cook until reduced, then add the lentils, mushroom stock and tomatoes. Bring to the boil, then reduce and simmer with a lid on.

STEP 3

Meanwhile, heat a large frying pan. Add the 1½ tbsp oil, then tip in all of the mushrooms. Fry until the water has evaporated and the mushrooms are golden. Pour in the soy sauce and stir, then add the mushrooms to the lentil pan.

STEP 4

Stir in the Marmite. Cook over a medium heat for 30-45 mins, stirring occasionally, until the lentils are cooked. Remove the thyme and season.

Brown butter chargrilled prawns

SERVES: 6 PREP TIME: -   COOK TIME: -
INGREDIENTS: 9   DIFFICULTY: EASY

INGREDIENTS
- 12 large king prawns, peeled, butterflied (tails intact)
- 2 tbs extra virgin olive oil
- 125g unsalted butter, chopped

TURMERIC PICKLE
- 100g turmeric, peeled, thinly sliced
- 1/4 cup (55g) caster sugar
- 10 curry leaves or 4 lemon myrtle leaves
- Juice of 1 lemon
- 1 1/2 tbs brown mustard seeds
- 1/4 cup (60ml) white vinegar

METHOD
STEP 1

For turmeric pickle, place turmeric in a heatproof bowl and set aside. Place sugar and vinegar in a small pan over medium heat, stirring until sugar dissolves. Bring to the boil, then remove from heat and pour over turmeric. Set aside to cool. Toss prawns with oil and season.

STEP 2

Heat a chargrill pan over high heat. Cook prawns, turning, for 3-4 minutes until just cooked through. Place on a serving platter.

STEP 3

Melt butter in a saucepan over medium heat. When the butter starts to foam, add curry leaves and cook for 2 minutes or until butter has browned and curry leaves are crisp.

STEP 4

Stir in lemon juice and mustard seed, then pour over prawns. Spoon turmeric pickle over prawns and serve.

Spiced pork chop schnitzel with pear and fennel slaw

SERVES: 4 PREP TIME: -   COOK TIME: -
INGREDIENTS: 14   DIFFICULTY: EASY

INGREDIENTS
- 1 cup (50g) panko breadcrumbs
- 1/2 cup chopped flat-leaf parsley leaves
- 1 1/2 tsp each coriander, fennel and cumin seeds, crushed
- 1 eggwhite
- 1/4 cup (70g) Dijon mustard
- 4 x 200g pork loin chops
- Sunflower oil, to shallow-fry
- Aioli, to serve

PEAR AND FENNEL SLAW
- 1 fennel bulb, thinly sliced
- 1 firm pear, cut into batons
- 1 tbs extra virgin olive oil
- Juice of 1/2 lemon
- 2 tbs thick Greek-style yoghurt
- 1 tsp nigella seeds

METHOD
- Combine panko, parsley and spices in a bowl. Whisk eggwhite and mustard in a separate bowl. Brush pork with mustard, then coat in breadcrumbs.
- Heat 1cm oil in a heavy-based frypan over medium-high heat. Cook pork for 3 minutes each side or until golden and cooked through. Drain on paper towel.
- Combine all slaw ingredients in a bowl.
- Serve pork chops with slaw and aioli.

Pepper salmon escalopes with dill pesto

SERVES: 4 PREP TIME: -   COOK TIME: -
INGREDIENTS: 13   DIFFICULTY: EASY

INGREDIENTS
- 800g salmon fillet (skin on), pin-boned
- Finely grated zest and juice of 1/2 lemon
- 2 tbs extra virgin olive oil
- 1/2 tsp ground white pepper
- Micro basil, to serve

DILL PESTO

- 1/2 cup dill, finely chopped
- 1 1/2 cups chopped flat-leaf parsley leaves
- 1/3 cup (25g) finely grated parmesan
- 150ml extra virgin olive oil
- 1/3 cup (55g) almonds, chopped
- 2 anchovy fillets in oil, drained, finely chopped
- 1 garlic clove, grated
- Juice of 1/2 lemon

METHOD

- 1.
  For the pesto combine all the ingredients in a bowl and season to taste. Set aside.
- 2.
  Slice salmon on a 45-degree angle into 2cm-thick slices. Combine lemon zest and juice, oil, pepper and 1/2 tsp salt in a bowl.
- 3.
  Brush over salmon. Heat a non-stick frypan over medium-high heat. In batches, cook salmon, skin-side down, for 1 1/2 minutes or until crisp, then turn and cook for a further 30 seconds or until cooked to your liking.
- 4.
  Scatter with basil and serve with pesto.

Healthy pumpkin, lentil and mushroom curry

SERVES: 4 PREP TIME: -   COOK TIME: -
INGREDIENTS: 14   DIFFICULTY: EASY

INGREDIENTS
- 2 tbs peanut or sunflower oil
- 1 onion, chopped
- 2 garlic cloves, chopped
- 3 tsp grated ginger
- 2 kaffir lime leaves, very finely shredded
- 1/4 cup (75g) red curry paste
- 1 tbs tomato paste
- 250g button mushrooms, halved
- 2 truss tomatoes, cut into wedges
- 400g can brown lentils, rinsed, drained
- 400ml can coconut milk
- 1/2 butternut pumpkin (800g), peeled, cut into 2cm pieces
- 150g baby spinach leaves
- Steamed rice, coriander leaves & thinly sliced red chilli, to serve

METHOD

- 1.
  Heat oil in a large pan over medium heat. Add onion and cook for 3-4 minutes until softened. Add the garlic, ginger, kaffir lime and curry and tomato pastes, and cook for 1-2 minutes until fragrant.
- 2.
  Add mushrooms and tomato wedges, and cook, stirring, for 2-3 minutes, then add the lentils and coconut milk. Rinse out coconut milk can with 1/2 cup (125ml) water and add to pan. Increase heat to medium-high and bring to a simmer. Season and cook for 5-6 minutes until the flavours have infused
- 3.
  Add the pumpkin and cook for 10 minutes or until just tender. Stir through the spinach and cook for a further 1 minute or until wilted.
- 4.
  Serve curry with steamed rice and sprinkled with coriander and chilli.

Roasted alla Norma with rigatoni

SERVES: 4 PREP TIME: -   COOK TIME: -
INGREDIENTS: 10   DIFFICULTY: EASY

INGREDIENTS
- 2 tbs tomato paste
- 2 tbs red wine vinegar
- 6 large roma tomatoes, cut into quarters lengthways
- 3 small eggplants, quartered lengthways
- 1/3 cup (80ml) extra virgin olive oil
- 1 tsp dried chilli flakes
- 2 tsp dried oregano
- 400g rigatoni
- 200g ricotta, crumbled
- Basil leaves, to serve

METHOD
- 1.
  Preheat oven to 200°C. Combine tomato paste, vinegar and tomatoes in a bowl, then place at one end of a roasting pan. Place the eggplant at the other end of the pan. Drizzle tomato and eggplant with oil, then sprinkle over chilli and oregano. Season, then roast for 30 minutes or until eggplant is tender and tomatoes collapse.
- 2.
  Meanwhile, cook the pasta in a pan of boiling salted water according to packet instructions until al dente. Drain, reserving 1/3 cup (80ml) cooking liquid.

- 3.
  Remove roasting dish from oven. Toss through pasta and reserved cooking liquid. Top with ricotta and basil to serve.

Christine Manfield's

SERVES: - PREP TIME: - COOK TIME: -
INGREDIENTS: 24   DIFFICULTY: EASY

INGREDIENTS
- 2 x 180g chicken breasts
- 1 tbs sunflower oil, plus extra to brush
- 200g vermicelli noodles, cooked according to packet instructions
- Thinly sliced long red chilli, to serve
- Sliced spring onions, to serve
- Sliced chives, to serve
- Mint leaves, to serve

TURMERIC SPICE PASTE
- 1 tbs finely grated galangal
- 1 1/2 tbs finely grated turmeric
- 2 small red chillies, chopped
- 6 candlenuts (hard, oily tropical nut – from Herbie's Spices) or 12 macadamias
- 3 lemongrass stalks (inner core only), finely grated
- 6 red (Asian) eschalots, chopped
- 5 kaffir lime leaves, shredded
- 4 garlic cloves, chopped
- 2 tbs sunflower oil
- 2 tbs sesame oil

TUMERIC LEMONGRASS BROTH
- 1.5L (6 cups) chicken stock
- 1 1/2 tbs tamarind puree
- 1/4 cup (60ml) fish sauce
- Juice of 1 lime
- 1 tbs palm sugar, grated
- 2 kaffir lime leaves
- 1/2 tsp freshly ground white pepper

METHOD
- 1.
  For the spice paste, whiz all ingredients in a food processor until a paste.
- 2.

Cut chicken in half lengthways. Rub 2 tbs spice paste into chicken. Chill for 1 hour.
- 3.
Heat oil in a pan over medium heat. Add remaining spice paste and cook, stirring occasionally, for 4-5 minutes until fragrant.
- 4.
Add all the broth ingredients, except the pepper, and bring to the boil. Reduce heat to low and simmer for 10 minutes or until slightly reduced.
- 5.
Strain, discarding solids. When ready to serve, reheat broth in a clean saucepan and stir through pepper.
- 6.
Brush a chargrill pan with oil and place over high heat. Grill chicken for 2 minutes each side or until cooked through. Cut chicken into thin strips.
- 7.
Divide noodles and broth among bowls. Top with chicken, chilli, spring onion, chives and mint to serve.

Spelt margherita pizza

SERVES: 4　PREP TIME: -　COOK TIME: 15MINS
INGREDIENTS: 9　　DIFFICULTY: EASY

INGREDIENTS
- 2 tbs extra virgin olive oil
- 400g can chickpeas, rinsed, drained
- 1 tsp each onion flakes, toasted and crushed fennel seeds, and brown mustard seeds
- 2 tsp smoked paprika (pimenton)
- 2 tsp dried chilli flakes
- 1 spelt pizza base (from health food stores)
- 1/3 cup (80ml) Ardmona Pureed Tomatoes
- 125g buffalo mozzarella ball, roughly torn
- 2 basil sprigs, leaves picked

METHOD
- 1.
Heat oil in a large frypan over high heat. Add chickpeas and spices with a good pinch of salt and cook, stirring, for 5 minutes or until golden and crisp. Remove from heat and keep warm.
- 2.

Preheat oven to 220°C. Place pizza base on a baking tray and spread with passata. Season and top with torn mozzarella. Bake for 10 minutes or until base is crisp and cheese has melted. Remove from oven and scatter with fried chickpeas and basil. Cut into wedges, to serve.

Matt Moran's grilled Hervey Bay scallops with togarashi & chilli syrup dressing

SERVES: 4 PREP TIME: 5MINS   COOK TIME: 10MINS
INGREDIENTS: 9   DIFFICULTY: EASY

INGREDIENTS
- 1/2 tsp cornflour
- 1/4 cup (55g) caster sugar
- 1 long red chilli, seeds removed, finely chopped
- 1/3 cup (80ml) rice vinegar
- 1 tsp grated ginger
- 2 pinches of shichimi togarashi (Japanese spice mix of salt, chilli, black pepper, sesame seeds, dried orange peel, poppyseeds and nori)
- 16 Hervey Bay scallops, roe removed
- 1 tbs olive oil
- Micro cress, to serve

METHOD
- 1.
  Combine the cornflour with 2 tsp cold water in a bowl. Set aside.
- 2.
  Place sugar, chilli and 2 tbs water in a small saucepan over medium heat. Bring to a simmer and cook for 1 minute. Add cornflour mixture and cook for a further 1 minute or until slightly thickened. Remove from heat and add the vinegar, ginger and togarashi. Set aside to cool.
- 3.
  Heat a large frypan over high heat. Toss scallops with the oil and season. In batches, sear scallops for 30 seconds each side until caramelised but still opaque in the centre.
- 4.
  Drizzle scallops with togarashi and chilli syrup dressing and scatter with micro cress to serve.

Beetroot, fennel and rhubarb salad

SERVES: 2　PREP TIME: 10MINS　COOK TIME: 1HR
INGREDIENTS: 13　　　DIFFICULTY: EASY

INGREDIENTS
- 2 tbs soy sauce
- 1 tbs rice wine vinegar
- 1 piece kombu (dried kelp seaweed – from Asian food stores)
- Juice of 1 lemon
- 1 tbs yuzu juice (Japanese citrus – from Asian food stores)
- 2 tbs olive oil
- 1 tsp sesame oil
- 2 (160g) beetroots
- 3 rhubarb stalks, thinly peeled using a vegetable peeler
- 1 tbs caster sugar
- 1 cup (120g) frozen podded edamame, blanched
- 1 small fennel, thinly sliced
- 2 cups baby beetroot leaves

METHOD
- 1.
  To make the dressing, place soy, vinegar, kombu and lemon juice in a bowl. Set aside overnight. The next day discard kombu, add yuzu and oils and whisk to combine.
- 2.
  Preheat oven to 180°C. Wrap beetroot in foil and bake for 1 hour or until a sharp knife pierces them easily. Remove and cool, then peel and cut into rough pieces.
- 3.
  Meanwhile, toss rhubarb with sugar and 1 tbs salt. Set aside for 5 minutes to pickle. Strain, then rinse under cold running water.
- 4.
  Toss beetroot, rhubarb, edamame, fennel and leaves with dressing. Serve.

Pear and coconut crumble with double-thick cream

SERVES: 6　PREP TIME: 15MINS　COOK TIME: 35MINS
INGREDIENTS: 10　　　DIFFICULTY: EASY

INGREDIENTS
- 5 beurre bosc pears
- 1 lemon, halved
- 125g pitted dates, chopped
- 1/3 cup (75g) coconut sugar
- 75g unsalted butter, melted, cooled slightly
- 1/3 cup (50g) self-raising flour
- 1 cup (100g) almond meal
- 1/2 cup (70g) slivered almonds
- 1 teaspoon ground cinnamon
- 300ml double-thick cream

METHOD
- 1.
  Preheat the oven to 200C.
- 2.
  Peel and core the pears, rubbing the flesh with half a lemon to prevent them from going brown. Cut into thin wedges, then place in a 22cm round baking dish. Add the dates, 1 tbs coconut sugar, juice from remaining lemon half and 2 tbs water, and toss well to coat. Cover with foil and bake for 15 minutes or until just tender.
- 3.
  Meanwhile, to make crumble, combine butter, flour, almond meal, almonds, cinnamon and remaining 1/4 cup (35g) coconut sugar in a bowl. Remove foil from baking dish and stir pears to coat in syrup. Sprinkle crumble over pear mixture, then return to oven and bake, uncovered, for a further 20 minutes or until crumble is dark golden and pears are tender.
- 4.
  Serve with double-thick cream.

Spiced crunchy salad

SERVES: 6 PREP TIME: -   COOK TIME: -
INGREDIENTS: 14   DIFFICULTY: EASY

INGREDIENTS
- 4 slices ciabatta (about 100g), torn
- 1/4 cup (60ml) olive oil
- 1 small cauliflower, quartered
- 50g baby spinach leaves
- 150g purple kale
- 1 head broccoli

DUKKAH
- 1/2 cup (75g) hazelnuts, skins removed
- 1 tbs sesame seeds
- 1 tsp coriander seeds
- 1 tsp cumin seeds

DRESSING
- 100g thick Greek-style yoghurt
- 20g feta, crumbled
- 1 tsp English mustard
- Zest and juice of 1 lemon

METHOD
- 1.
  Preheat oven to 200°C. Place bread on a baking tray, drizzle with oil and season. Bake for 15 minutes or until golden.
- 2.
  For the dukkah, toast hazelnuts and sesame seeds in a dry frypan over medium heat for 2 minutes or until golden. Remove from pan and set aside. Return frypan to medium heat, add coriander and cumin seeds, and toast for 1 minute or until fragrant. Transfer to a mortar with the hazelnuts and lightly crush with a pestle. Set aside.
- 3.
  For dressing, combine yoghurt, feta, mustard and lemon zest and juice in a large bowl. Season and set aside.
- 4.
  Using a mandoline or sharp knife, thinly slice the cauliflower quarters into a large bowl, then add spinach. Shred the kale and add to the bowl.
- 5.
  Heat a chargrill pan over high heat. Using a mandoline or sharp knife, thinly slice broccoli. Cook until lightly charred. Transfer to a bowl and spoon over half the dressing, then add to cauliflower mixture along with remaining dressing. Toss together and arrange on a platter. Serve scattered with dukkah and croutons.

Kelp noodles with poached chicken and miso

SERVES: 4 PREP TIME: -   COOK TIME: 35MINS
INGREDIENTS:14   DIFFICULTY: CAPABLE

INGREDIENTS
- 1L (4 cups) chicken stock
- 1 bunch coriander, leaves picked, roots reserved

- 10cm piece ginger, halved
- 1 tbs fish sauce
- 4 x 200g skinless chicken breast fillets
- 2 tbs each white (shiro) miso paste, brown rice vinegar and mirin (all from Asian food stores)
- 1 tbs coconut oil
- Juice of 1 lime
- 2 x 340g packets kelp noodles (we used Sea Tangle Kelp Noodles from Asian food stores), rinsed, drained
- 2 cups (100g) bean sprouts
- 2 long red chillies, thinly sliced on an angle
- 4 spring onions, thinly sliced on an angle
- 1 telegraph cucumber, halved, seeds removed, thinly sliced on an angle
- 4 sprigs Thai basil, leaves picked

METHOD

- 1.
  Bring the stock, coriander root, ginger, fish sauce and 1L (4 cups) water to the boil in a large saucepan. Add the chicken, remove pan from heat, then cover with a lid. Stand for 30 minutes or until chicken is white and cooked through.
- 2.
  Place miso, vinegar, mirin, coconut oil and 2 tbs poaching liquid in a saucepan over low heat and cook, stirring, for 4 minutes or until smooth. Remove from heat, stir in lime juice and cool slightly.
- 3.
  Remove chicken from pan, discarding liquid, and shred. Toss noodles, bean sprouts and half the chilli and dressing on a platter. Top with chicken, spring onion, cucumber, basil and coriander leaves, and remaining chilli. Drizzle with remaining dressing to serve.

Matt Moran's grilled sardines on toast

SERVES: 4 PREP TIME: - COOK TIME: 15MINS
INGREDIENTS: 12 DIFFICULTY: CAPABLE

INGREDIENTS

- 1/4 cup (60ml) extra virgin olive oil
- 8 thick slices sourdough
- 12 sardines, cleaned, butterflied
- 1 garlic clove, halved
- Baby sorrel or watercress, to serve

SALMORIGLIO
- 1 bunch oregano, leaves chopped
- 1 bunch flat-leaf parsley, leaves chopped
- Finely grated zest and juice of 1 lemon
- 1 garlic clove, finely chopped
- 2 long red chillies, seeds removed, chopped
- 2/3 cup (165ml) olive oil
- 2 tbs red wine vinegar

METHOD
- 1.
  For the salmoriglio, combine all the ingredients in a bowl. Season.
- 2.
  Preheat a barbecue or chargrill pan to high. Drizzle 2 tbs oil all over sourdough and cook on barbecue grill for 1-2 minutes each side until slightly charred. Remove from heat and rub cut side of garlic all over each toast. Keep warm and set aside.
- 3.
  Drizzle remaining 1 tbs oil over sardines and season. Place, skin-side down, on barbecue flat plate. Cook for 1-2 minutes each side until just cooked. (Alternatively, cook in a nonstick frypan over high heat.)
- 4.
  Divide toast among plates and top with sardines. Drizzle over salmoriglio and scatter with sorrel to serve.

Healthy broccolini, pea and asparagus breakfast gratin

SERVES: 6 PREP TIME: 5MINS   COOK TIME: 15MINS
INGREDIENTS: 11   DIFFICULTY: EASY

INGREDIENTS
- 100g speck, finely chopped
- 2 bunches broccolini, stalks sliced, florets reserved
- 3 cups (480g) fresh peas, blanched, refreshed in iced water
- 2 bunches asparagus, thinly sliced lengthways
- 150g baby spinach leaves
- 1 tsp dried chilli flakes
- 1 1/2 tbs extra virgin olive oil
- 400g ricotta, broken into large chunks
- 2 cups (220g) grated mozzarella
- 6 eggs, poached

- Micro or flat-leaf parsley, to serve

METHOD
- 1.
  Preheat grill to high. Place speck in a cold non-stick frypan and place over medium heat. Cook, stirring, for 5 minutes or until golden and crisp. Add broccolini stalks and cook, stirring, for 1-2 minutes until tender. Add broccolini florets, peas, asparagus and spinach, and cook for a further 1 minute or until spinach is just wilted. Transfer to a bowl and toss with chilli flakes and oil, then season. Stir through ricotta and half of the mozzarella.
- 2.
  Divide the mixture among six 400ml-capacity ovenproof gratin dishes, then scatter over remaining mozzarella. Grill for 8 minutes or until golden and bubbling. Serve each topped with a poached egg and parsley.

Vegan quinoa bircher with almond milk

SERVES: 6 PREP TIME: 10MINS   COOK TIME: -
INGREDIENTS: 12   DIFFICULTY: EASY

INGREDIENTS
- 5 pitted Medjool dates, finely chopped
- 2 cups (190g) quinoa flakes
- 1/2 cup (50g) LSA meal
- 1/2 cup (35g) shredded coconut
- 1/2 cup (80g) pumpkin seeds (pepitas)
- 1/2 cup (75g) slivered or chopped pistachios, plus extra to serve
- 1 tsp each ground cinnamon, ground cardamom and ground ginger
- 1 tsp vanilla extract
- Juice of 1 orange
- 3 cups (750ml) good-quality sugar-free almond milk
- 1 large green apple, grated, plus extra grated to serve
- Thinly sliced seedless green grapes and flaked coconut, to serve

METHOD
- 1.
  Begin this recipe at least 6 hours ahead.
- 2.
  Soak the dates in 1/2 cup (125ml) boiling water in a bowl until needed.
- 3.
  Combine the quinoa, LSA, shredded coconut, seeds, nuts, spices, vanilla, orange juice and almond milk in a bowl. Stir in the apple, then add the dates and soaking

liquid, and stir to combine. Cover with plastic wrap and chill for at least 6 hours or overnight to soak.

- 4.
Serve bircher topped with grapes, flaked coconut, and extra grated apple and pistachios.

Baked ocean trout with smashed cucumber salad

SERVES: 6　PREP TIME: 30MINS　COOK TIME: 15MINS
INGREDIENTS: 10　　DIFFICULTY: EASY

INGREDIENTS
- 2/3 cup (160ml) soy sauce
- 150ml maple syrup
- 3cm piece ginger, grated
- 3 garlic cloves, crushed
- 1kg skinless ocean trout fillet, pin-boned

SMASHED CUCUMBER SALAD
- 2 telegraph cucumbers
- 2 garlic cloves, finely chopped
- 1 red onion, halved, very thinly sliced
- 1/4 cup (70g) drained, finely shredded pickled ginger
- Micro herbs (optional), to serve

METHOD
- 1.
Line a large baking tray with baking paper. Place soy, maple syrup, ginger and garlic in a small bowl and stir to combine. Place trout on baking tray. Pour over marinade, then cover and refrigerate for 1 hour.
- 2.
Meanwhile, for the cucumber salad, peel and halve cucumbers lengthways, scoop out seeds and discard. Transfer cucumber to a large ziplock bag, seal, then bash with a rolling pin. Using your hands, break into chunks. Add garlic and 2 tsp salt to the bag and rub into cucumber. Add onion, shake to combine, then seal, removing as much air as possible. Chill for 15 minutes.
- 3.
Preheat the oven to 140°C. Cook the trout, uncovered, for 15 minutes or until just cooked through.
- 4.

Meanwhile, drain cucumber mixture, discarding liquid, then toss with ginger in a bowl. Serve trout with cucumber salad, topped with micro herbs, if using.

Herb-baked blue-eye on saffron and tomato potatoes

SERVES: 4 PREP TIME: 15MINS   COOK TIME: 35MINS
INGREDIENTS: 10   DIFFICULTY: CAPABLE

INGREDIENTS
- 1/4 cup (60ml) olive oil
- 4 garlic cloves, thinly sliced
- 250g vine-ripened tomatoes, peeled, quartered, seeds removed
- 900g floury potatoes (such as coliban), peeled, cut into 1cm slices
- 300ml vegetable stock
- A good pinch of saffron threads
- 50g unsalted butter, melted
- 1 tsp chopped fresh thyme leaves
- 1 tsp chopped flat-leaf parsley leaves
- 4 x 200g thick skinless blue-eye fillets

METHOD
- 1.
  Preheat the oven to 220°C.
- 2.
  Heat oil in a deep frypan over medium heat. Add garlic and cook, stirring, for 1 minute, then add tomato and cook for 2 minutes until tomato starts to soften. Reduce heat to low, add potato, stock, saffron and 1/2 tsp salt, then simmer for 15 minutes or until potato is almost tender. Transfer to a baking dish. Season.
- 3.
  Combine butter and chopped herbs in a bowl. Season fish, then coat well in herb butter. Place the fish on top of the potatoes and pour over any remaining herb butter. Bake for 10-12 minutes until the fish is just cooked through and potatoes are tender.
- 4.
  Spoon the potatoes into warmed bowls, then carefully place the fish on top.

Roasted fennel and pine nut polpette

SERVES: 4 PREP TIME: 40MINS   COOK TIME: 1HR15MINS
INGREDIENTS: 12   DIFFICULTY: CAPABLE

INGREDIENTS
- 1 large fennel bulb (400g), trimmed, cut into 3cm wedges, fronds reserved
- 1/2 cup (125ml) extra virgin olive oil
- 1 tbs pine nuts
- 1 tbs pumpkin seeds (pepitas)
- 1/2 long red chilli, seeds removed, roughly chopped
- 3 garlic cloves
- 2/3 cup (50g) grated parmesan
- 1 1/2 cups (105g) fresh breadcrumbs
- 1 egg yolk
- 1/2 bunch flat-leaf parsley, leaves picked, stalks finely chopped
- 400g can chopped tomatoes
- 1 tbs balsamic vinegar

METHOD
- 1.
  Preheat oven to 180°C. Place fennel in a roasting pan and drizzle with 1 tbs oil. Season, then roast for 30 minutes. Remove from oven and sprinkle over the pine nuts and pumpkin seeds. Return to oven for a further 8-10 minutes until fennel is cooked through and nuts are toasted.
- 2.
  Whiz chilli and 2 garlic cloves in a food processor until finely chopped. Add fennel, pine nuts and pumpkin seeds, and whiz until chopped but still chunky. Add parmesan, breadcrumbs and egg yolk. Season, then whiz until combined.
- 3.
  Grease a roasting tray with 1 tbs oil. Using wet hands, roll the mixture into 20 walnut-sized balls. Place on tray. Chill for 15 minutes to firm up. Preheat oven to 200°C. Drizzle polpette with oil and bake for 20-25 minutes until golden and crisp.
- 4.
  Meanwhile, to make tomato sauce, heat remaining 2 tbs oil in a pan over medium heat. Thinly slice remaining garlic clove and add to pan with parsley stalks. Cook for 1-2 minutes, then add tomatoes. Half-fill the can with water, then add to pan. Add balsamic and bring to the boil. Reduce heat to low and cook for 8-10 minutes until thickened. Cool slightly, then transfer to a food processor and whiz until smooth. Return to pan. Keep warm.
- 5.
  Divide sauce among plates. Top with polpette and sprinkle with chopped parsley and reserved fennel fronds.

Couscous with chickpeas, dried apricots, pistachios and marinated feta

SERVES: 6 PREP TIME: 5MINS   COOK TIME: 15MINS
INGREDIENTS: 10   DIFFICULTY: EASY

INGREDIENTS
- 1 1/2 cups (300g) couscous
- 350ml chicken or vegetable stock
- 1/2 tsp saffron threads, crumbled
- 150g dried apricots, roughly chopped
- 25g unsalted butter
- 400g can chickpeas, rinsed, drained
- 200g drained marinated feta, crumbled
- Handful of flat-leaf parsley, roughly chopped, plus extra sprigs to serve
- 1 preserved lemon quarter*, flesh and white pith removed, rind finely chopped
- 2/3 cup (100g) pistachio kernels

METHOD
- 1.
  Place the couscous in a large heatproof bowl and set aside. Place stock, saffron and a pinch of salt in a saucepan over medium-high heat and bring to the boil. Add apricot and simmer for 1-2 minutes. Remove from heat and stir in butter. Pour hot stock over couscous, cover with plastic wrap and stand for 10 minutes or until liquid has been absorbed.
- 2.
  Remove the plastic wrap and fluff couscous with a fork. Add chickpeas, feta, chopped parsley, preserved lemon rind and pistachios to the couscous, season with sea salt and freshly ground pepper and toss to combine. Garnish with parsley sprigs and serve.

Chicken kiev with cabbage slaw

SERVES: 4 PREP TIME: 30MINS   COOK TIME: 15MINS
INGREDIENTS: 15   DIFFICULTY: EASY

INGREDIENTS
- 100g unsalted butter, softened
- 3 garlic cloves, crushed
- 1/2 bunch parsley, finely chopped

- 4 (800g) chicken supremes
- 3 eggs, lightly beaten
- 1/3 cup (80ml) milk
- 2/3 cup (100g) plain flour
- 2 cups (200g) dried breadcrumbs
- Sunflower oil, to shallow-fry
- 1/4 savoy cabbage, thinly shaved
- 1 red onion, thinly sliced
- 100ml olive oil
- 2 tbs chardonnay vinegar or white wine vinegar
- 1/2 bunch chives, cut into 4cm lengths
- Juice of 2 lemons, plus wedges to serve

METHOD

- 1.
  Combine the butter, garlic and half the parsley in a bowl, then transfer to piping bag fitted with a 1 cm nozzle.
- 2.
  Preheat oven to 200°C. Remove the tenderloins and excess skin from chicken. Using a small sharp knife, starting at the top edge, make an incision through the centre of each breast, twisting the knife slightly to form a cavity. Pipe the butter into the cavity, then gently guide it down with your finger. Add more if necessary.
- 3.
  Whisk the eggs and milk in a bowl. Place the flour and breadcrumbs in two separate bowls. Dust the chicken first in flour, shaking off excess, then dip in egg mixture and finally coat in crumbs. Coat a second time in the egg and crumbs.
- 4.
  Heat 2 cm sunflower oil in a large deep fry pan over medium heat. Cook kievs, in batches, for 1 1/2 minutes each side or until golden. Transfer to a baking tray lined with baking paper and bake for 12 minutes or until cooked through.
- 5.
  Meanwhile, to make the slaw, toss the cabbage, onion, olive oil and vinegar in a bowl, then season and set aside.
- 6.
  Add the chives and remaining parsley, then toss to combine just before serving with chicken kievs and lemon wedges.

Chicken broth with kale, quinoa and preserved lemon

SERVES: 6 PREP TIME: 15MINS   COOK TIME: 1HR 10MINS
INGREDIENTS: 18   DIFFICULTY: EASY

INGREDIENTS
- 1 Lilydale Free Range Whole Chicken
- 2 tsp whole black peppercorns
- 1 onion, halved
- 2 carrots, halved
- 4 bay leaves
- 12 garlic cloves
- 10 lemon thyme or regular thyme sprigs
- 5 celery stalks
- 1 fennel bulb
- 1 cup (200g) white quinoa
- 2 tbs olive oil
- 4 anchovies in oil, drained
- 2 preserved lemon quarters, flesh removed, zest thinly sliced
- 1 long green chilli, thinly sliced on an angle
- 1/4 cup (60ml) verjuice
- 50g baby kale or 1/2 bunch torn kale leaves
- Juice of 1/2 lemon (optional)
- Toasted pumpkin seeds (pepitas – optional), to serve

METHOD
- 1.
  Place chicken, peppercorns, onion, carrot, bay leaves, 10 garlic cloves, 5 thyme sprigs, 2 celery stalks and 1 tbs salt in a stockpot and cover with water. Cut woody stalks from fennel and add to pot along with fronds, reserving fennel bulb. Place pot over high heat and bring to the boil, then reduce heat to medium-low and simmer for 1 hour or until chicken is cooked through. If chicken floats, top with a plate to keep it submerged. Cool chicken in pan, then transfer to a plate and set aside.
- 2.
  Strain stock through a sieve lined with muslin or clean Chux, discarding solids. When cool, skim any impurities on surface.
- 3.

Rinse quinoa under cold running water, then place in a saucepan with 2 cups (500ml) stock. Bring to the boil, then reduce heat to medium-low and cook, covered, for 10 minutes or until cooked but slightly al dente. Set aside.

- 4.
Heat the oil in a large saucepan over medium heat. Thickly slice the remaining 3 celery stalks on an angle and add to pan with anchovy and preserved lemon. Cook, stirring, for 2-3 minutes until slightly softened. Finely chop remaining 2 garlic cloves, then add to the pan with chilli and cook, stirring, for 1-2 minutes until starting to soften. Using a mandoline, thinly slice the fennel bulb, then add to the pan and cook for a further 1-2 minutes. Season well, then add verjuice and cook, stirring, for 2-3 minutes. Add remaining stock and 5 thyme sprigs. Bring to the boil, then reduce heat to medium-low and cook for 10 minutes or until warmed through.
- 5.
Remove breast meat and legs from the chicken and cut into thick slices, then add to the pan. Simmer for a further 5 minutes, then add kale and cooked quinoa. Cook for a final 5 minutes or until kale is wilted. Season and add lemon juice, if using. Sprinkle with pepitas, if using, to serve.

Seared tuna bruschetta

SERVES: 4 PREP TIME: 15MINS   COOK TIME: 10MINS
INGREDIENTS: 9   DIFFICULTY: EASY

INGREDIENTS
- 250g vine-ripened cherry tomatoes
- 1 tablespoon olive oil, plus extra to brush
- 1/2 cup (150g) whole-egg mayonnaise
- Juice of 1 lemon
- 4 slices woodfired or sourdough bread
- 1 garlic clove, halved
- 4 x 150g tuna steaks
- 1/3 cup (80g) black olive tapenade
- 1 cup wild rocket

METHOD
- 1.
Preheat the oven to 180°C.
- 2.
Place tomatoes on a baking tray, season and drizzle with oil. Roast for 6-8 minutes until softened. Combine mayonnaise and lemon juice in a bowl, then set aside.

- 3.
  Meanwhile, preheat a chargrill pan over medium-high heat. Brush bread with oil and cook for 1-2 minutes each side until charred. Rub bread with cut side of garlic. Brush tuna with oil and season. Chargrill for 1-2 minutes each side for medium rare.
- 4.
  Spread the bread with tapenade, top with the tuna, lemon mayonnaise and rocket, then serve with roasted tomatoes.

Pan-fried whiting with broccoli pesto

SERVES: 4 PREP TIME: 15MINS   COOK TIME: 10MINS
INGREDIENTS: 9   DIFFICULTY: EASY

INGREDIENTS
- 600g broccoli, cut into florets
- 1/3 cup (55g) whole almonds
- 3/4 cup (60g) finely grated parmesan
- 1 garlic clove, crushed
- 1 cup flat-leaf parsley leaves
- Finely grated zest and juice of 1 lemon, plus wedges to serve
- 1/2 cup (125ml) extra virgin olive oil
- 8 x 100g skinless whiting fillets
- 1/2 cup (75g) cornflour, seasoned

METHOD
- 1.
  Cook broccoli in boiling, salted water for 2-3 minutes until just tender, then drain and refresh in cold water. Finely chop broccoli and almonds in a food processor. Add cheese, garlic, parsley, zest, juice and 100ml oil. Pulse to a coarse pesto, then season and set aside.
- 2.
  Coat whiting in seasoned cornflour, shaking off excess. Heat remaining 1 tablespoon oil in a large non-stick frypan over medium-high heat. Add fish and cook, turning, for 4-5 minutes until golden. Serve the fish with the broccoli pesto and lemon wedges.

Farro, lentil and goat's cheese salad with avocado dressing

SERVES: 6 PREP TIME: 15MINS   COOK TIME: 20MINS

INGREDIENTS: 11   DIFFICULTY: EASY

INGREDIENTS
- 1 cup (200g) farro (from delis and gourmet shops)
- 1 cup (200g) dried green Puy-style lentils (from delis and gourmet shops)
- 1/2 avocado
- 1/2 cup (140g) natural yoghurt
- 1/2 cup (120g) sour cream
- Finely grated zest and juice of 1 lemon, plus wedges to serve
- 1 tablespoon extra virgin olive oil
- 1 1/4 cups (100g) flaked almonds, toasted
- Handful wild rocket leaves
- 300g goat's cheese, crumbled
- 1 bunch chives, chopped

METHOD
- 1.
  Place the farro in a saucepan of cold water over medium heat. Bring to a simmer, then cook for 15-20 minutes until tender. Drain and rinse under cold water.
- 2.
  Meanwhile, cook the lentils in a pan of boiling water over medium-high heat for 15 minutes or until tender. Drain and rinse under cold water.
- 3.
  Place the avocado, yoghurt, sour cream and lemon zest and juice in a food processor and whiz until smooth. Season with a little salt and lots of freshly ground black pepper. Set aside.
- 4.
  Place the farro, lentils and oil in a bowl, then season and toss to combine. Transfer to a serving dish, scatter over the almonds, rocket, goat's cheese and chives, then lightly toss to combine. Serve with the avocado dressing and lemon wedges.

Lasagne for spring

SERVES: 6 PREP TIME: 30 MINS   COOK TIME: 45 MINS
INGREDIENTS: 13   DIFFICULTY: EASY

INGREDIENTS
- 1kg butternut pumpkin, peeled, cut into small chunks
- 3 1/2 tablespoons olive oil, plus extra to serve
- 2 red capsicum
- 2 yellow capsicum

- 1kg small vine-ripened cherry tomatoes, 6 with stems intact
- 1 garlic clove, cut into slivers
- 18 (10 x 6cm) fresh green lasagne sheets
- 800g low-fat ricotta cheese
- 1/2 cup chopped basil leaves
- 1/4 cup chopped lemon thyme leaves
- 2 tablespoons chopped flat-leaf parsley
- 4 tablespoons grated parmesan
- Olive oil & balsamic vinegar, to serve

METHOD
- 1.
  Preheat the oven to 190°C.
- 2.
  Toss the pumpkin in 2 tablespoons olive oil, season with salt and pepper and place on a large baking tray. Roast for 25 minutes or until soft and lightly golden. At the same time, roast capsicum for 15 minutes or until skin is charred, then remove from oven and place in a plastic bag. Set aside until cooled completely, then remove and discard charred skin, seeds and core. Cut capsicum into 3cm-wide strips.
- 3.
  Mash the pumpkin and set aside.
- 4.
  Place tomatoes on a roasting tray, drizzle with 1 tablespoon olive oil and scatter the garlic slivers over the top. Roast 8 minutes or until slightly wilted. Reserve the 6 tomatoes with stems intact for garnish and place remaining tomatoes and garlic in a bowl. Roughly mash with a fork, then season with salt, pepper and a pinch of sugar.
- 5.
  Place lasagne sheets in a large pan of boiling, salted water and cook for 2-3 minutes or until al dente. Transfer to a bowl of cold water to stop lasagne cooking, then drain on a tea towel.
- 6.
  Combine the ricotta, fresh herbs and half the parmesan in a bowl, and season with salt and pepper.
- 7.
  To assemble, place a sheet of baking paper on a large baking tray. Place 6 sheets of lasagne on the tray. Layer the pumpkin on top, followed by half of the ricotta mixture, then the tomatoes. Add another layer of lasagne, followed by the roasted capsicum, then the remaining ricotta and finally a layer of lasagne. Brush the tops of the lasagne sheets with 1/2 tablespoon olive oil and sprinkle with the remaining parmesan. Cover the whole tray loosely with foil, place in the oven and heat for 10

minutes. The lasagne should be eaten warm, not hot. Use a fish slice to place each lasagne on a serving plate, drizzle with a little oil and balsamic, and serve with the reserved tomatoes.

Steak, corn and red bean salad

SERVES: 4 PREP TIME: 10MINS   COOK TIME: 10MINS
INGREDIENTS: 8   DIFFICULTY: EASY

INGREDIENTS
- 500g piece lean beef sirloin steak, trimmed of excess fat
- 1 tablespoon Worcestershire sauce
- 2 teaspoons ground cumin
- 1 tablespoon olive oil
- 1 cup frozen corn kernels
- 800g canned red kidney beans, rinsed, drained
- Juice of 1 lemon
- 2 spring onions, sliced on the diagonal

METHOD
- 1.
  Place the steak in a bowl and sprinkle over the Worcestershire sauce and 1 teaspoon of the ground cumin. Toss to coat the steak in the mixture.
- 2.
  Heat the olive oil in a frypan over medium-high heat. When the pan is hot, add the steak and cook for about 5 minutes each side for medium, or until cooked to your liking. Remove from the heat and set the steak aside in a warm place for a few minutes to rest, then slice.
- 3.
  Meanwhile, blanch the corn kernels in a pan of boiling water. Combine the drained kidney beans and corn in a bowl. Add the lemon juice and the remaining teaspoon of ground cumin to the bean mixture and toss to combine.
- 4.
  Add the sliced steak and the sliced spring onion to the salad and toss gently to combine.

Moroccan lamb with chickpea salad

SERVES: 4 PREP TIME:15MINS   COOK TIME: 5MINS

INGREDIENTS: 13   DIFFICULTY: EASY

INGREDIENTS
- 2 tablespoons Moroccan spice mix powder*
- 1/4 cup (60ml) extra virgin olive oil
- 2 x 250g lamb backstraps, trimmed
- 400g canned chickpeas, rinsed, drained
- 1 red onion, thinly sliced
- 2 tomatoes, seeds removed, chopped
- 2 tablespoons chopped coriander leaves
- 2 tablespoons chopped mint leaves
- 1/4 cup (3 tablespoons) tahini*
- 1 garlic clove, crushed
- 1/4 cup (60ml) lemon juice, plus wedges to serve
- Pita bread, to serve
- 2 cups baby salad leaves*

METHOD
- 1.
  In a bowl, mix the spice-mix powder with 1 tablespoon of the olive oil. Brush over the lamb and set aside.
- 2.
  Place chickpeas, onion, tomato, coriander and mint in a bowl. In a separate bowl, whisk tahini, garlic, lemon juice and 2 tablespoons water until you have a loose dressing. Toss salad with dressing.
- 3.
  Heat a chargrill pan or barbecue to medium-high heat and cook the lamb for 2-3 minutes each side until lightly charred, but still rare inside. Set aside to rest for 2-3 minutes in a warm place.
- 4.
  Lightly toast pita bread on the grill pan. Served the lamb sliced with the salad, grilled pita bread, baby salad leaves and lemon wedges on the side.

Cinnamon porridge

SERVES: 6 PREP TIME: 5MINS   COOK TIME: 10MINS
INGREDIENTS: 5   DIFFICULTY: EASY

INGREDIENTS
- 2 cups (180g) rolled oats (not instant)
- 1/4 teaspoon ground cinnamon, plus extra to dust
- 125g brown sugar

- 300ml thickened cream
- 2 bananas, sliced

METHOD
- 1.
  Place oats, cinnamon, 1L (4 cups) of water and a pinch of salt in a saucepan. Stir over low heat for 5 minutes, then leave to simmer for 5-6 minutes.
- 2.
  Meanwhile, place sugar in a saucepan with 2 tablespoons water and stir over low heat until sugar dissolves. Increase heat to medium and cook for 2-3 minutes until mixture has caramelised. Add 100ml cream and stir over low heat until smooth, then cool slightly.
- 3.
  Divide the porridge among 6 bowls. Toss bananas in caramel and place on top of porridge and serve with remaining cream and a dusting of cinnamon.

Blackened salmon with papaya mojo

SERVES: 6 PREP TIME: 10MINS   COOK TIME: 20MINS
INGREDIENTS: 12   DIFFICULTY: EASY

INGREDIENTS
- 1 tablespoon dried oregano
- 1 tablespoon sweet paprika
- 3 garlic cloves, crushed
- 1/4 cup (60ml) extra virgin olive oil
- 1kg piece skinless salmon fillet
- 2 tablespoons sunflower oil

PAPAYA MOJO
- 1/4 cup (60ml) extra virgin olive oil
- 1 small red onion, thinly sliced
- 1 papaya, cut into cubes
- 2 x 400g cans black turtle beans* (see note), drained, rinsed
- 1 bunch coriander, leaves roughly chopped, plus extra to serve
- Finely grated zest and juice of 2 limes, plus extra lime halves to serve

METHOD
- 1.
  Preheat the oven to 180°C.
- 2.
  Place the oregano, paprika, garlic and olive oil in a bowl and season. Place the fish on a chopping board and rub the marinade into the topside of the fish.

- 3.
  Place the sunflower oil in a flameproof, non-stick roasting pan over high heat. Warm for 1-2 minutes until the oil is smoking, then add the fish, marinated- side down, and cook for 5-6 minutes until the flesh has blackened. Transfer to the oven, then bake for 10 minutes or until just cooked, but still a little rare in the centre.
- 4.
  Meanwhile, for the papaya mojo, place all the ingredients in a bowl and season, then toss to combine. Set aside.
- 5.
  Invert the fish onto a platter and top with papaya mojo. Serve with extra coriander leaves and lime halves.

Grilled chicken salad with parmesan dressing

SERVES: 4 PREP TIME: 10MINS   COOK TIME: 8MINS
INGREDIENTS: 15   DIFFICULTY: EASY

INGREDIENTS
- 2 tablespoons extra virgin olive oil
- 4 x 200g chicken breast fillets, sliced 1cm thick on an angle
- 1/2 baguette, sliced 5mm thick
- 4 small zucchinis, trimmed, thinly sliced into ribbons with a mandoline
- 200g baby roma tomatoes, halved
- 1/4 cup flat-leaf parsley leaves
- 1/4 cup oregano leaves
- 1/4 cup finely shredded basil leaves

PARMESAN DRESSING (MAKES 200ML)
- 2 tbs sherry vinegar or red wine vinegar
- 1/4 cup (60ml) extra virgin olive oil
- 1/4 cup (20g) finely grated parmesan
- 1 eschalot, finely chopped
- 2 teaspoons finely chopped thyme
- 2 teaspoons Dijon mustard
- Finely grated zest and juice of 1 lemon

METHOD
- 1.
  For parmesan dressing, place all ingredients in a bowl and whisk to combine. Season with salt and freshly ground black pepper, then set aside.
- 2.

Preheat a barbecue or chargrill pan to medium-high. Drizzle chicken with 1 tablespoon oil and season. In batches, grill chicken for 2 minutes each side or until lightly charred and cooked through. Set aside.
- 3.
Brush bread slices with remaining 1 tablespoon oil, then grill for 1 minute each side or until lightly charred.
- 4.
Tear chicken into bite-sized pieces, then place in a large bowl and drizzle with half the parmesan dressing. Add zucchini, tomato, parsley, oregano, basil and half the chargrilled bread slices, then gently toss to combine.
- 5.
Divide salad among plates, drizzle with remaining parmesan dressing and serve with remaining bread slices.

Flat-roast chicken with lemon and herbs

SERVES: 4 PREP TIME: 45MINS   COOK TIME: 35MINS
INGREDIENTS: 9   DIFFICULTY: ADVANCED

INGREDIENTS
- 1.6kg whole chicken, boned, butterflied (or ask your butcher to do it)
- 2 tablespoons olive oil
- 2 tablespoons lemon juice, plus 1 lemon, sliced
- 2 garlic cloves, thinly sliced
- 1 long red chilli, deseeded, thinly sliced
- 1 teaspoon dried oregano
- 1 tablespoon chopped fresh thyme, plus 4 sprigs
- 8 marinated artichoke hearts with stem
- 200ml dry white wine

METHOD
- 1.
Preheat oven to 220°C.
- 2.
Place chicken, skin-side up, in an oiled roasting pan. Drizzle with oil and lemon juice, then scatter with lemon slices, garlic, chilli, oregano, chopped thyme and sprigs. Season well. Add artichokes to pan, then pour over the wine.
- 3.
Roast the chicken for 30-35 minutes until the skin is golden and the juices run clear when the thickest part is pierced (reduce oven to 200°C if it's browning too quickly).

- 4.
  Transfer chicken to a board and cut into 8 pieces. Pour pan juices into a jug.
- 5.
  Serve chicken with artichokes, drizzled with a spoonful of pan juices.

Herb-roasted turkey breast

SERVES: 6 PREP TIME: 5MINS   COOK TIME: 10MINS
INGREDIENTS: 6   DIFFICULTY: CAPABLE

INGREDIENTS
- 150g unsalted butter, plus extra to grease
- 12 fresh bay leaves
- 4 slices sourdough crusts, removed and torn apart
- 1 onion, chopped
- 1 tablespoon finely grated lemon zest
- 1 tablespoon chopped thyme leaves
- 1/3 cup flat-leaf parsley leaves
- 6 sage leaves, chopped
- 2 garlic cloves, chopped
- 1.5-2kg turkey breast with skin and wingbone attached (see note)

METHOD
- 1.
  Preheat oven to 180°C and grease a large baking dish. Place the butter and 6 bay leaves in a small pan over medium heat, until melted. Set aside.
- 2.
  Whiz bread, onion, zest, herbs and garlic in a food processor until combined. Season well, then add half the melted butter (reserving the bay leaves in the pan) and pulse until you have a coarse paste. Cool.
- 3.
  Carefully slide your fingers underneath turkey skin to form a pocket, taking carenot to tear the skin. Gently spread stuffing mixture between skin and meat, then secure in 4 or 5 places with kitchen string.
- 4.
  Lay remaining bay leaves in baking dish and place turkey on top. Brush with some bay butter and season well. Roast for 25 minutes, then baste with remaining butter. Bake for a further 35-40 minutes until golden and juices run clear. Loosely cover with foil and rest for 15 minutes, then thickly slice and serve.

Spicy kingfish with caramelised onion couscous

SERVES: 4 PREP TIME: 20MINS   COOK TIME: 20MINS
INGREDIENTS: 13   DIFFICULTY: EASY

INGREDIENTS
- 100ml extra virgin olive oil
- 1 tablespoon harissa, plus extra to serve
- 4 x 180g skinless kingfish fillets
- 2 red onions, thinly sliced
- 1/4 cup red wine vinegar
- 1 1/2 cups chicken or vegetable stock
- 1 1/2 cups couscous
- 2 cups mint leaves
- 1/4 cup currants
- 400g can chickpeas, rinsed, drained
- Juice of 1 lime, plus wedges to serve
- 1 long red chilli, seeds removed, finely chopped
- 1 cup flat-leaf parsley leaves, finely chopped

METHOD
- 1.
  Combine 2 tablespoons oil and 2 teaspoons of harissa in a bowl. Season, then add fish and coat in marinade. Cover and place in fridge for 30 minutes.
- 2.
  Meanwhile, heat 1 tablespoon of oil in a frypan over medium-low heat. Cook onion, stirring occasionally, for 10-15 minutes until lightly caramelised. Add vinegar and cook, stirring, for 2-3 minutes until evaporated. Season and set aside to cool.
- 3.
  Heat the stock in a pan over medium-high heat with remaining 2 teaspoon harissa, whisking to combine. Place the couscous in a bowl with teaspoon of sea salt and pour over the hot stock mixture. Cover with plastic wrap and stand for 10 minutes.
- 4.
  Finely chop 1 cup mint leaves. Fluff couscous with a fork, then stir through onion, currants, chickpeas, lime juice, chilli, parsley, chopped and whole mint leaves and 1 tablespoon of oil. Set mixture aside.
- 5.

Heat remaining tablespoon oil in a large non-stick frypan over medium-high heat. Cook fish 2-3 minutes each side until just cooked through. Serve with couscous, lime wedges and extra harissa.

Cajun chicken with avocado, lime and chilli salsa

SERVES: 4 PREP TIME: 20MINS   COOK TIME: 8MINS
INGREDIENTS: 9   DIFFICULTY: EASY

INGREDIENTS
- 4 small (180g each) Lilydale Free Range Chicken Breast
- 1 tablespoon sweet paprika
- Pinch of cayenne pepper
- 1 avocado, flesh cubed
- 2 tablespoons lime juice
- 1 long green chilli, seeds removed, thinly sliced lengthways
- 2 tablespoons freshly snipped chives
- Olive oil spray
- 250g steamed green beans

METHOD
- 1.
- Cut each breast into 3 thin escalopes, then toss in the combined paprika and cayenne to lightly coat. Set aside. Place avocado, lime, chilli and chives in a bowl. Season and stir gently to combine. Set aside.
- 2.
- Heat a large frypan over high heat and spray with oil. Cook chicken, in 2 batches, for 2 minutes each side until cooked. Stand for 3 minutes, then halve each piece on an angle. Serve chicken on beans and salsa, and drizzle with any resting juices.

Indian-spiced chicken with cucumber salad

SERVES: 4 PREP TIME: 25MINS   COOK TIME: 15MINS
INGREDIENTS: 12   DIFFICULTY: EASY

INGREDIENTS
- 3 Lebanese cucumbers (600g), roughly chopped
- 3/4 cup (200g) low-fat Greek yoghurt
- 1/2 teaspoon ground coriander

- 1 teaspoon ground cumin
- 1/4 cup (60ml) lemon juice, plus wedges to serve
- 1 teaspoon sweet paprika
- 1 teaspoon chilli powder
- 2 garlic cloves, crushed
- 2cm piece ginger, grated
- 4 Lilydale Free Range Chicken Breasts (skin and wingbone attached, optional)
- 2 teaspoons olive oil
- 2/3 cup coriander leaves

METHOD
- 1.
  Toss the cucumber with 1 teaspoon of salt.
- 2.
  Place in a colander to drain for 15 minutes.
- 3.
  Meanwhile, mix yoghurt, ground coriander, cumin and juice. Reserve a quarter of mixture for cucumber. Stir paprika, chilli, garlic and ginger into remaining yoghurt. Toss with chicken and marinate for 10 minutes.
- 4.
  Preheat oven to 190°C. Heat a lightly oiled chargrill or large frypan over medium heat. Brown chicken for 1-2 minutes each side, then transfer to a baking tray and roast for 6-8 minutes until cooked.
- 5.
  Meanwhile, rinse cucumber and drain well. Toss with reserved yoghurt mixture, oil and coriander leaves. Serve chicken on the cucumber salad, with lemon wedges.

Chargrilled swordfish with grape, almond & barley salad

SERVES: 4 PREP TIME: 35MINS   COOK TIME: 35MINS
INGREDIENTS: 11   DIFFICULTY: EASY

INGREDIENTS
- 1 1/4 cups (280g) pearl barley, rinsed
- Finely grated zest and juice of 1/2 lemon
- 2 tsp dried Italian herbs
- 100ml olive oil
- 4 x 220g swordfish fillets
- 1 1/2 tbs red wine vinegar

- 225g red seedless grapes, halved
- 1/2 cup (80g) roasted almonds, chopped
- 1/3 cup (60g) currants, soaked in warm water for 10 minutes, drained
- 1 bunch flat-leaf parsley, leaves picked
- 2 celery stalks, chopped

METHOD
- 1.
  Cook barley in a saucepan of boiling salted water for 25-30 minutes until tender. Drain, then set aside to cool.
- 2.
  Meanwhile, combine lemon zest, 1 tsp Italian herbs and 2 tbs oil in a bowl. Season, add the swordfish and turn to coat, then set aside for 15 minutes to marinate.
- 3.
  To make the dressing, whisk vinegar, lemon juice and remaining 1/4 cup (60ml) oil together, season and set aside.
- 4.
  Preheat a barbecue or chargrill pan to high. Cook swordfish for 3 minutes each side or until just cooked. Rest, loosely covered with foil, for 5 minutes.
- 5.
  Combine barley, grapes, almonds, currants, parsley, celery and remaining 1 tsp Italian herbs. Drizzle over dressing and toss to combine.
- 6.
  Serve salad topped with swordfish.

Roasted sweet potatoes with chilli and seeds

SERVES: 4 PREP TIME: -   COOK TIME: 20MINS
INGREDIENTS: 9   DIFFICULTY: EASY

INGREDIENTS
- 2 sweet potatoes
- 2/3 cup (165ml) sunflower oil
- 1 tbs each white and black sesame seeds
- 1 tsp each fennel and coriander seeds
- 1 tbs pumpkin seeds (pepitas)
- 2 tsp salt flakes
- 1 tsp dried chilli flakes
- 1 cup (250ml) natural yoghurt
- Juice of 1 lemon

METHOD

- 1.
  Place sweet potato in a microwave-safe dish and microwave on high, turning halfway, for 6 minutes or until cooked through. If still firm, continue cooking for 1 minute intervals until just cooked. Cut lengthways into eighths. Heat oil in a frypan over high heat. In batches, fry, turning halfway, for 10-12 minutes until crisp. Remove and drain on paper towel.
- 2.
  Meanwhile, toast sesame seeds in a dry frypan over medium-low heat, tossing frequently, for 3-4 minutes until white seeds are golden. Add remaining seeds and toast for 1-2 minutes until fragrant. Using a mortar and pestle, crush salt and chilli flakes. Combine with toasted seeds and roughly crush.
- 3.
  Combine the yoghurt and lemon in a bowl. Set aside.
- 4.
  Toss the sweet potato with seeds. Serve with lemon yoghurt.

Barbecued cuttlefish, fennel and soppressata salad

SERVES: 4 PREP TIME: -   COOK TIME: 7MINS
INGREDIENTS: 9   DIFFICULTY: EASY

INGREDIENTS
- 100g soppressata or other mild salami, finely chopped
- Juice of 1 lemon
- 2 bulbs baby fennel, thinly sliced using a mandoline, fronds reserved
- 2 pink lady apples, thinly sliced using a mandoline
- 1 tbs white wine vinegar
- 1/3 cup (80ml) extra virgin olive oil
- 1/4 cup nasturtium leaves or baby spinach
- 1 1/2 cups micro coriander
- 4 (about 500g) cuttlefish, cleaned

METHOD
- 1.
  Place the soppressata in a cold frypan and place over medium heat. When it begins to sizzle, cook for a further 4-5 minutes until crisp. Add the lemon juice and remove from heat. Set aside.
- 2.

Bring a saucepan of water to the boil over high heat. Add sliced fennel and blanch for 30 seconds. Refresh in iced water, then drain. Place in a bowl with the apple, vinegar and 2 tbs oil. Toss to combine. Place fennel fronds, nasturtium leaves and micro coriander in a separate bowl and set aside until ready to use.

- 3.
  Preheat a barbecue or chargrill pan to high. Toss the cuttlefish with the remaining 2 tbs oil and season. Cook for 2 minutes each side or until golden. Cool slightly, then slice tubes into thin rounds and roughly chop the tentacles.
- 4.
  Combine nasturtium mixture and apple mixture. Add cuttlefish and toss gently to combine, then transfer to a platter. Spoon over soppressata to serve.

Ocean perch with broad bean and cucumber salad

SERVES: 4   PREP TIME:-   COOK TIME: 15MINS
INGREDIENTS: 9   DIFFICULTY: EASY

INGREDIENTS
- 1kg whole ocean perch, cleaned, scaled
- 1/4 cup (60ml) extra virgin olive oil
- 500g broad beans, podded, blanched, peeled
- 4 baby Lebanese cucumbers (qukes), sliced lengthways
- Mixed salad leaves, to serve

SALAD DRESSING
- 1/4 cup (60ml) extra virgin olive oil
- 1 tbs lemon juice
- 2 tsp white wine vinegar
- 1 tsp fresh or bottled grated horseradish

METHOD
- 1.
  Preheat a barbecue with lid or large chargrill pan to medium-high.
- 2.
  Drizzle the fish with oil and season. Place on flat barbecue plate and close the lid. (Alternatively, enclose in baking paper, then foil and place on grill plate.) Cook for 7 minutes or until just cooked on one side. Using 2 large spatulas, carefully turn fish and cook for a further 7 minutes or until just cooked. Transfer to a platter and rest, loosely covered with foil, for 3-4 minutes.
- 3.
  For the salad dressing, combine all the ingredients in a bowl and season.

- 4.
  Toss the broad beans, cucumber and dressing in a bowl. Place around the fish and scatter over salad leaves to serve.

Roast chicken panzanella

SERVES: 4 PREP TIME: 10MINS   COOK TIME: 40MINS
INGREDIENTS: 11   DIFFICULTY: EASY

INGREDIENTS
- 8 Lilydale Free Range Chicken Thighs (bone in, skin on)
- 1/3 cup (55g) kalamata olives
- 1 red onion, thickly sliced into rings
- 200g baby red capsicums
- 2 tsp dried oregano
- 3 garlic cloves, finely grated
- 2 tbs red wine vinegar
- 100ml extra virgin olive oil
- 4 large slices ciabatta, roughly torn
- 4 large mixed tomatoes, halved
- 1/2 bunch basil, leaves picked

METHOD
- 1.
  Preheat oven to 200°C. Place chicken, olives, onion and capsicum in a large roasting dish. Combine oregano, garlic, vinegar and 1/3 cup (80ml) oil. Drizzle over dish. Season. Roast for 25 minutes or until chicken is slightly golden.
- 2.
  Drizzle remaining 1 tbs oil over bread, add to tray with tomato and roast for a further 10-15 minutes or until chicken is cooked through. Serve topped with basil.

Sticky pork and crispy noodle salad

SERVES: - PREP TIME: -   COOK TIME: -
INGREDIENTS: 12   DIFFICULTY: EASY

INGREDIENTS
- 2 tbs peanut oil
- 1 large onion, grated
- 500g pork mince
- 2 garlic cloves, crushed

- 1 tbs freshly grated ginger
- 1/4 cup (60ml) char siu sauce
- 1 tsp Chinese five spice powder
- 1/3 cup (80ml) Chinese rice wine (shaohsing)
- 100g packet Chang's fried noodles
- Chopped long red chilli, toasted
- cashews, coriander leaves, snipped, to serve
- chives and lime cheeks, to serve

METHOD
- 1.
  Heat oil in a frypan over medium-high heat. Cook onion, stirring, for 3-4 minutes until softened. Increase heat to high, add pork and cook, stirring, for 8-10 minutes until golden. Add garlic, ginger, char siu sauce and five spice, and cook for 2 minutes or until fragrant. Add the rice wine and cook for 3-4 minutes until caramelised.
- 2.
  Divide noodles among plates. Top with pork, chilli, cashews, coriander and chives. Serve with lime cheeks to squeeze over.

Double mint potato salad

SERVES: 4 PREP TIME: -   COOK TIME: -
INGREDIENTS: 8   DIFFICULTY: EASY

INGREDIENTS
- 800g small potatoes (a waxy variety such as kipfler, pink eye or nicola)
- 1/2 bunch mint, leaves torn
- 1/4 bunch flat-leaf parsley, leaves torn
- MINT DRESSING
- 2 tsp dried mint
- 1/2 tsp ground cumin
- 1/2 tsp salt flakes, plus extra, to serve
- Juice of 1/2 lemon
- 200g creme fraiche

METHOD
- 1.
  For the dressing, combine the dried mint, cumin, salt, lemon juice and creme fraiche. Chill, the longer the better, until ready to serve.
- 2.

Cook the potatoes in a large saucepan of boiling, salted water for 10 minutes or until tender. Drain, then place back into the warm, dry pan to dry and cool for 15 minutes.
- 3.
Cut the potatoes as you like (or leave whole if they're small). When cooled to room temperature, toss gently with the dressing until nicely coated.
- 4.
Scatter on the fresh herbs, finish with a sprinkle of salt and serve.

Matt Moran's grilled avocado with radish, cucumber and herb salad

SERVES: 4 PREP TIME: -   COOK TIME: -
INGREDIENTS: 9   DIFFICULTY: EASY

INGREDIENTS
- 2 Lebanese cucumbers, thinly sliced on the diagonal
- 1 1/2 tbs olive oil
- 2 firm, ripe avocados
- 1/2 bunch radishes, very thinly sliced
- 1/4 bunch each tarragon, dill, mint, & flat-leaf parsley, leaves picked
- CLASSIC DRESSING
- 2 tbs chardonnay vinegar or white wine vinegar
- 1 tbs lemon juice
- 1 tsp Dijon mustard
- 1/2 cup (125ml) grapeseed oil

METHOD
- 1.
For the dressing, whisk vinegar, lemon juice and mustard in a bowl. Whisking constantly, slowly add grapeseed oil until thick and emulsified. Season. Set aside.
- 2.
Combine cucumber in a bowl with half the olive oil and 1/4 tsp salt. Set aside.
- 3.
Preheat a chargrill pan to medium-high.
- 4.
Halve avocados lengthways and remove seeds, leaving skin intact, then halve lengthways again. Brush cut sides with remaining olive oil, then cook, cut-side down, for 2 minutes or until lightly charred.
- 5.

Turn and cook other cut side for a further 2 minutes. Set aside to cool for 5 minutes, then peel skin and discard.
- 6.
  To serve, combine all the ingredients on a platter, drizzle with dressing and season.

Bean, pea and lentil salad

SERVES: 8 PREP TIME: 25MINS   COOK TIME: 30MINS
INGREDIENTS: 9   DIFFICULTY: EASY

INGREDIENTS
- 1 cup French-style lentils
- 4 cups water
- 200g trimmed green beans
- 200g trimmed sugar-snap peas
- 1 cup frozen peas
- 1 finely chopped red onion
- 100ml olive oil
- 2 tbs lemon juice
- ¼ cup coarsely chopped mint.

METHOD
- 1.
  Place 1 cup French-style lentils and 4 cups water in a saucepan. Bring to the boil over high heat. Reduce heat to low and simmer for 25 minutes or until just tender. Drain and set aside.
- 2.
  Meanwhile cook 200g trimmed green beans in a saucepan of boiling, salted water for 2 minutes. Add 200g trimmed sugar-snap peas and cook for 2 minutes. Add 1 cup frozen peas.Cook for a further 2 minutes. Drain. Place in iced water for 5 minutes. Drain and combine with lentils and 1 finely chopped red onion. Whisk 100ml olive oil with 2 tbs lemon juice and season with salt and pepper. Toss gently through salad. Scatter over ¼ cup coarsely chopped mint. Serve.

Mint, bean and feta salad

SERVES: 8 PREP TIME: 15MINS   COOK TIME: 10MINS
INGREDIENTS: 7   DIFFICULTY: EASY

INGREDIENTS

- 2 x 500g pkts frozen broad beans
- 250g frozen peas
- ⅓ cup extra virgin olive oil
- 3 zucchinis, diced
- 1 lemon, finely zested, juiced
- mint leaves, torn
- 100g Persian feta, crumbled

METHOD
- 1.
Add beans and peas to a saucepan of boiling water for 3-4 minutes until bright green. Drain and refresh under cold water. Drain, peel beans and discard skins. Transfer to a large bowl.
- 2.
Heat 1½ tbs of the oil in a small frying pan and cook zucchini over mediumhigh heat for 5 minutes until golden and tender. Add to bowl with beans and peas, along with lemon zest, mint and feta.
- 3.
Whisk lemon juice and remaining oil together in a jug. Season with pepper. Pour over salad and serve.

Radish and tuna salad with wasabi dressing

SERVES: 4 PREP TIME: 15MINS   COOK TIME: 5MINS
INGREDIENTS: 13   DIFFICULTY: CAPABLE

INGREDIENTS
- 1 tbs mirin
- 1/4 cup (60ml) extra virgin olive oil
- 2 tsp wasabi paste
- Juice of 1 lime
- 4 x 160g tuna steaks
- 1 tbs sesame oil
- 2 garlic cloves, crushed
- 2 tbs dark soy sauce
- 75g snow pea tendrils
- 4 red radishes, sliced on a mandoline
- 1 cup (120g) edamame, blanched
- 1 Lebanese cucumber, thinly sliced
- 1 tbs black sesame seeds, toasted

METHOD

- 1.
  To make the wasabi dressing, combine the mirin, olive oil, wasabi and lime juice in a bowl. Set aside.
- 2.
  Place a frypan over high heat until smoking. Place the tuna in a bowl with sesame oil, garlic and soy, and toss to coat. Drain. Cook tuna for 45 seconds each side or until seared but still rare in the centre. Remove from pan and rest, loosely covered with foil, for 5 minutes.
- 3.
  Toss snow pea tendrils, radish, edamame and cucumber in a bowl. Divide among serving bowls, then drizzle with the wasabi dressing.
- 4.
  Thinly slice tuna and divide among bowls. Scatter with sesame to serve.

Sticky barbecued prawn salad

SERVES: - PREP TIME: 15MINS   COOK TIME: 10MINS
INGREDIENTS: 15   DIFFICULTY: EASY

INGREDIENTS
- 4 cloves of garlic
- 4 spring onions
- 1 fresh green chilli
- ½ a bunch of fresh basil
- 12 large unpeeled raw banana prawns
- 1 lemon
- Olive oil
- 75ml sweet chilli sauce
- 8 thin slices of focaccia bread
- 2 large ripe tomatoes
- 1 handful of ripe mixed-colour cherry tomatoes
- Balsamic vinegar
- 2 ripe avocados
- 1 lime
- Extra virgin olive oil

METHOD
- 1.
  Light the barbecue and prepare a hot side and a cool side. Meanwhile, prep all the ingredients so you're ready to go: peel and finely slice 3 of the garlic cloves and slice the spring onions diagonally into 1 cm pieces. Halve, deseed and chop the

chilli, then pick the basil leaves and finely chop the stalks. Pull off and discard the little legs from the underside of the prawns. Halve the lemon.
- 2.
When you're ready to cook, place a heatproof pan over a high heat. Add a splash of oil, the garlic and spring onions and cook for a few seconds until sizzling and smelling great, then add the chilli and basil stalks. After a minute or so, add the chilli sauce and a splash of water, then cook for 5 to 10 minutes or until thickened and reduced, stirring regularly. Place on the cool side of the grill until needed.
- 3.
Toast the focaccia slices on both sides until crisp and golden. Halve the remaining garlic clove and rub all over the toasted focaccia, then keep warm until needed. Slice the tomatoes into random chunks, and halve and quarter the cherry tomatoes, then place in a bowl. Drizzle with the balsamic and toss to coat. Halve and destone the avocados, slice the flesh and place in a bowl, then squeeze over the lime juice and toss together. Drizzle the prawns with oil and place on the hot side of the barbecue along with the lime, cut-side down. Grill for around 4 minutes on each side, or until crisp on the outside and cooked through – the exact timing will depend on how hot your barbecue is, so use your instincts and keep a close eye.
- 4.
Place the garlicky focaccia onto a nice serving platter. Arrange the tomatoes and avocado on top. Drizzle everything with a little extra virgin olive oil. Once cooked, transfer the prawns to the pan of glaze using tongs, then squeeze in the grilled lemon (making sure to avoid adding the pips). Toss a couple of times to coat, then carefully add to the top of the salad, drizzling the excess sauce in and around the platter. Tear over the basil leaves, then serve.

New nicoise salad

SERVES: 4 PREP TIME: 10MINS   COOK TIME: 15MINS
INGREDIENTS: 12   DIFFICULTY: EASY

INGREDIENTS
- 500g small kipfler potatoes
- 2 tbs extra virgin olive oil
- 4 eggs
- 4 small Lebanese cucumbers, sliced lengthways into thin wedges
- 6 mixed heirloom tomatoes, sliced
- 250g can tuna in oil, drained
- 2 eschalots, thinly sliced
- 150g snow pea shoots

- OLIVE TAPENADE DRESSING
- 1/4 cup (60ml) extra virgin olive oil
- 2 tbs red wine vinegar
- 1/3 cup (50g) pitted kalamata olives, finely chopped
- 1/2 garlic clove, finely grated

METHOD
- 1.
  Place potatoes in a saucepan, cover with cold water and bring to the boil over high heat. Reduce heat to medium-low and cook for 15 minutes or until tender. Rinse under cold water and drain.
- 2.
  For the olive tapenade dressing, combine all ingredients and season.
- 3.
  Heat oil in a large pan over medium-high heat. Break eggs into pan and fry for 2 minutes or until cooked to your liking.
- 4.
  Halve potatoes if large. Divide among plates with cucumber, tomato, tuna, eschalot and snow pea shoots. Drizzle with dressing and top with an egg to serve.

Barbecue beef salad with beer vinaigrette

SERVES: 4 PREP TIME: 5MINS   COOK TIME: 10MINS
INGREDIENTS: 12   DIFFICULTY: EASY

INGREDIENTS
- 2 tbs extra virgin olive oil, plus extra to drizzle
- 1 tsp smoked paprika (pimenton), plus extra to sprinkle
- 2 garlic cloves, finely grated
- 4 corn cobs, husks removed
- 4 x 200g beef sirloin steaks
- 2 baby cos lettuces, quartered lengthways
- 50g sharp cheddar cheese, crumbled
- 2 limes, halved

BEER VINAIGRETTE
- 375ml beer (we used golden ale)
- 1/4 cup (60ml) extra virgin olive oil
- 1 tbs apple cider or white wine vinegar
- 1 tbs maple syrup

METHOD
- 1.

For the beer vinaigrette, place beer in a small saucepan over medium heat. Bring to a simmer and cook for 4-5 minutes until reduced to 1/3 cup (80ml). Set aside to cool completely
- 2.
Preheat barbecue or chargrill pan to high heat. Combine oil, paprika and garlic in a bowl, season and brush over corn and steak. Chargrill corn, turning, for 4-5 minutes until lightly charred. Add steak and cook, turning, for 2 minutes each side for medium-rare or until cooked to your liking. Rest steak, loosely covered with foil, for 4 minutes. Slice kernels off corn cobs.
- 3.
Meanwhile, combine the reduced beer, oil, vinegar and maple syrup in a bowl and season.
- 4.
Slice steak and divide among plates with corn, cos and cheese. Drizzle with the vinaigrette and oil. Sprinkle over paprika and serve with lime halves.

BAKED CHICKEN WITH PEACHES

Servings: 8 | Prep: 15m | Cooks: 30m | Total: 45m

NUTRITION FACTS

Calories: 248 | Carbohydrates: 30.3g | Fat: 2.8g | Protein: 24.6g | Cholesterol: 67mg

INGREDIENTS

- 8 skinless, boneless chicken breast halves
- 1/8 teaspoon ground ginger
- 1 cup brown sugar
- 1/8 teaspoon ground cloves
- 4 fresh peaches - peeled, pitted, and sliced
- 2 tablespoons fresh lemon juice

DIRECTIONS

1. Preheat oven to 350 degrees F (175 degrees C). Lightly grease a 9x13 inch baking dish.
2. Place chicken in the prepared baking dish, and sprinkle with 1/2 cup of brown sugar. Place peach slices over chicken, then sprinkle with remaining 1/2 cup brown sugar, ginger, cloves, and lemon juice.

3. Bake for about 30 minutes in the preheated oven, basting often with juices, until chicken is cooked through and juices run clear.

SUMMER CORN SALAD

Servings: 4 | Prep: 25m | Cooks: 20m | Total: 45m

NUTRITION FACTS

Calories: 305 | Carbohydrates: 42.8g | Fat: 15.6g | Protein: 6.2g | Cholesterol: 0mg

INGREDIENTS

- 6 ears corn, husked and cleaned
- 1/4 cup olive oil
- 3 large tomatoes, diced
- 2 tablespoons white vinegar
- 1 large onion, diced
- salt and pepper to taste
- 1/4 cup chopped fresh basil

DIRECTIONS

1. Bring a large pot of lightly salted water to a boil. Cook corn in boiling water for 7 to 10 minutes, or until desired tenderness. Drain, cool, and cut kernels off the cob with a sharp knife.
2. In a large bowl, toss together the corn, tomatoes, onion, basil, oil, vinegar, salt and pepper. Chill until serving.

HONEY WHEAT BREAD

Servings: 24 | Prep: 30m | Cooks: 30m | Total: 2h

NUTRITION FACTS

Calories: 171 | Carbohydrates: 31.2g | Fat: 3.5g | Protein: 4.3g | Cholesterol: 0mg

INGREDIENTS

- 2 cups warm water (110 degrees F/45 degrees C)
- 1/3 cup honey

- 2 cups whole wheat flour
- 1/3 cup vegetable oil
- 1 tablespoon active dry yeast
- 5 cups all-purpose flour
- 1 teaspoon salt

DIRECTIONS

1. Dissolve yeast in warm water. Add honey, and stir well. Mix in whole wheat flour, salt, and vegetable oil. Work all-purpose flour in gradually. Turn dough out onto a lightly floured surface, and knead for at least 10 to 15 minutes. When dough is smooth and elastic, place it in a well oiled bowl. Turn it several times in the bowl to coat the surface of the dough, and cover with a damp cloth. Let rise in a warm place until doubled in bulk, about 45 minutes.
2. Punch down the dough. Shape into two loaves, and place into two well greased 9 x 5 inch loaf pans. Allow to rise until dough is 1 to 1 1/2 inches above pans.
3. Bake at 375 degrees F (190 degrees C) for 25 to 30 minutes.

CREAMY ITALIAN WHITE BEAN SOUP

Servings: 4 | Prep: 20m | Cooks: 30m | Total: 50m

NUTRITION FACTS

Calories: 245 | Carbohydrates: 38.1g | Fat: 4.9g | Protein: 12g | Cholesterol: 2mg

INGREDIENTS

- 1 tablespoon vegetable oil
- 1/4 teaspoon ground black pepper
- 1 onion, chopped
- 1/8 teaspoon dried thyme
- 1 stalk celery, chopped
- 2 cups water
- 1 clove garlic, minced
- 1 bunch fresh spinach, rinsed and thinly sliced
- 2 (16 ounce) cans white kidney beans, rinsed and drained
- 1 tablespoon lemon juice
- 1 (14 ounce) can chicken broth

DIRECTIONS

1. In a large saucepan, heat oil. Cook onion and celery in oil for 5 to 8 minutes, or until tender. Add garlic, and cook for 30 seconds, continually stirring. Stir in beans, chicken broth, pepper, thyme and 2 cups water. Bring to a boil, reduce heat, and then simmer for 15 minutes.
2. With slotted spoon, remove 2 cups of the bean and vegetable mixture from soup and set aside.
3. In blender at low speed, blend remaining soup in small batches until smooth, (it helps to remove the center piece of the blender lid to allow steam to escape.) Once blended pour soup back into stock pot and stir in reserved beans.
4. Bring to a boil, occasionally stirring. Stir in spinach and cook 1 minute or until spinach is wilted. Stir in lemon juice and remove from heat and serve with fresh grated Parmesan cheese on top.

TURKEY CARCASS SOUPS

Servings: 12 | Prep: 45m | Cooks: 2h | Total: 2h45m

NUTRITION FACTS

Calories: 133 | Carbohydrates: 27.7g | Fat: 1.3g | Protein: 4.2g | Cholesterol: 2mg

INGREDIENTS

- 1 turkey carcass
- 1 tablespoon Worcestershire sauce
- 4 quarts water
- 1 1/2 teaspoons salt
- 6 small potatoes, diced
- 1 teaspoon dried parsley
- 4 large carrots, diced
- 1 teaspoon dried basil
- 2 stalks celery, diced
- 1 bay leaf
- 1 large onion, diced
- 1/4 teaspoon freshly cracked black pepper
- 1 1/2 cups shredded cabbage
- 1/4 teaspoon paprika
- 1 (28 ounce) can whole peeled tomatoes, chopped   1/4 teaspoon poultry seasoning

- 1/2 cup uncooked barley
- 1 pinch dried thyme

DIRECTIONS

1. Place the turkey carcass into a large soup pot or stock pot and pour in the water; bring to a boil, reduce heat to a simmer, and cook the turkey frame until the remaining meat falls off the bones, about 1 hour. Remove the turkey carcass and remove and chop any remaining turkey meat. Chop the meat.
2. Strain the broth through a fine mesh strainer into a clean soup pot. Add the chopped turkey to the strained broth; bring the to a boil, reduce heat, and stir in the potatoes, carrots, celery, onion, cabbage, tomatoes, barley, Worcestershire sauce, salt, parsley, basil, bay leaf, black pepper, paprika, poultry seasoning, and thyme. Simmer until the vegetables are tender, about 1 more hour. Remove bay leaf before serving.

LOWER FAT BANANA BREAD

Servings: 12 | Prep: 15m | Cooks: 1h | Total: 1h15m

NUTRITION FACTS

Calories: 178 | Carbohydrates: 31.2g | Fat: 4.3g | Protein: 3.9g | Cholesterol: 31mg

INGREDIENTS

- 2 eggs
- 1 tablespoon vanilla extract
- 2/3 cup white sugar
- 1 3/4 cups all-purpose flour
- 2 very ripe bananas, mashed
- 2 teaspoons baking powder
- 1/4 cup applesauce
- 1/2 teaspoon baking soda
- 1/3 cup nonfat milk
- 1/2 teaspoon salt
- 1 tablespoon vegetable oil
- 1/3 cup chopped walnuts

DIRECTIONS

1. Preheat oven to 325 degrees F (165 degrees C). Spray a bread pan with non-stick cooking spray, and lightly dust with flour.
2. In a large bowl, beat eggs and sugar in a large bowl until light and fluffy, about 5 minutes. Beat in bananas, applesauce, milk, oil and vanilla.
3. In a separate bowl, sift together flour, baking powder, baking soda and salt. Stir flour mixture into banana mixture, mixing just until blended. Fold in walnuts. Pour batter into prepared pan.
4. Bake in preheated pan until golden and a toothpick inserted into center of the loaf comes out clean, about 1 hour. Turn bread out onto a wire rack and let cool.

SLOW COOKER CHICKEN CREOLE

Servings: 4 | Prep: 10m | Cooks: 12h | Total: 12h10m

NUTRITION FACTS

Calories: 189 | Carbohydrates: 13.8g | Fat: 1.9g | Protein: 29.6g | Cholesterol: 68mg

INGREDIENTS

- 4 skinless, boneless chicken breast halves
- 1 green bell pepper, diced
- salt and pepper to taste
- 3 cloves garlic, minced
- Creole-style seasoning to taste
- 1 onion, diced
- 1 (14.5 ounce) can stewed tomatoes, with liquid
- 1 (4 ounce) can mushrooms, drained
- 1 stalk celery, diced
- 1 fresh jalapeno pepper, seeded and chopped

DIRECTIONS

1. Place chicken breasts in slow cooker. Season with salt, pepper, and Creole-style seasoning to taste. Stir in tomatoes with liquid, celery, bell pepper, garlic, onion, mushrooms, and jalapeno pepper.
2. Cook on Low for 10 to 12 hours, or on High for 5 to 6 hours.

GRANOLA BARS

Servings: 20 | Prep: 15m | Cooks: 25m | Total: 40m

NUTRITION FACTS

Calories: 212 | Carbohydrates: 32.2g | Fat: 8.6g | Protein: 3.4g | Cholesterol: 9mg

INGREDIENTS

- 2 cups quick cooking oats
- 1/2 teaspoon ground cinnamon
- 1 cup all-purpose flour
- 1/2 cup chopped English walnuts
- 3/4 cup packed brown sugar
- 1/2 cup vegetable oil
- 3/4 cup raisins
- 1/2 cup honey
- 1/2 cup wheat germ
- 1 egg
- 1/2 teaspoon salt
- 2 teaspoons vanilla extract

DIRECTIONS

1. Preheat oven to 350 degrees F (175 degrees C). Line a 9x13 inch baking pan with aluminum foil or parchment paper, and spray with vegetable oil spray.
2. In a large bowl, stir together oats, flour, brown sugar, raisins, wheat germ, salt, cinnamon, and walnuts. In a smaller bowl, thoroughly blend oil, honey, egg, and vanilla; pour into the flour mixture, and mix by hand until the liquid is evenly distributed. Press evenly into the prepared baking pan.
3. Bake 25 to 30 minutes in the preheated oven, or until the edges are golden. Cool completely in pan before turning out onto a cutting board and cutting into bars.

OATMEAL WHOLE WHEAT QUICK BREAD

Servings: 12 | Prep: 20m | Cooks: 20m | Total: 40m

NUTRITION FACTS

Calories: 88 | Carbohydrates: 15.1g | Fat: 2.2g | Protein: 2.9g | Cholesterol: 2mg

INGREDIENTS

- 1 cup rolled oats
- 1 1/2 tablespoons honey
- 1 cup whole wheat flour
- 1 tablespoon vegetable oil
- 2 teaspoons baking powder
- 1 cup milk
- 1/2 teaspoon salt

DIRECTIONS

1. Preheat oven to 450 degrees F (230 degrees C).
2. Grind oatmeal in a food processor or blender. In a large bowl, combine oatmeal, flour, baking powder and salt. In a separate bowl, dissolve honey in vegetable oil then stir in the milk. Combine both mixtures and stir until a soft dough is formed. Form the dough into a ball and place on a lightly oiled baking sheet.
3. Bake in preheated oven for about 20 minutes, or until bottom of loaf sounds hollow when tapped.

OAT APPLESAUCE MUFFINS

Servings: 12| Prep: 10m | Cooks: 30m | Total: 2h40m

NUTRITION FACTS

Calories: 101 | Carbohydrates: 20g | Fat: 1.2g | Protein: 3.5g | Cholesterol: 16mg

INGREDIENTS

- 1 cup rolled oats
- 1/2 teaspoon baking soda

- 1 cup buttermilk
- 1/2 cup brown sugar
- 1 cup whole wheat flour
- 1/2 cup applesauce
- 1 teaspoon baking powder
- 1 egg

DIRECTIONS

1. Place oats in a small bowl, pour in buttermilk. Let sit for two hours at room temperature.
2. Preheat oven to 375 degrees F (190 degrees C). Grease 12 muffin cups or line with paper muffin liners.
3. In a large bowl, stir together whole wheat flour, baking powder, baking soda and brown sugar. Stir in oat/buttermilk mixture, applesauce and egg; mix well. Pour batter into prepared muffin cups.
4. Bake in preheated oven for 30 minutes, until a toothpick inserted into center of muffin comes out clean.

FRESH TOMATO MARINARA SAUCE

Servings: 6 | Prep: 15m | Cooks: 1h10m | Total: 1h25m

NUTRITION FACTS

Calories: 147 | Carbohydrates: 16.5g | Fat: 7.4g | Protein: 2.7g | Cholesterol: 0mg

INGREDIENTS

- 3 tablespoons olive oil
- 1 teaspoon oregano
- 1/2 onion, chopped
- 1 teaspoon dried marjoram
- 8 large tomatoes, peeled and cut into big chunks
- 1 teaspoon salt
- 6 cloves garlic, minced
- 1/2 teaspoon ground black pepper
- 1 bay leaf
- 1/4 teaspoon fennel seed
- 1/2 cup red wine

- 1/4 teaspoon crushed red pepper
- 1 tablespoon honey
- 2 teaspoons balsamic vinegar, or more to taste
- 2 teaspoons dried basil

DIRECTIONS

1. Heat olive oil in a stockpot over medium heat. Cook and stir onion in hot oil until softened, about 5 minutes; add tomatoes, garlic, and bay leaf. Bring the liquid from the tomatoes to a boil, reduce to medium-low, and simmer mixture until tomatoes are softened, about 30 minutes.
2. Stir red wine, honey, basil, oregano, marjoram, salt, black pepper, fennel seed, and crushed red pepper into the tomato mixture; bring again to a simmer and cook until herbs have flavored the sauce, about 30 minutes more.
3. Stir balsamic vinegar into the sauce.

CHICKEN BROCCOLI CA - UNIENG'S STYLE

Servings: 6 | Prep: 10m | Cooks: 25m | Total: 35m

NUTRITION FACTS

Calories: 170 | Carbohydrates: 9.8g | Fat: 7.9g | Protein: 16.2g | Cholesterol: 33mg

INGREDIENTS

- 12 ounces boneless, skinless chicken breast halves, cut into bite-sized pieces
- 1/2 cup water
- 1 tablespoon oyster sauce
- 1 teaspoon ground black pepper
- 2 tablespoons dark soy sauce
- 1 teaspoon white sugar
- 3 tablespoons vegetable oil
- 1/2 medium head bok choy, chopped
- 2 cloves garlic, chopped
- 1 small head broccoli, chopped
- 1 large onion, cut into rings
- 1 tablespoon cornstarch, mixed with equal parts water

DIRECTIONS

1. In a large bowl, combine chicken, oyster sauce and soy sauce. Set aside for 15 minutes.
2. Heat oil in a wok or large heavy skillet over medium heat. Saute garlic and onion until soft and translucent. Increase heat to high. Add chicken and marinade, then stir-fry until light golden brown, about 10 minutes. Stir in water, pepper and sugar. Add bok choy and broccoli, and cook stirring until soft, about 10 minutes. Pour in the cornstarch mixture, and cook until sauce is thickened, about 5 minutes.

SPICY TUNA FISH CAKES

Servings: 4 | Prep: 20m | Cooks: 30m | Total: 50m

NUTRITION FACTS

Calories: 237 | Carbohydrates: 20.7g | Fat: 5.6g | Protein: 25.2g | Cholesterol: 72mg

INGREDIENTS

- 1 large potato, peeled and cubed
- 1 1/2 teaspoons garlic powder
- 4 (3 ounce) cans tuna, drained
- 1 teaspoon Italian seasoning
- 1 egg
- 1/4 teaspoon cayenne pepper
- 1/4 cup chopped onion
- salt and ground black pepper to taste
- 1 tablespoon Dijon mustard
- 1 tablespoon olive oil
- 1 tablespoon dry breadcrumbs, or as needed

DIRECTIONS

1. Place the potato into a small pot and cover with salted water. Bring to a boil over high heat, then reduce heat to medium-low, cover, and simmer until tender, about 20 minutes. Drain and allow to steam dry for a minute or two, then mash the potato with a potato masher or fork in a large bowl.
2. Mix the tuna, egg, onion, Dijon mustard, bread crumbs, garlic powder, Italian seasoning, cayenne pepper, salt, and pepper into the mashed potato until well-blended. Divide the tuna mixture into 8 equal portions and shape into patties.

3. Heat the olive oil in a skillet over medium heat. Pan fry the tuna patties until browned and crisp, about 3 minutes on each side.

TEXAS CAVIAR

Servings: 16 | Prep: 15m | Cooks: 1h | Total: 1h15m

NUTRITION FACTS

Calories: 107 | Carbohydrates: 11.8g | Fat: 5.4g | Protein: 3.5g | Cholesterol: 0mg

INGREDIENTS

- 1/2 onion, chopped
- 1 (8 ounce) bottle zesty Italian dressing
- 1 green bell pepper, chopped
- 1 (15 ounce) can black beans, drained
- 1 bunch green onions, chopped
- 1 (15 ounce) can black-eyed peas, drained
- 2 jalapeno peppers, chopped
- 1/2 teaspoon ground coriander
- 1 tablespoon minced garlic
- 1 bunch chopped fresh cilantro
- 1 pint cherry tomatoes, quartered

DIRECTIONS

1. In a large bowl, mix together onion, green bell pepper, green onions, jalapeno peppers, garlic, cherry tomatoes, zesty Italian dressing, black beans, black-eyed peas and coriander. Cover and chill in the refrigerator approximately 2 hours. Toss with desired amount of fresh cilantro to serve.

FRESH STRAWBERRY PIE

Servings: 16 | Prep: 15m | Cooks: 15m | Total: 2h30m | Additional: 2h

NUTRITION FACTS

Calories: 167 | Carbohydrates: 31.6g | Fat: 4.4g | Protein: 1.7g | Cholesterol: 0mg

INGREDIENTS

- 2 (8 inch) pie shells, baked
- 2 tablespoons cornstarch
- 2 1/2 quarts fresh strawberries
- 1 cup boiling water
- 1 cup white sugar
- 1 (3 ounce) package strawberry flavored Jell-O®

DIRECTIONS

1. In a saucepan, mix together the sugar and corn starch; make sure to blend corn starch in completely. Add boiling water, and cook over medium heat until mixture thickens. Remove from heat. Add gelatin mix, and stir until smooth. Let mixture cool to room temperature.
2. Place strawberries in baked pie shells; position berries with points facing up. Pour cooled gel mixture over strawberries.
3. Refrigerate until set. Serve with whipped cream, if desired.

MANDARIN CHICKEN PASTA SALAD

Servings: 6 | Prep: 45m | Cooks: 8m | Total: 53m

NUTRITION FACTS

Calories: 425 | Carbohydrates: 44.7g | Fat: 18.9g | Protein: 21.8g | Cholesterol: 35mg

INGREDIENTS

- 1 teaspoon finely chopped, peeled fresh ginger
- 1/2 cucumber - scored, halved lengthwise, seeded, and sliced
- 1/3 cup rice vinegar
- 1/2 cup diced red bell pepper
- 1/4 cup orange juice
- 1/2 cup coarsely chopped red onion
- 1/4 cup vegetable oil
- 2 diced Roma tomatoes
- 1 teaspoon toasted sesame oil
- 1 carrot, shredded
- 1 (1 ounce) package dry onion soup mix

- 1 (6 ounce) bag fresh spinach
- 2 teaspoons white sugar
- 1 (11 ounce) can mandarin orange segments, drained
- 1 clove garlic, pressed
- 2 cups diced cooked chicken
- 1 (8 ounce) package bow tie (farfalle) pasta
- 1/2 cup sliced almonds, toasted

DIRECTIONS

1. To make the dressing, whisk together the ginger root, rice vinegar, orange juice, vegetable oil, sesame oil, soup mix, sugar, and garlic until well blended. Cover, and refrigerate until needed.
2. Bring a large pot of lightly salted water to a boil. Add the bowtie pasta and cook for 8 to 10 minutes or until al dente; drain, and rinse under cold water. Place pasta in a large bowl.
3. To make the salad, toss the cucumber, bell pepper, onion, tomatoes, carrot, spinach, mandarin oranges, chicken, and almonds with the pasta. Pour the dressing over the salad mixture, and toss again to coat evenly. Serve immediately.

SPINACH LENTIL SOUP

Servings: 8 | Prep: 15m | Cooks: 35m | Total: 50m

NUTRITION FACTS

Calories: 150 | Carbohydrates: 22.7g | Fat: 2.4g | Protein: 10.1g | Cholesterol: 10mg

INGREDIENTS

- 1/3 cup uncooked white rice
- 1/2 teaspoon crushed red pepper flakes
- 2/3 cup water
- 6 cups water
- 1 teaspoon vegetable oil
- 2 cups reduced sodium chicken broth
- 4 ounces turkey kielbasa, chopped
- 1 cup dry lentils
- 1 onion, minced
- 1 (10 ounce) bag fresh spinach, torn

- 1 carrot, chopped

DIRECTIONS

1. In a pot, bring the rice and water to a boil. Reduce heat to low, cover, and simmer 20 minutes.
2. Heat the oil in a large pot over medium heat, and cook the turkey kielbasa until lightly browned. Mix in onion and carrot, and season with red pepper. Cook and stir until tender. Pour in the water and broth, and mix in lentils. Bring to a boil, reduce heat to low, and simmer 25 minutes.
3. Stir the cooked rice and spinach into the soup, and continue cooking 5 minutes before serving.

RASPBERRY SAUCE

Servings: 8 | Prep: 10m | Cooks: 5m | Total: 15m

NUTRITION FACTS

Calories: 53 | Carbohydrates: 13g | Fat: 0.2g | Protein: 0.4g | Cholesterol: 0mg

INGREDIENTS

- 1 pint fresh raspberries
- 2 tablespoons cornstarch
- 1/4 cup white sugar
- 1 cup cold water
- 2 tablespoons orange juice

DIRECTIONS

1. Combine the raspberries, sugar, and orange juice in a saucepan. Whisk the cornstarch into the cold water until smooth. Add the mixture to the saucepan and bring to a boil.
2. Simmer for about 5 minutes, stirring constantly, until the desired consistency is reached. The sauce will thicken further as it cools.
3. Puree the sauce in a blender or with a handheld immersion blender and strain it through a fine sieve. Serve warm or cold. The sauce will keep in the refrigerator for up to two weeks.

SPICY BLACK BEAN CAKES

Servings: 8 | Prep: 20m | Cooks: 15m | Total: 35m

NUTRITION FACTS

Calories: 219 | Carbohydrates: 31.3g | Fat: 6.7g | Protein: 9.4g | Cholesterol: 29mg

INGREDIENTS

- 1/2 cup reduced fat sour cream
- 6 cloves garlic, pressed
- 2 teaspoons fresh lime juice
- 2 fresh jalapeno peppers, finely diced
- 1 small fresh jalapeno pepper, minced
- 1 tablespoon ground cumin
- salt to taste
- 2 (14.5 ounce) cans black beans, drained and rinsed
- 2 tablespoons olive oil, divided
- salt and black pepper to taste
- 4 green onions, thinly sliced
- 2 cups grated raw sweet potato
- 1/2 cup reduced fat sour cream
- 1 egg, lightly beaten

DIRECTIONS

1. To prepare lime sour cream, mix the sour cream, lime juice, 1 small minced jalapeno, and salt together in a small bowl. Cover, and refrigerate.
2. Heat 1 tablespoon olive oil in a small skillet over medium heat. Cook green onions until softened, about 1 minute. Stir in garlic, 2 diced jalapenos, and cumin; cook until fragrant, about 30 seconds.
3. Transfer contents of skillet to a large bowl. Stir in black beans, and mash with a fork. Season with salt and pepper to taste. Mix in sweet potatoes, egg, and bread crumbs. Divide into 8 balls, and flatten into patties.
4. In the oven, set cooking rack about 4 inches from heat source. Set oven to broil. Lightly grease baking sheet with 1 tablespoon oil.
5. Place bean patties on baking sheet, and broil 8 to 10 minutes. Turn cakes over, and broil until crispy, about 3 minutes more. Serve with lime sour cream.

ALFREDO LIGHT

Servings: 8 | Prep: 20m | Cooks: 20m | Total: 40m

NUTRITION FACTS

Calories: 292 | Carbohydrates: 50.5g | Fat: 4.1g | Protein: 13.9g | Cholesterol: 6mg

INGREDIENTS

- 1 onion, chopped
- 1/2 teaspoon salt
- 1 clove garlic, minced
- 1/4 teaspoon ground black pepper
- 2 teaspoons vegetable oil
- 1/2 cup grated Parmesan cheese
- 2 cups skim milk
- 16 ounces dry fettuccine pasta
- 1 cup chicken broth
- 1 (16 ounce) package frozen broccoli florets
- 3 tablespoons all-purpose flour

DIRECTIONS

1. In a medium saucepan, heat oil over medium heat. Add onion and garlic, and saute until golden brown.
2. In a small saucepan, stir together milk, chicken broth, flour, salt and pepper over low heat until smooth and thick. Stir into onion mixture. Continue to cook over medium low heat, stirring frequently, until the sauce is thick. Stir in Parmesan cheese.
3. Meanwhile, cook pasta in boiling water. Add broccoli to the pasta for the last several minutes of cooking. Continue cooking until the pasta is al dente.
4. Drain the pasta and vegetables, and transfer to a large bowl. Toss with sauce. Serve.

AUNT JEWEL'S CHICKEN DRESSING CASSEROLE

Servings: 12 | Prep: 15m | Cooks: 45m | Total: 1h

NUTRITION FACTS

Calories: 236 | Carbohydrates: 15.8g | Fat: 5.2g | Protein: 29.5g | Cholesterol: 73mg

INGREDIENTS

- 3 pounds skinless, boneless chicken breast meat
- 1 (10.75 ounce) can milk
- 1 (10.75 ounce) can condensed cream of chicken soup
- 1 1/2 cups chicken broth
- 1 (10.75 ounce) can condensed cream of celery soup
- 1 (6 ounce) package seasoned cornbread stuffing mix

DIRECTIONS

1. Place chicken in a large saucepan full of lightly salted water. Bring to a boil; boil for about 30 minutes, or until chicken is cooked through (juices run clear). Remove chicken from pan, reserving broth. Cut chicken into bite size pieces and place in bottom of a 9x13 inch baking dish.
2. Preheat oven to 350 degrees F (175 degrees C).
3. In a medium bowl mix together cream of chicken soup and cream of celery soup. Fill one empty soup can with milk, and mix milk with soups. Pour mixture over chicken. In a small bowl combine stuffing and broth; mix together and spoon mixture over casserole.
4. Bake in the preheated oven for 45 minutes.

BLACK BEAN CHILI

Servings: 8 | Prep: 20m | Cooks: 20m | Total: 40m

NUTRITION FACTS

Calories: 164 | Carbohydrates: 28g | Fat: 2.8g | Protein: 9g | Cholesterol: < 1mg

INGREDIENTS

- 1 tablespoon olive oil
- 1 teaspoon ground black pepper
- 1 onion, chopped
- 1 teaspoon ground cumin
- 2 red bell pepper, seeded and chopped
- 1 tablespoon chili powder
- 1 jalapeno pepper, seeded and minced
- 2 (15 ounce) cans black beans, drained and rinsed
- 10 fresh mushrooms, quartered 1
- 1/2 cups chicken broth or vegetable broth
- 6 roma (plum) tomatoes, diced
- 1 teaspoon salt
- 1 cup fresh corn kernels

DIRECTIONS

1. Heat oil in a large saucepan over medium-high heat. Saute the onion, red bell peppers, jalapeno, mushrooms, tomatoes and corn for 10 minutes or until the onions are translucent. Season with black pepper, cumin, and chili powder. Stir in the black beans, chicken or vegetable broth, and salt. Bring to a boil.
2. Reduce heat to medium low. Remove 1 1/2 cups of the soup to food processor or blender; puree and stir the bean mixture back into the soup. Serve hot by itself or over rice.

DELICIOUS APPLE SAUCE

Servings: 2 | Prep: 15m | Cooks: 30m | Total: 45m

NUTRITION FACTS

Calories: 152 | Carbohydrates: 39.9g | Fat: 0.2g | Protein: 0.4g | Cholesterol: 0mg

INGREDIENTS

- 2 apples - peeled, cored and shredded
- 1/4 cup water
- 1 teaspoon ground cinnamon
- 3 tablespoons brown sugar

DIRECTIONS

1. Place shredded apples in a medium saucepan over medium low heat. Sprinkle with cinnamon, then add water and cook until the apple bits become soft and mushy.
2. Stir in brown sugar and mix well; if desired, top with ice cream and serve.

OVEN FRIES

Servings: 6 | Prep: 15m | Cooks: 30m | Total: 45m

NUTRITION FACTS

Calories: 156 | Carbohydrates: 34.1g | Fat: 1g | Protein: 3.8g | Cholesterol: 0mg

INGREDIENTS

- 2 1/2 pounds baking potatoes
- 1 teaspoon salt
- 1 teaspoon vegetable oil
- 1 pinch ground cayenne pepper
- 1 tablespoon white sugar

DIRECTIONS

1. Preheat oven to 450 degrees F (230 degrees C). Line a baking sheet with foil, and coat well with vegetable cooking spray. Scrub potatoes well and cut into 1/2 inch thick fries.
2. In a large mixing bowl, toss potatoes with oil, sugar, salt and red pepper. Spread on baking sheet in one layer.
3. Bake for 30 minutes in the preheated oven, until potatoes are tender and browned. Serve immediately.

SWISS CHARD WITH GARBANZO BEANS AND FRESH TOMATOES

Servings: 4 | Prep: 10m | Cooks: 15m | Total: 25m

NUTRITION FACTS

Calories: 122 | Carbohydrates: 13.3g | Fat: 7.3g | Protein: 3.2g | Cholesterol: 0mg

INGREDIENTS

- 2 tablespoons olive oil
- salt and pepper to taste
- 1 shallot, chopped
- 1 bunch red Swiss chard, rinsed and chopped
- 2 green onions, chopped
- 1 tomato, sliced
- 1/2 cup garbanzo beans, drained
- 1/2 lemon, juiced

DIRECTIONS

1. Heat olive oil in a large skillet. Stir in shallot and green onions; cook and stir for 3 to 5 minutes, or until soft and fragrant. Stir in garbanzo beans, and season with salt and pepper; heat through. Place chard in pan, and cook until wilted. Add tomato slices, squeeze lemon juice over greens, and heat through. Plate, and season with salt and pepper to taste.

DEVIL'S STEAK SAUCE

Servings: 4 | Prep: 10m | Cooks: 15m | Total: 25m

NUTRITION FACTS

Calories: 62 | Carbohydrates: 15.9g | Fat: 0g | Protein: 0.1g | Cholesterol: 0mg

INGREDIENTS

- 2 tablespoons raspberry jam
- 2 tablespoons malt vinegar
- 2 tablespoons brown sugar
- 5 drops hot pepper sauce
- 2 tablespoons Worcestershire sauce
- salt and freshly ground black pepper to taste
- 2 tablespoons tomato sauce

DIRECTIONS

1. In a saucepan over high heat, blend raspberry jam, brown sugar, Worcestershire sauce, tomato sauce, malt vinegar, hot pepper sauce, salt, and pepper. Bring to a boil over high heat, reduce heat to low, and simmer 10 minutes, or until thickened.

BUTTERNUT SQUASH FRIES

Servings: 4 | Prep: 15m | Cooks: 20m | Total: 35m

NUTRITION FACTS

Calories: 102| Carbohydrates: 26.5g | Fat: 0.2g | Protein: 2.3g | Cholesterol: 0mg

INGREDIENTS

- 1 (2 pound) butternut squash, halved and seeded
- salt to taste

DIRECTIONS

1. Preheat the oven to 425 degrees F (220 degrees C).
2. Use a sharp knife to carefully cut away the peel from the squash. Cut the squash into sticks like French fries. Arrange squash pieces on a baking sheet and season with salt.
3. Bake for 20 minutes in the preheated oven, turning the fries over halfway through baking. Fries are done when they are starting to brown on the edges and become crispy.

CAJUN PASTA FRESCA

Servings: 8 | Prep: 5m | Cooks: 20m | Total: 25m

NUTRITION FACTS

Calories: 294 | Carbohydrates: 46.2g | Fat: 7.5g | Protein: 12.2g | Cholesterol: 9mg

INGREDIENTS

- 1 pound vermicelli pasta
- 1 tablespoon chopped fresh parsley
- 2 tablespoons olive oil

- 1 tablespoon Cajun seasoning
- 1 teaspoon minced garlic
- 1/2 cup shredded mozzarella cheese
- 13 roma (plum) tomatoes, chopped
- 1/2 cup grated Parmesan cheese
- 1 tablespoon salt

DIRECTIONS
1. Bring a large pot of lightly salted water to a boil. Add pasta and cook for 8 to 10 minutes or until al dente; drain.
2. While the pasta water is boiling, in a large skillet over medium heat, briefly saute garlic in oil. Stir in tomatoes and their juice and sprinkle with salt. When tomatoes are bubbly, mash slightly with a fork. Stir in parsley, reduce heat and simmer 5 minutes more.
3. Toss hot pasta with tomato sauce, Cajun seasoning, mozzarella and Parmesan.

SUPERFAST ASPARAGUS

Servings: 3 | Prep: 5m | Cooks: 10m | Total: 15m

NUTRITION FACTS
Calories: 32 | Carbohydrates: 6.3g | Fat: 0.2g | Protein: 3.4g | Cholesterol: 0mg

INGREDIENTS
- 1 pound asparagus
- 1 teaspoon Cajun seasoning

DIRECTIONS
1. Preheat oven to 425 degrees F (220 degrees C).
2. Snap the asparagus at the tender part of the stalk. Arrange spears in one layer on a baking sheet. Spray lightly with nonstick spray; sprinkle with the Cajun seasoning.
3. Bake in the preheated oven until tender, about 10 minutes.

RANCH CRISPY CHICKEN

Servings: 8 | Prep: 15m | Cooks: 30m | Total: 45m

NUTRITION FACTS
Calories: 162 | Carbohydrates: 6.1g | Fat: 1.7g | Protein: 27.8g | Cholesterol: 68mg

INGREDIENTS
- 8 skinless, boneless chicken breast halves

- 1/4 cup dry bread crumbs
- 2 (1 ounce) packages ranch dressing mix

DIRECTIONS
1. Preheat oven to 375 degrees F (190 degrees C).
2. Combine dressing mix and bread crumbs in a plastic bag. Add chicken and shake until coated.
3. Place coated chicken pieces on an ungreased cookie sheet and bake in preheated oven for 25 to 30 minutes, or until chicken is cooked through and juices run clear. Serve with rice or potatoes, if desired.

ROSEMARY TURKEY MEATLOAF

Servings: 8 | Prep: 15m | Cooks: 1h | Total: 1h15m

NUTRITION FACTS
Calories: 362 | Carbohydrates: 47.1g | Fat: 9.8g | Protein: 20.9g | Cholesterol: 93mg

INGREDIENTS
- 1 1/2 pounds ground turkey
- 1 teaspoon salt
- 2 cups dry bread crumbs
- 1 teaspoon pepper
- 1 onion, chopped
- 1 1/2 tablespoons chopped fresh rosemary
- 1 egg, beaten
- 1 cup canned tomato sauce
- 1 cup milk
- 3/4 cup brown sugar
- 1/2 cup balsamic vinegar
- 1 tablespoon Dijon mustard
- 1 clove garlic, minced

DIRECTIONS
1. Preheat oven to 350 degrees F (175 degrees C). Lightly grease a 9x5 inch loaf pan.
2. In a large mixing bowl, mix together the ground turkey, bread crumbs, onion, egg and milk. Season with balsamic vinegar, salt, pepper and rosemary. Press into the prepared

pan. Blend together the tomato sauce, brown sugar and mustard; pour evenly over the top of the loaf.
3. Bake for 1 hour in the preheated oven, or until juices run clear when pricked with a knife.

QUINOA WITH CHICKPEAS AND TOMATOES

Servings: 6 | Prep: 20m | Cooks: 20m | Total: 40m

NUTRITION FACTS
Calories: 185 | Carbohydrates: 28.8g | Fat: 5.4g | Protein: 6g | Cholesterol: 0mg

INGREDIENTS
- 1 cup quinoa
- 3 tablespoons lime juice
- 1/8 teaspoon salt
- 4 teaspoons olive oil
- 1 3/4 cups water
- 1/2 teaspoon ground cumin
- 1 cup canned garbanzo beans (chickpeas), drained 1 pinch
- salt and pepper to taste
- 1 tomato, chopped
- 1/2 teaspoon chopped fresh parsley
- 1 clove garlic, minced

DIRECTIONS
1. Place the quinoa in a fine mesh strainer, and rinse under cold, running water until the water no longer foams. Bring the quinoa, salt, and water to a boil in a saucepan. Reduce heat to medium-low, cover, and simmer until the quinoa is tender, 20 to 25 minutes.
2. Once done, stir in the garbanzo beans, tomatoes, garlic, lime juice, and olive oil. Season with cumin, salt, and pepper. Sprinkle with chopped fresh parsley to serve.

PENNE WITH SHRIMP

Servings: 8 | Prep: 10m | Cooks: 25m | Total: 35m

NUTRITION FACTS

Calories: 385 | Carbohydrates: 48.5g | Fat: 8.5g | Protein: 24.5g | Cholesterol: 95mg

INGREDIENTS
- 1 (16 ounce) package penne pasta
- 1/4 cup white wine
- 2 tablespoons olive oil
- 2 (14.5 ounce) cans diced tomatoes
- 1/4 cup chopped red onion
- 1 pound shrimp, peeled and deveined
- 1 tablespoon chopped garlic
- 1 cup grated Parmesan cheese

DIRECTIONS
1. Bring a large pot of lightly salted water to a boil. Add pasta and cook for 8 to 10 minutes or until al dente; drain.
2. Heat the oil in a skillet over medium heat. Stir in onion and garlic, and cook until onion is tender. Mix in wine and tomatoes, and continue cooking 10 minutes, stirring occasionally.
3. Mix shrimp into the skillet, and cook 5 minutes, or until opaque. Toss with pasta and top with Parmesan cheese to serve.

'CHINESE BUFFET' GREEN BEANS

Servings: 6 | Prep: 15m | Cooks: 10m | Total: 25m

NUTRITION FACTS
Calories: 55 | Carbohydrates: 8.1g | Fat: 2.3g | Protein: 1.6g | Cholesterol: 0mg

INGREDIENTS
- 1 tablespoon oil, peanut or sesame
- 1 tablespoon white sugar
- 2 cloves garlic, thinly sliced
- 2 tablespoons oyster sauce
- 1 pound fresh green beans, trimmed
- 2 teaspoons soy sauce

DIRECTIONS
1. Heat peanut oil in a wok or large skillet over medium-high heat. Stir in the garlic, and cook until the edges begin to brown, about 20 seconds. Add the green beans; cook and stir until the green beans begin to soften, about 5 minutes. Stir in the sugar, oyster

sauce, and soy sauce. Continue cooking and stirring for several minutes until the beans have attained the desired degree of tenderness.

HONEY WHEAT BREAD

Servings: 24 | Prep: 30m | Cooks: 30m | Total: 2h

NUTRITION FACTS
Calories: 171 | Carbohydrates: 31.2g | Fat: 3.5g | Protein: 4.3g | Cholesterol: 0mg

INGREDIENTS
- 2 cups warm water (110 degrees F/45 degrees C)
- 1/3 cup honey
- 2 cups whole wheat flour
- 1/3 cup vegetable oil
- 1 tablespoon active dry yeast
- 5 cups all-purpose flour
- 1 teaspoon salt

DIRECTIONS
1. Dissolve yeast in warm water. Add honey, and stir well. Mix in whole wheat flour, salt, and vegetable oil. Work all-purpose flour in gradually. Turn dough out onto a lightly floured surface, and knead for at least 10 to 15 minutes. When dough is smooth and elastic, place it in a well oiled bowl. Turn it several times in the bowl to coat the surface of the dough, and cover with a damp cloth. Let rise in a warm place until doubled in bulk, about 45 minutes.
2. Punch down the dough. Shape into two loaves, and place into two well greased 9 x 5 inch loaf pans. Allow to rise until dough is 1 to 1 1/2 inches above pans.
3. Bake at 375 degrees F (190 degrees C) for 25 to 30 minutes.

JAMIE'S SWEET AND EASY CORN ON THE COB

Servings: 6 | Prep: 5m | Cooks: 10m | Total: 15m

NUTRITION FACTS
Calories: 94 | Carbohydrates: 21.5g | Fat: 1.1g | Protein: 2.9g | Cholesterol: 0mg

INGREDIENTS

- 2 tablespoons white sugar
- 6 ears corn on the cob, husks and silk removed
- 1 tablespoon lemon juice

DIRECTIONS
1. Fill a large pot about 3/4 full of water and bring to a boil. Stir in sugar and lemon juice, dissolving the sugar. Gently place ears of corn into boiling water, cover the pot, turn off the heat, and let the corn cook in the hot water until tender, about 10 minutes.

CAJUN STYLE BAKED SWEET POTATO

Servings: 4 | Prep: 10m | Cooks: 1h | Total: 1h10m

NUTRITION FACTS
Calories: 229 | Carbohydrates: 49.1g | Fat: 2.3g | Protein: 4.8g | Cholesterol: 0mg

INGREDIENTS
- 1 1/2 teaspoons paprika
- 1/4 teaspoon dried rosemary
- 1 teaspoon brown sugar
- 1/4 teaspoon garlic powder
- 1/4 teaspoon black pepper
- 1/8 teaspoon cayenne pepper
- 1/4 teaspoon onion powder
- 2 large sweet potatoes
- 1/4 teaspoon dried thyme
- 1 1/2 teaspoons olive oil

DIRECTIONS
1. Preheat oven to 375 degrees F (190 degrees C).
2. In a small bowl, stir together paprika, brown sugar, black pepper, onion powder, thyme, rosemary, garlic powder, and cayenne pepper.
3. Slice the sweet potatoes in half lengthwise. Brush each half with olive oil. Rub the seasoning mix over the cut surface of each half. Place sweet potatoes on a baking sheet, or in a shallow pan.
4. Bake in preheated oven until tender, or about 1 hour.

SLOW COOKER OATS

Servings: 6 | Prep: 15m | Cooks: 6h | Total: 6h15m

NUTRITION FACTS
Calories: 208 | Carbohydrates: 37.2g | Fat: 5.6g | Protein: 3.9g | Cholesterol: 10mg

INGREDIENTS
- 1 cup steel cut oats
- 2 tablespoons butter
- 3 1/2 cups water
- 1 tablespoon ground cinnamon
- 1 cup peeled and chopped apple
- 2 tablespoons brown sugar
- 1/2 cup raisins
- 1 teaspoon vanilla extract

DIRECTIONS
1. Place the steel cut oats, water, apple, raisins, butter, cinnamon, brown sugar, and vanilla extract into a slow cooker, and stir to combine and dissolve the sugar. Cover the cooker, set to Low, and allow to cook 6 to 7 hours (for firm oats) or 8 hours (for softer texture).

ROASTED ASPARAGUS AND MUSHROOMS

Servings: 6 | Prep: 10m | Cooks: 15m | Total: 25m

NUTRITION FACTS
Calories: 38 | Carbohydrates: 4.3g | Fat: 1.8g | Protein: 2.8g | Cholesterol: 0mg

INGREDIENTS
- 1 bunch fresh asparagus, trimmed
- 2 teaspoons olive oil
- 1/2 pound fresh mushrooms, quartered
- kosher salt to taste
- 2 sprigs fresh rosemary, minced
- freshly ground black pepper to taste

DIRECTIONS
1. Preheat oven to 450 degrees F (230 degrees C). Lightly spray a cookie sheet with vegetable cooking spray.

2. Place the asparagus and mushrooms in a bowl. Drizzle with the olive oil, then season with rosemary, salt, and pepper; toss well. Lay the asparagus and mushrooms out on the prepared pan in an even layer. Roast in the preheated oven until the asparagus is tender, about 15 minutes.

BAKED FRENCH FRIES

Servings: 4 | Prep: 20m | Cooks: 25m | Total: 45m

NUTRITION FACTS
Calories: 145 | Carbohydrates: 28.2g | Fat: 1.6g | Protein: 5.2g | Cholesterol: 4mg

INGREDIENTS
- 3 russet potatoes, sliced into
- 1/4 inch strips
- 1/4 cup grated Parmesan cheese
- cooking spray
- salt and pepper to taste
- 1 teaspoon dried basil

DIRECTIONS
1. Preheat oven to 400 degrees F (200 degrees C). Lightly grease a medium baking sheet.
2. Arrange potato strips in a single layer on the prepared baking sheet, skin sides down. Spray lightly with cooking spray, and sprinkle with basil, Parmesan cheese, salt and pepper.
3. Bake 25 minutes in the preheated oven, or until golden brown.

SPICED SLOW COOKER APPLESAUCE

Servings: 8 | Prep: 10m | Cooks: 6h30m | Total: 6h40m

NUTRITION FACTS
Calories: 150 | Carbohydrates: 39.4g | Fat: 0.2g | Protein: 0.4g | Cholesterol: 0mg

INGREDIENTS
- 8 apples - peeled, cored, and thinly sliced
- 3/4 cup packed brown sugar
- 1/2 cup water
- 1/2 teaspoon pumpkin pie spice

DIRECTIONS
1. Combine the apples and water in a slow cooker; cook on Low for 6 to 8 hours. Stir in the brown sugar and pumpkin pie spice; continue cooking another 30 minutes.

LEMON CHICKEN ORZO SOUP

Servings: 12 | Prep: 20m | Cooks: 1h | Total: 1h20m

NUTRITION FACTS
Calories: 167 | Carbohydrates: 21.7g | Fat: 4.1g | Protein: 12.1g | Cholesterol: 20mg

INGREDIENTS
- 8 ounces orzo pasta 1 bay leaf
- 1 teaspoon olive oil 3 (32 ounce) cartons fat-free, low-sodium chicken broth
- 3 carrots, chopped, or more to taste 1/2 cup fresh lemon juice
- 3 ribs celery, chopped 1 lemon, zested
- 1 onion, chopped 8 ounces cooked chicken breast, chopped
- 2 cloves garlic, minced 1 (8 ounce) package baby spinach leaves
- 1/2 teaspoon dried thyme 1 lemon, sliced for garnish (optional)
- 1/2 teaspoon dried oregano 1/4 cup grated Parmesan cheese (optional)
- salt and ground black pepper to taste

DIRECTIONS
1. Bring a large pot of lightly salted water to a boil. Cook orzo in the boiling water until partially cooked through but not yet soft, about 5 minutes; drain and rinse with cold water until cooled completely.
2. Heat olive oil in a large pot over medium heat. Cook and stir carrots, celery, and onion in hot oil until the vegetables begin to soften and the onion becomes translucent, 5 to 7 minutes. Add garlic; cook and stir until fragrant, about 1 minute more. Season mixture with thyme, oregano, salt, black pepper, and bay leaf; continue cooking another 30 seconds before pouring chicken broth into the pot.
3. Bring the broth to a boil. Partially cover the pot, reduce heat to medium-low, and simmer until the vegetables are just tender, about 10 minutes.
4. Stir orzo, lemon juice, and lemon zest into the broth; add chicken. Cook until the chicken and orzo are heated through, about 5 minutes. Add baby spinach; cook until

the spinach wilts into the broth and the orzo is tender, 2 to 3 minutes. Ladle soup into bowls; garnish with lemon slices and Parmesan cheese.

Asian eggs

SERVES: 4 PREP TIME: 5MINS COOK TIME: 25MINS
INGREDIENTS: 11   DIFFICULTY: EASY

INGREDIENTS
- 1&1/2 cups (300g) long-grain rice
- 1/2 cup (75g) unsalted peanuts
- 100ml sunflower or peanut oil
- 8 eggs
- 1 bunch each coriander & Thai basil, leaves picked
- Bean sprouts, chopped birdseye chilli & lime wedges to serve

CHILLI PASTE
- 2 tsp chilli flakes
- 2 tbs each chilli oil, olive oil, soy sauce
- 1 garlic clove, crushed
- 2 tsp grated ginger
- 2 tsp fish sauce

METHOD
- 1. Preheat oven to 180°C. Cook rice to packet instructions, then set aside.
- 2. Place peanuts on a baking tray and roast for 10 minutes or until light golden then remove, cool and roughly chop.
- 3. For the chilli paste, combine ingredients in a bowl and set aside.
- 4. Heat oil in a wok over medium-high heat. Crack one egg into a cup, then when the oil is hot, use the cup to pour the egg into the centre. Cook for 1 minute or until the outside starts to go golden but the yolk is still runny. Remove with a slotted spoon and repeat with remaining eggs.
- 5. Spoon rice onto dishes, top with eggs, peanuts, herbs and chilli sauce. Serve with bean sprouts, extra chilli and lime wedges.

Leek, almond and bruised tomato galette

SERVES: 6 PREP TIME: -   COOK TIME: 2HR
INGREDIENTS: 13   DIFFICULTY: EASY

INGREDIENTS
- 5 over-ripe or bruised truss or roma tomatoes, chopped
- 3 leeks, thinly sliced
- 1/2 bunch hard herbs, such as thyme or rosemary
- 1/3 cup (80ml) extra virgin olive oil
- 1 bunch micro basil, leaves picked
- 1/3 cup (55g) roasted almonds, chopped
- 2/3 cup (50g) finely grated parmesan, plus extra to serve
- 2 tbs baby capers in vinegar, drained
- 1 egg, lightly beaten
- Sliced mixed tomatoes (heirloom and vine-ripened cherry tomatoes), to serve

SPELT PASTRY
- 22/3 cups (400g) white spelt flour
- 200g cold unsalted butter, chopped
- 1/4 cup (60ml) apple cider vinegar

METHOD
- 1.
  For the pastry, place flour and 1 tsp salt flakes in a bowl. Add butter and toss to coat. Using a flat-bladed knife or pastry cutter, roughly cut in butter, leaving plenty of big pieces of butter. Combine vinegar and 1/2 cup (125ml) iced water in a jug. In 3 batches, add to flour mixture, stirring to combine. Turn out onto a clean work surface and gently knead until the dough comes together. Enclose in plastic wrap and chill for 3 hours.
- 2.
  Preheat oven to 200°C. Line a baking tray with foil and place bruised tomato, leek and hard herbs on top. Drizzle with oil and season. Roast for 40 minutes or until leek is very tender. Transfer mixture to a colander set over a bowl and set aside to drain and cool, reserving the liquid. Discard the herb sprigs.
- 3.
  Meanwhile, roughly chop half the basil leaves and place in a bowl with almonds, parmesan and capers. Roll out pastry on a lightly floured work surface until 3mm-

thick, 30cm round and place on a baking paper-lined baking tray. Scatter over basil mixture, leaving a 7cm border, and top with leek mixture. Fold over pastry border to partially enclose filling. Brush with egg and cook for 50 minutes or until pastry is crisp and golden. Cool slightly.
- 4.
  Serve tart topped with sliced heirloom tomatoes, cherry tomatoes, remaining basil leaves and extra parmesan. Drizzle with reserved roasting juices and serve.

Sesame butter radishes with lemon

SERVES: 6 PREP TIME: 5MINS   COOK TIME: 10MINS
INGREDIENTS: 6   DIFFICULTY: EASY

INGREDIENTS
- 100g unsalted butter, chopped
- 2 tsp sesame oil
- 3 bunches mixed radishes, washed, trimmed
- Juice of 1 lemon, plus extra lemon wedges to serve
- 1 tbs each toasted black and white sesame seeds
- Red vein sorrel, baby radish leaves, baby shiso and sourdough, to serve

METHOD
- 1.
  Melt butter and oil in large frypan over medium-high heat and cook for 3 minutes or until nut brown. Add radish and cook, tossing pan, for 6-8 minutes or until tender. Spoon into a serving bowl.
- 2.
  Drizzle over lemon juice and scatter with sesame seeds and salad leaves. Serve with sourdough and extra lemon.

Egg noodles with Sichuan pepper chicken and cucumber

SERVES: 4 PREP TIME: -   COOK TIME: 40MINS
INGREDIENTS: 17   DIFFICULTY: CAPABLE

INGREDIENTS
- 3 x 180g chicken breasts
- 2/3 cup (165ml) light soy sauce

- 2 x 1cm-thick slices ginger
- 1 1/2 tsp Sichuan peppercorns
- 2 star anise
- 1/2 bunch spring onions
- 500g fresh thin egg noodles
- 2 small Lebanese cucumbers, thinly sliced
- 1 tbs rice vinegar
- 1/4 cup (60ml) Chinese sesame paste (from Asian grocers)
- 2 tbs Chinese black vinegar (chinkiang)
- 1 tsp caster sugar
- Coriander leaves, white sesame seeds and pickled green chillies (from Asian grocers), to serve

GREEN CHILLI OIL
- 2 long green chillies, chopped
- 1 bunch chives, choppe
- 1/2 bunch flat-leaf parsley, leaves chopped
- 3/4 cup (180ml) peanut oil

METHOD
- 1.
  For the green chilli oil, combine all the ingredients except peanut oil in a food processor with 1/2 tsp salt and whiz to a rough paste. Add peanut oil and whiz until smooth. Set aside for 20 minutes to infuse. Strain through a muslin-lined sieve.
- 2.
  Place chicken, 1/2 cup (125ml) soy sauce, ginger, 1 tsp Sichuan peppercorns, star anise and chopped spring onions in a pan. Add enough water to just cover, then bring to a simmer over medium-high heat and cook for 5 minutes. Remove from heat and set aside for 20 minutes to cook through. Remove chicken, reserving 2 tbs poaching liquid, and slice. Set aside.
- 3.
  Meanwhile, cook noodles according to packet instructions, then drain and refresh in iced water. Combine cucumber and 1 tsp salt in a bowl. Set aside for 10 minutes to remove excess water. Drain, then combine with rice vinegar.
- 4.
  Combine with the sesame paste, black vinegar, sugar, reserved poaching liquid and remaining 2 tbs soy sauce. Toss the sauce with the noodles.
- 5.
  Divide noodles, chicken and cucumber among bowls. Drizzle over chilli oil and top with coriander and sesame seeds. Serve with pickled chillies on the side.

Quick chicken roast

SERVES: 4 PREP TIME: 15MINS   COOK TIME: 55MINS
INGREDIENTS: 11   DIFFICULTY: EASY

INGREDIENTS
- 6 thyme sprigs, leaves picked
- 4 anchovies in oil, drained, chopped
- 2 teaspoons dried oregano
- 1 teaspoon chilli flakes
- 2 tablespoons olive oil
- 2 garlic cloves, chopped
- Finely grated zest of 1 lemon
- 8 Lilydale Free Range Chicken Thighs (bone in, skin on)
- 800g baby kipfler potatoes, halved lengthways
- 100g speck or streaky bacon, cut into 5mm-thick batons
- 250g baby truss tomatoes

METHOD
- 1.
  Preheat the oven to 200C.
- 2.
  Combine the thyme, anchovies, oregano, chilli, oil, garlic and lemon zest in a bowl. Add the chicken and turn to coat. Add the potatoes and toss to combine. Place on a large baking tray and scatter over the speck.
- 3.
  Cut the zested lemon into wedges and add to the tray. Season and roast for 40 minutes or until chicken is golden and potatoes tender. Remove from the oven and top with tomatoes. Roast for a further 10-15 minutes until tomatoes are blistered.
- 4.
  Squeeze over roasted lemon juice to serve.

Eggplant kasundi warm rice salad

SERVES: 4 PREP TIME: 10MINS   COOK TIME: 45MINS
INGREDIENTS: 18   DIFFICULTY: EASY

INGREDIENTS
- ½ cup (125ml) olive oil

- 1 tsp each cumin seeds, caraway seeds, fennel seeds and nigella seeds
- 1 tbs brown mustard seeds
- 24 fresh curry leaves
- 1 onion, finely chopped
- 1 tbs finely grated ginger
- 3 garlic cloves, crushed
- 600g eggplant, cut into 1cm pieces
- 2 tbs each curry powder, brown sugar and white vinegar
- 2 x 400g cans cherry tomatoes
- 400g can chickpeas, rinsed, drained
- ½ cup (140g) thick Greek-style yoghurt
- Juice of ½ a lemon
- 1 Lebanese cucumber, thinly sliced into rounds
- Mint leaves, to serve

CARDAMOM RICE
- 250g basmati rice
- 4 cardamom pods
- 2 star anise

METHOD
- 1.
  Heat oil in a saucepan over medium heat. Add seeds and curry leaves. Cook for 2 minutes or until mustard seeds start to pop. Add the onion, ginger and two-thirds garlic. Cook 3-4 minutes until onion has softened. Add eggplant, curry powder and sugar. Cook 8-10 minutes until eggplant has softened slightly.
- 2.
  Stir in vinegar, half the tomatoes and 1 cup (250ml) water. Bring to the boil. Reduce heat to mediumlow and simmer, loosely covered, for 25 minutes or until eggplant is very tender. Stir in chickpeas and remaining tomatoes.
- 3.
  For the rice, combine all ingredients with 2 cups (500ml) cold water and 1 tsp salt flakes in a pan over high heat. Bring to the boil. Reduce heat to low, cover and cook, without stirring, for 12 minutes or until water has been absorbed and rice is tender. Uncover and stir with a fork.
- 4.
  For dressing, combine yoghurt, lemon juice and remaining garlic in a small bowl.
- 5.
  Place rice in a bowl. Top with eggplant and cucumber. Drizzle over dressing and scatter with mint. Toss to serve.

Taleggio sourdough salad with simple salsa verde

SERVES: 4 PREP TIME: 15MINS   COOK TIME: 5MINS
INGREDIENTS: 13   DIFFICULTY: EASY

INGREDIENTS
- 1 sourdough loaf, cut on an angle into 1cm-thick slices
- 2 tbs olive oil
- 1 garlic clove, halved
- 100g Taleggio (from delis – substitute brie), rind removed, thickly sliced
- 2 bunches broccolini, trimmed, halved lengthways, blanched, refreshed
- 1 bunch asparagus, trimmed, halved lengthways, blanched, refreshed
- 1/2 cup loosely packed watercress sprigs
- 1/2 cup (70g) roasted hazelnuts, chopped
- Lemon wedges, to serve

SIMPLE SALSA VERDE
- 1 bunch tarragon, leaves picked, plus extra to serve
- 1 bunch flat-leaf parsley, leaves picked
- 1/2 cup (125ml) extra virgin olive oil
- Juice of 1 lemon

METHOD
- 1.
  For the simple salsa verde, place all ingredients and 1/2 tsp salt flakes in a food processor and whiz until smooth. Set aside.
- 2.
  Heat the oven grill to high heat. Rub sourdough slices with oil and place on a large baking tray. Grill, checking often, for 90 seconds each side or until golden. Rub toasted sourdough with cut side of garlic. Return sourdough to tray, placing some slices on their sides and some lying flat. Arrange Taleggio on top. Grill, checking often, for 1-2 minutes or until cheese has melted.
- 3.
  Arrange sourdough on a serving platter with broccolini, asparagus, watercress and hazelnuts. Drizzle with a little salsa verde and scatter with extra tarragon. Serve with lemon wedges and remaining salsa verde.

Prawn and spinach angel hair pasta with prawn oil

SERVES: 4 PREP TIME: -   COOK TIME: -
INGREDIENTS: 16   DIFFICULTY: CAPABLE

INGREDIENTS
- 400g angel hair pasta
- 1kg green prawns, peeled (tails intact), deveined, shells reserved
- 250g cherry tomatoes, halved
- 100g baby spinach leaves
- Micro basil, to serve

PRAWN OIL
- 1 cup (250ml) olive oil
- 5 lemon thyme sprigs, leaves picked
- 4 garlic cloves, bruised
- 1 each carrot and onion, roughly chopped
- 1 celery stalk, roughly chopped
- 2 bay leaves
- 1 tsp each fennel and coriander seeds
- 1 tbs tomato paste
- 6 flat-leaf parsley stalks
- 2 basil stalks
- 1 tsp sweet smoked paprika (pimenton)

METHOD
- 1.
  For the prawn oil, heat 1/2 cup (125ml) oil in a large saucepan over high heat.
- 2.
  Add reserved prawn shells, thyme leaves, garlic, vegetables, bay leaves, and fennel and coriander seeds.
- 3.
  Cook, stirring, for 5-6 minutes until shells are crisp and dry.
- 4.
  Add the tomato paste and cook, stirring, for 2-3 minutes until slightly darkened and caramelised.
- 5.
  Add the parsley, basil stalks and paprika, and stir to combine.
- 6.

- Add the remaining 1/2 cup (125ml) oil.
- 7.
Reduce heat to low, and cook, stirring occasionally, for 15 minutes or until flavours infuse.
- 8.
Remove from heat and allow to infuse for a further 15 minutes.
- 9.
Strain the oil through a sieve, pressing down on the shells to extract as much oil as possible.
- 10.
Discard solids and set aside.
- 11.
Cook the pasta in a large saucepan of boiling salted water according to packet instructions. Drain.
- 12.
Meanwhile, heat 2 tbs prawn oil in a large frypan over medium-high heat.
- 13.
Add the prawns and cook, stirring, for 2-3 minutes until just cooked through.
- 14.
Add tomato and spinach, and cook for a further 1 minute or until tomato is warmed through and spinach is wilted.
- 15.
Add drained pasta to pan with reserved prawn oil. Season and toss to combine.
- 16.
Divide among serving plates and top with micro basil to serve.

Orecchiette with hot-smoked salmon, peas and beurre blanc sauce

SERVES: 4 PREP TIME: 10MINS   COOK TIME: 20MINS
INGREDIENTS: 9   DIFFICULTY: EASY

INGREDIENTS
- 400g orecchiette or other short dried pasta
- 1/3 cup (80ml) white wine
- 1/3 cup (80ml) white wine vinegar
- 2 eschalots, finely chopped
- 175g chilled unsalted butter, chopped
- 1 cup (120g) frozen peas

- 250g hot-smoked salmon or trout fillets, skin removed, flaked
- 2 tbs thickened cream
- 2 tbs chopped dill, plus extra sprigs to serve

METHOD
- 1.
  Cook pasta in a saucepan of boiling salted water according to the packet instructions until al dente. Drain, reserving 1/4 cup (60ml) cooking liquid.
- 2.
  Meanwhile, to make beurre blanc sauce, place wine, vinegar and eschalot in a saucepan over medium-low heat. Cook for 3-4 minutes until liquid is reduced to 1 tbs. Whisking constantly, add the butter, 1 piece at a time, until mixture is thick. Remove from heat and cover to keep warm. Blanch peas in boiling salted water for 1 minute. Refresh under cold running water, then drain well.
- 3.
  Combine pasta with the beurre blanc sauce in a serving bowl, adding a little of the reserved cooking liquid to loosen, if necessary. Add peas, salmon, cream and dill, then gently toss to combine. Serve garnished with extra dill sprigs.

Valli Little's Cajun ocean trout with pineapple salad

SERVES: 4 PREP TIME: 20MINS   COOK TIME: 10MINS
INGREDIENTS: 8   DIFFICULTY: EASY

INGREDIENTS
- 1 tsp each ground cumin, coriander, sweet smoked paprika (pimenton) and fennel seeds
- 2 tbs olive oil
- 4 x 150g ocean trout fillets, skin removed, pin-boned
- 1/2 pineapple, peeled, cored, thinly sliced
- 2 Lebanese cucumbers, cut into thin wedges
- 1 long red chilli, seeds removed, thinly sliced
- Juice of 1 lime
- 1/2 cup coriander leaves

METHOD
- 1.
  Combine the spices, 1 tbs oil and 1 tsp salt in a large bowl. Add the fish, turning to coat, then set aside for 15 minutes to marinate.
- 2.

Heat the remaining 1 tbs oil in a frypan over medium heat and cook the fish for 2-3 minutes each side until almost cooked through. Remove from the pan, loosely cover with foil, then set aside to rest for 5 minutes.

- 3.
Meanwhile, place the pineapple, cucumber, chilli and lime juice in a bowl, season, then toss to combine. Place on a serving platter and flake the trout over the top. Sprinkle with coriander to serve.

Chopped chilli chicken stir fry

SERVES: 4 PREP TIME:-   COOK TIME: 20MINS
INGREDIENTS: 10   DIFFICULTY: EASY

INGREDIENTS
- 1/4 cup (60ml) peanut or sunflower oil
- 250g purple eggplants, chopped if large
- 100g pea eggplants (from Asian grocers), blanched
- 1 bunch spring onion, sliced
- 1/4 cup (75g) gluten-free chilli paste or chilli sauce
- 2 long red chillies, thinly sliced
- 1 bunch Thai basil, leaves picked
- 500g Lilydale Free Range Chicken Mince
- Steamed rice, to serve
- Fried eggs, to serve

METHOD
- 1.
Heat 2 tbs oil in a wok or large frypan over medium-high heat. Add eggplants, season and cook, stirring, for 3-4 minutes until golden. Remove from pan and set aside. Return pan to medium-high heat with remaining 1 tbs oil. Cook onion, chilli paste and half the chilli and basil, stirring, for 2-3 minutes until softened. Add chicken and cook, breaking up with a spoon, for 10 minutes or until browned. Return the eggplant to pan and toss to warm through.
- 2.
Divide rice, chicken and eggs among plates. Top with remaining basil and chilli.

Minty lamb with beetroot and charred broccoli

SERVES: 4　PREP TIME: 15MINS　COOK TIME: 20MINS
INGREDIENTS:13　　　DIFFICULTY: EASY

INGREDIENTS
- 1/2 bunch mint, leaves chopped
- 1/2 bunch flat-leaf parsley, leaves chopped
- 1/4 cup (40g) pine nuts, toasted
- 2 tbs grated parmesan
- 1 garlic clove, finely chopped
- 2/3 cup (165ml) olive oil, plus extra to brush
- 12 x French-trimmed lamb cutlets
- 3 tsp dried mint
- 1 Kurrawong Organics broccoli, sliced lengthways
- 1 1/2 tbs lemon juice
- 100g watercress
- 2 Kurrawong Organics beetroots, cut into thin matchsticks
- 120g marinated feta, drained, crumbled

METHOD
- 1.
Whiz the fresh mint, parsley, pine nuts, parmesan and garlic in a food processor until a paste. Gradually add 1/2 cup (125ml) oil and whiz until combined. Set aside.
- 2.
Brush lamb with a little extra oil, then season and coat in dried mint. In a separate bowl, toss broccoli and 1 tbs oil. Preheat a chargrill pan to medium-high heat.
- 3.
Cook broccoli, turning, for 3-4 minutes until lightly charred. Set aside. Cook lamb for 4 minutes each side for medium-rare or until cooked to your liking.
- 4.
Whisk the lemon juice and remaining 1 tbs oil together in a bowl. Season.
- 5.
Arrange broccoli, watercress, beetroot and feta on a platter. Top with the lamb, then drizzle over lemon dressing and mint pesto to serve.

Sardines stuffed with kale, pine nuts and raisins

SERVES: 4   PREP TIME: 20MINS   COOK TIME: 50MINS
INGREDIENTS: 9   DIFFICULTY: EASY

INGREDIENTS
- 2 cups (50g) shredded kale
- 2 tbs each raisins and pine nuts
- 1 garlic clove, crushed
- Finely grated zest of 1/2 lemon, plus 2 lemons, halved
- 12 sardines, cleaned
- 2 (600g) sweet potatoes, peeled, cut into 8mm matchsticks
- 1/3 cup (80ml) olive oil, plus extra to brush
- 1 tbs finely chopped flat-leaf parsley leaves
- 2 tbs panko breadcrumbs

METHOD
- 1.
  Preheat the oven to 200°C. Place the kale in a heatproof bowl and cover with 1 cup (250ml) boiling water. Stand for 1 minute, then drain and refresh under cold running water. Squeeze to remove excess liquid. Transfer to a large chopping board, or food processor with raisins, pine nuts, garlic and lemon zest, and roughly chop, tossing to combine. Stuff sardine cavities with kale mixture, then place on a baking paper-lined baking tray. Set aside.
- 2.
  To make fries, combine sweet potato and 2 tbs oil in a bowl. Season. Divide between 2 baking paper-lined baking trays. Roast for 25-30 minutes, tossing once, until golden. Toss with chopped parsley. Keep warm.
- 3.
  Increase heat to 210°C. Sprinkle sardines with breadcrumbs and drizzle with the remaining 2 tbs oil. Roast for 10-15 minutes until golden and cooked through.
- 4.
  Meanwhile, preheat a chargrill pan over medium-high heat. Brush the cut sides of halved lemons with extra oil. Cook, cut-side down, for 2-3 minutes until lightly charred.
- 5.

Serve sardines with sweet potato fries and chargrilled lemons to squeeze over.

Raw pad Thai

SERVES: 6 PREP TIME: 20MINS   COOK TIME: -
INGREDIENTS: 15   DIFFICULTY: EASY

INGREDIENTS
- 1 small zucchini, spiralised or grated
- 2 carrots, spiralised or grated
- 1 red capsicum, seeds removed, very thinly sliced
- 1 cup (80g) finely shredded white cabbage
- 100g snow peas, trimmed, thinly sliced lengthways
- 1 cup (80g) bean sprouts, trimmed
- 1 cup (150g) frozen podded edamame, thawed
- 1 cup Thai (holy) basil leaves
- tbs toasted seed mix in shoyu (from health food shops)

PAD THAI DRESSING
- 1 garlic clove, crushed
- 1/4 cup (70g) almond butter or pure peanut butter
- 2 tbs lime juice
- 2 1/2 tbs pure maple syrup
- 1/2 tbs sesame oil
- 1 tsp grated ginger

METHOD
- 1.
  For the dressing, place all the ingredients in a blender with 2 tbs filtered water and whizz to combine, adding a little more water to thin the mixture if necessary. Season and set aside.
- 2.
  Place the zucchini, carrot, capsicum, cabbage, snow peas, bean sprouts and edamame in a large bowl. Add the dressing and toss to combine. Divide among serving plates, top with the basil and serve with toasted seed mix.

Seared tuna with Fijian-Style potato curry

SERVES: 4 PREP TIME: -   COOK TIME: -
INGREDIENTS: 16   DIFFICULTY: CAPABLE

INGREDIENTS
- 800g sebago potatoes, peeled, cut into 4cm pieces
- 2 tbs ghee
- 1 onion, finely chopped
- 1 long green chilli, seeds removed, finely chopped, plus extra to serve
- 2cm piece ginger, grated
- 1 garlic clove, crushed
- 1 tsp mild curry powder
- 1 tsp ground turmeric
- 3 tsp brown mustard seeds
- 1/2 tsp chilli powder
- 10 fresh curry leaves, plus extra fried leaves (optional), to serve
- 1 1/2 tsp caster sugar
- 1/3 cup (60ml) rice vinegar
- 1 red onion, thinly sliced into rounds
- 4 x 180g tuna steaks
- Coriander leaves, to serve

METHOD
- 1.
  Place potato in a pan of cold salted water, bring to the boil over high heat. Cook for 3-4 minutes until par-cooked. Drain.
- 2.
  Heat the ghee in a frypan with a lid over medium heat.
- 3.
  Add onion and cook, stirring, for 2-3 minutes until softened.
- 4.
  Add chilli, ginger, garlic and spices, and cook for a further 1 minute or until fragrant.
- 5.
  Add the potatoes, curry leaves and 1 cup (250ml) water.
- 6.
  Cover and cook for 10 minutes, shaking to prevent catching, then remove lid and cook for a further 5-10 minutes until potatoes start to crisp
- 7.
  Remove from heat. Stir in 1/2 tsp sugar and season. Keep warm.

- 8.
  Combine the vinegar, 1/2 tsp salt and remaining 1 tsp sugar in a bowl, stirring until dissolved.
- 9.
  Add red onion and toss to combine. Set aside.
- 10.
  Heat a chargrill pan or barbecue to high.
- 11.
  Season tuna and grill for 1 minute each side or until seared but still rare in the centre.
- 12.
  Remove from pan. Rest, loosely covered with foil, for 5 minutes.
- 13.
  Drain red onion. Add coriander leaves and toss to combine. Season.
- 14.
  Divide tuna and potato curry among plates.
- 15.
  Top with onion mixture, extra chilli and fried curry leaves, if using, to serve.

Thai red fish curry with noodles

SERVES: 4 PREP TIME: 15MINS   COOK TIME: 10MINS
INGREDIENTS: 13   DIFFICULTY: EASY

INGREDIENTS
- 200g Pad Thai rice noodles
- 1/4 cup (60ml) peanut oil
- 600g firm boneless white fish fillets (such as ling), cut into 2cm thick slices
- 2 garlic cloves, finely chopped
- 1/2 bunch spring onions, chopped, dark and pale parts separated
- 1 bunch coriander, leaves picked, roots chopped
- 1/4 cup (60ml) Thai red curry paste
- 1 tablespoon fish sauce
- 150g sugar snap peas
- 2/3 cup (165ml) coconut cream
- 1/2 cup (75g) chopped peanuts
- Bean sprouts, to serve
- Lime wedges, to serve

METHOD
- 1.

- Soak noodles in hot water for 10 minutes or until soft, then drain. Set aside.
- 2.
Heat 1 tablespoon oil in a wok over high heat and season the fish. Stir-fry half the fish for 2 minutes or until slightly golden, then transfer to a plate. Repeat with another 1 tbs oil and remaining fish.
- 3.
Heat the remaining 1 tablespoon oil in the pan, then and add the garlic, white spring onion and coriander root. Stir-fry for 1-2 minutes until softened. Add the curry paste and stir-fry for a further 2 minutes or until fragrant, then add the fish sauce, sugar snap peas, 1/4 cup (60ml) water and cook for a further 2 minutes or until sauce is slightly reduced. Return the fish to the wok with coconut cream and remaining spring onion, then toss to combine and warm through.
- 4.
Divide the noodles among 4 bowls and top with the fish curry. Serve immediately with coriander leaves, peanuts, bean sprouts and lime wedges.

Char siu beef with broccolini

SERVES: 4 PREP TIME: 15MINS   COOK TIME: 10MINS
INGREDIENTS: 11   DIFFICULTY: EASY

INGREDIENTS
- 100g thin rice noodles
- 1 tablespoon sunflower oil
- 2 garlic cloves, chopped
- 400g beef mince
- 2cm piece ginger, grated
- 1/4 cup (60ml) Chinese rice wine (shaohsing)(see note)
- 1/4 cup (60ml) char siu sauce (Chinese barbecue sauce)(see note)
- 2 bunches broccolini, trimmed, blanched, refreshed
- 1/3 cup (50g) unsalted roasted peanuts, chopped
- 1 long red chilli, sliced
- Coriander leaves, to serve

METHOD
- 1.
Cook noodles according to packet instructions. Drain. Set aside.
- 2.
Meanwhile, heat oil in a large frypan or wok over high heat. Add the garlic, beef and ginger, then cook, breaking up the beef with a wooden spoon, for 3-4 minutes

until the beef is browned. Add the rice wine and char sui sauce, then simmer for 1 minute. Add the broccolini and stir until warmed through.
- 3.
Divide the noodles among plates and top with the beef mixture. Garnish with peanuts, chilli and coriander, then serve.

Broad bean and pecorino bruschetta

SERVES: 4 PREP TIME: 35MINS   COOK TIME: 25MINS
INGREDIENTS: 7   DIFFICULTY: CAPABLE

INGREDIENTS
- 2kg fresh broad beans, podded (to give about 400g) (see Notes)
- 1/3 cup (80ml) olive oil, plus extra to brush
- 3 rosemary sprigs
- 3 garlic cloves, roughly chopped, plus 1 extra garlic clove, halved
- 1 loaf ciabatta, cut into 8 thick slices
- 2 tablespoons roughly chopped flat-leaf parsley
- 100g Pecorino Sardo or Pecorino Romano, shaved

METHOD
- 1.
Blanch broad beans in boiling salted water for 1 minute, then plunge into iced water and squeeze beans from skins. Set aside.
- 2.
Warm oil, rosemary and chopped garlic in a pan over very low heat for 15-20 minutes, stirring occasionally, to infuse oil. Don't allow garlic to colour.
- 3.
Add beans, 1 tablespoon water and 1/2 teaspoon each salt and pepper. Increase heat to medium and cook for 2 minutes or until beans are cooked and bright green.
- 4.
Meanwhile, preheat a chargrill pan or grill to high. Brush ciabatta with oil, then grill for 1-2 minutes each side until golden and charred. Rub halved garlic over toasts.
- 5.
Top toasts with beans and a drizzle of oil. Sprinkle with parsley, cheese and black pepper, then serve immediately.

Mixed mushroom noodles with tea-marbled eggs

SERVES: 4 PREP TIME: -   COOK TIME: 10MINS
INGREDIENTS: 17   DIFFICULTY: EASY

INGREDIENTS
- 1 tsp Chinese five-spice powder
- 1/2 cup (125ml) dark soy sauce
- 2 tsp brown sugar
- 3 star anise
- 2 black tea bags (we used English breakfast)
- 4 eggs
- 500g yang chun dried wheat noodles (from Asian grocers)
- 1 bunch bok choy, quartered lengthways
- 1/3 cup (80ml) peanut oil
- 500g mixed Asian mushrooms, such as enoki, oyster and shiitake
- 2 garlic cloves, crushed
- Black sesame seeds and micro radish, to serve

GINGER DRESSING
- 1 garlic clove, crushed
- 2 tbs each rice vinegar and peanut oil
- 1 tbs soy sauce
- 2 tsp each sesame oil, chilli oil and finely grated ginger
- 1 tsp caster sugar

METHOD
- 1.
  Place five-spice powder, soy sauce, sugar, star anise, tea bags and 1.5L (6 cups) water (or enough to cover eggs) in a pan and bring to the boil over medium heat. Add eggs and cook for 3 minutes to par-cook, then remove from pan and cool slightly under cold running water. Using the back of a spoon, lightly crack shells, keeping shells intact (this creates veins). Carefully return eggs to boiling liquid and cook for a further 2 minutes. Remove pan from heat and set aside to cool in liquid (residual heat will continue cooking eggs). Chill for at least 2 hours or overnight. Discard liquid. Peel eggs and set aside.
- 2.
  Cook the noodles according to packet instructions, then drain and refresh in iced water. Chill until ready to use.
- 3.

Blanch bok choy in a saucepan of boiling salted water for 30 seconds, then drain and refresh in iced water.
- 4.
 For the dressing, combine all the ingredients in a bowl and set aside.
- 5.
 Heat 2 tbs oil in a large frypan over high heat. Add half the mushrooms, then season and cook for 3 minutes or until slightly charred. Add garlic and cook for 30 seconds or until fragrant, then transfer to a bowl. (If using enoki mushrooms, cook separately for 1 minute.) Repeat with remaining 2 tbs oil and mushrooms.
- 6.
 Divide noodles, bok choy, mushrooms and eggs among bowls. Drizzle with dressing and sprinkle with sesame seeds and micro radish to serve.

Valli Little's rolled rice noodles with crispy chilli tofu

SERVES:4 PREP TIME: -   COOK TIME: 10MINS
INGREDIENTS: 15   DIFFICULTY: EASY

INGREDIENTS
- 100ml sunflower oil
- 400g banh cuon rolled rice noodles (from Asian grocers), cut into 6cm lengths
- 1/2 tsp dried chilli flakes
- 2 tsp sea salt flakes
- 2 tbs each rice flour and self-raising flour
- 250g very firm tofu, crumbled
- 1 bunch broccolini, blanched, halved lengthways
- 1 cup (160g) peas, blanched
- 1/2 cup (50g) fried Asian shallots
- Chopped pickled red chillies (from Asian grocers), to serve

SESAME DRESSING
- 2 tbs each soy sauce and rice vinegar
- 1 tbs each sesame oil and peanut oil
- 1 tsp caster sugar
- 2 tsp grated ginger
- 1 garlic clove, crushed

METHOD
- 1.
 Heat 2 tbs sunflower oil in a frypan over medium-high heat. Cook rolled rice rolls for 3-4 minutes on one side until slightly golden and crisp. Turn, then add 1/4 cup

(60ml) water to pan and immediately cover with a lid. Cook for 2 minutes or until tender. Remove noodles from pan and set aside to cool completely.
- 2.
To make crispy tofu, using a mortar and pestle, crush chilli flakes, then combine with salt flakes. Combine the flours in a separate bowl and season with salt. Add tofu and toss to coat, then discard excess flour. Heat remaining 1/4 cup (60ml) oil in a frypan over medium-high heat. Add tofu and cook, stirring, for 4 minutes or until golden and crisp. Drain on paper towel, then toss in chilli salt.
- 3.
For the dressing, place all ingredients and 2 tbs water in a bowl. Stir to combine.
- 4.
Divide the noodle rolls among plates and drizzle over sauce. Top with crispy chilli tofu, broccolini, peas, fried Asian shallots and pickled chilli to serve.

Quick and easy chicken cacciatore

SERVES: 4 PREP TIME: 5MINS   COOK TIME: 25MINS
INGREDIENTS: 11   DIFFICULTY: EASY

INGREDIENTS
- 1 tbs olive oil
- 4 Lilydale Free Range Chicken Thighs
- 1 onion, chopped
- 2 garlic cloves, crushed
- 2 tsp chopped rosemary leaves
- 1 red capsicum, cut into strips
- 1 cup (120g) pitted green olives
- 1 cup (250ml) red wine
- 400g can chopped tomatoes
- 1 tbs chopped flat-leaf parsley leaves
- 1 cup (170g) instant polenta, cooked to packet instructions (optional)

METHOD
- 1.
Heat oil in a large, deep frypan over medium heat. Pat the chicken dry with paper towel, then season and place, skin-side down, in the pan. Cook for 4 minutes or until skin is golden, then turn and cook for a further 1 minute or until browned. Transfer to a plate.
- 2.

Return the pan to medium heat with the onion and cook, stirring, for 2 minutes or until softened. Add the garlic and rosemary, then cook for a further 1 minute or until fragrant. Add the capsicum, olives and red wine, then cook for 3-4 minutes until the liquid is reduced by half. Add tomato, then return the chicken, skin-side up, to the pan. Bring to a simmer and cook for 12 minutes or until chicken is cooked through.
- 3.
Garnish with parsley and serve with polenta, if desired.

Garlic and spinach gnocchi with lemon and pecorino

SERVES: 4 PREP TIME: 20MINS   COOK TIME: 1HR 15MINS
INGREDIENTS: 8   DIFFICULTY: CAPABLE

INGREDIENTS
- 900g evenly sized maris piper or King Edward potatoes
- 100g garlic cloves
- 200g baby spinach
- 300g Tipo 00 flour, plus extra for dusting
- 2 large egg yolks
- 75g butter
- Juice of 1/2 lemon
- 50g pecorino, plus extra to serve

METHOD
- 1.
Preheat oven to 180°C. Wash the potatoes and dry well, then prick all over with a fork. Place in a roasting pan and bake for 1 hour or until cooked through.
- 2.
Meanwhile, sit a steamer over a pan of boiling water. Add garlic, then cover and steam for 8 minutes. Add 75g spinach and steam for a further 2 minutes or until garlic is tender and spinach is wilted. Transfer to food processor and whiz to a puree. If mixture feels too wet, spoon into a muslin or clean tea towel and squeeze out excess liquid. Set aside.
- 3.
Cool potatoes slightly, then peel and pass through a potato ricer while hot onto a clean work surface. (The potatoes need to be hot or the gnocchi will be stodgy.) Pile the flour on top of the potato, in a mound, and season generously. Make a well in the middle. Whisk the egg yolks and garlic puree together, then pour into the well. Using your hands, lightly bring all the ingredients together (don't overwork

the mixture or it will become tough). As soon as it comes together, clean and dry your hands and worktop for the next step.
- 4.
  Roll out gnocchi on a lightly floured surface to a rectangle, 1cm thick. Cut into 2cm strips, then cut into 2cm pieces.
- 5.
  Bring a large pan of salted water to the boil. Shred remaining 125g spinach leaves. Melt butter in a frypan over low heat and add the spinach. Cook gnocchi in two batches, for 2-3 minutes until they rise to the surface. Remove with a slotted spoon and add to the frypan of spinach. Repeat with remaining gnocchi. Add lemon juice, grate over pecorino, season and toss together. Serve with extra pecorino.

Fish tacos with avocado salsa

SERVES:4   PREP TIME: 20MINS   COOK TIME: 15MINS
INGREDIENTS: 17   DIFFICULTY: EASY

INGREDIENTS
- 600g skinless white fish fillets (such as flathead), pin-boned
- Large pinch of cayenne pepper
- 1 teaspoon ground cumin
- 1 tablespoon olive oil
- 8 taco shells
- 1 baby cos lettuce, finely shredded
- Coriander leaves, to serve

SALSA
- 2 ripe tomatoes
- 1 green capsicum, finely chopped
- 1 avocado, flesh finely chopped
- 1 tablespoon pickled sliced jalapeño chillies, drained, finely chopped
- 1/2 red onion, thinly sliced
- 2 tablespoons coriander leaves
- 1 garlic clove, crushed
- 1/2 teaspoon ground cumin
- 1 tablespoon lime juice
- 1 tablespoon olive oil

METHOD
- 1.
  Preheat the oven to 180°C.
- 2.

For salsa, halve the tomatoes, squeeze out and discard the seeds and juice, then finely chop the flesh. Place in a bowl with the remaining salsa ingredients, season with salt and pepper and mix to combine.
- 3.
Stack taco shells upright in a baking dish and heat in the oven for 5 minutes.
- 4.
Meanwhile, dust the fish with the cayenne, cumin, salt and pepper. Heat oil in a non-stick frypan and sear the fish for 1-2 minutes on each side until just cooked through.
- 5.
Fill each taco shell with a layer of cos lettuce, top with the fish and spoon the avocado salsa over the top. Scatter with the coriander leaves and serve.

Chicken quesadillas with chipotle relish and mango salsa

SERVES: 4 PREP TIME: 10MINS   COOK TIME: 1HR
INGREDIENTS: 16   DIFFICULTY: EASY

INGREDIENTS
- 1 1/2 tablespoons olive oil
- 1 large onion (200g), finely chopped
- 8 garlic cloves, finely chopped
- 2 tablespoons chopped chipotle chillies in adobo (smoked, pickled jalapenos in sauce)
- 400g can chopped tomatoes
- 1/4 cup (70g) tomato paste
- 1 cup (250ml) malt vinegar
- 120g caster sugar
- 2 mangoes, flesh cut into 2cm cubes
- 1 avocado, flesh cut into 2cm cubes
- 1 long red chilli, seeds removed, finely chopped
- Juice of 1/2 lime, plus extra lime wedges to serve
- 1 cup finely chopped coriander, plus extra leaves, to serve
- 8 flour tortillas
- 1 small barbecued chicken, meat shredded, skin and bones discarded
- 2 1/2 cups (250g) grated mozzarella

METHOD
- 1.

Heat oil in a pan over medium heat. Add onion and garlic, and cook, stirring, for 5 minutes or until softened. Add chipotle, tomato, paste, vinegar, sugar, 1 cup (250ml) water and 2 teaspoons salt. Bring to a simmer, reduce heat to low and cook, stirring occasionally, for 45 minutes or until reduced and thickened. Cool. If not using immediately, transfer to a sterilised jar, seal and store in the fridge for up to 2 weeks.

- 2.
Combine mango, avocado, chilli, lime juice and coriander in a bowl. Set aside.
- 3.
Preheat an oiled barbecue or large frypan to high. Spread half the tortillas with chipotle relish and top with chicken and mozzarella. Sandwich with remaining tortillas, then cook, weighted with a heavy pan or pressing down with a spatula, in batches if necessary, for 2 minutes each side. Cut quesadillas into quarters and serve with mango salsa, extra coriander leaves and lime wedges.

Zucchini carpaccio

SERVES: 6 PREP TIME: 15MINS   COOK TIME: -
INGREDIENTS: 5   DIFFICULTY: EASY

INGREDIENTS
- 500g mixed green and yellow zucchinis
- 100ml olive oil
- 2 tsp finely grated lemon zest, plus 2 tbs lemon juice
- 100g wild rocket leaves
- 1 1/4 cups (100g) shaved parmesan

METHOD
- 1.
Using a mandoline, thinly slice zucchini lengthways and place on a serving platter.
- 2.
Whisk the oil, lemon zest and juice in a bowl and season.
- 3.
Scatter rocket and parmesan over the zucchini, drizzle with dressing and season with freshly ground black pepper to serve.

Shannon Bennett's Welsh rarebit

SERVES: 4 PREP TIME: 15MINS   COOK TIME: -
INGREDIENTS: 13   DIFFICULTY: EASY

INGREDIENTS
- 8 slices sourdough
- 85g unsalted butter
- 2/3 cup (100g) plain flour
- 2 cups (500ml) apple cider
- 400g mature cheddar cheese, grated
- 100g gruyere cheese, grated
- 1 tbs chopped flat-leaf parsley leaves
- 2 tsp Worcestershire sauce
- 8 eggs, plus 2 extra egg yolks
- 1/4 cup (70g) Dijon mustard
- 1/4 cup (60ml) extra virgin olive oil
- Juice of 1 lemon
- Watercress and mixed leaves, to serve

METHOD
- 1.
  Preheat oven grill to high. Place sourdough slices in a single layer on a baking tray. Grill, turning, for 2 minutes or until golden.
- 2.
  Melt butter in a pan over low heat. Add flour and whisk to combine. Cook, stirring, for 1 minute, then increase heat to medium and gradually add cider, whisking constantly, until a thick paste forms. Remove from heat, add cheese, parsley, Worcestershire sauce, egg yolks and 2 tbs mustard. Season. Return pan to medium heat and cook, stirring, for 2 minutes or until thick and smooth. Set aside.
- 3.
  In two batches, heat 2 tsp oil in a frypan over medium heat. Break 4 eggs into pan. Fry for 2-3 minutes until whites are set and yolks are runny. Remove from pan and set aside. Repeat with another 2 tsp oil and remaining 4 eggs. Place 1 egg on each slice of toast and spoon over cheese sauce. Grill for 3-4 minutes until golden.
- 4.
  Meanwhile, combine lemon juice, and remaining 30g mustard and 2 tbs olive oil in bowl. Season and toss with salad leaves.
- 5.
  Serve rarebit topped with a salad.

Rigatoni with a spicy sausage sauce

SERVES: 4 PREP TIME: -   COOK TIME: -
INGREDIENTS: 13   DIFFICULTY: EASY

INGREDIENTS
- 2 tbs extra virgin olive oil
- 6 Italian pork sausages (about 400g), skin removed, broken into large pieces
- 2 garlic cloves, finely chopped
- 2 small red chillies, finely chopped
- 2 baby fennel bulbs, chopped
- 1/2 cup (125ml) dry white wine
- 400g can chopped tomatoes
- 1/2 cup (125ml) chicken stock
- 2 tsp finely chopped oregano leaves
- 2 tsp caster sugar
- 400g rigatoni or other short pasta
- Grated pecorino or parmesan, to serve
- Shredded flat-leaf parsley, to serve

METHOD
- 1.
  Heat oil in a frypan over medium heat. Add meat, stirring until browned. Add garlic, chilli and fennel. Continue cooking for 3-4 minutes, stirring, until fragrant. Increase heat to medium-high, add wine, tomatoes, chicken stock, oregano and sugar, stirring. Bring to boil, then reduce to a simmer and cook for 15 minutes, or until slightly thickened. Season.
- 2.
  Meanwhile, cook the pasta in a large saucepan of salted boiling water according to packet instructions, or until al dente. Drain well and return to the pan with the sauce and toss until well combined.
- 3.
  Divide pasta among serving bowls, then serve with pecorino and shredded parsley.

Mexican eggs with potato hash

SERVES: 4 PREP TIME: 15MINS   COOK TIME: 25MINS
INGREDIENTS: 10   DIFFICULTY: EASY

INGREDIENTS
- 1/4 cup (60ml) olive oil
- 1 onion, finely chopped
- 400g beef mince
- 1/4 cup (60ml) chipotle chilli sauce (see notes) or other hot sauce
- 400g can chopped tomatoes

- 1/3 cup roughly chopped coriander, plus extra to serve
- 1kg (about 4) desiree potatoes (unpeeled), scrubbed, coarsely grated
- 50g unsalted butter, melted
- 4 eggs
- 1 jalapeno chilli or long green chilli, thinly sliced

METHOD
- 1.
Heat 1 tablespoon oil in a large frypan (with a lid) over medium-high heat. Add onion and a pinch of salt, then cook, stirring, for 3-4 minutes until soft. Add the beef and cook, stirring, for 5 minutes or until browned. Stir in the chipotle sauce, tomatoes and coriander, season with freshly ground black pepper and reduce heat to medium. Cook for a further 5-6 minutes until slightly thickened.
- 2.
Meanwhile, to make the potato hash, place grated potato in a clean tea towel and squeeze to remove excess water. Place potato in a bowl with the melted butter, then season and stir to combine. Heat another 1 tablespoon oil in a separate frypan over medium heat. Using a 1/3 cup (80ml) measuring cup, place 4 mounds of potato in the pan, flatten with a spoon and cook for 3-4 minutes each side until golden and cooked through. Repeat with the remaining 1 tablespoon oil and potato mixture.
- 3.
Using a spoon, make 4 indents in the beef, then crack an egg into each. Cover and cook for 7 minutes or until whites are cooked. Garnish with the chilli and extra coriander, then serve with the hash.

Ricotta dumplings with orecchiette, peas and prosciutto

SERVES: 4 PREP TIME: 15MINS   COOK TIME: 25MINS
INGREDIENTS: 13   DIFFICULTY: EASY

INGREDIENTS
- 2 cups orecchiette pasta
- 1/4 cup (60ml) olive oil, plus extra to drizzle
- 1 cup freshly podded or frozen peas

- 1/2 onion, thinly sliced
- 1/4 cup (60ml) dry white wine
- 4 thin slices prosciutto or ham, sliced
- 2 tablespoons mint leaves

RICOTTA DUMPLINGS
- 250g fresh ricotta
- 2 tablespoons grated parmesan, plus extra to serve
- 1/3 cup (50g) plain flour
- 1 egg, plus 1 extra yolk
- 2 tablespoons finely chopped flat-leaf parsley
- Large pinch freshly grated nutmeg

METHOD
1. For the ricotta dumplings, briefly process all the ingredients in a food processor with salt and pepper until smooth. Chill until needed.
2. Cook pasta in a pan of boiling salted water according to packet instructions, adding peas for the final 2 minutes of cooking time, then drain. Rinse briefly in cold water to cool slightly, then drain again. Toss with 1 tablespoon of the oil.
3. Heat remaining oil in a large pan over medium-low heat. Add onion and cook for 5 minutes or until soft. Add the wine, prosciutto, peas and pasta and lightly toss for 1 minute or until pasta is heated through. Arrange the contents of the pan with its juices in a single layer over a large serving platter.
4. Meanwhile, bring a pan of salted water to the boil. Drop the ricotta batter by the teaspoon into the boiling water, cooking 6 at a time, and simmer for 2 minutes. Drain on paper towel while you cook remaining dumplings, then scatter over the pasta. Season well with sea salt and freshly ground black pepper, scatter with mint and a little extra parmesan, then drizzle with extra oil and serve warm.

Miso salmon with eggplant

SERVES: 4 PREP TIME: 15MINS   COOK TIME: 5MINS
INGREDIENTS: 9   DIFFICULTY: EASY

INGREDIENTS
- 4 tablespoons white miso paste*
- 2 tablespoons honey
- 4 small (100g) skinless salmon fillets
- 2 tablespoons rice vinegar*

- 1 tablespoon peanut oil
- 100g snow peas, blanched
- 150g snow pea sprouts, trimmed
- 12 chargrilled eggplant slices, halved
- 1 tablespoon toasted sesame seeds

METHOD
- 1.
- Mix together half the miso paste and half the honey and brush over fish.
- 2.
- Preheat a lightly oiled chargrill or barbecue to medium-high and cook salmon for 2 minutes each side until just cooked.
- 3.
- Meanwhile, mix the remaining miso paste and honey with vinegar and oil.
- 4.
- Combine the vegetables in a bowl and toss with dressing. Flake salmon and toss through the salad. Divide between bowls and top with sesame seeds.

Fish bread with quick pickled vegetables

SERVES: 4 PREP TIME: 45MINS   COOK TIME: 15MINS
INGREDIENTS: 15   DIFFICULTY: EASY

INGREDIENTS
- 1 teaspoon ground turmeric
- 2 tablespoons plain flour
- 1/3 cup (80ml) milk
- 2 tablespoons fresh dill, chopped
- 500g firm boneless white fish fillets (such as blue eye), cut into 2cm pieces
- 2 tablespoons coconut oil
- 1 thick baguette, split
- 1 Lebanese cucumber, thinly sliced
- 1 cup fresh coriander
- 1 cup Thai basil leaves
- 1 lime, halved

QUICK PICKLED VEGETABLES
- 1/3 cup (75g) coconut sugar
- 1/3 cup (80ml) rice vinegar
- 1 carrot, cut into matchsticks
- 1 small daikon (Asian white radish), cut into matchsticks

METHOD

- 1.
  For the quick pickled vegetables, combine sugar and vinegar in a small saucepan over low heat, stirring until the sugar dissolves, then set aside to cool. Add carrot and daikon, and set aside for a further 30 minutes to pickle, then drain.
- 2.
  Meanwhile, combine the turmeric and flour in a bowl, then season. Combine the milk and dill in a separate bowl. Dip the fish in the milk mixture, then in the flour mixture, shaking off any excess.
- 3.
  Heat the oil in a frypan over medium heat. Cook the fish, in batches, turning, for 3-4 minutes or until golden.
- 4.
  Brush the inside of the baguette with some of the oil from the pan. Fill the baguette with the fish, cucumber, pickled vegetables, coriander and Thai basil. Squeeze over lime juice to serve.

Thai fish and pumpkin soup

SERVES: 4   PREP TIME: 30MINS   COOK TIME: 25MINS
INGREDIENTS: 14   DIFFICULTY: EASY

INGREDIENTS
- 1 tablespoon sunflower oil
- 3 tablespoons Thai red curry paste
- 200ml light coconut milk
- 3 cups (750ml) salt-reduced chicken or fish stock
- 4 Asian (red) eschalots, thinly sliced
- 1 long red chilli, thinly sliced
- 2 kaffir lime leaves, finely shredded (optional)
- 250g pumpkin, peeled, cut into 2cm pieces
- 1 green capsicum, cut into strips
- 2 tablespoons tamarind puree
- 2 tablespoons fish sauce
- 1 tablespoon brown sugar
- 600g skinless chunky fish fillets (such as blue eye, ling or snapper), cut into 3cm pieces
- 100g baby spinach leaves

METHOD
- 1.

Heat oil in a saucepan over medium-high heat. Add curry paste and cook, stirring, for 2 minutes or until fragrant.
- 2.
Add the coconut milk, stock, eschalot, chilli and kaffir lime leaves, if using, and stir to combine. Add pumpkin, capsicum, tamarind, fish sauce, sugar and a pinch of salt and cook for 20 minutes or until the pumpkin is tender.
- 3.
Add fish and simmer for 5 minutes or until the fish is opaque.
- 4.
Place half the spinach in 4 warm bowls and top with the fish and veg. Scatter with remaining spinach, then ladle the sauce over the top and serve.

Satay beef fillet with watercress and cucumber

SERVES: 4 PREP TIME: 35MINS   COOK TIME: 20MINS
INGREDIENTS: 13   DIFFICULTY: EASY

INGREDIENTS
- 1/4 cup (60ml) peanut oil
- 2 long red chillies, seeds removed, finely chopped
- 3 garlic cloves, finely chopped
- 600g centre-cut beef eye fillet
- 2 Asian (red) eschalots, finely chopped
- 2 teaspoons grated ginger
- 1 1/2 tablespoons light soy sauce
- 1 cup (250ml) coconut milk
- 1 tablespoon caster sugar
- 1/3 cup (95g) crunchy peanut butter
- 1 bunch watercress, leaves picked
- 2 Lebanese cucumbers, halved, sliced lengthways into thin wedges
- Coriander leaves, to serve

METHOD
- 1.
Combine 2 tablespoons oil, half the chilli and one-third of the garlic in a bowl and brush over the beef. Season, then set aside at room temperature for 30 minutes.
- 2.
Meanwhile, heat remaining 1 tablespoon oil in a saucepan over medium heat. Add eschalot and cook, stirring, for 3 minutes or until softened but not browned. Add

ginger and remaining garlic, and cook for a further 1 minute or until fragrant. Add soy sauce, coconut milk and sugar, stirring until sugar dissolves, then bring to a simmer and cook for 1 minute or until slightly reduced and thickened. Add peanut butter and stir until melted and combined. Set aside.

- 3.
Preheat a barbecue or chargrill pan to high. Cook beef, turning, for 10-12 minutes until lightly charred but rare in the centre, or until cooked to your liking. Rest, loosely covered with foil, for 5 minutes.
- 4.
Meanwhile, gently reheat peanut sauce over low heat. Thinly slice beef and arrange on a serving plate with watercress and cucumber wedges. Drizzle over spoonfuls of peanut sauce, and serve scattered with coriander leaves.

Sri Lankan salmon curry

SERVES: 4 PREP TIME: 5MINS   COOK TIME: 20MINS
INGREDIENTS: 13   DIFFICULTY: EASY

INGREDIENTS
- 2 garlic cloves
- 3cm piece ginger, sliced
- 2 tsp each panch phoran and whole coriander seeds
- 1 tbs mild madras curry powder
- 2 small green chillies, chopped
- 2 tbs sunflower oil
- 1 onion, chopped
- 4 tomatoes, chopped
- 10 curry leaves
- 1 bunch broccolini
- 270ml can coconut milk
- 600g skinless salmon fillets, cut into 3cm pieces
- Shredded coconut, lime wedges, chutney and warmed roti, to serve

METHOD
- 1.
To make the curry paste, place the garlic, ginger, spices and chilli in a mortar and pestle and grind to a paste. Set aside.
- 2.

Heat oil in a saucepan over medium heat. Add onion and cook for 3-4 minutes until softened. Add the curry paste and cook, stirring, for 2 minutes or until fragrant. Add the tomato, curry leaves and broccolini, then cook for a further 2 minutes. Add the coconut milk and 1/2 cup (125ml) water, then bring to a simmer.
- 3.
Add the salmon, season and cook for a final 5 minutes or until the salmon is just cooked.
- 4.
Garnish the curry with shredded coconut and serve immediately with lime wedges, chutney and warmed roti.

Pumpkin and goat's cheese bruschetta with sage burnt butter

SERVES: 6 PREP TIME: 10MINS   COOK TIME: 30MINS
INGREDIENTS: 9   DIFFICULTY: EASY

INGREDIENTS
- 1/2 butternut pumpkin (500g), peeled, cut into 1.5cm pieces
- 2 tablespoons olive oil
- 1/2 teaspoon dried chilli flakes
- 6 slices sourdough bread
- 1 garlic clove, halved
- 150g soft goat's cheese
- 3/4 cup (250g) caramelised onion jam
- 50g unsalted butter
- 12 sage leaves

METHOD
- 1.
Preheat the oven to 180C. Place the pumpkin on a baking paper-lined baking tray and drizzle with 1 tbs oil, season and sprinkle with chilli flakes. Roast for 20 minutes or until golden and tender.
- 2.
Heat a chargrill pan over high heat. Toast bread slices for 1-2 minutes each side until lightly charred. While still warm, rub both sides with garlic halves. Place toast on a baking tray. Spread each slice with goat's cheese, top with caramelised onion and scatter with pumpkin pieces. Bake for 2 minutes or until warmed through.
- 3.

Meanwhile, melt butter and remaining 1 tablespoons oil in a small frypan over medium heat. Add sage leaves and cook for 1 minute or until butter is browned and sage is crisp.

- 4.
Drizzle bruschetta with sage burnt butter, and serve immediately.

Harissa lamb with roast carrots and quinoa pilaf

SERVES: 4 PREP TIME: 10MINS   COOK TIME: 40MINS
INGREDIENTS: 11   DIFFICULTY: EASY

INGREDIENTS
- 1/4 cup (60ml) olive oil
- 3 garlic cloves, crushed
- Finely grated zest of 1/2 lemon
- 3 teaspoons ground cumin
- 1 1/2 tablespoons harissa
- 2 x 6-cutlet untrimmed lamb racks, fat scored
- 1 bunch baby (Dutch) carrots
- 1 1/4 cups (250g) quinoa, rinsed, drained
- 1 cup (250ml) Massel Chicken Style Liquid Stock
- 400g can chickpeas, rinsed, drained
- Coriander leaves, to serve

METHOD
- 1.
Preheat the oven to 190C. Line a baking tray with baking paper.
- 2.
Combine oil, garlic, lemon zest, 2 teaspoons cumin, 1 tablespoon harissa and 2 teaspoons salt in a bowl, then rub over the lamb. Place the carrots on baking tray and top with lamb.
- 3.
Roast for 40 minutes for medium or until cooked to your liking. Remove from oven and rest lamb, loosely covered with foil, for 5 minutes.
- 4.
Meanwhile, to make the quinoa pilaf, combine quinoa, stock, chickpeas, remaining 1 teaspoon cumin, 1/2 tablespoon harissa, 1 teaspoon salt and 3/4 cup (185ml) hot water in an ovenproof dish. Cover with foil and roast on the bottom shelf (underneath the lamb) for 25 minutes or until all the liquid is absorbed. Transfer to a serving bowl. Drizzle over the lamb resting juices.

- 5.
  Scatter lamb with coriander and serve with carrots and quinoa pilaf.

Cheat's blinis with jamon and figs

SERVES: 32 PREP TIME: 3HR   COOK TIME: -
INGREDIENTS: 7   DIFFICULTY: EASY

INGREDIENTS
- 16 dried dessert figs, halved
- 1/4 cup (60ml) Pedro Ximenez sherry or other sweet sherry
- 2 x 140g packets pikelet bites (see note)
- 250g mascarpone cheese
- 100g sliced jamon (see note) or prosciutto, cut into strips
- Olive oil, to drizzle
- Chervil (see note) or flat-leaf parsley sprigs, to garnish

METHOD
- 1.
- Soak the dried dessert figs in the sherry for 2 hours or until they have absorbed all the liquid.
- 2.
- Place the pikelets on a platter and spread each with a little mascarpone. Add a small scroll of jamon and a piece of fig. Sprinkle with sea salt and freshly ground black pepper, drizzle over oil and garnish with chervil or parsley.

Hawker-style stir-fried noodles

SERVES: 6 PREP TIME: 25MINS   COOK TIME: 10MINS
INGREDIENTS: 15   DIFFICULTY: EASY

INGREDIENTS
- 1 tablespoon chilli paste
- 1/4 cup (60ml) oyster sauce
- Juice of 1/2 a lime
- 2 eschalots, halved, thinly sliced
- 4 spring onions, cut into 3-4cm lengths
- 2 garlic cloves, thinly sliced
- 1 bunch choy sum, cut into 4cm lengths
- 200g fresh thin egg noodles
- 1/4 cup (60ml) canola or sunflower oil

- 150g firm fried tofu, thinly sliced
- 200g packet fried or steamed fish balls, rinsed, drained
- 200g boneless Chinese barbecued duck or soy-braised chicken meat
- 1 1/2 cups (120g) bean sprouts
- 4 kaffir lime leaves, thinly sliced
- Fried Asian shallots, to serve

METHOD
- 1.
- Combine paste, oyster sauce, lime juice and 2 tablespoons water in a small bowl. Set aside. Combine eschalots, spring onion, garlic and choy sum in a bowl.
- 2.
- Cook noodles according to packet instructions, drain and toss with 1 tablespoon oil.
- 3.
- Heat remaining 2 tablespoons oil in a large wok over high heat. Add choy sum mixture and toss well for 1 minute. Add tofu, fish balls and duck or chicken and cook, tossing, for a further minute. Add noodles and sauce mixture and cook for a further 2 minutes or until noodles are heated through. Remove from heat, add sprouts and lime leaves, and toss to combine. Serve in bowls and scatter with fried shallots.

Spiced coconut eggs

SERVES: 4 PREP TIME: 10MINS   COOK TIME: 10MINS
INGREDIENTS: 13   DIFFICULTY: EASY

INGREDIENTS
- 100g unsalted butter
- 2 onions, thinly sliced
- 3 teaspoons good-quality mild curry powder
- 6-8 fresh curry leaves
- 200ml hollandaise sauce
- 200ml coconut cream
- 200ml thick cream
- 100ml vegetable stock
- 2 tablespoons lemon juice
- 8 hard-boiled eggs, peeled
- 4 spring onions, sliced on the diagonal
- Toasted shaved coconut and paprika, to garnish
- Steamed basmati rice and pappadams, to serve

METHOD

- 1.
  Place butter in a pan, add onions and cook over low heat, stirring, for 6-8 minutes until softened but not coloured. Add curry powder and leaves and cook for a further minute.
- 2.
  Stir in hollandaise, coconut cream, thick cream, stock and lemon juice.
- 3.
  Add eggs to warm through with half of the onion. Serve with rice and/or pappadams, and garnish with coconut, remaining onion and paprika.

Korean barbecue chicken fried rice

SERVES: 4 PREP TIME: -   COOK TIME: -
INGREDIENTS: 17   DIFFICULTY: EASY

INGREDIENTS

- 100ml peanut oil
- 2 eggs, lightly beaten
- 1 barbecue chicken, meat shredded
- 1 long red chilli, finely chopped, plus extra to serve
- 1/2 bunch spring onions, white and pale green parts chopped
- 1/4 savoy cabbage, outer leaves discarded, finely shredded
- 2 garlic cloves, chopped
- 11/3 cups (120g) long-grain rice, cooked to packet instructions, cooled
- 1 bunch coriander, leaves picked
- 1 tbs black sesame seeds

KOREAN BARBECUE SAUCE

- 1/4 cup (60ml) light soy sauce
- 1/4 cup (60g) brown sugar
- 2 garlic cloves, crushed
- 3 tsp chilli paste
- 3 tsp grated ginger
- 1 tbs rice wine vinegar
- 2 tsp sesame oil

METHOD

- 1.
  For the barbecue sauce, combine all the ingredients in a bowl and season with pepper. Heat 1 tbs oil in a wok or large frypan over high heat. Add the egg and

cook, stirring, for 1 minute or until softly scrambled. Remove from pan and set aside.
- 2.
Add another 2 tbs oil to the pan with the chicken and half the barbecue sauce. Stir-fry for 5-6 minutes until caramelised. Remove from pan and set aside.
- 3.
Add remaining 2 tbs oil to pan with chilli, spring onion, cabbage and garlic. Stir-fry for 1 minute or until fragrant. Add the rice and remaining barbecue sauce, and cook, stirring, for 1-2 minutes to warm through.
- 4.
Increase heat to high and cook for a further 6 minutes or until rice begins to crisp around the edges. Remove from heat and stir through reserved chicken, egg and half the coriander.
- 5.
Divide rice among bowls. Serve topped with sesame, extra chilli and remaining coriander.

Quick tomato and salami pizzas

SERVES: 2 PREP TIME: -   COOK TIME: 8MINS
INGREDIENTS: 10   DIFFICULTY: EASY

INGREDIENTS
- 2 Lebanese breads
- 1/3 cup (90g) basil pesto
- 2 x 150g buffalo mozzarella balls, torn
- 1 tsp dried chilli flakes
- 1 long green chilli, thinly sliced
- 10 slices hot salami
- 250g mixed cherry tomatoes, some halved
- 1/3 cup (40g) pitted green olives
- Basil leaves, to serve
- Extra virgin olive oil, to serve

METHOD
- 1.
Preheat the oven to 250°C. Place breads on a large baking tray or individual trays. Spread pesto evenly over each bread, then top with mozzarella, dried chilli, green chilli, salami, tomatoes, and olives. Bake for 8 minutes or until base is crisp and cheese has melted.
- 2.

Season with black pepper, drizzle with olive oil and top with basil to serve.

Black pepper prawns

SERVES: 4 PREP TIME: 15MINS   COOK TIME: 20MINS
INGREDIENTS: 15   DIFFICULTY: EASY

INGREDIENTS
- 1 tbs dried shrimp*
- 1/2 cup (100g) jasmine rice
- 2 garlic cloves, roughly chopped
- 2cm piece ginger, peeled
- 1 long red chilli, seeds removed, roughly chopped
- 2 tbs whole black peppercorns
- 1 cup (250ml) chicken stock
- 2 tbs kecap manis (Indonesian sweet soy sauce)*
- 2 tbs oyster sauce
- 2 cups (500ml) sunflower oil
- 800g green prawns, peeled (heads and tails intact), deveined
- 1/4 cup fresh curry leaves*
- 6 spring onions, thinly sliced on an angle
- 50g unsalted butter
- 2 tbs coriander leaves

METHOD
- 1.
Soak the dried shrimp in 1/2 cup (125ml) boiling water for 10 minutes.
- 2.
Meanwhile, cook the jasmine rice in boiling water according to packet instructions. Drain and keep warm.
- 3.
Drain the shrimp, then place in a mortar and pestle with the garlic, ginger, red chilli and whole black peppercorns. Pound until you have a smooth paste, then set aside.
- 4.
Combine the chicken stock, kecap manis and oyster sauce in a small bowl, then set aside.
- 5.
Heat the sunflower oil in a wok over medium-high heat. In 3 batches, add the prawns to the wok, being careful as the oil may spit. Cook the prawns, carefully

- 6.
  Drain all but 2-3 tablespoons oil from the wok. Add the shrimp paste and half the spring onions to the wok, then cook, stirring, for 1-2 minutes until fragrant. Stir in the stock mixture, bring to the boil, then whisk in butter.
- 7.
  Reduce heat to medium, then return the prawns and curry leaves to the wok and toss to combine. Cook, stirring, for 1-2 minutes until heated through.
- 8.
  Divide the rice and prawns among plates, garnish with coriander leaves and remaining spring onion, then serve.

Gwyneth Paltrow's seared scallops with watercress and asparagus

SERVES: 4 PREP TIME: 10MINS   COOK TIME: 4MINS
INGREDIENTS: 9   DIFFICULTY: EASY

INGREDIENTS
- 16 scallops, roe removed
- Juice of 1 small lemon, plus lemon wedges to serve
- Splash of champagne vinegar or white wine vinegar
- 1 tbs finely chopped eschalot
- 1/3 cup (80ml) olive oil
- 12 asparagus spears, trimmed
- 1 bunch watercress
- Large handful sugar snap peas, cut into 1cm pieces (about 1 cup)
- 55g unsalted butter

METHOD
- 1.
  Dry scallops well with paper towel, then generously season.
- 2.
  Combine the lemon juice, vinegar, eschalot, and 1 tbs oil in a large bowl.
- 3.
  Using a peeler, shave 4 of the asparagus spears into strips. Add to the bowl with the watercress. Cut the remaining 8 asparagus spears into 1cm pieces and set aside.
- 4.

Heat 1 tbs oil in a large frypan over medium-high heat. Add the sugar snap peas and asparagus pieces, season, and cook for 1-2 minutes until just cooked. Add to the bowl with the watercress and toss to combine.
- 5.
  Return pan to medium-high heat with remaining 2 tbs oil. Add the scallops, and cook (on one side only) for 3-5 minutes until very crispy and almost cooked through. Turn scallops, reduce the heat to low and add the butter (the butter will immediately sizzle and start to turn brown). Turn off the heat (the residual heat will finish cooking the scallops).
- 6.
  Divide the salad among four plates, top with seared scallops and drizzle over brown butter. Serve with lemon wedges on the side, if desired.

Gwyneth Paltrow's Singapore rice noodles

SERVES: 4 PREP TIME: 15MINS   COOK TIME: 10MINS
INGREDIENTS: 13   DIFFICULTY: EASY

INGREDIENTS
- 100g thin rice noodles
- 1/3 cup (80ml) peanut oil
- 2 tbs toasted sesame oil
- 1 onion, thinly sliced
- ½ cup finely chopped broccoli
- ½ cup chopped green beans (1cm pieces)
- ½ cup (60g) fresh or frozen peas
- 200g firm tofu, cut into 1cm pieces
- 1 tsp madras curry powder, or more to taste
- 1 large egg
- ¼ cup (60ml) tamari
- 2 spring onions, thinly sliced
- ¼ cup chopped fresh coriander

METHOD
- 1.
  Soak the rice noodles in hot water for 10 minutes or according to packet instructions. Drain and set aside.
- 2.
  Meanwhile, heat 1 tbs each peanut and sesame oils in a wok or large nonstick frypan over medium-high heat. When oils are hot but not smoking, add the onion

and cook, without stirring, for 1 minute to sear. Reduce heat to medium and cook, stirring occasionally, for 4 minutes or until golden. Transfer the onion to a bowl.
- 3.
Add the broccoli, green beans, peas, tofu, and another 1 tbs peanut oil to pan. Cook over high heat for 2 minutes or until the vegetables are just cooked and the tofu is beginning to brown. Add vegetable mixture to onion bowl.
- 4.
Add 1 tbs peanut oil, curry powder, remaining 1 tbs sesame oil and 2 tbs water to the pan. Add noodles and stir combine. Make a well in the centre of the noodles, add the remaining 1 tbs peanut oil, and crack in the egg. Stir vigorously with a wooden spoon and let scramble until almost cooked through, then mix in with the noodles.
- 5.
Add the tamari, spring onion, and coriander and stir to combine. Season to taste, then serve.

Floating market fish soup

SERVES: 4 PREP TIME: 25MINS   COOK TIME: 15MINS
INGREDIENTS: 13   DIFFICULTY: EASY

INGREDIENTS
- 600g white fish fillets (such as blue-eye or snapper)
- 100g bean thread vermicelli (glass noodles)
- 2 lemongrass stems
- 1.2 litres chicken stock
- 3 eschalots, finely sliced
- 1 long red chilli, sliced
- 2 tablespoons tamarind puree
- 2 tablespoons fish sauce
- 1 tablespoon sugar
- 100g bean sprouts
- 2 tomatoes, chopped
- Small handful of Thai basil (or mint) and coriander leaves
- 1 lime, quartered

METHOD
- 1.
Cut the fish into bite-sized chunks and toss with salt and pepper. Put noodles in a bowl, pour over boiling water to cover and leave for 4 minutes, then drain.
- 2.

Trim lemongrass to inner, tender white part and finely slice. Put stock, eschalot, chilli, tamarind and lemongrass in a pan. Bring to a boil over medium-high heat, then simmer for 10 minutes over medium heat.

- 3.
Stir in fish, fish sauce and sugar. Simmer over medium-high heat, covered, for 5 minutes. Add sprouts, noodles and tomatoes. Simmer for 1 minute or until hot.
- 4.
Divide among warm bowls. Scatter with herbs and serve with lime wedges.

Korean fish stir-fry

SERVES: 4 PREP TIME: 20MINS   COOK TIME: 10MINS
INGREDIENTS: 13   DIFFICULTY: EASY

INGREDIENTS
- 600g ling fillets, cut into 3cm pieces
- 180g rice stick noodles
- 2 teaspoons sunflower or rice bran oil
- 4 spring onions, finely chopped
- 2 green capsicums, thinly sliced
- 1 red capsicum, thinly sliced
- 2 cups watercress sprigs

MARINADE
- 2 garlic cloves, crushed
- 1/2 teaspoon chilli powder
- 2 tablespoons soy sauce
- 1 tablespoon Chinese rice wine (shaohsing)
- 2 teaspoons sesame seeds, toasted
- 2 teaspoons sesame oil

METHOD
- 1.
Combine marinade ingredients in a bowl, add fish and turn to coat. Stand for 10 minutes. Cook the noodles according to packet instructions, then drain.
- 2.
Heat the oil in a wok over high heat. Add drained fish (reserving marinade), and stir-fry for 1 minute. Add onion and capsicum and stir-fry for 2 minutes. Add reserved marinade and simmer for 2-3 minutes until fish is cooked and sauce is slightly thickened. Remove from the heat and fold in watercress, then serve the stir-fry on the noodles.

Moroccan swordfish

SERVES: 4 PREP TIME: 40MINS   COOK TIME: 10MINS
INGREDIENTS: 13   DIFFICULTY: EASY

INGREDIENTS
- 1 teaspoon saffron threads
- 2 tomatoes, peeled, seeded, thinly sliced
- 1 red capsicum, roasted, peeled, seeded, thinly sliced
- 1 yellow capsicum, roasted, peeled, seeded, thinly sliced
- 1 teaspoon ground coriander
- 1/2 teaspoon ground cumin
- 1 small red chilli, seeded, thinly sliced
- 2 large garlic cloves, crushed
- 150ml extra virgin olive oil, plus extra to brush
- 20ml (1 tablespoon) lemon juice
- 4 (about 150g each) swordfish fillets
- 1 tablespoon chopped fresh mint
- 1 tablespoon chopped fresh coriander

METHOD
- 1.
  Place saffron threads in a bowl with two tablespoons of warm water and set aside for five minutes.
- 2.
  Place tomato, capsicum, coriander, cumin, chilli, garlic, oil, lemon juice and saffron and its soaking liquid in a pan. Heat gently through.
- 3.
  Preheat a chargrill or non-stick frying pan to high. Season the fish, brush with oil and fry for 1-2 minutes (the centre should remain rare).
- 4.
  Place on serving plates, add the herbs to the sauce and divide the sauce between the plates.

Kingfish skewers with chargrilled tomatoes and chillies

SERVES: 4 PREP TIME: 25MINS   COOK TIME: 10MINS
INGREDIENTS: 8   DIFFICULTY: EASY

INGREDIENTS
- 1/4 cup (60ml) lemon juice
- 5-6 parsley sprigs, leaves roughly chopped
- 1/2 tsp dried chilli flakes
- 1 1/2 tbs olive oil
- 800g skinless kingfish fillets, pinboned, cut into 3cm cubes
- 3 long red chillies
- 3 long green chillies
- 250g vine-ripened cherry tomatoes

METHOD
- 1.
Soak 8 wooden skewers in water for 10 minutes. Combine juice, parsley, dried chilli, 2 tsp oil and fish in a bowl. Cover and refrigerate for 10 minutes, then thread onto skewers.
- 2.
Meanwhile, toss chillies and tomatoes in remaining olive oil. Heat an oiled chargrill or barbecue over medium-high heat. When hot, cook chillies for 10 minutes, turning to blacken. The skin should pop and crack open. Cut each chilli open down one side and remove seeds (unless you like it really spicy).
- 3.
Add the kingfish skewers to the chargrill or barbecue and cook for 6-8 minutes, turning once, or until just cooked. Add the tomatoes and cook for the final 5 minutes, or until softened and lightly charred.
- 4.
Serve 2 skewers per person with chargrilled tomatoes and chillies.

Baked ocean trout with tahini and herb salad

SERVES: 6　PREP TIME: 55MINS　COOK TIME: 20MINS
INGREDIENTS: 11　　　　DIFFICULTY: EASY

INGREDIENTS
- 800g skinless ocean trout fillet, pin-boned
- 1 tablespoon extra virgin olive oil
- 1/2 cup (140g) thick Greek-style yoghurt
- 1 tablespoon tahini
- 1 tablespoon lemon juice
- 2 teaspoons sumac (see note)

- 2 preserved lemon quarters, flesh and white pith discarded, rind finely chopped (see note)
- 1 bunch coriander, leaves finely chopped
- 1 bunch flat-leaf parsley, leaves finely chopped
- 1/4 cup (40g) toasted pine nuts
- Roast potatoes, to serve

METHOD

1. Preheat the oven to 140°C and line a large tray with baking paper. Place trout on the tray, brush with oil and season. Bake for 20 minutes. Remove from oven and cool completely. Transfer to a large platter.
2. Meanwhile, combine yoghurt, tahini, lemon juice and 1 teaspoon sumac, and season.
3. In a separate bowl, combine preserved lemon rind, herbs, pine nuts and remaining 1 teaspoon sumac.
4. Spread fish with tahini sauce and scatter with herb mixture. Serve with potatoes.

Healthy turmeric and coconut fish curry

SERVES: 4 PREP TIME: 20MINS   COOK TIME: 35MINS
INGREDIENTS: 18   DIFFICULTY: EASY

INGREDIENTS

- 4 garlic cloves, chopped
- 4 small green chillies, chopped
- 1 tbs finely chopped ginger
- 2 tsp finely chopped fresh turmeric
- 2 tbs sunfower oil
- 1 onion, finely chopped
- 2 tsp ground coriander
- 2 tsp ground turmeric
- 1 tsp ground cumin
- 1/4 tsp ground cloves
- 6 green cardamom pods, cracked
- 12 curry leaves, plus extra deep-fried leaves to serve
- 400ml can coconut milk
- 1 cup (250ml) fish stock

- 600g sand whiting fillets or whiting fillets (skin on), cut into 4cm pieces
- Juice of 1 lime
- Steamed basmati rice, to serve
- Coriander leaves, to serve

METHOD
- 1.
  Using a mortar and pestle, pound the garlic, chilli, ginger and turmeric to a paste.
- 2.
  Heat oil in a deep frypan over medium heat. Cook onion, stirring, for 3-4 minutes until softened. Add chilli paste and cook, stirring, for 3-4 minutes until fragrant. Add spices and curry leaves, and cook, stirring, for a further 2 minutes. Add coconut milk and stock, then bring to a simmer.
- 3.
  Cook, stirring occasionally, for 10 minutes or until slightly reduced. Add fish and cook for 4 minutes or until just cooked. Remove from heat. Season with lime juice and salt.
- 4.
  Serve curry with rice, topped with coriander and deep-fried curry leaves.

Cured kingfish with pickled baby beetroot

SERVES: 4 PREP TIME: 10MINS   COOK TIME: 5MINS
INGREDIENTS: 15   DIFFICULTY: EASY

INGREDIENTS
- 1 tsp each black peppercorns, coriander seeds and fennel seeds, crushed
- 1/2 cup (110g) sea salt fakes
- 1/2 cup (110g) caster sugar
- 1/2 cup chopped dill, plus sprigs to serve
- 500g skinless sashimi-grade kingfish fillet
- 100g sour cream
- 1/3 cup (80ml) milk
- 2 tsp lemon juice
- Flat-leaf parsley leaves, to serve

PICKLED BABY BEETROOT
- 1/3 cup (80ml) white wine vinegar
- 2 bay leaves
- 1 tsp coriander seeds
- 2 tbs caster sugar
- 3 tsp lime juice

- 1 bunch raw baby beetroot, peeled, very thinly sliced

METHOD
- 1.
Combine the spices, salt, sugar and dill in a bowl. Add fish and turn to coat. Cover and chill for 3-4 hours. Rinse and pat dry.
- 2.
For the beetroot, combine vinegar, bay, coriander seeds, sugar, 1/3 cup (80ml) water and 2 tsp salt in a pan over medium heat. Bring to the boil, then remove from heat and stir in lime. Place beetroot in a bowl and pour over pickling liquid. Season with pepper. Stand for 2 hours to pickle. Drain.
- 3.
Whisk sour cream, milk and lemon juice in a bowl until combined. Season.
- 4.
Thinly slice fish and serve with beetroot, dill and parsley drizzled with dressing.

Quick filo fish pie

SERVES: 4 PREP TIME: 10MINS   COOK TIME: 30MINS
INGREDIENTS: 12   DIFFICULTY: EASY

INGREDIENTS
- 1 cup (250ml) milk
- 2 eggs, lightly beaten
- 1 tablespoon dill, chopped
- 1/2 cup (140g) thick Greek-style yoghurt
- 1/2 teaspoon smoked paprika (pimenton)
- 16 green prawns, peeled, deveined
- 2 x 150g hot-smoked salmon fillets, flaked
- 1 cup (120g) frozen peas, thawed
- 1 baby fennel bulb, very finely chopped
- 8 sheets filo pastry
- 100g unsalted butter, melted, cooled slightly
- Lemon wedges, to serve

METHOD
- 1.
Preheat the oven to 180C.
- 2.
Combine the milk, eggs, dill, yoghurt and paprika in a bowl. Divide the prawns, salmon, peas and fennel among four 350ml ovenproof dishes, then pour in the milk mixture. Lay 2 sheets of filo on a clean work surface. Brush with butter, then

scrunch together and lightly place on top of a pie filling. Repeat with remaining filo and pies.
- 3.
  Bake for 30 minutes or until pastry is golden and crisp, and prawns are just cooked. Cool slightly. Serve pies with lemon wedges.

15-minute jacket sweet potatoes

SERVES: 4 PREP TIME: 5MINS   COOK TIME: 15MINS
INGREDIENTS: 8   DIFFICULTY: EASY

INGREDIENTS
- 4 x 350g sweet potatoes (skin-on)
- 400g can chickpeas, rinsed, drained
- 2 tbs harissa paste
- 150g marinated feta, drained, crumbled
- 2 truss tomatoes, roughly chopped
- 1/2 bunch coriander, leaves chopped
- 1 tbs finely chopped preserved lemon rind, white pith removed
- 2 tbs extra virgin olive oil

METHOD
- 1.
  Pierce potatoes all over with a fork. Place on a plate and microwave on high, turning halfway, for 8 minutes or until tender.
- 2.
  Meanwhile, preheat oven grill to high. Combine chickpeas and harissa in a bowl, then place on a baking tray and grill for 4 minutes or until crisp.
- 3.
  Slice potatoes lengthways, leaving them attached on one end to form a 'pocket'. Place on a baking tray. Top with chickpeas and feta. Grill for 4 minutes or until golden.
- 4.
  Combine tomato, coriander, preserved lemon and oil in a bowl. Season.
- 5.
  Top potatoes with salsa to serve.

Chermoula kingfish with moroccan beans

SERVES: 4 PREP TIME: 20MINS   COOK TIME: 15MINS

INGREDIENTS: 19   DIFFICULTY: EASY

INGREDIENTS
- 4 x 180g skinless kingfish fillets
- 2 tablespoons olive oil
- 1 onion, finely chopped
- 2 garlic cloves, crushed
- 720g can mixed beans, rinsed, drained
- 1/4 cup sliced roasted capsicum
- 1/2 cup (125ml) chicken stock
- 1/2 cup coriander leaves

CHERMOULA
- 2 teaspoons sweet paprika
- 1 teaspoon finely grated ginger
- 1 teaspoon dried chilli flakes
- 1 teaspoon ground cumin
- 1 teaspoon ground coriander
- 1 teaspoon ground white pepper
- 1/2 teaspoon ground cardamom
- 1/2 teaspoon ground cinnamon
- 1/2 teaspoon ground all spice
- 2 tablespoons lemon juice
- 1/4 cup (60ml) olive oil

METHOD
- 1.
  For the chermoula, place all the ingredients in a large bowl and stir to combine.
- 2.
  Add the kingfish to the chermoula and toss to coat well. Set aside to marinate for 15 minutes.
- 3.
  Heat 1 tablespoon oil in a large saucepan and add the onion. Cook, stirring, for 2-3 minutes until softened, then add the garlic and cook for a further 2 minutes or until fragrant. Remove from heat.
- 4.
  Place 1/2 cup mixed beans in a food processor and whiz until smooth. Add the bean puree to the saucepan with the capsicum, chicken stock and remaining beans. Cook for a further 2-3 minutes until warmed through. Keep warm.
- 5.
  Heat the remaining 1 tablespoon oil in a frypan over medium heat. Cook the kingfish fillets for 2-3 minutes each side until just cooked through.
- 6.

Serve the kingfish with the Moroccan bean mixture and garnish with coriander

Fish with yoghurt tartar sauce and grain salad

SERVES: 4 PREP TIME: 15MINS   COOK TIME: 20MINS
INGREDIENTS: 15   DIFFICULTY: CAPABLE

INGREDIENTS
- 1 egg, chilled
- 1 cup (150g) arrowroot
- 1 tsp ground turmeric
- Finely grated zest of 1 lemon, plus 2 tbs lemon juice
- 1 cup (280g) low-fat thick Greek-style yoghurt
- 2 tbs low-fat mayonnaise
- 16 cornichons, finely chopped
- 2 tbs chopped dill, plus extra sprigs, to serve
- 2 tbs baby capers, rinsed, drained, chopped
- 1 cup (200g) wholemeal couscous
- 1 tbs finely chopped flat-leaf parsley leaves
- 1/2 red onion, thinly sliced
- Coconut or sunflower oil, to deep-fry
- 8 x 110g flathead fillets
- Lemon wedges, to serve

METHOD
- 1.
  Lightly whisk the egg, arrowroot, turmeric, 2 tsp lemon zest, a pinch of salt and 1/2 cup (125ml) iced water in a bowl. Set aside.
- 2.
  To make the yoghurt tartar sauce, combine the yoghurt, mayonnaise, lemon juice, cornichons, dill and capers in a bowl and season. Set aside.
- 3.
  Cook the couscous according to packet instructions, then fluff with a fork. Add the parsley, onion and remaining lemon zest, then season and stir to combine. Cover and keep warm.
- 4.
  Half-fill a large saucepan with the oil and heat to 160°C (a cube of bread will turn golden in 45 seconds when the oil is hot enough). Season the fish, then dip in the batter, shaking off any excess. Deep-fry for 2-4 minutes until golden and cooked through. Drain on paper towel.

- 5.
  Divide lemon couscous among serving plates and top with fish. Serve with the sauce, extra dill and lemon wedges.

Chargrilled swordfish with grape, almond & barley salad

SERVES: 4 PREP TIME: 35MINS COOK TIME: 35MINS
INGREDIENTS: 11   DIFFICULTY: EASY

INGREDIENTS
- 1 1/4 cups (280g) pearl barley, rinsed
- Finely grated zest and juice of 1/2 lemon
- 2 tsp dried Italian herbs
- 100ml olive oil
- 4 x 220g swordfish fillets
- 1 1/2 tbs red wine vinegar
- 225g red seedless grapes, halved
- 1/2 cup (80g) roasted almonds, chopped
- 1/3 cup (60g) currants, soaked in warm water for 10 minutes, drained
- 1 bunch flat-leaf parsley, leaves picked
- 2 celery stalks, chopped

METHOD
- 1.
  Cook barley in a saucepan of boiling salted water for 25-30 minutes until tender. Drain, then set aside to cool.
- 2.
  Meanwhile, combine lemon zest, 1 tsp Italian herbs and 2 tbs oil in a bowl. Season, add the swordfish and turn to coat, then set aside for 15 minutes to marinate.
- 3.
  To make the dressing, whisk vinegar, lemon juice and remaining 1/4 cup (60ml) oil together, season and set aside.
- 4.
  Preheat a barbecue or chargrill pan to high. Cook swordfish for 3 minutes each side or until just cooked. Rest, loosely covered with foil, for 5 minutes.
- 5.
  Combine barley, grapes, almonds, currants, parsley, celery and remaining 1 tsp Italian herbs. Drizzle over dressing and toss to combine.
- 6.
  Serve salad topped with swordfish.

Whole baked snapper with ginger and chilli

SERVES: 4 PREP TIME: 10MINS   COOK TIME: 30MINS
INGREDIENTS: 8   DIFFICULTY: EASY

INGREDIENTS
- 4 lemons, sliced, plus wedges to serve
- 6cm piece ginger, thinly sliced
- 2 garlic cloves, thinly sliced
- 2 long red chillies, sliced
- 1 cup coriander leaves, plus extra to serve
- 1/3 cup (80ml) olive oil
- 2 whole snapper, cleaned (ask your fishmonger to do this), skin scored
- Thinly sliced spring onion and mint leaves, to serve

METHOD
- 1.
  Preheat a barbecue or chargrill to high.
- 2.
  Place 2 sheets of foil on a workbench and top each with a sheet of baking paper.
- 3.
  Divide half the lemon slices, ginger, garlic, chilli, coriander and oil between the paper and top with the fish. Cover with remaining lemon slices, ginger, garlic, chilli, coriander and oil, then season. Seal the parcels and cook on the barbecue for 25-30 minutes until cooked.
- 4.
  Open the parcels and top with spring onion, herbs and lemon wedges.

Spiced pork chop schnitzel with pear and fennel slaw

SERVES: 4 PREP TIME: -   COOK TIME: -
INGREDIENTS: 14   DIFFICULTY: EASY

INGREDIENTS
- 1 cup (50g) panko breadcrumbs
- 1/2 cup chopped flat-leaf parsley leaves
- 1 1/2 tsp each coriander, fennel and cumin seeds, crushed
- 1 eggwhite

- 1/4 cup (70g) Dijon mustard
- 4 x 200g pork loin chops
- Sunflower oil, to shallow-fry
- Aioli, to serve

PEAR AND FENNEL SLAW
- 1 fennel bulb, thinly sliced
- 1 firm pear, cut into batons
- 1 tbs extra virgin olive oil
- Juice of 1/2 lemon
- 2 tbs thick Greek-style yoghurt
- 1 tsp nigella seeds

METHOD
1. Combine panko, parsley and spices in a bowl. Whisk eggwhite and mustard in a separate bowl. Brush pork with mustard, then coat in breadcrumbs.
2. Heat 1cm oil in a heavy-based frypan over medium-high heat. Cook pork for 3 minutes each side or until golden and cooked through. Drain on paper towel.
3. Combine all slaw ingredients in a bowl.
4. Serve pork chops with slaw and aioli.

Aubergine & chickpea stew

Prep: 15 mins **Cook:** 8 hrs - 10 hrs plus overnight soaking

Serves 4-6

Ingredients

- 200g dried chickpeas, soaked for 6-8 hours
- 2 tbsp extra virgin olive oil, plus extra to serve (optional)
- 2 onions, finely sliced
- 6 garlic cloves, crushed
- 1 tbsp baharat
- 1 tsp ground cinnamon
- 1 small bunch of flat-leaf parsley, stalks finely chopped, leaves roughly chopped, to serve
- 3 medium aubergines, sliced into 2cm rounds
- 2 x 400g cans chopped tomatoes
- 1 lemon, juiced
- 50g pine nuts, toasted, to serve

- pitta breads or flatbreads, to serve (optional)

Method

STEP 1

Drain the chickpeas and bring to the boil in a pan of salted water. Cook for 10 mins, then drain.

STEP 2

Heat the oil in a frying pan over a medium heat and fry the onions for 10 mins, or until beginning to soften. Stir in the garlic, baharat and cinnamon and cook for 1 min. Tip the onion mixture into a slow cooker and add the chickpeas, parsley stalks, aubergines, tomatoes and a can of water. Season. Cover and cook on high for 2 hrs, then turn the heat to low and cook for 6-8 hrs more until the mixture has reduced slightly and the chickpeas and aubergines are really tender.

STEP 3

Stir in the lemon juice, then scatter over the pine nuts and parsley leaves. Drizzle over some extra olive oil and serve with pitta breads or flatbreads, if you like.

Lamb jalfrezi with cumin rice

Prep:20 mins Cook:40 mins

Serves 4

Ingredients

- 2 tsp cold-pressed rapeseed oil
- 600g lean lamb leg steak , trimmed of all visible fat, diced
- 1 large onion , finely chopped
- 2 large garlic cloves , chopped
- 50g ginger , shredded
- 2 tsp ground coriander
- 2 tsp cumin seeds
- 400g can chopped tomatoes
- 1 tbsp vegetable bouillon powder
- 2 large peppers , seeded and diced
- 1 medium onion , cut into wedges
- 1 red or green chilli , deseeded and sliced
- 25g fresh coriander , chopped

For the rice

- 250g brown basmati rice

- 1-2 tsp cumin seeds

Method

STEP 1

Heat 1 tsp oil a large wide non-stick frying pan and fry the lamb for about 4 mins, stirring until browned. Scoop from the pan and set aside.

STEP 2

Add the chopped onion, garlic and half the shredded ginger to the pan and fry for 5 mins until softened. If the onions start to catch, add a splash of water. Add the spices and cook for a minute more. Tip in the tomatoes and half a can of water along with the bouillon, then blitz everything in the pan with a hand blender until really smooth. Stir in the lamb, then cover and simmer over a low-medium heat for 25 mins until tender.

STEP 3

Meanwhile boil the rice with the cumin seeds in a pan of water for 25 mins until tender. Drain.

STEP 4

Heat the remaining oil in a non-stick wok. Add the peppers, onion wedges, chilli and remaining ginger, and stir-fry everything together for around 5 mins, or until tender, but still with some bite. Stir into the curry with the coriander and serve with the rice. If you're following our Healthy Diet Plan, eat two portions of the curry and rice now, then chill the rest for another day. To serve the second night, just reheat portions in the microwave on plates.

Chicken & sweetcorn tacos

Prep: 30 mins **Cook:** 30 mins

Serves 4, plus 2 lunchboxes

Ingredients

- 250g plain flour , plus extra for dusting
- 2 tbsp rapeseed oil
- 2 tbsp taco or fajita seasoning (see tip, below)
- 5-6 skinless chicken breasts, sliced

- ¼ red cabbage, finely shredded
- 3 limes, 1 juiced, 2 cut into wedges
- small bunch of coriander, chopped
- 4 sweetcorn cob, kernels sliced off, or 400g frozen sweetcorn
- 400g can black beans, drained and rinsed
- 2 garlic cloves, crushed
- 4 tbsp fat-free yogurt, to serve
- chilli sauce, to serve

Method

STEP 1

Combine the flour with half the oil and a small pinch of salt in a bowl. Pour over 125-150ml warm water, then bring together into a soft dough with your hands. Cut into six equal pieces, then cut four of the pieces in half again, so you have eight small pieces and two large. Roll all the pieces out on a floured work surface until they're as thin as you can get them.

STEP 2

Heat a dry frying pan over a medium-high heat and cook the small and large tortillas for 2-3 mins on each side until golden and toasted (do this one at a time). Leave the large tortillas to cool, then cover and reserve for use in the lunchboxes (see tip below). Keep the small tortillas warm in foil.

STEP 3

Sprinkle the taco seasoning over the chicken in a bowl, and toss to combine. Toss the cabbage with the lime juice, half the coriander and some seasoning in another bowl, then leave to pickle.

STEP 4

Meanwhile, heat two frying pans over a high heat. Divide the remaining oil between the pans and fry the sweetcorn and a pinch of salt until sizzling and turning golden, stirring occasionally – you want the sweetcorn to char slightly, as this adds flavour, so you may need to leave it to cook undisturbed for a bit. While the sweetcorn cooks and chars, fry the chicken in the larger pan until cooked through and golden (you may need to do this in batches).

STEP 5

Tip the black beans and garlic into the sweetcorn and stir to warm through. Squeeze over two of the lime wedges.

STEP 6

Reserve two spoonfuls each of the chicken (about 1 chicken breast) and sweetcorn mix for use in the lunchboxes (see tip, below), then serve the rest in bowls alongside the cabbage, yogurt, lime wedges, remaining coriander, chilli sauce and tortillas for everyone to dig into.

Red pepper, squash & harissa soup

Prep: 15 mins **Cook:** 1 hr

Serves 6

Ingredients

- 1 small butternut squash (about 600-700g), peeled and cut into chunks
- 2 red pepper, roughly chopped
- 2 red onion, roughly chopped
- 3 tbsp rapeseed oil
- 3 garlic cloves in their skins
- 1 tbsp ground coriander
- 2 tsp ground cumin
- 1.2l chicken or vegetable stock
- 2 tbsp harissa paste
- 50ml double cream

Method

STEP 1

Heat oven to 180C/160C fan/gas 4. Put all the veg on a large baking tray and toss together with rapeseed oil, garlic cloves in their skins, ground coriander, ground cumin and some seasoning. Roast for 45 mins, moving the veg around in the tray after 30 mins, until soft and starting to caramelise. Squeeze the garlic cloves out of their skins. Tip everything into a large pan. Add the chicken or vegetable stock, harissa paste and double cream. Bring to a simmer and bubble for a few mins. Blitz the soup in a blender, check the seasoning and add more liquid if you need to. Serve swirled with extra cream and harissa.

Roast chicken traybake

Prep: 10 mins **Cook:** 1 hr and 5 mins

Serves 2

Ingredients

- 2 red onions (320g), sliced across into rings
- 1 large red pepper, deseeded and chopped into 3cm pieces
- 300g potatoes, peeled and cut into 3cm chunks
- 2 tbsp rapeseed oil
- 4 bone-in chicken thighs, skin and any fat removed
- 1 lime, zested and juiced
- 3 large garlic cloves, finely grated
- 1 tsp smoked paprika
- 1 tsp thyme leaves
- 2 tsp vegetable bouillon powder
- 200g long stem broccoli, stem cut into lengths if very thick

Method

STEP 1

Heat the oven to 200C/180C fan/gas 6. Put the onion, pepper, potatoes and oil in a non-stick roasting tin and toss everything together. Roast for 15 mins while you rub the chicken with the lime zest, garlic, paprika and thyme. Take the veg from the oven, stir, then snuggle the chicken thighs among the veg, covering them with some of the onions so they don't dry out as it roasts for 40 mins.

STEP 2

As you approach the end of the cooking time, mix 200ml boiling water with the bouillon powder. Take the roasting tin from the oven, add the broccoli to the tin, and pour over the hot stock followed by the lime juice, then quickly cover with the foil and put back in the oven for 10 more mins until the broccoli is just tender.

Lemon dressed salmon with leek & broad bean purée

Prep: 10 mins **Cook:** 20 mins

Serves 2

Ingredients

- ½ lemon, zested and juiced
- 1 tbsp drained capers
- 1 tbsp rapeseed oil, plus 1 tsp
- 1 large leek (about 275g), sliced
- 200g frozen baby broad beans
- 2 skin-on wild salmon fillets
- 250g bag spinach
- 12 small basil leaves

- 170g baby potatoes (halved if larger), boiled

Method

STEP 1

Mix the lemon zest and juice with the capers and 1 tbsp oil to make the dressing. Boil the leek and beans together with a little salt for 6-8 mins until tender. Lift them out with a slotted spoon, set aside, then add the spinach to the pan to wilt for 1-2 mins.

STEP 2

Meanwhile, heat 1 tsp oil in a non-stick pan over a medium heat and fry the salmon, skin-side down for 4 mins. Turn to cook the other side for 2-4 mins, or until just cooked through. Add a couple of spoonfuls of the broad beans to the dressing then, using a hand blender, small food processor or a fork, blitz the rest of the beans with the leek to a purée, adding a splash of cooking water if it's too thick. Drain the spinach well and divide between plates, spoon on the purée, then top with salmon. Spoon over the dressing, scatter over the basil and serve with potatoes.

Healthier potato salad

Prep: 10 mins **Cook:** 10 mins

Serves 6

Ingredients

- 750g Charlotte new potato , skins left on
- 2 tbsp good-quality mayonnaise (we used Hellmann's)
- 3 tbsp natural yogurt
- 3 tbsp half-fat crème fraîche
- 1 tsp Dijon mustard
- 1 tbsp semi-skimmed milk
- 8 spring onions , ends trimmed, halved lengthways and sliced
- 3 tbsp snipped chive
- 1 tbsp chopped tarragon

Method

STEP 1

Cut the potatoes into 2.5-3cm chunks (step 1), so that they are all the same size and will cook evenly. Put them in a pan of boiling water. Once the water has returned to the boil, lower the heat slightly and cook for about 10 mins or until just cooked and still keeping their shape. Tip them into a colander to drain well, then transfer to a large bowl.

STEP 2

While the potatoes are cooking, mix together the mayonnaise, yogurt, crème fraîche, mustard and milk. Add the spring onions, then most of the chives and tarragon to the potatoes (step 2). Season with pepper and a pinch of salt.

STEP 3

Spoon the dressing over the potatoes while they are still warm (step 3), then toss gently together so that they are well coated but don't break up. Tip the potato salad into a serving bowl and scatter over the remaining chives and tarragon. Serve cold – but the flavour is best if not served straight from the fridge.

Cabbage soup

Prep: 20 mins **Cook:** 50 mins

Serves 6

Ingredients

- 2 tbsp olive oil
- 1 large onion , finely chopped
- 2 celery sticks , finely chopped
- 1 large carrot , finely chopped
- 70g smoked pancetta , diced (optional)
- 1 large Savoy cabbage , shredded
- 2 fat garlic cloves , crushed
- 1 heaped tsp sweet smoked paprika
- 1 tbsp finely chopped rosemary
- 1 x 400g can chopped tomatoes
- 1.7l hot vegetable stock
- 1 x 400g can chickpeas , drained and rinsed
- shaved parmesan (or vegetarian alternative), to serve (optional)
- crusty bread , to serve (optional)

Method

STEP 1

Heat the oil in a casserole pot over a low heat. Add the onion, celery and carrot, along with a generous pinch of salt, and fry gently for 15 mins, or until the veg begins to soften. If you're using pancetta, add it to the pan, turn up the heat and fry for a few mins more until turning golden brown. Tip in the cabbage and fry for 5 mins, then stir through the garlic, paprika and rosemary and cook for 1 min more.

STEP 2

Tip the chopped tomatoes and stock into the pan. Bring to a simmer, then cook, uncovered, for 30 mins, adding the chickpeas for the final 10 mins. Season generously with salt and black pepper.

STEP 3

Ladle the soup into six deep bowls. Serve with the shaved parmesan and crusty bread, if you like.

Red cabbage, cauliflower & coconut dhal

Prep: 20 mins **Cook:** 1 hr and 10 mins

Serves 4

Ingredients

- 1 small cauliflower , broken into small florets
- 2 tbsp rapeseed oil
- 1 onion , finely chopped
- 200g red cabbage , sliced
- thumb-sized piece of ginger , peeled and grated
- 2 garlic cloves , crushed
- ½ tsp chilli powder
- ½ tsp turmeric
- 1 tsp garam masala
- 1 tsp black mustard seeds
- small handful of curry leaves
- 300g split red lentils
- 1.25 litres hot low-salt vegetable stock
- 1 lime , juiced
- 2 tbsp coconut flakes, toasted
- coriander leaves and chopped chilli, to serve (optional)

Method

STEP 1

Heat the oven to 180C/160C fan/gas 4. Toss the cauliflower, 1 tbsp of the oil and some seasoning in a roasting tin. Roast for 25-30 mins, then set aside.

STEP 2

Heat the remaining oil in a large saucepan and add the onion and cabbage. Fry gently over a medium heat for 10 mins. Add the ginger, garlic, spices and curry leaves and fry for 2 mins. Stir through the lentils and most of the cauliflower. Pour over the stock, bring to the boil, lower to a simmer and cook uncovered for 40 mins. Stir through the lime juice and season to taste. Ladle into bowls, top with the remaining cauliflower, toasted coconut and coriander and chilli, if using.

Swedish meatballs

Prep: 10 mins **Cook:** 25 mins plus cooling and chilling

Serves 4

Ingredients

- 2 tbsp rapeseed oil
- 1 onion , finely chopped
- 1 small garlic clove , finely grated
- 375g lean pork mince
- 1 medium egg yolk
- grating of nutmeg
- 50g fine fresh breadcrumbs
- 300ml hot low-salt beef stock
- ½ tbsp Dijon mustard
- 2 tbsp fat-free natural yogurt
- 400g spring greens , shredded
- lingonberry or cranberry sauce , to serve

Method

STEP 1

Put 1 tbsp rapeseed oil in a frying pan over a medium heat. Add the onion and fry for 10 mins or until soft and translucent. Add the garlic and cook for 1 min. Leave to cool.

STEP 2

Mix the cooled onions, pork mince, egg yolk, a good grating of nutmeg and the breadcrumbs in a bowl with your hands until well combined. Form into 12 balls and chill for 15 mins.

STEP 3

Heat the remaining oil in a frying pan and fry the meatballs for 5 mins over a medium heat, turning often until golden. Pour over the stock and bubble for 8-10 mins or until it has reduced a little. Stir through the mustard and yogurt.

STEP 4

Steam the greens for 5 mins or until tender. Serve the meatballs with the greens and a dollop of the sauce.

Linguine with avocado, tomato & lime

Prep: 20 mins **Cook:** 10 mins

Serves 2

Ingredients

- 115g wholemeal linguine
- 1 lime, zested and juiced
- 1 avocado, stoned, peeled, and chopped
- 2 large ripe tomatoes, chopped
- ½ pack fresh coriander, chopped
- 1 red onion, finely chopped
- 1 red chilli, deseeded and finely chopped (optional)

Method

STEP 1

Cook the pasta according to pack instructions – about 10 mins. Meanwhile, put the lime juice and zest in a medium bowl with the avocado, tomatoes, coriander, onion and chilli, if using, and mix well.

STEP 2

Drain the pasta, toss into the bowl and mix well. Serve straight away while still warm, or cold.

Blackberry & apple oat bake

Prep: 15 mins **Cook:** 50 mins

Serves 6

Ingredients

- 500ml semi-skimmed milk
- 2 small cinnamon sticks
- 6 cardamom pods , bashed
- 2 Gala apples , peeled, cored and cut into 1cm cubes
- 200g jumbo porridge oats
- 1 egg , beaten

- 1 tsp vanilla extract
- 1 tsp baking powder
- 100g pecans, roughly chopped
- 320g blackberries
- milk or fat-free yogurt and maple syrup, to serve

Method

STEP 1

Heat the oven to 200C/180C fan/gas 6. Put the milk, spices and apple in a small saucepan. Cover, gently bring to the boil and simmer for 10-12 mins. Set aside to infuse for at least 15 mins.

STEP 2

Remove and discard the spices, then pour the apples and milk into a large bowl and roughly crush the apples with the back of a fork. Mix in the oats, egg, vanilla, baking powder, pecans and blackberries.

STEP 3

Tip into a 2-litre ovenproof dish and bake for about 30-35 mins until piping hot in the middle. Serve with milk or yogurt and maple syrup, if you like.

Salmon pesto traybake with baby roast potatoes

Prep: 5 mins **Cook:** 45 mins

Serves 2 adults + 2 children

Ingredients

- 500g baby new potatoes, cut in half
- 1 tsp olive oil
- 2 large courgettes, cut into small chunks
- 1 red pepper, cut into small chunks
- 1 spring onion, finely sliced
- 25g pine nuts
- 3-4 salmon fillets
- juice ½ lemon
- 1½ - 2 tbsp pesto

Method

STEP 1

Boil the potatoes for 10 mins until tender, then drain. Heat oven to 200C/180C fan/gas 6. Toss the potatoes in the oil, then transfer to a baking tray. Roast for 20 mins. Push the potatoes to one side and put the courgette, pepper, spring onion and pine nuts down the middle of the tray. Put the salmon on the other side. Squeeze lemon juice over the fillets and the vegetables (not including the potatoes). Season everything with pepper. Spread each of the salmon fillets with pesto and return the tray to the oven for 12-15 mins until everything is cooked through.

Easy butter chicken

Prep: 15 mins **Cook:** 35 mins plus at least 1 hr marinating

Serves 4

Ingredients

- 500g skinless boneless chicken thighs

For the marinade

- 1 lemon, juiced
- 2 tsp ground cumin
- 2 tsp paprika
- 1-2 tsp hot chilli powder
- 200g natural yogurt

For the curry

- 2 tbsp vegetable oil
- 1 large onion, chopped
- 3 garlic cloves, crushed
- 1 green chilli, deseeded and finely chopped (optional)
- thumb-sized piece ginger, grated
- 1 tsp garam masala
- 2 tsp ground fenugreek
- 3 tbsp tomato purée
- 300ml chicken stock
- 50g flaked almonds, toasted

To serve (optional)

- cooked basmati rice
- naan bread
- mango chutney or lime pickle
- fresh coriander
- lime wedges

Method

STEP 1

In a medium bowl, mix all the marinade ingredients with some seasoning. Chop the chicken into bite-sized pieces and toss with the marinade. Cover and chill in the fridge for 1 hr or overnight.

STEP 2

In a large, heavy saucepan, heat the oil. Add the onion, garlic, green chilli, ginger and some seasoning. Fry on a medium heat for 10 mins or until soft.

STEP 3

Add the spices with the tomato purée, cook for a further 2 mins until fragrant, then add the stock and marinated chicken. Cook for 15 mins, then add any remaining marinade left in the bowl. Simmer for 5 mins, then sprinkle with the toasted almonds. Serve with rice, naan bread, chutney, coriander and lime wedges, if you like.

Curried chicken & new potato traybake

Prep: 15 mins **Cook:** 45 mins plus marinating

Serves 4

Ingredients

- 8 chicken drumsticks
- 3 tbsp olive oil
- 1 tsp garlic paste
- 1 tsp ginger paste
- 1 tsp garam masala
- 1 tsp turmeric
- 150ml pot natural yogurt
- 500g new potatoes, halved
- 4 large tomatoes, roughly chopped
- 1 red onion, finely chopped
- small pack coriander, roughly chopped

Method

STEP 1

Put the drumsticks in a large bowl with 1 tbsp oil, the garlic, ginger, garam masala, turmeric and 2 tbsp yogurt. Toss together with your hands until coated. Leave to marinate for at least 30 mins (can be left in the fridge overnight). Heat oven to 180C/160C fan/gas 4.

STEP 2

Put the potatoes in a large roasting tin with the remaining oil and plenty of seasoning. Add the chicken drumsticks and bake for 40-45 mins until cooked and golden.

STEP 3

Scatter the tomatoes, onion, coriander and some seasoning over the chicken and potatoes, with the remaining yogurt served on the side.

Italian borlotti bean, pumpkin & farro soup

Prep: 15 mins **Cook:** 35 mins

Serves 6

Ingredients

- 4 tbsp extra virgin olive oil , plus extra to serve
- 1 onion , finely chopped
- 1 celery stick , cut into chunks
- 750g pumpkin or squash, peeled, deseeded and cut into small chunks
- 1 carrot , peeled and cut into chunks
- 3 garlic cloves , chopped
- 3 tbsp tomato purée
- 1.2l chicken stock or vegetable stock
- 75g farro or mixed grains (such as barley or spelt)
- 50-80g parmesan rinds or vegetarian alternative (optional), plus a few shavings to serve
- 400g can borlotti beans , drained
- 2 handfuls baby spinach
- 2 tbsp chopped parsley or 8 whole sage leaves

Method

STEP 1

Heat the oil in a heavy-bottomed saucepan. Add the onion, celery, pumpkin or squash and carrot and cook until the vegetables have some colour. Add a splash of water and some seasoning, then cover the pan and let the vegetables cook over a very low heat for 5 mins.

STEP 2

Add the garlic and cook for another couple of mins, then add the tomato purée, stock, mixed grains, parmesan rinds, if using, and some seasoning. Simmer for about 15 mins (or until the grains are cooked), adding the beans for the final 5 mins. In the last few mins, add the spinach, then taste for seasoning.

STEP 3

If you want to use sage, fry the leaves whole in a little olive oil before adding to the soup. If you prefer to use parsley, you can just add it directly to the soup. Serve with shavings of parmesan and a drizzle of extra virgin olive oil on top of each bowlful. Remove the parmesan rinds and serve.

Chana masala with pomegranate raita

Prep:10 mins **Cook:**35 mins

Serves 2

Ingredients

- 1 tbsp rapeseed oil
- 2 onions , halved and thinly sliced
- 1 tbsp chopped ginger
- 2 large garlic cloves , finely grated or crushed
- 1 green chilli , halved, deseeded and thinly sliced
- ½ tsp cumin seeds
- ½ tsp mustard seeds
- ½ tsp garam masala
- ½ tsp turmeric
- 1 tsp ground coriander
- 400g can chickpeas , undrained
- 4 small tomatoes (about 160g), cut into wedges
- 2 tsp vegetable bouillon powder
- cooked wholegrain rice , to serve (optional)

For the pomegranate raita

- 150ml plain bio yogurt
- 25g pomegranate seeds
- 2 tbsp finely chopped coriander , plus extra leaves to serve

Method

STEP 1

Heat the oil in a large non-stick pan, then cook the onions, ginger, garlic and chilli for 15-20 mins.

STEP 2

Add the spices, chickpeas, the liquid from the can, ¾ can cold water, the tomatoes and bouillon. Cover and simmer for 10 mins.

STEP 3

Meanwhile, mix the ingredients for the raita in a small bowl, reserving a few coriander leaves. Roughly mash some of the curry to thicken it. Spoon into bowls with rice, if you like. Scatter over the reserved coriander and serve with the raita on the side.

Leek, pea & watercress soup

Prep: 10 mins **Cook:** 22 mins

Serves 4

Ingredients

- 1 tbsp olive oil , plus a drizzle to serve
- 2 leeks , finely sliced
- 4 small garlic cloves , crushed
- 650-800ml hot veg stock
- 80g watercress
- 400g frozen peas
- 1 small lemon , zested and juiced
- small bunch of parsley , finely chopped
- dairy-free crème fraîche and crusty bread, to serve (optional)

Method

STEP 1

Heat the oil in a large saucepan over a medium heat. Add the leeks and garlic and fry for 7-10 mins or until softened and translucent.

STEP 2

Pour in the hot stock and simmer for 5-10 mins. Stir through the watercress, reserving a few leaves for garnish, then the peas, and cook for 5 mins until wilted. Use a hand blender or processor and whizz until smooth. Stir through the lemon juice and zest, then season to taste. Stir through half the parsley. Ladle into bowls and top with the remaining parsley, reserved watercress and a drizzle of olive oil. Swirl through some crème fraîche, then serve with crusty bread, if you like.

Saucy bean baked eggs

Prep: 5 mins Cook: 20 mins

Serves 2

Ingredients

- 2 x 400g cans cherry tomatoes
- 400g can mixed bean salad, drained
- 200g baby spinach
- 4 medium eggs
- 50g thinly sliced smoked ham, torn
- wholemeal rye bread, to serve (optional)

Method

STEP 1

Tip the tomatoes and bean salad into an ovenproof frying pan or shallow flameproof casserole dish. Simmer for 10 mins, or until reduced. Stir in the spinach and cook for 5 mins more until wilted.

STEP 2

Heat the grill to medium. Make four indentations in the mixture using the back of a spoon, then crack one egg in each. Nestle the ham in the mixture, then grill for 4-5 mins, or until the whites are set and the yolks runny. Serve with rye bread, if you like.

Crunchy oat clusters with peach & yogurt

Prep: 5 mins Cook: 15 mins - 20 mins

Serves 6

Ingredients

- 50g (about 7) soft ready-to-eat dried apricots (we used Crazy Jack organic, because they are sulphur-free)
- ½ tbsp rapeseed oil
- 3 large eggs, whites only (see tip to use up the yolks)

- 200g porridge oats
- 1 tbsp cinnamon
- 1 tbsp vanilla extract
- 25g desiccated coconut
- 25g flaked almonds
- 25g pumpkin seeds
- 3 x 120g pots bio yogurt
- 3 peaches, to serve

Method

STEP 1

Heat oven to 180C/160C fan/gas 4 and line a large baking tray with baking parchment.

STEP 2

Tip the apricots, oil and egg whites into a bowl (see tip box for how to use up the egg yolks), then blitz with a hand blender until very smooth. Stir in the oats, cinnamon and vanilla, then fold through the desiccated coconut, almonds and pumpkin seeds.

STEP 3

Pinch clusters of the mixture together to create texture in the granola, then scatter over the lined baking tray in a single layer. Bake for 15 mins, then toss (turning the larger pieces) and bake for a further 10 mins until golden and crunchy.

STEP 4

Cool the granola completely on the tray, then pack into a large airtight jar or container. If you're following our Healthy Diet Plan, serve two portions over three days, filling the base of each bowl with yogurt (½ pot for each portion) and topping with half a peach, sliced.

Overnight oats

Prep: 10 mins **Serves 1**

Ingredients

- ¼ tsp ground cinnamon
- 50g rolled porridge oats
- 2 tbsp natural yogurt
- 50g mixed berries
- drizzle of honey
- ½ tbsp nut butter (we used almond)

Method

STEP 1

The night before serving, stir the cinnamon and 100ml water (or milk) into your oats with a pinch of salt.

STEP 2

The next day, loosen with a little more water (or milk) if needed. Top with the yogurt, berries, a drizzle of honey and the nut butter.

Moroccan chicken with fennel & olives

Prep: 10 mins **Cook:** 45 mins

Serves 2

Ingredients

- ½ lemon
- 1 tbsp rapeseed oil
- 1 large onion , finely chopped
- 1 fennel bulb , halved and thinly sliced, fronds reserved
- thumb-sized piece ginger , finely chopped
- 2 large garlic cloves , chopped
- 4 skinless chicken thigh fillets, halved and any fat trimmed
- ½ tsp ground cinnamon
- ½ tsp turmeric
- 1 tsp ground cumin
- 1 tsp ground coriander
- 400ml hot vegetable stock , made with 2 tsp bouillon powder
- 2 tomatoes , cut into wedges
- 6 Kalamata or green olives , pitted and halved
- generous handful coriander , chopped, plus extra to serve
- 70g wholewheat couscous
- 400g can chickpeas , drained and rinsed

Method

STEP 1

Squeeze the lemon over a bowl and set the bowl aside. Cut the lemon in two, remove the pith from one half and chop the rind.

STEP 2

Heat the oil in a non-stick frying pan and fry the onion, fennel, ginger and garlic until soft. Add the chicken and fry for a few mins more until just browned.

STEP 3

Add the lemon rind and spices, then pour in the stock. Cover and simmer for 25 mins, then add the tomatoes, olives, coriander and half the lemon juice. Cook for 5 mins more until the fennel and chicken are tender and the sauce reduced.

STEP 4

Meanwhile, cook the couscous following pack instructions and stir in the chickpeas. Add more lemon juice to taste, then serve the tagine with the couscous, extra coriander and fennel fronds.

Beetroot, cumin & coriander soup with yogurt and hazelnut dukkah

Prep: 10 mins **Cook:** 1 hr and 10 mins

Serves 4

Ingredients

- 2 tbsp olive oil
- 2 red onions , cut into wedges
- 1kg raw beetroot , peeled and cut into wedges
- 1 tsp chilli flakes
- 1 tbsp cumin seeds , plus 1 tsp
- 1 ½ tbsp coriander seeds
- 1 tbsp red wine vinegar
- 1.2l vegetable stock (we used Bouillon)
- 30g hazelnuts
- 1 tbsp sesame seeds
- 4 tbsp natural yogurt

Method

STEP 1

Heat the oil in a large saucepan. Add the onions, beetroot and a pinch of salt and cook for 10 mins, then turn up the heat and add the chilli flakes and 1 tbsp each of the cumin and coriander seeds. Cook until aromatic, then add the vinegar and give everything a good stir. Pour in the stock and bring to the boil, then cover and simmer for 45 mins-1 hr until a knife can be easily inserted into a beetroot wedge; uncover the pan halfway through cooking to reduce the soup.

STEP 2

Meanwhile, make the dukkah. Put the hazelnuts, sesame seeds and the remaining cumin and coriander into a dry frying pan and gently toast until the hazelnuts are golden. Add a pinch of salt and crush with a pestle and mortar (alternatively, use a knife to roughly chop the nuts).

STEP 3

Blitz the soup with a hand blender and season to taste. Divide between four bowls, then top with a swirl of the yogurt and a sprinkling of hazelnut dukkah.

Caesar pitta

Prep: 10 mins No cook

Serves 1

Ingredients

- 1 tsp lemon juice
- ½ small garlic clove, crushed
- 1 tbsp fat-free Greek yogurt
- 1 tbsp lighter mayonnaise
- ¼ tsp mustard powder
- 1 brown anchovy, rinsed and finely chopped
- ½ tbsp grated parmesan
- 1 small skinless cooked chicken breast, or 80g cooked chicken, shredded
- ¼ small cucumber, cubed
- 3 cherry tomatoes, halved
- 4 Little Gem lettuce leaves, shredded
- 1 wholemeal pitta bread

Method

STEP 1

Whisk the lemon juice, garlic, yogurt, mayonnaise, mustard powder, anchovy, parmesan and 2-3 tbsp water together with a good grinding of black pepper. Toss in the chicken, cucumber, tomatoes and lettuce, until everything is well coated. Toast the pitta and split, then stuff with the salad and chicken mixture.

Peanut butter overnight oats

Prep: 5 mins plus overnight soaking, no cook

Serves 1

Ingredients

- 80g frozen raspberries
- 50g rolled porridge oats
- 1 tsp maple syrup
- 1 tbsp peanut butter

Method

STEP 1

Stir the frozen raspberries into your oats with 150ml water and a pinch of salt, then cover and chill in the fridge overnight.

STEP 2

The next day, mix in the maple syrup, then top the oats with the peanut butter.

Herb & ricotta chicken with mushroom rice

Prep: 10 mins **Cook:** 35 mins

Serves 2

Ingredients

- 2 ½ tsp rapeseed oil
- 2 leeks, washed and sliced
- 180g closed cup mushrooms, roughly sliced
- 125g brown basmati rice
- 3 thyme sprigs
- 2 tsp vegetable bouillon powder
- 60g ricotta
- good handful basil, chopped, plus a few small leaves, to serve
- 1 garlic clove, finely grated
- 10g parmesan, finely grated
- 2 skinless chicken breast fillets
- handful chopped parsley, plus extra to serve

Method

STEP 1

Heat 1 tsp oil in a large pan, then add the leeks and stir-fry until softened and charred around the edges. Tip in the mushrooms and cook until softened.

STEP 2

Stir in the rice and thyme sprigs with the bouillon powder, then pour in 700ml boiling water. Cover and leave to simmer for 30 mins.

STEP 3

While the rice is cooking, mix the ricotta with the basil, garlic and parmesan. Cut a slash in the top of each chicken breast, then slightly open out and spoon on the ricotta mix. Heat the remaining 1½ tsp oil in a small frying pan, then add the chicken, ricotta-side up. Cover with a lid and cook over a low heat for 10 mins. Once cooked, turn off the heat and leave while you wait for the rice to finish cooking.

STEP 4

Pour any juices from the chicken into the rice, then cook for 5 mins more to get rid of any excess moisture. Stir the parsley through the rice, remove the thyme sprigs and spoon onto two plates, top with the chicken, and scatter over the basil and more parsley leaves.

Indian chickpeas with poached eggs

Prep: 5 mins **Cook:** 10 mins

Serves 2

Ingredients

- 1 tbsp rapeseed oil
- 2 garlic cloves, chopped
- 1 yellow pepper, deseeded and diced
- ½ - 1 red chilli, deseeded and chopped
- ½ bunch spring onions (about 5), tops and whites sliced but kept separate
- 1 tsp cumin, plus a little extra to serve (optional)
- 1 tsp coriander
- ½ tsp turmeric
- 3 tomatoes, cut into wedges
- ⅓ pack coriander, chopped
- 400g can chickpeas in water, drained but liquid reserved
- ½ tsp reduced-salt bouillon powder (we used Marigold)
- 4 large eggs

Method

STEP 1

Heat the oil in a non-stick sauté pan, add the garlic, pepper, chilli and the whites from the spring onions, and fry for 5 mins over a medium-high heat. Meanwhile, put a large pan of water on to boil.

STEP 2

Add the spices, tomatoes, most of the coriander and the chickpeas to the sauté pan and cook for 1-2 mins more. Stir in the bouillon powder and enough liquid from the chickpeas to moisten everything, and leave to simmer gently.

STEP 3

Once the water is at a rolling boil, crack in your eggs and poach for 2 mins, then remove with a slotted spoon. Stir the spring onion tops into the chickpeas, then very lightly crush a few of the chickpeas with a fork or potato masher. Spoon the chickpea mixture onto plates, scatter with the reserved coriander and top with the eggs. Serve with an extra sprinkle of cumin, if you like.

Ricotta, broccoli, & new potato frittata

Prep: 5 mins **Cook:** 25 mins

Serves 2, plus 2 lunchboxes

Ingredients

- 100g new potatoes
- 200g long-stem broccoli
- 200g green beans , trimmed and halved
- 400g can mixed beans , drained
- 3 tsp rapeseed oil
- 2 garlic cloves , crushed
- pinch of chilli flakes , cumin seeds or fennel seeds
- 4 large eggs
- 50g ricotta
- 1 tsp sherry vinegar
- ½ small bunch of basil , roughly chopped (optional)

Method

STEP 1

Boil the potatoes for 10-15 mins until tender. Add the broccoli for the last 2 mins of cooking. Drain and thickly slice the potatoes.

STEP 2

Meanwhile, put the green beans and mixed beans in a pan and cover with water. Bring to a simmer and cook for 3-4 mins, or until the green beans are tender. Drain and leave to steam-dry in the pan.

STEP 3

Heat the grill to high. Heat 2 tsp of the oil in a medium non-stick frying pan and fry the garlic for 1 min, then add the chilli flakes or cumin or fennel seeds and cook for 1 min more. Add the potatoes, broccoli and seasoning, and toss to coat in the flavoured oil.

STEP 4

Beat the eggs in a jug, season and pour over the potato mix. Cook over a medium heat for 2 mins, or until the base is set. Dollop teaspoons of the ricotta on top, then grill for 4-5 mins until cooked through.

STEP 5

Meanwhile, drizzle another 1 tsp oil over the bean mixture with the vinegar. Stir in the basil, if using, and season. Slice the frittata into four wedges, and serve two with half the bean salad on the side. Chill the remaining wedges and bean salad to use in the lunchboxes below.

Steaks with goulash sauce & sweet potato fries

Prep: 10 mins **Cook:** 25 mins

Serves 2

Ingredients

- 3 tsp rapeseed oil , plus extra for the steaks
- 250g sweet potatoes , peeled and cut into narrow chips
- 1 tbsp fresh thyme leaves
- 2 small onions , halved and sliced (190g)
- 1 green pepper , deseeded and diced
- 2 garlic cloves , sliced
- 1 tsp smoked paprika
- 85g cherry tomatoes , halved
- 1 tbsp tomato purée
- 1 tsp vegetable bouillon powder
- 2 x 125g fillet steaks , rubbed with a little rapeseed oil
- 200g bag baby spinach , wilted in a pan or the microwave

Method

STEP 1

Heat oven to 240C/220C fan/gas 7 and put a wire rack on top of a baking tray. Toss the sweet potatoes and thyme with 2 tsp oil in a bowl, then scatter them over the rack and set aside until ready to cook.

STEP 2

Heat 1 tsp oil in a non-stick pan, add the onions, cover the pan and leave to cook for 5 mins. Take off the lid and stir – they should be a little charred now. Stir in the green pepper and garlic, cover the pan and cook for 5 mins more. Put the potatoes in the oven and bake for 15 mins.

STEP 3

While the potatoes are cooking, stir the paprika into the onions and peppers, pour in 150ml water and stir in the cherry tomatoes, tomato purée and bouillon. Cover and simmer for 10 mins.

STEP 4

Pan-fry the steak in a hot, non-stick pan for 2-3 mins each side depending on their thickness. Rest for 5 mins. Spoon the goulash sauce onto plates and top with the beef. Serve the chips and spinach alongside.

Hake & seafood cataplana

Prep: 15 mins **Cook:** 35 mins

Serves 2

Ingredients

- 2 tbsp cold-pressed rapeseed oil
- 1 onion , halved and thinly sliced
- 250g salad potatoes , cut into chunks
- 1 large red pepper , deseeded and chopped
- 1 courgette (200g), thickly sliced
- 2 tomatoes , chopped (150g)
- 2 large garlic cloves , finely grated
- 1 tbsp cider vinegar (optional)
- 2 tsp vegetable bouillon powder
- 2 skinless hake fillets (pack size 240g)
- 150g pack ready-cooked mussels (not in shells)
- 60g peeled prawns
- large handful of parsley , chopped

Method

STEP 1

Heat the oil in a wide non-stick pan with a tight-fitting lid. Fry the onions and potatoes for about 5 mins, or until starting to soften. Add the peppers, courgettes, tomatoes and garlic, then stir in the vinegar, if using, the bouillon and 200ml water. Bring to a simmer, cover and cook for 25 mins, or until the peppers and courgettes are very tender (if your pan doesn't have a tight-fitting lid, wet a sheet of baking parchment and place over the stew before covering – this helps keep in the juices).

STEP 2

Add the hake fillets, mussels and prawns, then cover and cook for 5 mins more, or until the fish flakes easily when tested with a fork. Scatter over the parsley and serve.

Paneer jalfrezi with cumin rice

Prep: 20 mins **Cook:** 30 mins

Serves 4

Ingredients

- 2 tsp cold-pressed rapeseed oil
- 1 large and 1 medium onion , large one finely chopped and medium one cut into wedges
- 2 large garlic cloves , chopped
- 50g ginger , peeled and shredded
- 2 tsp ground coriander
- 2 tsp cumin seeds
- 400g can chopped tomatoes
- 1 tbsp vegetable bouillon powder
- 135g paneer , chopped
- 2 large peppers , seeded and chopped
- 1 red or green chilli , deseeded and sliced
- 25g coriander , chopped

For the rice

- 260g brown basmati rice
- 1 tsp cumin seeds

Method

STEP 1

Heat 1 tsp oil a large non-stick frying pan and fry the chopped onions, garlic and half the ginger for 5 mins until softened. Add the ground coriander and cumin seeds and cook for 1 min more, then tip in the tomatoes, half a can of water and the bouillon. Blitz everything together with a stick blender until very smooth, then bring to a simmer. Cover and cook for 15 mins.

STEP 2

Meanwhile, cook the rice and cumin seeds in a pan of boiling water for 25 mins, or until tender.

STEP 3

Heat the remaining oil in a non-stick wok and fry the paneer until lightly coloured. Remove from the pan and set aside. Add the peppers, onion wedges and chilli to the pan and stir-fry until the veg is tender, but still retains some bite. Mix the stir-fried veg and paneer into the sauce with the chopped coriander, then serve with the rice. If you're following our Healthy Diet Plan, eat two portions of the curry and rice, then chill the rest for another day. Will keep for up to three days, covered, in the fridge. To serve on the second night, reheat the leftover portions in the microwave until piping hot.

Sweet & sour tofu

Prep: 10 mins **Cook:** 15 mins

Serves 1

Ingredients

- 1 tbsp rapeseed or vegetable oil
- 75g extra-firm tofu , cut into 2cm chunks
- ½ onion , cut into thin wedges
- ½ red pepper , chopped into chunks
- 1 large garlic clove , finely sliced
- 80g fresh pineapple chunks
- 1 tbsp low-salt ketchup
- 1 tbsp rice wine vinegar
- ½ tbsp dark soy sauce
- cooked basmati rice , to serve
- sesame seeds , to serve

Method

STEP 1

Heat half the oil in a non-stick frying pan over a medium heat. Add the tofu and fry for 5 mins, turning regularly, until golden brown on all sides. Remove to a plate with a slotted spoon and set aside.

STEP 2

Heat the remaining oil in the pan over a high heat. Fry the onion, pepper and garlic for 5-6 mins, or until the veg begins to soften. Add the pineapple, ketchup, vinegar, soy sauce and 50ml water, and simmer for 1 min, or until slightly reduced. Stir the tofu back into the pan.

STEP 3

Cook the basmati rice following pack instructions. Serve the tofu in bowls with the rice and a sprinkling of sesame seeds.

Herby fish fingers with Chinese-style rice

Prep: 10 mins **Cook:** 35 mins

Serves 2

Ingredients

- 100g brown basmati rice
- 160g frozen peas
- 50g French beans
- 3 spring onions , finely chopped
- ½ tsp dried chilli flakes
- good handful coriander , roughly chopped
- 2 tsp tamari
- few drops sesame oil
- 1 tbsp cold-pressed rapeseed oil
- 2 large eggs
- 280g pack skinless cod loins cut into chunky strips (cut into 4 strips per loin)

Method

STEP 1

Cook the rice in a pan of water for 25 mins, adding the peas and beans for the last 6 mins. Drain, then return to the pan and stir in the spring onions, chilli flakes, all but 1 tbsp chopped coriander, the tamari and sesame oil. Cover.

STEP 2

Meanwhile, heat a large non-stick pan with the rapeseed oil Beat the eggs with the remaining 1 tbsp coriander. Cut the fish into chunky strips, then coat them in the egg and fry in the oil for a couple of mins each side until golden. Remove the fish from the pan and tip in the rice with any remaining egg and stir. Serve in bowls, topped with the fish.

Winter vegetable & lentil soup

Prep: 10 mins **Cook:** 30 mins

Serves 2

Ingredients

- 85g dried red lentils
- 2 carrots, quartered lengthways then diced
- 3 sticks celery, sliced
- 2 small leeks, sliced
- 2 tbsp tomato purée
- 1 tbsp fresh thyme leaves
- 3 large garlic cloves, chopped
- 1 tbsp vegetable bouillon powder
- 1 heaped tsp ground coriander

Method

STEP 1

Tip all the ingredients into a large pan. Pour over 1½ litres boiling water, then stir well.

STEP 2

Cover and leave to simmer for 30 mins until the vegetables and lentils are tender.

STEP 3

Ladle into bowls and eat straightaway, or if you like a really thick texture, blitz a third of the soup with a hand blender or in a food processor.

Spiced salmon & tomato traybake

Prep: 5 mins **Cook:** 25 mins

Serves 2

Ingredients

- 1 red onion , sliced
- 200g cherry tomatoes
- 3 tbsp mild or madras curry paste
- 400g can chickpeas , drained and rinsed
- 2 skinless salmon fillets
- 1 large or 2 small naan breads
- 2 tbsp fat-free yogurt
- lemon wedges and a few coriander leaves, to serve (optional)

Method

STEP 1

Heat the oven to 200C/180C fan/gas 6. Toss the onion, tomatoes, 2 tbsp curry paste, the chickpeas and 200ml water together in a deep 20 x 25cm roasting tin. Roast for 15 mins until the onions are tender and the tomatoes are just bursting.

STEP 2

Stir everything, then season. Brush the remaining curry paste over the salmon fillets and season. Nestle the salmon into the veg in the tin and roast for another 8-10 mins, or until cooked to your liking.

STEP 3

Meanwhile, warm the naan breads – you can do this by putting them directly on the oven rack below the roasting tin. Cut the warmed naan breads into wedges. Swirl the yogurt into the veg in the tin, then serve with the naan wedges for dunking, a few coriander leaves sprinkled over, if you like, and the lemon wedges, if using, for squeezing over.

Courgette, leek & goat's cheese soup

Prep: 8 mins **Cook:** 17 mins

Serves 4

Ingredients

- 1 tbsp rapeseed oil
- 400g leeks, well washed and sliced
- 450g courgettes, sliced
- 3 tsp vegetable bouillon powder, made up to 1 litre with boiling water
- 400g spinach
- 150g tub soft vegetarian goat's cheese
- 15g basil, plus a few leaves to serve
- 8 tsp omega seed mix (see tip)
- 4 x 25g portions wholegrain rye bread

Method

STEP 1

Heat the oil in a large pan and fry the leeks for a few mins to soften. Add the courgettes, then cover the pan and cook for 5 mins more. Pour in the stock, cover and cook for about 7 mins.

STEP 2

Add the spinach, then cover the pan and cook for 5 mins so that it wilts. Take off the heat and blitz until really smooth with a hand blender. Add the goat's cheese and basil, then blitz again.

STEP 3

If you're making this recipe as part of our two-person Summer Healthy Diet Plan, spoon half the soup into two bowls or large flasks, then cool and chill the remainder for another day. Reheat in a pan or microwave to serve. If serving in bowls, scatter with some extra basil leaves and the seeds, and eat with the rye bread.

Salmon salad with sesame dressing

Prep: 7 mins **Cook:** 16 mins

Serves 2

Ingredients

For the salad

- 250g new potatoes , sliced
- 160g French beans , trimmed
- 2 wild salmon fillets
- 80g salad leaves
- 4 small clementines , 3 sliced, 1 juiced
- handful of basil , chopped
- handful of coriander , chopped

For the dressing

- 2 tsp sesame oil
- 2 tsp tamari
- ½ lemon , juiced
- 1 red chilli , deseeded and chopped
- 2 tbsp finely chopped onion (1/4 small onion)

Method

STEP 1

Steam the potatoes and beans in a steamer basket set over a pan of boiling water for 8 mins. Arrange the salmon fillets on top and steam for a further 6-8 mins, or until the salmon flakes easily when tested with a fork.

STEP 2

Meanwhile, mix the dressing ingredients together along with the clementine juice. If eating straightaway, divide the salad leaves between two plates and top with the warm potatoes and beans and the clementine slices. Arrange the salmon fillets on top, scatter over the herbs and spoon over the dressing. If taking to work, prepare the potatoes, beans and salmon the night before, then pack into a rigid airtight container with the salad leaves kept separate. Put the salad elements together and dress just before eating to prevent the leaves from wilting.

Cod with cucumber, avocado & mango salsa salad

Prep: 5 mins **Cook:** 8 mins

Serves 2

Ingredients

- 2 x skinless cod fillets
- 1 lime , zested and juiced
- 1 small mango , peeled, stoned and chopped (or 2 peaches, stoned and chopped)
- 1 small avocado , stoned, peeled and sliced
- ¼ cucumber , chopped
- 160g cherry tomatoes , quartered
- 1 red chilli , deseeded and chopped
- 2 spring onions , sliced
- handful chopped coriander

Method

STEP 1

Heat oven to 200C/180C fan/gas 6. Put the fish in a shallow ovenproof dish and pour over half the lime juice, with a little of the zest, then grind over some black pepper. Bake for 8 mins or until the fish flakes easily but is still moist.

STEP 2

Meanwhile, put the rest of the ingredients, plus the remaining lime juice and zest, in a bowl and combine well. Spoon onto plates and top with the cod, spooning over any juices in the dish.

Butternut biryani with cucumber raita

Prep: 15 mins **Cook:** 30 mins

Serves 2

Ingredients

- 20g dried porcini mushrooms, roughly chopped
- 1 tbsp rapeseed oil
- 2 onions, sliced (160g)
- 2 garlic cloves, shredded
- 1 tbsp chopped fresh ginger
- 1 red chilli, deseeded and chopped
- 85g brown basmati rice
- 160g diced butternut squash (prepared weight)
- 1 tsp cumin seeds
- 1 tsp ground coriander
- 1 tsp vegetable bouillon
- 10cm length cucumber, grated, core removed
- 125g bio yogurt
- 2 tbsp chopped mint, plus a few leaves
- one third of a pack fresh coriander, chopped
- 25g toasted flaked almonds

Method

STEP 1

Pour 425ml boiling water over the dried mushrooms and set aside.

STEP 2

Heat the oil in a non-stick pan. Add the onions, garlic, ginger and chilli and stir-fry briefly over a high heat so they start to soften. Add the rice and squash and stir for a few mins. Tip in the cumin and coriander then stir in the mushrooms and their water with the bouillon.

STEP 3

Cover the pan and simmer for 20 mins until the rice is tender. Meanwhile mix the cucumber and yogurt with the mint to make a raita. Stir the coriander and almonds into the rice when it is ready and serve with the raita and a few extra leaves of mint or coriander.

Smoky chickpeas on toast

Prep: 2 mins **Cook:** 10 mins

Serves 2

Ingredients

- 1 tsp olive oil or vegetable oil, plus a drizzle
- 1 small onion or banana shallot, chopped
- 2 tsp chipotle paste
- 250ml passata
- 400g can chickpeas, drained
- 2 tsp honey
- 2 tsp red wine vinegar
- 2-4 slices good crusty bread
- 2 eggs

Method

STEP 1

Heat ½ tsp of the oil in a pan. Tip in the onion and cook until soft, about 5-8 mins, then add the chipotle paste, passata, chickpeas, honey and vinegar. Season and bubble for 5 mins.

STEP 2

Toast the bread. Heat the remaining oil in a frying pan and fry the eggs. Drizzle the toast with a little oil, then top with the chickpeas and fried eggs.

Chicken & lemon skewers

Prep: 20 mins **Cook:** 25 mins

Serves 4

Ingredients

- 1 small pack mint, leaves picked
- 150g natural yogurt, plus extra to serve (optional)
- 1 lemon, zested and juiced
- ½ tsp ground cumin
- ½ tsp ground coriander
- 2cm piece ginger, grated
- 4 skinless chicken breasts, each cut into 6 pieces
- 4 wholemeal flatbreads or pittas
- 2 Little Gem lettuces, sliced
- 1 small red onion, sliced, to serve

- pickled red cabbage , chilli sauce and
- hummus, to serve (all optional)

You will need

4 metal or wooden skewers

Method

STEP 1

Chop half the mint and put in a bowl with the yogurt, half the lemon juice, all the lemon zest, spices and ginger. Mix well and season with lots of black pepper and a pinch of salt. Add the chicken pieces, mix well and put in the fridge for 20-30 mins. Meanwhile, soak 4 large wooden skewers in water for at least 20 mins (or use metal ones).

STEP 2

When you're ready to cook the chicken, heat your grill to a medium heat and line the grill tray with foil. Thread the chicken onto the soaked wooden or metal skewers and grill for 15-20 mins, turning halfway through, until browned and cooked through.

STEP 3

Warm the flatbreads under the grill for a couple of seconds, then serve them topped with the lettuce, chicken, red onion, remaining lemon juice and mint, and any optional extras such as extra yogurt or pickled cabbage, chilli sauce and hummus.

Greek-style roast fish

Prep: 10 mins **Cook:** 50 mins

Serves 2

Ingredients

- 5 small potatoes (about 400g), scrubbed and cut into wedges
- 1 onion, halved and sliced
- 2 garlic cloves, roughly chopped
- ½ tsp dried oregano or 1/2 tbsp chopped fresh oregano
- 2 tbsp olive oil
- ½ lemon, cut into wedges
- 2 large tomatoes, cut into wedges
- 2 fresh skinless pollock fillets (about 200g)
- small handful parsley, roughly chopped

Method

STEP 1

Heat oven to 200C/180C fan/gas 6. Tip the potatoes, onion, garlic, oregano and olive oil into a roasting tin, season, then mix together with your hands to coat everything in the oil. Roast for 15 mins, turn everything over and bake for 15 mins more.

STEP 2

Add the lemon and tomatoes, and roast for 10 mins, then top with the fish fillets and cook for 10 mins more. Serve with parsley scattered over.

Chickpea tagine soup

Prep: 10 mins **Cook:** 30 mins

Serves 4

Ingredients

- 2 red peppers
- 1 tbsp rapeseed oil
- 1 red onion , thinly sliced
- 2 large garlic cloves , crushed
- 2 tsp ground coriander
- 1 tsp ground cumin
- 2 tbsp rose harissa paste
- 2 x 400g cans chickpeas , drained and rinsed
- 1 ½l low-salt veg stock
- 150g kale , chopped
- 1 lemon , zested and juiced
- 50g dried apricots , finely chopped
- 1/2 small bunch parsley , finely chopped
- fat-free natural yogurt , to serve (optional)

Method

STEP 1

Heat the grill to its highest setting. Halve and deseed the peppers, then lay cut-side down on a baking sheet lined with foil. Grill for 10-15 mins, or until blistered and softened. Leave until cool enough to handle, then remove and discard the skins. Slice the roasted peppers into thin strips.

STEP 2

Heat the oil in a large saucepan over a low heat. Fry the onion for 8-10 mins until softened. Stir through the garlic, coriander, cumin and harissa paste and cook for 1 min more. Add the chickpeas and stock, bring to the boil and simmer for 15 mins, covered.

STEP 3

Stir the peppers through the soup with the kale, lemon zest and juice, and apricots and cook, covered, for another 5 mins. Ladle the soup into bowls and serve with the chopped parsley scattered over and a dollop of yogurt, if you like.

Toddler recipe: Sweetcorn & spinach fritters

Prep: 10 mins **Cook:** 6 mins

Makes 12 fritters (3 toddler portions or 14 small portions)

Ingredients

- 1 x small can no-salt sweetcorn, drained
- small handful baby spinach leaf
- 1 small garlic clove, crushed
- 1 spring onion, chopped
- 50g plain flour
- ½ tsp baking powder
- 1 egg
- 50ml milk
- 1 tsp rapeseed oil, for frying

Method

STEP 1

Pulse all the ingredients except the oil in a food processor until fairly but not completely smooth.

STEP 2

Heat a little oil in a frying pan until hot and dollop four spoonfuls of the mixture into the pan leaving space around them. Fry for just under 1 min on each side until lightly golden. When you flip the fritter, flatten with a spatula to ensure even cooking the whole way through. Cook in three batches, placing the cooked fritters on a plate covered with kitchen roll. Serve warm.

STEP 3

You can freeze any fritters you don't need. Lay them on a baking sheet, then once frozen, transfer to a freezer bag. Reheat the frozen fritters in the oven (180C/160fan/gas 4) for around 10 mins until piping hot. Allow to cool to lukewarm before serving.

Cumin roast veg with tahini dressing

Prep: 10 mins **Cook:** 45 mins - 50 mins

Serves 4

Ingredients

- 3 large carrots , roughly chopped
- 3 peeled raw beetroots , roughly chopped
- 1 sweet potato , sliced
- 3 red onions , cut into wedges
- 250g cauliflower florets
- 1 tsp cumin seeds

- 2 tbsp rapeseed oil
- 1 tbsp balsamic vinegar
- 2-3 tbsp chopped mint
- 2-3 tbsp chopped coriander
- 400g can chickpeas
- 2 hard-boiled eggs , halved
- 100g young spinach leaves

For the dressing

- 3 tbsp tahini
- 1 tbsp crunchy peanut butter
- 1 lemon , zested and juiced

- 1 tsp ground coriander
- 1 garlic clove , finely grated

Method

STEP 1

Heat oven to 200C/180C fan/gas 6. Tip all of the vegetables into a large roasting tin. Add the cumin seeds, oil and balsamic vinegar, then toss together. Roast for 45-50 mins until the veg is tender and starting to char.

STEP 2

Meanwhile, mix the tahini and peanut butter with the lemon juice, coriander, garlic and about 4-5 tbsp water to make a dressing.

STEP 3

When the veg is ready, leave to cool a little. Add the mint, coriander, lemon zest and chickpeas, then toss well.

STEP 4

If you're following our Healthy Diet Plan, serve two portions now with the eggs, some dressing and half the spinach, then serve the remainder on another day without the eggs.

Cumin roast veg with tahini dressing

Prep: 10 mins **Cook:** 45 mins - 50 mins

Serves 4

Ingredients

- 3 large carrots , roughly chopped
- 3 peeled raw beetroots , roughly chopped
- 1 sweet potato , sliced
- 3 red onions , cut into wedges
- 250g cauliflower florets
- 1 tsp cumin seeds

For the dressing

- 3 tbsp tahini
- 1 tbsp crunchy peanut butter
- 1 lemon , zested and juiced

- 2 tbsp rapeseed oil
- 1 tbsp balsamic vinegar
- 2-3 tbsp chopped mint
- 2-3 tbsp chopped coriander
- 400g can chickpeas
- 2 hard-boiled eggs , halved
- 100g young spinach leaves

- 1 tsp ground coriander
- 1 garlic clove , finely grated

Method

STEP 1

Heat oven to 200C/180C fan/gas 6. Tip all of the vegetables into a large roasting tin. Add the cumin seeds, oil and balsamic vinegar, then toss together. Roast for 45-50 mins until the veg is tender and starting to char.

STEP 2

Meanwhile, mix the tahini and peanut butter with the lemon juice, coriander, garlic and about 4-5 tbsp water to make a dressing.

STEP 3

When the veg is ready, leave to cool a little. Add the mint, coriander, lemon zest and chickpeas, then toss well.

STEP 4

If you're following our Healthy Diet Plan, serve two portions now with the eggs, some dressing and half the spinach, then serve the remainder on another day without the eggs.

Leek, kale & potato soup topped with shoestring fries

Prep: 15 mins **Cook:** 30 mins

Serves 4 - 6

Ingredients

- 4 large potatoes (around 500g), 3 peeled and cubed, 1 left whole with skin on
- 1 tbsp cold pressed rapeseed oil
- 15g butter
- 5 leeks (around 500g), washed and sliced into half moons
- 2 garlic cloves, sliced
- 1 ½l vegetable stock (we used Bouillon)
- 200g kale
- 2 tbsp half-fat crème fraîche

Method

STEP 1

Heat oven to 220C/200C fan/ gas 7 and line a baking tray with parchment. Cut the whole potato into matchsticks using a julienne peeler, or shave thin slices using a vegetable peeler, then cut into matchsticks. Pat dry using kitchen paper, then toss with the oil and some seasoning. Spread out on the tray and roast for 15-18 mins.

STEP 2

Melt the butter in a large saucepan. Add the leeks, chopped potatoes and a pinch of salt, then cook gently for 10 mins until the leeks have softened. Stir in the garlic and cook for 1 min more, then pour in the stock. Simmer for 10-12 mins until the potatoes are soft, then add the kale and cook for 2-3 mins to wilt.

STEP 3

Stir in the crème fraîche, then blitz with a hand blender and season to taste. Divide the soup between bowls and top with the shoestring fries.

Miso salmon with ginger noodles

Prep: 10 mins **Cook:** 12 mins

Serves 2

Ingredients

- 2 nests wholemeal noodles (100g)
- 1 ½ tsp brown miso
- 2 tsp balsamic vinegar
- ½ tsp smoked paprika
- 2 skinless wild salmon fillets (230g)
- 1 tbsp rapeseed oil
- 30g ginger, cut into matchsticks
- 1 green pepper, deseeded and cut into strips
- 2 leeks (165g), thinly sliced
- 3 garlic cloves, finely grated
- 160g baby spinach

Method

STEP 1

Put the noodles in a bowl, cover with boiling water and set aside to soften. Heat the grill to medium and place a piece of foil on the grill rack. Mix 1 tsp of the miso with the vinegar, paprika and 1 tbsp water. Spread over the salmon and grill for 6-8 mins until flaky and cooked.

STEP 2

Heat the oil in a wok and stir-fry the ginger, pepper and leeks over a high heat for a few mins until softened. Add the garlic and cook for 1 min more. Drain the noodles, reserve 2 tbsp water and mix with the remaining miso.

STEP 3

Add the drained noodles, miso liquid and spinach to the wok and toss over the heat until the spinach wilts. Pile onto plates, top with the salmon and any juices and serve.

Slow-cooker Bolognese

Prep: 15 mins **Cook:** 7 hrs and 30 mins - 9 hrs and 30 mins

Serves 12

Ingredients

- 4 tbsp olive oil
- 6 smoked bacon rashers, chopped
- 1 ½kg lean minced beef (or use half beef, half pork mince)
- 4 onions, finely chopped
- 3 carrots, finely chopped
- 4 celery sticks, finely chopped
- 8 garlic cloves, crushed
- 500g mushrooms, sliced
- 4 x 400g cans chopped tomatoes
- 6 tbsp tomato purée
- 2 tbsp dried mixed herbs
- 2 bay leaves
- large glass red wine (optional)
- 4 tbsp red wine vinegar
- 1 tbsp sugar
- cooked spaghetti, to serve
- parmesan, to serve

Method

STEP 1

Heat the oil in a large pan and fry the bacon and mince in batches until browned. Add to your slow cooker.

STEP 2

Add the onions, carrots, celery, garlic, mushrooms, tomatoes, tomato purée, herbs, wine (if using), vinegar, sugar and seasoning to the slow cooker. Cover and cook on Low for 6-8 hours, then uncover, turn to High and cook for another hour until thick and saucy.

STEP 3

Serve with cooked spaghetti and grated or shaved parmesan. To cook this entire recipe on the hob, check out our big-batch Bolognese recipe.

Butter bean, mushroom & bacon pot pies

Prep: 15 mins **Cook:** 50 mins

Serves 4

Ingredients

- 3 tbsp rapeseed oil
- 2 red onions, thinly sliced
- 500g mushrooms, thickly sliced
- 70g smoked streaky bacon, sliced into thin strips
- 2 tbsp plain flour
- 500ml low-salt vegetable stock
- 250g kale, roughly sliced
- 3 tsp wholegrain mustard
- 2 tbsp reduced-fat crème fraîche
- 1 tbsp finely chopped tarragon
- 1 lemon, zested and juiced
- 2 x 400g cans butter beans, drained and rinsed

Method

STEP 1

Heat 2 tbsp of the oil in a saucepan or large flameproof casserole dish. Fry the onions for 10 mins until soft, then add the mushrooms and bacon and fry for another 5 mins until golden. Stir in the flour and cook for 2 mins more. Gradually pour in the stock, then bring to the boil and bubble for 2 mins. Add the kale and cook for another 5 mins, then stir in the mustard, crème fraîche, half the tarragon and the lemon juice. Spoon the mushroom mixture into four small baking dishes.

STEP 2

Heat the oven to 180C/160C fan/gas 4. Put the butter beans in a food processor with the remaining oil and tarragon and the lemon zest. Blitz until chunky, adding 2-3 tbsp water to loosen if needed.

STEP 3

Spoon the butter bean mixture over the filling, smoothing with the back of a spoon. Bake for 20-25 mins until golden. Leave to cool slightly, then serve.

Spaghetti puttanesca with red beans & spinach

Prep: 10 mins **Cook:** 17 mins

Serves 2

Ingredients

- 100g wholemeal spaghetti
- 1 large onion , finely chopped
- 1 tbsp rapeseed oil
- 1 red chilli , deseeded and sliced
- 2 garlic cloves , chopped
- 200g cherry tomatoes , halved
- 2 tsp cider vinegar
- 1 tbsp capers
- 5 Kalamata olives , halved
- 1 tsp smoked paprika
- 210g can kidney beans , drained
- 160g spinach leaves
- small handful of chopped parsley
- small handful of basil leaves

Method

STEP 1

Cook the spaghetti in simmering water for 10-12 mins until al dente. Meanwhile, fry the onion in the oil in a large non-stick frying pan with a lid until tender and turning golden. Stir in the chilli, garlic and cherry tomatoes.

STEP 2

Add the vinegar, capers, olives and paprika with a ladleful of pasta water. Stir in the beans and cook until warmed through.

STEP 3

Add the spinach to the pasta water to wilt, then drain well. Toss with the tomato and bean mixture and the parsley and basil, then pile onto plates or in shallow bowls to serve.

Raspberry chia jam

Prep: 5 mins **Cook:** 15 mins

Makes 1 jar (about 400g)

Ingredients

- 500g raspberries
- 1 tsp vanilla bean paste
- 3 tbsp honey
- 3 tbsp chia seeds

Method

STEP 1

Put the raspberries in a pan with the vanilla and honey, then cook over a low heat for 5 mins or until the berries have broken down.

STEP 2

Stir through the chia and cook for 10 mins. Set aside to cool completely (it will thicken significantly as it cools). Spoon into a bowl or sterilised jar. Great on toast, swirled through porridge or in yogurt. Will keep in the fridge for up to one week.

Asparagus & lemon spaghetti with peas

Prep: 7 mins **Cook:** 12 mins

Serves 2

Ingredients

- 150g wholemeal spaghetti
- 160g asparagus, ends trimmed and cut into lengths
- 2 tbsp rapeseed oil
- 2 leeks (220g), cut into lengths, then thin strips
- 1 red chilli, deseeded and finely chopped
- 1 garlic clove, finely grated
- 160g frozen peas
- 1 lemon, zested and juiced, plus wedges to serve

Method

STEP 1

Boil the spaghetti for 12 mins until al dente, adding the asparagus for the last 3 mins. Meanwhile, heat the oil in a large non-stick frying pan, add the leeks and chilli and cook for 5 mins. Stir in the garlic, peas and lemon zest and juice and cook for a few mins more.

STEP 2

Drain and add the pasta to the pan with ¼ mug of the pasta water and toss everything together until well mixed. Spoon into shallow bowls and serve with lemon wedges for squeezing over, if you like.

Mexican-style bean soup with shredded chicken & lime

Prep: 10 mins **Cook:** 20 mins

Serves 2

Ingredients

- 2 tsp rapeseed oil
- 1 large onion , finely chopped
- 1 red pepper , cut into chunks
- 2 garlic cloves , chopped
- 2 tsp mild chilli powder
- 1 tsp ground coriander
- 1 tsp ground cumin
- 400g can chopped tomatoes
- 400g can black beans
- 1 tsp vegetable bouillon powder
- 1 cooked skinless chicken breast , about 125g, shredded
- handful chopped coriander
- 1 lime , juiced
- ½ red chilli , deseeded and finely chopped (optional)

Method

STEP 1

Heat the oil in a medium pan, add the onion and pepper, and fry, stirring frequently, for 10 mins. Stir in the garlic and spices, then tip in the tomatoes and beans with their liquid, half a can of water and the bouillon powder. Simmer, covered, for 15 mins.

STEP 2

Meanwhile, tip the chicken into a bowl, add the coriander and lime juice with a little chilli (if using, or see tip below for guacamole alternative) and toss well. Ladle the soup into two bowls, top with the chicken and serve.

Quick chicken hummus bowl

Prep: 10 mins **Serves 2**

Ingredients

- 200g hummus
- 1 small lemon , zested and juiced
- 200g pouch cooked mixed grains (we used Merchant Gourmet red rice & quinoa)
- 150g baby spinach , roughly chopped
- 1 small avocado , halved and sliced
- 1 cooked chicken breast , sliced at an angle
- 100g pomegranate seeds
- ½ red onion , finely sliced
- 2 tbsp toasted almonds

Method

STEP 1

Mix 2 tbsp of the hummus with half the lemon juice, the lemon zest and enough water to make a drizzly dressing. Squeeze the grain pouch to separate the grains, then divide between two shallow bowls and toss through the dressing. Top each bowl with a handful of the spinach.

STEP 2

Squeeze the remaining lemon juice over the avocado halves, then add one half to each bowl. Divide the chicken, pomegranate seeds, onion, almonds and remaining hummus between the two bowls and gently mix everything together just before eating.

Swedish meatballs with beetroot & apple salad

Cook: 20 mins **Serves 4**

Ingredients

For the meatballs

- 500g lean pork mince (5% fat)
- 100g coarsely grated courgette , squeezed of excess juice
- 1 onion , grated
- 4 tbsp chopped fresh dill
- 2 garlic cloves , finely grated
- 1 egg
- 1 tbsp rapeseed oil

- 1 tsp thyme leaves
- 2 tsp vegetable bouillon powder, made up to 300ml with boiling water
- 2 tbsp half-fat crème fraîche

For the salad

- 1 large apple, chopped
- 1 red onion, halved and thinly sliced
- 4 tbsp chopped parsley
- 2 tsp capers
- ½ lemon, juiced
- 320g cooked beetroot, cut into strips

Method

STEP 1

To make the meatballs, tip the pork into a bowl and add the grated courgette and onion, half the dill, half the garlic and plenty of black pepper. Break in the egg and mix well with your hands. When everything is well combined, break off walnut-size pieces and roll into balls – you should end up with about 28. The mixture will be very soft.

STEP 2

Heat the oil in a large non-stick frying pan then gently fry the meatballs in two batches until firm and pale golden, turning them every now and then so they brown evenly. Each batch should take 6-8 mins.

STEP 3

Wipe out the pan to remove excess fat and add the remaining garlic and thyme, then pour in the bouillon and bring to the boil. Turn off the heat, stir in the crème fraîche and remaining dill, then return the meatballs to the pan and turn them in the mixture until coated.

STEP 4

For the salad, mix the apple, onion, parsley and capers with the lemon, then stir through the beetroot. Serve the salad alongside the meatballs. If you're cooking for two people, eat half the meatballs and salad now, and chill the rest for another day – it will keep in the fridge for up to three days. Reheat the meatballs in the microwave until piping hot.

Vegan pumpkin soup

Prep: 25 mins **Cook:** 40 mins

Serves 6

Ingredients

- 1 medium pumpkin or large squash (about 1½kg)
- 1 tbsp rapeseed oil
- ½ tsp ground allspice
- 1 large onion, finely chopped

For the coconut & pumpkin seed relish

- 3 tbsp coconut flakes
- 3 tbsp pumpkin seeds
- 1 red chilli, deseeded and finely chopped
- 1 tbsp chopped ginger
- 2 garlic cloves, crushed
- 1-1.2 litres vegan stock
- 1 tbsp vegan white miso
- 3 tbsp soya cream or coconut yogurt
- ½ small bunch of coriander, chopped
- 1 lime, zested and juiced

Method

STEP 1

Heat the oven to 200C/180C fan/gas 6. Peel, deseed and chop the pumpkin into 3cm chunks (reserve the seeds for the relish – see tip). Tip the pumpkin onto a baking tray, drizzle over half the oil, scatter with the allspice and toss well. Season and roast for 30 mins until golden and tender. Meanwhile, toast the coconut flakes for the relish in a dry frying pan over a low heat for a few minutes until lightly golden. Remove from the pan and leave to cool, then stir in the pumpkin seeds, chilli, coriander and lime zest.

STEP 2

Heat the remaining oil in a large saucepan over a medium heat, and fry the onion for 5 mins until tender but not golden. Add the ginger and garlic and fry for another minute, then tip in 1 litre stock and the miso. Put the roasted pumpkin in the pan, then bring to a simmer. Remove from the heat and blend the soup with a stick blender until smooth. If you prefer a thinner soup, add the remaining stock. Return the soup to a gentle simmer, then season well and stir in the lime juice. Ladle into bowls, and serve topped with a swirl of the soya cream and a sprinkle of the relish.

Mint & basil griddled peach salad

Prep: 10 mins **Cook:** 25 mins

Serves 2

Ingredients

- 1 lime , zested and juiced
- 1 tbsp rapeseed oil
- 2 tbsp finely chopped mint , plus a few whole leaves to serve
- 2 tbsp basil , chopped
- 2 peaches (300g), quartered
- 75g quinoa
- 160g fine beans , trimmed and halved
- 1 small red onion , very finely chopped
- 1 large Little Gem lettuce (165g), roughly chopped
- ½ x 60g pack rocket
- 1 small avocado , stoned and sliced

Method

STEP 1

Mix the lime zest and juice, oil, mint and basil, then put half in a bowl with the peaches. Meanwhile, cook the quinoa following pack instructions.

STEP 2

Cook the beans for 3-4 mins until just tender. Meanwhile, griddle the peaches for 1 min on each side. If you don't have a griddle pan, use a large non-stick frying pan with a drop of oil.

STEP 3

Drain the quinoa and divide between shallow bowls. Toss the warm beans and onion in the remaining mint mixture and pile on top of the quinoa with the lettuce and rocket. Top with the avocado and peaches and scatter over the mint leaves. Serve while still warm.

Punchy spaghetti

Prep: 10 mins **Cook:** 15 mins

Serves 1

Ingredients

- 75g wholemeal spaghetti
- 2 anchovies, in oil
- 1 fat garlic clove, finely chopped
- 1 tbsp olive oil
- ½ tsp smoked paprika
- 1 small courgette, cut into cubes
- 100g cherry tomatoes, halved
- large handful rocket
- ½ lemon, juiced

Method

STEP 1

Bring a pan of water to the boil and cook the pasta for 1 min less than the pack instructions.

STEP 2

Meanwhile, cook the anchovies and garlic in a frying pan with the oil, until the anchovies have broken down. Add the paprika and courgette, then cook for 5 mins until the courgette is mostly softened. Tip in the cherry tomatoes and turn up the heat a little so they begin to burst.

STEP 3

Transfer the pasta straight to the frying pan using tongs (a little water will help create a smooth sauce). Take the pan off the heat, add a good grinding of black pepper and a squeeze of lemon juice to taste, then toss through the rocket. Mix everything to combine and pile into your bowl.

Burrito bowl with chipotle black beans

Prep: 15 mins **Cook:** 15 mins

Serves 2

Ingredients

- 125g basmati rice
- 1 tbsp olive oil
- 2 garlic cloves, chopped
- 400g can black beans, drained and rinsed
- 1 tbsp cider vinegar
- 1 tsp honey
- 1 tbsp chipotle paste
- 100g chopped curly kale
- 1 avocado, halved and sliced
- 1 medium tomato, chopped
- 1 small red onion, chopped

To serve (optional)

- chipotle hot sauce
- coriander leaves
- lime wedges

Method

STEP 1

Cook the rice following pack instructions, then drain and return to the pan to keep warm. In a frying pan, heat the oil, add the garlic and fry for 2 mins or until golden. Add the beans, vinegar, honey and chipotle. Season and warm through for 2 mins.

STEP 2

Boil the kale for 1 min, then drain, squeezing out any excess water. Divide the rice between big shallow bowls and top with the beans, kale, avocado, tomato and onion. Serve with hot sauce, coriander and lime wedges, if you like.

Mushroom hash with poached eggs

Prep: 10 mins **Cook:** 17 mins

Serves 4

Ingredients

- 1 ½ tbsp rapeseed oil
- 2 large onions, halved and sliced
- 500g closed cup mushrooms, quartered
- 1 tbsp fresh thyme leaves, plus extra for sprinkling
- 500g fresh tomatoes, chopped
- 1 tsp smoked paprika
- 4 tsp omega seed mix (see tip)
- 4 large eggs

Method

STEP 1

Heat the oil in a large non-stick frying pan and fry the onions for a few mins. Cover the pan and leave the onions to cook in their own steam for 5 mins more.

STEP 2

Tip in the mushrooms with the thyme and cook, stirring frequently, for 5 mins until softened. Add the tomatoes and paprika, cover the pan and cook for 5 mins until pulpy. Stir through the seed mix.

STEP 3

If you're making this recipe as part of our two-person Summer Healthy Diet Plan, poach two of the eggs in lightly simmering water to your liking. Serve on top of half the hash with a sprinkling of fresh thyme and some black pepper. Chill the remaining hash to warm in a pan and eat with freshly poached eggs on another day. If you're serving four people, poach all four eggs, divide the hash between four plates, sprinkle with thyme and black pepper and serve with the eggs on top.

Hearty lamb stew

Prep: 10 mins **Cook:** 1 hr and 40 mins

Serves 4

Ingredients

- 1 tbsp vegetable oil
- 500g cubed stewing lamb
- 1 onion, thickly sliced
- 2 carrots, thickly sliced
- 2 leeks, thickly sliced
- 400ml hot vegetable or chicken stock
- 1 tsp dried rosemary or 1 fresh sprig
- 400g cannellini bean, rinsed and drained
- crusty bread or boiled potatoes to serve (optional)

Method

STEP 1

Heat the oil in a large casserole. Tip in the lamb and cook for 5 mins until any liquid has disappeared, then add the onion, carrots and leeks. Cook for 5 mins more, stirring often, until the veg is starting to soften.

STEP 2

Pour over the stock, add the rosemary, cover with a lid and cook over a low heat for 1 hr. Stir in the beans and cook for 30 mins more, topping up with water if necessary, until the lamb is tender and cooked through. Serve with some crusty bread or potatoes, if you like.

Avocado & black bean eggs

Prep: 5 mins **Cook:** 5 mins

Serves 2

Ingredients

- 2 tsp rapeseed oil
- 1 red chilli, deseeded and thinly sliced
- 1 large garlic clove, sliced
- 2 large eggs
- 400g can black beans
- ½ x 400g can cherry tomatoes
- ¼ tsp cumin seeds
- 1 small avocado, halved and sliced
- handful fresh, chopped coriander
- 1 lime, cut into wedges

Method

STEP 1

Heat the oil in a large non-stick frying pan. Add the chilli and garlic and cook until softened and starting to colour. Break in the eggs on either side of the pan. Once they start to set, spoon the beans (with their juice) and the tomatoes around the pan and sprinkle over the cumin seeds. You're aiming to warm the beans and tomatoes rather than cook them.

STEP 2

Remove the pan from the heat and scatter over the avocado and coriander. Squeeze over half of the lime wedges. Serve with the remaining wedges on the side for squeezing over.

Ginger chicken & green bean noodles

Prep: 10 mins **Cook:** 15 mins

Serves 2

Ingredients

- ½ tbsp vegetable oil
- 2 skinless chicken breasts, sliced
- 200g green beans, trimmed and halved crosswise

- thumb-sized piece of ginger, peeled and cut into matchsticks
- 2 garlic cloves, sliced
- 1 ball stem ginger, finely sliced, plus 1 tsp syrup from the jar
- 1 tsp cornflour, mixed with 1 tbsp water
- 1 tsp dark soy sauce, plus extra to serve (optional)
- 2 tsp rice vinegar
- 200g cooked egg noodles

Method

STEP 1

Heat the oil in a wok over a high heat and stir-fry the chicken for 5 mins. Add the green beans and stir-fry for 4-5 mins more until the green beans are just tender, and the chicken is just cooked through.

STEP 2

Stir in the fresh ginger and garlic, and stir-fry for 2 mins, then add the stem ginger and syrup, the cornflour mix, soy sauce and vinegar. Stir-fry for 1 min, then toss in the noodles. Cook until everything is hot and the sauce coats the noodles. Drizzle with more soy, if you like, and serve.

Goan-style vegetable curry with kitchari

Prep: 10 mins **Cook:** 40 mins

Serves 4

Ingredients

For the kitchari

- 225g brown basmati rice
- 1 tsp rapeseed oil
- 1 tsp ground coriander
- 390g can green lentils, drained

For the curry

- 1 tbsp rapeseed oil
- 2 large onions (330g), 1 finely chopped, 1 sliced
- 2 red chillies, deseeded and sliced
- 25g ginger, finely chopped
- 1 tsp ground turmeric
- 1 tsp smoked paprika
- 1 tsp ground cumin

- 3 tsp ground coriander
- 3 garlic cloves, chopped
- 1 tbsp vegetable bouillon powder (check it's vegan if you need it to be), made up with 500ml boiling water
- 360g cauliflower florets (about 1/4 cauliflower)
- 1 ½ tsp tamarind
- 320g fine beans, trimmed and halved if large
- 4 large tomatoes, cut into wedges
- 2 large courgettes (320g), halved lengthways and thickly sliced
- 100g coconut yogurt
- ½ x 30g pack fresh coriander, chopped, to serve

Method

STEP 1

Boil the rice in a pan of water for 25 mins until tender, then drain.

STEP 2

Meanwhile, make the curry. Heat the oil in a large pan and fry the onions, chillies and ginger for 8-10 mins until softened. Add the spices and garlic, stir briefly, then pour in the bouillon and stir in the cauliflower. Cover and simmer for 5 mins.

STEP 3

Stir in the tamarind with the beans, tomatoes and courgettes, then cover the pan and cook for 10-15 mins more until the veg are tender, but still retain a little bite. Remove the lid for the last 5 mins to reduce the sauce a little. Remove from the heat and stir in the yogurt and half the fresh coriander.

STEP 4

Meanwhile, for the kitchari, heat the oil in a non-stick pan and add the ground coriander. Warm briefly, then tip in the rice and drained lentils. Warm through for 1 min, then stir through the remaining fresh coriander.

STEP 5

If you're following our Healthy Diet Plan, serve half the curry and rice now, then chill the rest to eat another night (cool the rice quickly on a wide tray, then chill immediately). Reheat the rice and curry in the microwave or on the hob. You may need to add a drop of water to the rice to stop it sticking.

Chicken, sweet potato & pea curry

Prep: 10 mins **Cook:** 30 mins

Serves 4

Ingredients

- 1 tbsp rapeseed oil
- 1 tbsp korma paste
- 2 skinless chicken breast fillets, each cut into 8-10 pieces
- 320g sweet potatoes, chopped into bite-sized pieces
- 6 tbsp red lentils
- 325ml can light coconut milk (freeze the rest for later)
- 200g frozen peas
- 220g cherry tomatoes
- 300g cooked rice or roti, to serve

Method

STEP 1

Heat the oil in a deep frying pan or wok, stir in the curry paste and fry for 30 seconds until it becomes fragrant. Stir in the chicken, then add the sweet potatoes and lentils and keep stirring to coat everything in the paste. Add 300ml water and the coconut milk. Bring to the boil, then simmer for 15-20 mins or until the chicken and sweet potato are cooked through and the consistency of the sauce is slightly thickened.

STEP 2

Tip in the peas, bring back to the boil and simmer for a further 2 mins, then add the tomatoes and cook for 2 mins more. Serve with steamed rice, or roti.

Feta & kale loaded sweet potato

Prep: 10 mins **Cook:** 50 mins

Serves 2

Ingredients

- 2 sweet potatoes
- 210g can chickpeas, drained
- 1 small red onion, thinly sliced
- 2 tbsp red wine vinegar
- 30g feta, cut into small cubes
- 1 tbsp extra virgin olive oil

- pinch chilli flakes
- 100g kale
- 1 tbsp pumpkin seeds, toasted
- 80g bag rocket

Method

STEP 1

Heat oven to 200C/180C fan/gas 6. Prick the sweet potatoes all over with a fork, then put them in a roasting tin and roast for 40 mins. Add the chickpeas to the tray, then roast for 10 mins more, until the potatoes are completely tender and the chickpeas have crisped a little.

STEP 2

Meanwhile, mix the onion with the vinegar and a pinch of sugar and salt, and set aside to quick pickle. In another bowl, marinate the feta with the oil and chilli flakes.

STEP 3

When the potatoes are nearly cooked, cook the kale in a pan with 50ml water for 3 mins until wilted, then season to taste. Halve the potatoes, divide between two plates and top each with the kale, chickpeas, red onion (reserving the vinegar), marinated feta and pumpkin seeds. Toss the rocket with the reserved vinegar, then serve on the side.

Hearty lamb & barley soup

Prep: 10 mins **Cook:** 25 mins

Serves 4

Ingredients

- 1 tsp olive oil
- 200g lamb neck fillet, trimmed of fat and cut into small pieces
- ½ large onion, finely chopped
- 50g pearl barley
- 600g mixed root vegetable (we used potato, parsnip and swede, cubed)
- 2 tsp Worcestershire sauce
- 1 ¾ 1 litre lamb or beef stock
- 1 thyme sprig
- 100g green bean (frozen are fine), finely chopped

Method

STEP 1

Heat the oil in a large saucepan. Season the lamb, then fry for a few mins until browned. Add the onion and barley, then gently fry for 1 min. Add the veg, cook for 2 more mins, then add the Worcestershire sauce, stock and thyme. Cover, then simmer for 20 mins.

STEP 2

When everything is cooked, spoon about a quarter of the soup into a separate pan. Purée with a stick blender (or put into a normal blender and whizz), then stir it back into the rest of the soup. Add the green beans, simmer for 3 mins, then ladle the soup into bowls and serve with granary bread.

Cocoa & cherry oat bake

Prep: 15 mins **Cook:** 25 mins - 30 mins

Serves 6

Ingredients

- 75g dried cherries
- 1 tbsp chia seeds
- 500ml hazelnut milk
- 200g jumbo porridge oats
- 3 tbsp cocoa powder
- 1 tbsp cocoa nibs
- 1 tsp baking powder
- 1 tsp vanilla extract
- 50g blanched hazelnuts
- fat-free yogurt and sugar-free cherry compote, to serve (optional)

Method

STEP 1

Heat the oven to 200C/180C fan/gas 6. Cover the cherries with boiling water and set aside for 10 mins. Meanwhile, mix the chia seeds with 3 tbsp warm water.

STEP 2

Drain the cherries and put in a large bowl with the soaked chia and the remaining ingredients, except the hazelnuts. Tip into a 2-litre ovenproof dish and scatter over the hazelnuts, then bake for 25-30 mins until piping hot in the middle. Serve with yogurt and cherry compote, if you like.

Easy vegan tacos

Prep: 10 mins **Cook:** 30 mins

Serves 2

Ingredients

- 175g pack baby corn
- 1 large red onion , sliced (190g)
- 1 red pepper , deseeded and roughly chopped
- ½ tsp cumin seeds
- 2 tsp rapeseed oil
- 1 large ripe kiwi , halved lengthways (110g)
- 1 large tomato , halved (115g)
- 100g wholemeal flour , plus extra for rolling
- 1 large garlic clove
- 15g fresh coriander , chopped
- 1 tsp vegan bouillon powder
- ½ tsp smoked paprika
- 85g red cabbage , finely shredded

Method

STEP 1

Heat oven to 220C/200C fan/gas 7. Pile the corn, red onion and pepper into a large shallow roasting tin and toss with the cumin seeds and oil. Add the kiwi and tomato on one side of the tin and roast for 20 mins.

STEP 2

Meanwhile, mix 60ml water into the flour with the blade of a knife to make a dough. Knead briefly until smooth, then cut equally into four and roll out each piece on a lightly floured surface into a 16cm round tortilla. Cover with a tea towel to stop them drying out.

STEP 3

Remove the cooked tomato and kiwi from the tin and return the veg to the oven for 10 mins. Remove the skin from the kiwi and scoop the flesh into a bowl with the tomato, garlic, half the coriander, bouillon and paprika. Use a hand blender to blitz to a smooth salsa.

STEP 4

Heat a large non-stick frying pan, without oil, and cook the tortillas one at a time for a minute on one side and about 10 seconds on the other, until you see them puff up a little. Spread a tortilla with some salsa, top with cabbage and roasted veg, then scatter with the remaining coriander. Add a spoonful more salsa and eat with your hands.

Smashed chicken with corn slaw

Prep: 10 mins **Cook:** 5 mins

Serves 4

Ingredients

For the chicken

- 4 skinless chicken breast fillets
- 1 lime, zested and juiced
- 2 tbsp bio yogurt
- 1 tsp fresh thyme leaves
- ¼ tsp turmeric
- 2 tbsp finely chopped coriander
- 1 garlic clove, finely grated
- 1 tsp rapeseed oil

For the slaw

- 1 small avocado
- 1 lime, zested and juiced
- 2 tbsp bio yogurt
- 2 tbsp finely chopped coriander
- 160g corn, cut from 2 cobs
- 1 red pepper, deseeded and chopped
- 1 red onion, halved and finely sliced
- 320g white cabbage, finely sliced
- 150g new potatoes, boiled, to serve

Method

STEP 1

Cut the chicken breasts in half, then put them between two sheets of baking parchment and bash with a rolling pin to flatten. Mix the lime zest and juice with the yogurt, thyme, turmeric, coriander and garlic in a large bowl. Add the chicken and stir until well coated. Leave to marinate while you make the slaw.

STEP 2

Mash the avocado with the lime juice and zest, 2 tbsp yogurt and the coriander. Stir in the corn, red pepper, onion and cabbage.

STEP 3

Heat a large non-stick frying pan or griddle pan, then cook the chicken in batches for a few mins each side – they'll cook quickly as they're thin. Serve the hot chicken with the slaw and the new potatoes. If you're cooking for two, chill half the chicken and slaw for lunch another day (eat within two days).

Pork souvlaki with Greek salad & rice

Prep: 15 mins Cook: 35 mins

Serves 2

Ingredients

- 1 garlic clove, finely grated
- 4 tsp olive oil
- ½ lemon, zested and juiced
- ¾ tsp dried oregano
- 250g lean pork tenderloin, cut into chunks
- 1 onion, finely chopped
- 85g brown basmati rice
- ½ tsp dried mint
- 1 tsp vegetable bouillon powder
- 2 tbsp chopped fresh dill
- 3 tomatoes, chopped
- 10cm chunk of cucumber, chopped
- 1 red onion, halved and thinly sliced
- 4 Kalamata olives, halved
- 1 tsp red wine vinegar
- 25g feta, crumbled

Method

STEP 1

Mix the garlic with 2 tsp of the oil, the lemon zest and 1 tsp juice, lots of black pepper, and ½ tsp oregano in a large bowl. Tip in the pork and mix so the meat is well coated. Set aside to marinate for 30 mins if you have time.

STEP 2

Heat 1 tsp olive oil in a non-stick pan. Add the chopped onion, cover and cook for 5 mins, then remove the lid and stir in the rice, dried mint and bouillon. Pour in 300ml boiling water. Cover and cook for 30-35 mins until the liquid has been absorbed and the rice is tender. Stir in the dill and a squeeze of lemon juice.

STEP 3

Meanwhile, heat the grill to high or light your barbecue. Thread the pork onto two skewers. Mix the tomatoes, cucumber, red onion and olives in a bowl with the remaining oregano, vinegar, remaining oil and a squeeze of lemon. Pile onto plates and top with the feta.

STEP 4

Grill the souvlaki for about 4 mins each side until they are cooked, but still juicy. Serve with the salad and rice.

Sausage, mustard & apple hash

Prep: 5 mins **Cook:** 30 mins

Serves 2

Ingredients

- 450g white potatoes , peeled and cut into 2cm cubes
- 30g butter
- olive oil , for frying
- 2 small Cox's apples , cored and cut into wedges
- 4 herby pork sausages , cut into chunks
- 2 tsp wholegrain mustard
- 3 thyme sprigs , leaves picked
- watercress salad , to serve

Method

STEP 1

Bring a large pan of salted water to the boil. Add the potatoes and cook for 4 mins. Drain and leave to steam dry in a colander.

STEP 2

Heat half the butter and 1 tbsp olive oil in a large frying pan or shallow casserole dish over a medium-high heat. Add the apple wedges and fry on each side for 5 mins or until golden brown and starting to caramelise. Remove with a slotted spoon and set aside on a plate.

STEP 3

In the same pan, heat the remaining butter and a little more oil over a medium heat and add the potatoes and sausage chunks. Fry for 10-15 mins, turning every so often until the potatoes and sausage are crisp and golden brown. Season to taste. Stir through the mustard and the apple wedges, then scatter over some thyme leaves, and serve with watercress salad.

Mushroom & potato soup

Prep: 15 mins **Cook:** 30 mins

Serves 4

Ingredients

- 1 tbsp rapeseed oil
- 2 large onions, halved and thinly sliced
- 20g dried porcini mushrooms
- 3 tsp vegetable bouillon powder
- 300g chestnut mushrooms, chopped
- 3 garlic cloves, finely grated
- 300g potato, finely diced
- 2 tsp fresh thyme
- 4 carrots, finely diced
- 2 tbsp chopped parsley
- 8 tbsp bio yogurt
- 55g walnut pieces

Method

STEP 1

Heat the oil in a large pan. Tip in the onions and fry for 10 mins until golden. Meanwhile, pour 1.2 litres boiling water over the dried mushrooms and stir in the bouillon.

STEP 2

Add the fresh mushrooms and garlic to the pan with the potatoes, thyme and carrots, and continue to fry until the mushrooms soften and start to brown.

STEP 3

Pour in the dried mushrooms and stock, cover the pan and leave to simmer for 20 mins. Stir in the parsley and plenty of pepper. Ladle into bowls and serve each portion topped with 2 tbsp yogurt and a quarter of the walnuts. The rest can be chilled and reheated the next day.

Quinoa salad with avocado mayo

Prep: 10 mins **Cook:** 18 mins

Serves 2

Ingredients

- 70g quinoa
- 75g avocado, halved and stoned

- 1 small garlic clove, finely grated
- ½ tsp mustard powder
- 1 lemon, juiced and half zested
- 198g can sweetcorn, drained
- 160g cherry tomatoes, halved
- 2 x 5cm chunks cucumber, diced
- 2 spring onions, finely sliced
- 2 tbsp chopped mint
- 2 tbsp pumpkin seeds
- 100g cooked chicken (optional)

Method

STEP 1

Put the quinoa in a pan of boiling water and simmer for about 18 mins until the grains burst. Tip into a sieve and rinse under cold water.

STEP 2

Meanwhile, scoop the avocado into a bowl and add the garlic, mustard and 2 tbsp lemon juice, then blitz with a hand blender or in a food processor until smooth. Add 1-2 tbsp cold water if it's too thick.

STEP 3

Stir the lemon zest into the quinoa, along with the corn, salad vegetables, mint and pumpkin seeds, then flavour with a little more lemon juice. Tip onto plates or into containers. Top with the chicken, if using, and spoon over the avocado mayo.

Guacamole & mango salad with black beans

Cook: 15 mins No cook

Serves 2

Ingredients

- 1 lime, zested and juiced
- 1 small mango, stoned, peeled and chopped
- 1 small avocado, stoned, peeled and chopped
- 100g cherry tomatoes, halved
- 1 red chilli, deseeded and chopped
- 1 red onion, chopped
- ½ small pack coriander, chopped
- 400g can black beans, drained and rinsed

Method

STEP 1

Put the lime zest and juice, mango, avocado, tomatoes, chilli and onion in a bowl, stir through the coriander and beans.

Egyptian courgettes with dukkah sprinkle

Prep: 10 mins **Cook:** 25 mins

Serves 4

Ingredients

- 1 tbsp rapeseed oil
- 2 onions, halved and sliced
- 2 tsp ground coriander
- 2 tsp smoked paprika
- 400g can chopped tomatoes
- 2 tsp vegetable bouillon powder
- 2 large courgettes, sliced
- 400g can butter beans, drained
- 180g cherry tomatoes
- 160g frozen peas
- 15g coriander, chopped

For the dukkah

- 1 tsp coriander seeds
- 1 tsp cumin seeds
- 1 tbsp sesame seeds
- 25g flaked almonds

Method

STEP 1

Heat the oil in a large non-stick pan and fry the onions for 5 mins, stirring occasionally until starting to colour. Stir in the ground coriander and paprika, then tip in the tomatoes with a can of water. Add the bouillon powder and courgettes, cover and cook for 6 mins.

STEP 2

Meanwhile, make the dukkah. Warm the whole spices, sesame seeds and almonds in a pan until aromatic, stirring frequently, then remove the pan from the heat.

STEP 3

Add the butter beans, tomatoes and peas to the courgettes, cover and cook for 5 mins more. Stir in the coriander, then spoon into bowls. Crush the spices and almonds using a pestle and mortar and scatter on top. If you're cooking for two people, put half the seed mix in a jar and chill half the veg for another day.

Spanish chicken stew

Prep: 10 mins **Cook:** 30 mins

Serves 4

Ingredients

- 2 tbsp olive oil
- 500g skinless boneless chicken thighs
- 1 red pepper , cut into chunky pieces
- 1 large onion , sliced
- 2 garlic cloves , chopped
- 1 tbsp white wine vinegar
- 1 tbsp smoked paprika
- 400ml chicken stock
- large handful black olives (such as couchillo)
- 50g flaked almonds , toasted
- cooked rice or crusty bread, to serve

Method

STEP 1

In a large saucepan, heat 1 tbsp of the oil. Season the chicken and brown on both sides for 7-8 mins until golden, then set aside on a plate. Put the remaining 1 tbsp oil in the pan with the pepper, onion and garlic. Fry on a medium heat for 8 mins or until slightly golden. Add the vinegar and cook for 1 min.

STEP 2

Return the chicken to the pan with the paprika and stock. Bring to the boil, then turn down to simmer for 25 mins until the chicken is cooked through. Add the olives and almonds, and serve with rice or crusty bread.

Mexican beans & avocado on toast

Prep: 20 mins **Cook:** 10 mins

Serves 4

Ingredients

- 270g cherry tomatoes, quartered
- 1 red or white onion, finely chopped
- ½ lime, juiced
- 4 tbsp olive oil
- 2 garlic cloves, crushed
- 1 tsp ground cumin

- 2 tsp chipotle paste or 1 tsp chilli flakes
- 2 x 400g cans black beans, drained
- small bunch coriander, chopped
- 4 slices bread
- 1 avocado, finely sliced

Method

STEP 1

Mix the tomatoes, ¼ onion, lime juice and 1 tbsp oil and set aside. Fry the remaining onion in 2 tbsp oil until it starts to soften. Add the garlic, fry for 1 min, then add the cumin and chipotle and stir until fragrant. Tip in the beans and a splash of water, stir and cook gently until heated through. Stir in most of the tomato mixture and cook for 1 min, season well and add most of the coriander.

STEP 2

Toast the bread and drizzle with the remaining 1 tbsp oil. Put a slice on each plate and pile some beans on top. Arrange some slices of avocado on top, then sprinkle with the remaining tomato mixture and coriander leaves to serve.

Caponata bake

Prep: 15 mins **Cook:** 35 mins

Makes 2 (serves 4)

Ingredients

- 700g medium potatoes (about 6), thinly sliced
- 4 tbsp milk
- 85g mature cheddar, finely grated
- 1 tbsp rapeseed oil
- 2 onions (320g), finely chopped
- 4 tsp balsamic vinegar
- 2 tsp vegetable bouillon powder
- 2 x 400g cans chopped tomatoes
- 2 aubergines, cut into chunks
- 2 red peppers (540g), deseeded and chopped
- 30g pack basil, leaves picked and finely chopped
- 3 garlic cloves, finely grated
- 10 Kalamata olives, pitted and halved
- 2 tsp capers
- ⅓ x 30g pack flat-leaf parsley, chopped
- 320g broccoli florets

Method

STEP 1

Heat the grill to high. Boil the potato slices for 10 mins, then drain, tip into a bowl (don't worry if they break up a little) and add the milk and half the cheese. Mix together.

STEP 2

Meanwhile, heat the oil in a large frying pan and cook the onion until softened. Spoon in the balsamic vinegar and bouillon powder, then stir in the tomatoes, aubergine, peppers, basil and garlic. Cover and cook for 20 mins, stirring frequently and adding a little water if necessary, until the aubergine is tender when tested with a knife.

STEP 3

Remove from the heat and stir in the olives, capers and parsley. Tip into two shallow baking dishes. Cover with the potatoes and sprinkle with the remaining cheese.

STEP 4

If you are following our Healthy Diet Plan, grill the one you are eating now until golden. While it's grilling, steam or boil half the broccoli to serve with the bake. To reheat on the second day, heat oven to 180C/160C fan/gas 4 and bake for 30-40 mins until bubbling and golden. Cook the remaining broccoli to serve with it.

Prosciutto, kale & butter bean stew

Prep: 5 mins **Cook:** 20 mins

Serves 4

Ingredients

- 80g pack prosciutto , torn into pieces
- 2 tbsp olive oil
- 1 fennel bulb , sliced
- 2 garlic clove , crushed
- 1 tsp chilli flakes
- 4 thyme sprigs
- 150ml white wine or chicken stock
- 2 x 400g cans butter beans
- 400g can cherry tomatoes
- 200g bag sliced kale

Method

STEP 1

Fry the prosciutto in a dry saucepan over a high heat until crisp, then remove half with a slotted spoon and set aside. Turn the heat down to low, pour in the oil and tip in the fennel with a pinch of salt. Cook for 5 mins until softened, then throw in the garlic, chilli flakes and thyme and cook for a further 2 mins, then pour in the wine or stock and bring to a simmer.

STEP 2

Tip both cans of butter beans into the stew, along with their liquid, then add the tomatoes, season well and bring everything to a simmer. Cook, undisturbed, for 5 mins, then stir through the kale. Once wilted, ladle the stew into bowls, removing the thyme sprigs and topping each portion with the remaining prosciutto.

Chicken bhuna

Prep: 15 mins **Cook:** 50 mins

Serves 6

Ingredients

- 3 medium onions, 2 finely chopped, 1 roughly chopped
- 100ml vegetable oil
- 1 tbsp ginger and garlic purée
- 1 tbsp mild curry powder
- 1 tsp turmeric
- 1 tsp chilli powder
- 800g chicken thighs, diced
- 100ml natural yogurt
- 4 tbsp tomato purée
- 2 tsp garam masala

Method

STEP 1

To make the onion purée, bring a small pan of water to the boil and add half the roughly chopped onion. Boil until soft (about 10 mins), drain and puree with a hand blender or mini food processor.

STEP 2

Heat a large saucepan on a high heat. Once it's hot add the oil and finely chopped onions and reduce to a low heat. Cook the onions slowly and gently until golden brown in colour, and season.

STEP 3

Add the ginger and garlic purée, curry powder, turmeric, chilli powder and a splash of water to the pan of onions and stir in well. Fry for a couple of mins. Add the diced chicken thighs and stir in well.

STEP 4

Mix the yogurt, tomato purée and onion purée together in a jug with 300ml water. Pour into the saucepan and mix well. Turn up the heat until the sauce begins to boil. Simmer for 15 to 20 mins, stirring occasionally.

STEP 5

Finally, sprinkle in the garam masala and stir in well for the final 2 mins before serving.

Veggie tahini lentils

Prep: 10 mins **Cook:** 10 mins

Serves 4

Ingredients

- 50g tahini
- zest and juice 1 lemon
- 2 tbsp olive oil
- 1 red onion, thinly sliced
- 1 garlic clove, crushed
- 1 yellow pepper, thinly sliced
- 200g green beans, trimmed and halved
- 1 courgette, sliced into half moons
- 100g shredded kale
- 250g pack pre-cooked puy lentils

Method

STEP 1

In a jug, mix the tahini with the zest and juice of the lemon and 50ml of cold water to make a runny dressing. Season to taste, then set aside.

STEP 2

Heat the oil in a wok or large frying pan over a medium-high heat. Add the red onion, along with a pinch of salt, and fry for 2 mins until starting to soften and colour. Add the garlic, pepper, green beans and courgette and fry for 5 min, stirring frequently.

STEP 3

Tip in the kale, lentils and the tahini dressing. Keep the pan on the heat for a couple of mins, stirring everything together until the kale is wilted and it's all coated in the creamy dressing.

Green minestrone with tortellini

Prep: 5 mins **Cook:** 25 mins

Serves 4

Ingredients

- 2 tbsp olive or rapeseed oil
- 1 onion , chopped
- 1 small leek , chopped
- 1 celery stick , chopped
- 3 garlic cloves , crushed
- 2 bay leaves
- 1l good-quality chicken or vegetable stock
- 100g shredded spring veg or cabbage
- 50g frozen peas
- 1 lemon , zested
- 250g tortellini

Method

STEP 1

Heat the olive or rapeseed oil in a large pan. Add the onion, leek and celery stick. Cook for 8-10 mins until softened, then stir in the garlic and bay leaves. Pour in the chicken or vegetable stock, then cover and simmer for 10 mins. Add the spring veg or cabbage, peas, lemon zest and tortellini (spinach tortellini works well). Cover and cook for another 3 mins, season well and ladle into bowls.

Khatti dhal

Prep: 15 mins **Cook:** 1 hr and 15 mins - 1 hr and 30 mins plus soaking

Serves 4 - 6

Ingredients

For the dhal

- 430g toor dhal or red split lentils
- ½ tsp turmeric
- 2 large tomatoes, chopped (better if you remove the skin but not essential)
- 5cm piece ginger, peeled and grated

- 2 garlic cloves, crushed or grated
- 2 green chillies, chopped (deseeded if you don't like it very hot)

For the tempering

- 2 tbsp oil or ghee (or a mixture of oil and unsalted butter)
- ½ tsp cumin seeds
- 8 garlic cloves, sliced
- 2 tbsp tamarind paste
- 1 tsp hot chilli powder
- 2 tsp ground coriander
- 3 dried chillies (I use Kashmiri), roughly broken
- 12 curry leaves, fresh or frozen (optional)

Method

STEP 1

Soak the toor dhal for about 40 mins, then rinse well. Put it in a large heavy-bottomed saucepan with the turmeric, tomatoes, ginger, garlic and chillies. Add 1.7 litres of water and bring to the boil. Turn the heat down low and cook until you have a thick purée, adding water if it gets too dry. Dhal can be quite soupy or quite thick, depending on how you like it. Simply reduce it to thicken it, or add water to thin it. Season to taste.

STEP 2

When the dhal is at a thickness you like, add the tamarind, chilli powder (unless it's already hot enough), and the ground coriander and check the seasoning.

STEP 3

Tempering is the last phase for a dhal. Heat the oil or ghee in a frying pan and add the cumin seeds. Cook over a medium heat for about 30 secs, then add the garlic and cook for about 10 secs (the garlic should eventually become golden but not brown so don't overdo it at this point), then add the dried chillies and the curry leaves, if using. Fry until the dried chillies have changed colour slightly and the curry leaves are crisp. Pour this over the dhal and stir. Cover and leave to sit for a few mins before serving.

Roasted new potato, kale & feta salad with avocado

Prep: 15 mins **Cook:** 35 mins

Serves 2

Ingredients

- 200g Jersey Royal potatoes, halved
- 2 garlic cloves
- 2 tbsp cold-pressed rapeseed oil
- 1 lemon, juiced
- 1 banana shallot, chopped
- 200g bag kale
- 1 small ripe avocado, flesh scooped out
- ½ tsp Dijon mustard
- 25g feta (or vegetarian alternative), crumbled
- ½-1 tsp chilli flakes
- 1 tbsp pumpkin seeds, toasted

Method

STEP 1

Heat oven to 200C/180C fan/gas 6. Boil the potatoes for 10 mins until mostly tender, drain and leave to steam dry. Toss the potatoes in a large roasting tin with the garlic, drizzle over 1 tbsp oil and season. Roast for 20 mins.

STEP 2

While the potatoes are roasting, squeeze half the lemon juice over the shallot and half of the kale, season, then massage gently to encourage the kale to soften.

STEP 3

Remove the garlic cloves from the oven. Put the rest of the kale on top of the potatoes, drizzle over a little oil, season and return to the oven for 5 mins until crisp.

STEP 4

Meanwhile, blitz the garlic, avocado, mustard, remaining oil and lemon juice together, add enough water to create a smooth dressing and season to taste. Mix the potatoes and cooked kale into the raw kale salad and tip onto a platter. Drizzle over the dressing, then top with the feta, chilli flakes and pumpkin seeds.

Baked banana porridge

Prep: 5 mins **Cook:** 25 mins

Serves 2

Ingredients

- 2 small bananas, halved lengthways
- 100g jumbo porridge oats
- ¼ tsp cinnamon
- 150ml milk of your choice, plus extra to serve
- 4 walnuts, roughly chopped

Method

STEP 1

Heat oven to 190C/170C fan/gas 5. Mash up one banana half, then mix it with the oats, cinnamon, milk, 300ml water and a pinch of salt, and pour into a baking dish. Top with the remaining banana halves and scatter over the walnuts.

STEP 2

Bake for 20-25 mins until the oats are creamy and have absorbed most of the liquid.

All-in-one chicken with wilted spinach

Prep: 20 mins **Cook:** 1 hr

Serves 2

Ingredients

- 2 beetroot, peeled and cut into small chunks
- 300g celeriac, cut into small chunks
- 2 red onions, quartered
- 8 garlic cloves, 4 crushed, the rest left whole, but peeled
- 1 tbsp rapeseed oil
- 1½ tbsp fresh thyme leaves, plus extra to serve
- 1 lemon, zested and juiced
- 1 tsp fennel seeds
- 1 tsp English mustard powder
- 1 tsp smoked paprika
- 4 tbsp bio yogurt
- 4 bone-in chicken thighs, skin removed
- 260g bag spinach

Method

STEP 1

Heat oven to 200C/180C fan/gas 6. Tip the beetroot, celeriac, onions and whole garlic cloves into a shallow roasting tin. Add the oil, 1 tbsp thyme, half the lemon zest, fennel seeds and a squeeze of lemon juice, then toss together. Roast for 20 mins while you prepare the chicken.

STEP 2

Stir the mustard powder and paprika into 2 tbsp yogurt in a bowl. Add half the crushed garlic, the remaining lemon zest and thyme, and juice from half the lemon. Add the chicken and toss well until it's coated all over. Put the chicken in the tin with the veg and roast for 40 mins until the chicken is cooked through and the vegetables are tender.

STEP 3

About 5 mins before the chicken is ready, wash and drain the spinach and put it in a pan with the remaining crushed garlic. Cook until wilted, then turn off the heat and stir in the remaining yogurt. Scatter some extra thyme over the chicken and vegetables, then serve.

Miso beansprout rolls

Prep: 10 mins **Cook:** 10 mins

Serves 2

Ingredients

- 50g brown basmati rice
- 1 ½ tbsp finely chopped ginger , plus 2 slices
- 4 tsp rapeseed oil
- 1 yellow pepper , deseeded and cut into strips
- 4 garlic cloves , grated
- 160g beansprouts
- 4 spring onions , shredded
- 1 large carrot , cut into thin strips with a julienne peeler
- 1 red chilli , seeded and chopped (optional)
- 2 tsp miso paste
- 4 large eggs

Method

STEP 1

Boil the rice with the sliced ginger for 25 mins until tender – use just enough water so that it cooks, but it's not swamped. Drain well and remove the ginger.

STEP 2

Heat 2 tsp oil in a large wok, then stir-fry the chopped ginger, pepper and garlic for about 1 min. Tip in the beansprouts, spring onions, carrots and chilli, if using, then stir-fry until the veg has softened and started to char. Remove from the heat.

STEP 3

Stir the miso with 2 tsp water to dilute it a little, then beat in the eggs. Heat 1 tsp oil in a large non-stick frying pan. Pour in half the egg mixture and scatter over half the rice. Allow the mixture to set to an omelette. While still a little moist, tip half of the vegetables on top and cook for a few seconds more. Carefully roll up, and repeat with the remaining egg, rice and vegetables.

Leek & butter bean soup with crispy kale & bacon

Prep: 10 mins **Cook:** 30 mins

Serves 4

Ingredients

- 4 tsp olive oil
- 500g leeks , sliced
- 4 thyme sprigs , leaves picked
- 2 x 400g cans butter beans
- 500ml vegetable bouillon stock
- 2 tsp wholegrain mustard
- ½ small pack flat-leaf parsley
- 3 rashers streaky bacon
- 40g chopped kale , any tough stems removed
- 25g hazelnuts , roughly chopped

Method

STEP 1

Heat 1 tbsp oil in a large saucepan over a low heat. Add the leeks, thyme and seasoning. Cover and cook for 15 mins until softened, adding a splash of water if the leeks start to stick. Add the butter beans with the water from the cans, the stock and mustard. Bring to the boil and simmer for 3-4 mins until hot. Blend the soup in a food processor or with a stick blender, stir through the parsley and check the seasoning.

STEP 2

Put the bacon in a large, non-stick frying pan over a medium heat. Cook for 3-4 mins until crispy, then set side to cool. Add the remaining 1 tsp oil to the pan, and tip in the kale and hazelnuts. Cook for 2 mins, stirring until the kale is wilted and crisping at the edges and the hazelnuts are toasted. Cut the bacon into small pieces, then stir into the kale mixture.

STEP 3

Reheat the soup, adding a splash of water if it is too thick. Serve in bowls sprinkled with the bacon & kale mixture.

Herb omelette with fried tomatoes

Prep: 5 mins **Cook:** 5 mins

Serves 2

Ingredients

- 1 tsp rapeseed oil
- 3 tomatoes, halved
- 4 large eggs
- 1 tbsp chopped parsley
- 1 tbsp chopped basil

Method

STEP 1

Heat the oil in a small non-stick frying pan, then cook the tomatoes cut-side down until starting to soften and colour. Meanwhile, beat the eggs with the herbs and plenty of freshly ground black pepper in a small bowl.

STEP 2

Scoop the tomatoes from the pan and put them on two serving plates. Pour the egg mixture into the pan and stir gently with a wooden spoon so the egg that sets on the base of the pan moves to enable uncooked egg to flow into the space. Stop stirring when it's nearly cooked to allow it to set into an omelette. Cut into four and serve with the tomatoes.

Curried mango & chickpea pot

Prep: 15 mins **Serves 1**

Ingredients

- 200g chickpeas, drained and rinsed
- 2 tbsp fat-free Greek yogurt
- ½ lemon, juiced
- 1 heaped tbsp korma curry paste
- ½ carrot, julienned or grated
- 70g red cabbage, shredded
- 50g baby spinach, shredded
- 40g mango, finely diced
- ½ tsp nigella seeds

- ½ small red chilli, finely sliced (deseeded if you want less heat)

Method

STEP 1

Combine the chickpeas, yogurt, lemon and korma paste in a bowl, then toss with the carrot, cabbage, spinach and mango. Tip into your lunchbox or an airtight container and scatter with the nigella seeds and red chilli.

Triangular bread thins

Prep: 8 mins **Cook:** 10 mins - 12 mins

Makes 6

Ingredients

- 190g plain wholemeal spelt flour, plus extra for dusting
- ½ tsp bicarbonate of soda
- 1 tsp baking powder
- 75ml live bio yogurt made up to 150ml with cold water

Method

STEP 1

Heat oven to 200C/180C fan/gas 6 and line a baking sheet with baking parchment. Mix the flour, bicarbonate of soda and baking powder in a bowl, then stir in the diluted yogurt with the blade of a knife until you have a soft, sticky dough, adding a little water if the mix is dry.

STEP 2

Tip the dough onto a lightly floured surface and shape and flatten with your hands to make a 20cm round. Take care not to over-handle as it can make the bread tough. Lift onto the baking sheet and cut into six triangles, slightly easing them apart with the knife. Bake for about 10-12 mins – they don't have to be golden, but should feel firm. Leave to cool on a wire rack.

STEP 3

Use to make our wild salmon & avocado triangles and goat's cheese, tomato & olive triangles. The rest can be packed into a food bag to use later in the week, or frozen until needed.

Spiced chicken, spinach & sweet potato stew

Prep: 15 mins **Cook:** 40 mins

Serves 4

Ingredients

- 3 sweet potatoes, cut into chunks
- 190g bag spinach
- 1 tbsp sunflower oil

For the spice paste

- 2 onions, chopped
- 1 red chilli, chopped
- 1 tsp paprika
- thumb-sized piece ginger, grated

To serve

- 8 chicken thighs, skinless and boneless
- 500ml chicken stock

- 400g can tomatoes
- 2 preserved lemons, deseeded and chopped

- pumpkin seeds, toasted
- 2-3 preserved lemons, deseeded and chopped
- 4 naan bread, warmed

Method

STEP 1

Put the sweet potato in a large, deep saucepan over a high heat. Cover with boiling water and boil for 10 mins. Meanwhile, put all the paste ingredients in a food processor and blend until very finely chopped. Set aside until needed.

STEP 2

Put the spinach in a large colander in the sink and pour the sweet potatoes and their cooking water over it to drain the potatoes and wilt the spinach at the same time. Leave to steam-dry.

STEP 3

Return the saucepan to the heat (no need to wash it first), then add the oil, followed by the spice paste. Fry the paste for about 5 mins until thickened, then add the chicken. Fry for 8-10 mins until the chicken starts to colour. Pour over the stock, bring to the boil and leave to simmer for 10 mins, stirring occasionally.

STEP 4

Check the chicken is cooked by cutting into one of the thighs and making sure it's white throughout with no signs of pink. Season with black pepper, then add the sweet potato. Leave to simmer for a further 5 mins. Meanwhile, roughly chop the spinach and add to the stew. At this point you can leave the stew to cool and freeze for up to 3 months, if you like.

STEP 5

Scatter over the pumpkin seeds and preserved lemons, and serve with warm naan bread on the side.

Leek, tomato & barley risotto with pan-cooked cod

Prep: 10 mins **Cook:** 20 mins

Serves 2

Ingredients

- 2 tsp rapeseed oil
- 1 large leek (315g), thinly sliced
- 2 garlic cloves, chopped
- 400g can barley (don't drain)
- 2 tsp vegetable bouillon
- 1 tsp finely chopped sage
- 1 tbsp thyme leaves, plus a few extra to serve
- 160g cherry tomatoes
- 50g finely grated parmesan
- 2 skin-on cod fillets or firm white fish fillets

Method

STEP 1

Heat 1 tsp oil in a non-stick pan and fry the leek and garlic for 5-10 mins, stirring frequently until softened, adding a splash of water to help it cook if you need to.

STEP 2

Tip in the barley with its liquid, then stir in the bouillon, sage and thyme. Simmer, stirring frequently for 3-4 mins. Add the tomatoes and cook about 4-5 mins more until they soften and start to split, adding a drop more water if necessary. Stir in the parmesan.

STEP 3

Meanwhile, heat the remaining oil in a non-stick pan and fry the cod, skin-side down, for 4-5 mins. Flip the fillets over to cook briefly on the other side. Spoon the risotto into two bowls. Serve the cod on top with a few thyme leaves, if you like.

Miso mushroom & tofu noodle soup

Prep: 10 mins **Cook:** 15 mins

Serves 1

Ingredients

- 1 tbsp rapeseed oil
- 70g mixed mushrooms, sliced
- 50g smoked tofu, cut into small cubes
- ½ tbsp brown rice miso paste
- 50g dried buckwheat or egg noodles
- 2 spring onions, shredded

Method

STEP 1

Heat half the oil in a frying pan over a medium heat. Add the mushrooms and fry for 5-6 mins, or until golden. Transfer to a bowl using a slotted spoon and set aside. Add the remaining oil to the pan and fry the tofu for 3-4 mins, or until evenly golden.

STEP 2

Mix the miso paste with 325ml boiling water in a jug. Cook the noodles following pack instructions, then drain and transfer to a bowl. Top with the mushrooms and tofu, then pour over the miso broth. Scatter over the spring onions just before serving.

Green chowder with prawns

Prep: 10 mins **Cook:** 20 mins - 30 mins

Serves 4

Ingredients

- 1 tbsp olive oil
- 1 onion , finely chopped
- 1 celery stick , finely chopped
- 1 garlic clove
- 300g petit pois
- 200g pack sliced kale
- 2 potatoes , finely chopped
- 1 low-salt chicken stock cube (we used Kallo)
- 100g cooked North Atlantic prawns

Method

STEP 1

Heat the oil in a saucepan over a medium heat. Add the onion and celery and cook for 5-6 mins until softened but not coloured. Add the garlic and cook for a further min. Stir in the petit pois, kale and potatoes, then add the stock cube and 750ml water. Bring to the boil and simmer for 10-12 mins until the potatoes are soft.

STEP 2

Tip ¾ of the mixture into a food processor and whizz until smooth. Add a little more water or stock if it's too thick. Pour the mixture back into the pan and add half the prawns.

STEP 3

Divide between four bowls and spoon the remaining prawns on top. Can be frozen for up to a month. Add the prawns once defrosted.

Little spicy veggie pies

Prep: 10 mins **Cook:** 55 mins

Serves 4

Ingredients

- 2 tbsp rapeseed oil
- 2 tbsp finely chopped ginger
- 3 tbsp Korma curry powder
- 3 large garlic cloves , grated
- 2 x 400g cans chickpeas , undrained
- 320g carrots , coarsely grated
- 160g frozen sweetcorn
- 1 tbsp vegetable bouillon powder
- 4 tbsp tomato purée
- 250g bag spinach , cooked

For the topping

- 750g potatoes, peeled and cut into 3cm chunks
- 1 tsp ground coriander
- 10g fresh coriander, chopped
- 150g coconut yogurt

Method

STEP 1

To make the topping, boil the potatoes for 15-20 mins until tender then drain, reserving the water, and mash with the ground and fresh coriander and yogurt until creamy.

STEP 2

While the potatoes are boiling, heat the oil in a large pan, add the ginger and fry briefly, tip in the curry powder and garlic, stirring quickly as you don't want it to burn, then tip in a can of chickpeas with the water from the can. Stir well, then mash in the pan to smash them up a bit, then tip in the second can of chickpeas, again with the water from the can, along with the carrots, corn, bouillon and tomato purée. Simmer for 5-10 mins, adding some of the potato water, if needed, to loosen.

STEP 3

Heat the oven to 200C/180C fan/gas 6. Spoon the filling into four individual pie dishes (each about 10cm wide, 8cm deep) and top with the mash, smoothing it to seal round the edges of the dishes. If you're following our Healthy Diet Plan, bake two for 25 mins until golden, and cook half the spinach, saving the rest of the bag for another day. Cover and chill the remaining two pies to eat another day. Will keep in the fridge for four days. If freezing, to reheat, bake from frozen for 40-45 mins until golden and piping hot.

Sesame salmon, purple sprouting broccoli & sweet potato mash

Prep: 10 mins **Cook:** 15 mins

Serves 2

Ingredients

- 1 ½ tbsp sesame oil
- 1 tbsp low-salt soy sauce
- thumb-sized piece ginger, grated
- 1 garlic clove, crushed
- 1 tsp honey

- 2 sweet potatoes, scrubbed and cut into wedges
- 1 lime, cut into wedges
- 2 boneless skinless salmon fillets
- 250g purple sprouting broccoli
- 1 tbsp sesame seeds
- 1 red chilli, thinly sliced (deseeded if you don't like it too hot)

Method

STEP 1

Heat oven to 200C/180 fan/ gas 6 and line a baking tray with parchment. Mix together 1/2 tbsp sesame oil, the soy, ginger, garlic and honey. Put the sweet potato wedges, skin and all, into a glass bowl with the lime wedges. Cover with cling film and microwave on high for 12-14 mins until completely soft.

STEP 2

Meanwhile, spread the broccoli and salmon out on the baking tray. Spoon over the marinade and season. Roast in the oven for 10-12 mins, then sprinkle over the sesame seeds.

STEP 3

Remove the lime wedges and roughly mash the sweet potato using a fork. Mix in the remaining sesame oil, the chilli and some seasoning. Divide between plates, along with the salmon and broccoli.

Slow cooker pork fillet with apples

Prep: 15 mins **Cook:** 4 hrs

Serves 4

Ingredients

- ½ tbsp rapeseed oil
- 500g pork fillet, sliced into medallions
- 1 medium onion, finely chopped
- 3 eating apples
- 150ml low-salt chicken stock
- 1 tbsp Dijon mustard
- 4 sage leaves, finely sliced
- 2 tbsp half-fat crème fraîche

Method

STEP 1

Heat the slow cooker. Heat the oil in a large frying pan, fry the pork medallions on each side for 2 mins until they pick up a little colour. Fry the onion for a few mins, then add the stock and mustard to the pan and stir. Tip the pork and sauce into the slow cooker.

STEP 2

Core and cut the apples into quarters, add them to the pot with the sage. Season with black pepper. Cook on Low for 4 hours or until the meat is tender, then stir in the crème fraîche.

Easy chicken stew

Prep: 10 mins **Cook:** 50 mins

Serves 4

Ingredients

- 1 tbsp olive oil
- 1 bunch spring onions, sliced, white and green parts separated
- 1 small swede (350g), peeled and chopped into small pieces
- 400g potatoes, peeled and chopped into small pieces
- 8 skinless boneless chicken thighs
- 1 tbsp Dijon mustard
- 500ml chicken stock
- 200g Savoy cabbage or spring cabbage, sliced
- 2 tsp cornflour (optional)
- crusty bread or cheese scones, to serve (optional)

Method

STEP 1

Heat the oil in a large saucepan. Add the white spring onion slices and fry for 1 min to soften. Tip in the swede and potatoes and cook for 2-3 mins more, then add the chicken, mustard and stock. Cover and cook for 35 mins, or until the vegetables are tender and the chicken cooked through.

STEP 2

Add the cabbage and simmer for another 5 mins. If the stew looks too thin, mix the cornflour with 1 tbsp cold water and pour a couple of teaspoonfuls into the pan; let the stew bubble and thicken, then check again. If it's still too thin, add a little more of the cornflour mix and let the stew bubble and thicken some more.

STEP 3

Season to taste, then spoon the stew into deep bowls. Scatter over the green spring onion slices and serve with crusty bread or warm cheese scones, if you like.

One-pan egg & veg brunch

Prep: 5 mins **Cook:** 25 mins

Serves 2 adults + 2 children

Ingredients

- 300g baby new potatoes , halved
- ½ tbsp rapeseed oil
- 1 knob of butter
- 1 courgette , cut into small chunks
- 1 yellow pepper , cut into small chunks
- 1 red pepper , cut into small chunks
- 2 spring onions , finely sliced
- 1 garlic clove , crushed
- 1 sprig thyme , leaves picked
- 4 eggs
- toast , to serve

Method

STEP 1

Boil the new potatoes for 8 mins, then drain.

STEP 2

Heat the oil and butter in a large non-stick frying pan, then add the courgette, peppers, potatoes and a little salt and pepper. Cook for 10 mins, stirring from time to time until everything is starting to brown. Add the spring onions, garlic and thyme and cook for 2 mins more.

STEP 3

Make four spaces in the pan and crack in the eggs. Cover with foil or a lid and cook for around 4 mins, or until the eggs are cooked (with the yolks soft for dipping into). Sprinkle with more thyme leaves and ground black pepper if you like. Serve with toast.

Sesame chicken & prawn skewers

Prep: 15 mins **Cook:** 5 mins Plus marinating

Makes 20

Ingredients

- thumb-sized piece ginger , grated
- 1 large garlic clove , grated
- 1 tsp honey
- 1½ tsp soy sauce
- 1 tsp sesame oil
- ½ lime , juiced
- 1 tbsp sesame seeds
- 1 skinless chicken breast , cut into 10 pieces
- 10 raw king prawns
- 1 broccoli head , cut into 20 florets
- 20 cocktail skewers

Method

STEP 1

Combine the ginger, garlic, honey, soy sauce, sesame oil, lime juice and sesame seeds. Divide between two bowls, then add the chicken pieces to one and the prawns to the other. Toss both mixtures well, then leave to marinate in the fridge for 15 mins.

STEP 2

Cook the chicken in a frying pan over a medium-high heat for 3 mins, then push to one side and add the prawns to the other side of the pan. Cook for 2 mins until the prawns are pink and the chicken is cooked through (use two separate pans if anyone you're cooking for has an allergy or is a pescatarian). Put the broccoli in a microwaveable bowl with a splash of water, then cover and cook on high for 5 mins.

STEP 3

Thread half of the skewers with chicken and broccoli and the other half with prawns and broccoli.

Clementine & vanilla porridge with citrus salsa

Prep: 10 mins **Cook:** 5 mins plus overnight soaking

Serves 4

Ingredients

- 4 clementines
- 2 tsp vanilla extract
- 140g porridge oats
- 1 grapefruit , peeled, seeded and chopped
- small handful mint leaves
- 2 tbsp sunflower seeds
- 6 walnut halves , broken
- 4 x 120g pots bio yogurt

Method

STEP 1

Peel the clementines, then finely chop 1 tbsp of the peel. Put the peel in a large bowl with the vanilla, oats and 800ml water. Cover and set aside to soak overnight.

STEP 2

To make the salsa, chop the clementines and mix in a bowl with the grapefruit and mint leaves. Cover and chill.

STEP 3

The next morning, tip the porridge into a pan and cook until bubbling and thick.

STEP 4

If you're following our Healthy Diet Plan, pour half of the porridge into two bowls and tip the remainder into a container ready to chill, topped with half the salsa, seeds and nuts. Divide the other half of the salsa between the two bowls of porridge along with half the yogurt. Scatter with the remaining nuts and seeds. The leftover porridge can be reheated the next day with a splash of water. Top with the remaining salsa and yogurt.

Oat pancakes

Prep: 10 mins **Cook:** 25 mins

Serves 2

Ingredients

- 1 orange , zested and juiced
- 120g frozen berries
- 1 small Pink Lady apple , finely diced
- 100g porridge oats

- 1 tsp baking powder
- 1 tsp cinnamon
- 100ml oat milk
- 1 medium egg, lightly beaten
- 1 tbsp cold pressed rapeseed oil
- 50g fat-free Greek yogurt

Method

STEP 1

To make the compote, put the orange juice, berries and apple in a small saucepan and gently simmer over a medium heat for 10-12 mins until the berries begin to burst and the apple has softened. Remove from the heat and leave to cool a little. Add a splash of water to loosen, if you like.

STEP 2

Blitz the oats in a food processor to form a coarse flour consistency, then tip into a mixing bowl. Add the baking powder, cinnamon and orange zest and stir well. Whisk together the oat milk and egg in a jug, then pour into the dry ingredients and combine to create a thick batter.

STEP 3

Heat a little of the oil in a non-stick frying pan, then pour in 2 tbsp of the batter to make a small pancake. Cook over a medium heat for 2 mins, or until small bubbles start to appear on the surface. Flip the pancake over and cook on the other side for 1 min, then transfer to a plate. Repeat with the remaining oil and batter (you should end up with six pancakes). Stack the pancakes on two warm plates, spoon over the compote and top with a dollop of the Greek yogurt.

Mushroom brunch

Prep: 5 mins **Cook:** 12 mins - 15 mins

Serves 4

Ingredients

- 250g mushrooms
- 1 garlic clove
- 1 tbsp olive oil
- 160g bag kale
- 4 eggs

Method

STEP 1

Slice the mushrooms and crush the garlic clove. Heat the olive oil in a large non-stick frying pan, then fry the garlic over a low heat for 1 min. Add the mushrooms and cook until soft. Then, add the kale. If the kale won't all fit in the pan, add half and stir until wilted, then add the rest. Once all the kale is wilted, season.

STEP 2

Now crack in the eggs and keep them cooking gently for 2-3 mins. Then, cover with the lid to for a further 2-3 mins or until the eggs are cooked to your liking. Serve with bread.

Cumin-spiced halloumi with corn & tomato slaw

Prep: 10 mins **Cook:** 5 mins

Serves 4

Ingredients

- 1 lime , zested and juiced
- 1 tsp rapeseed oil
- 1 tsp fresh thyme leaves
- ¼ tsp turmeric

For the slaw

- 1 lime , zested and juiced
- 3 tbsp bio yogurt
- 3 tbsp finely chopped coriander
- 1 red chilli , deseeded and chopped
- 160g corn , cut from 2 fresh cobs
- 1 red pepper , deseeded and chopped

- ¼ tsp cumin seeds
- 1 tbsp finely chopped coriander
- 1 garlic clove , finely grated
- 100g halloumi , thinly sliced

- 100g fine green beans , blanched, trimmed and halved
- 200g cherry tomatoes , halved
- 1 red onion , halved and finely sliced
- 320g white cabbage , finely sliced

Method

STEP 1

Mix the lime zest and juice with the oil, thyme, turmeric, cumin, coriander and garlic together in a bowl. Add the halloumi and carefully turn it until coated – take care as it breaks easily.

STEP 2

To make the slaw, mix the lime juice and zest, yogurt, coriander and chilli together, then stir in the corn, red pepper, beans, tomatoes, onion and cabbage.

STEP 3

Heat a large non-stick frying pan or griddle pan and fry the cheese in batches for 1 min each side. Serve the slaw on plates with the halloumi slices on top. If you're cooking for two people, serve half of the halloumi and slaw and chill the rest for lunch another day.

Carrot & ginger soup

Prep: 15 mins **Cook:** 25 mins - 30 mins

Serves 4

Ingredients

- 1 tbsp rapeseed oil
- 1 large onion, chopped
- 2 tbsp coarsely grated ginger
- 2 garlic cloves, sliced
- ½ tsp ground nutmeg
- 850ml vegetable stock
- 500g carrot (preferably organic), sliced
- 400g can cannellini beans (no need to drain)

Supercharged topping

- 4 tbsp almonds in their skins, cut into slivers
- sprinkle of nutmeg

Method

STEP 1

Heat the oil in a large pan, add the onion, ginger and garlic, and fry for 5 mins until starting to soften. Stir in the nutmeg and cook for 1 min more.

STEP 2

Pour in the stock, add the carrots, beans and their liquid, then cover and simmer for 20-25 mins until the carrots are tender.

STEP 3

Scoop a third of the mixture into a bowl and blitz the remainder with a hand blender or in a food processor until smooth. Return everything to the pan and heat until bubbling. Serve topped with the almonds and nutmeg.

Veggie okonomiyaki

Prep: 15 mins **Cook:** 10 mins

Serves 2

Ingredients

- 3 large eggs
- 50g plain flour
- 50ml milk
- 4 spring onions , trimmed and sliced
- 1 pak choi , sliced
- 200g Savoy cabbage , shredded
- 1 red chilli , deseeded and finely chopped, plus extra to serve
- ½ tbsp low-salt soy sauce
- ½ tbsp rapeseed oil
- 1 heaped tbsp low-fat mayonnaise
- ½ lime , juiced
- sushi ginger , to serve (optional)
- wasabi , to serve (optional)

Method

STEP 1

Whisk together the eggs, flour and milk until smooth. Add half the spring onions, the pak choi, cabbage, chilli and soy sauce. Heat the oil in a small frying pan and pour in the batter. Cook, covered, over a medium heat for 7-8 mins. Flip the okonomiyaki into a second frying pan, then return it to the heat and cook for a further 7-8 mins until a skewer inserted into it comes out clean.

STEP 2

Mix the mayonnaise and lime juice together in a small bowl. Transfer the okonomiyaki to a plate, then drizzle over the lime mayo and top with the extra chilli and spring onion and the sushi ginger, if using. Serve with the wasabi on the side, if you like.

Tuna, avocado & quinoa salad

Prep: 5 mins **Cook:** 20 mins

Serves 2

Ingredients

- 100g quinoa
- 3 tbsp extra virgin olive oil
- juice 1 lemon
- ½ tbsp white wine vinegar
- 120g can tuna, drained
- 1 avocado, stoned, peeled and cut into chunks
- 200g cherry tomatoes on the vine, halved
- 50g feta, crumbled
- 50g baby spinach
- 2 tbsp mixed seeds, toasted

Method

STEP 1

Rinse the quinoa under cold water. Tip into a saucepan, cover with water and bring to the boil. Reduce the heat and simmer for 15 mins until the grains have swollen but still have some bite. Drain, then transfer to a bowl to cool slightly.

STEP 2

Meanwhile, in a jug, combine the oil, lemon juice and vinegar with some seasoning.

STEP 3

Once the quinoa has cooled, mix with the dressing and all the remaining ingredients and season. Divide between plates or lunchboxes.

Chilli chicken & peanut pies

Prep: 15 mins **Cook:** 1 hr

Makes 2 pies, each serves 2

Ingredients

For the mash

- 500g potatoes, peeled and chopped
- 2 x 400g cans cannellini beans, drained
- 3 tbsp chopped fresh coriander
- 1 tsp chilli powder

For the chicken filling

- 2 tsp rapeseed oil
- 2 tbsp finely chopped ginger
- 1 red chilli, deseeded for less spice
- 2 tbsp cumin seeds
- 2 tbsp ground coriander
- 1 tsp chilli powder
- 400g leeks, thickly sliced
- 1 red pepper, deseeded and diced
- 1 green pepper, deseeded and diced
- 2 large skinless chicken breasts, about 400g, diced
- 400g can chopped tomatoes
- 2 tbsp tomato purée
- 2 tsp vegetable bouillon
- 3 tbsp peanut butter (with no sugar or palm oil)
- 320g broccoli, to serve

Method

STEP 1

Heat oven to 200C/180C fan/gas 6. Cook the potatoes in a steamer for 15 mins until tender. Meanwhile, start the chicken filling. Heat the oil in a non-stick pan, add the ginger and chilli, and stir over a medium heat until starting to soften. Stir in the dried spices, leeks and peppers. Cook, stirring frequently, until softened.

STEP 2

Add the chicken and stir-fry until it begins to colour, then tip in the tomatoes, squeeze in some tomato purée and add the bouillon and 150ml water. Cover and simmer for 10 mins.

STEP 3

Mix the peanut butter with 100ml water, then stir into the stew and cook for 5 mins more. Spoon the mixture equally into two 24 x 18cm shallow pie dishes.

STEP 4

For the mash, tip the beans into a bowl, add the coriander and chilli powder and mash well. Add the steamed potatoes and roughly mash into the beans so it still has a little texture. Pile on top of the filling in the pie dishes and carefully spread over the filling to enclose it. Bake one of the pies for 35 mins.

STEP 5

Meanwhile, cook half of the broccoli and serve with the pie. Chill the other pie with the remaining broccoli for another day. Will keep chilled for up to three days. Reheat the remaining pie as above, adding an extra 15 mins to the cooking time.

Curried chicken & baked dhal

Prep: 20 mins **Serves 2**

Ingredients

- 2 garlic cloves
- thumb-sized piece ginger
- 100g red split lentils
- 2 red onions, cut into small wedges
- 1 small cauliflower, cut into florets
- ½ tsp turmeric
- 2 tsp cumin seeds
- 4 boneless and skinless chicken thighs
- 1 tsp cold pressed rapeseed oil
- 2 tsp medium curry powder
- 100g baby leaf spinach
- 2 tomatoes, chopped
- ½ lemon, cut into wedges
- 2 tbsp natural yogurt

Method

STEP 1

Heat oven to 200C/180C fan/gas 6. Grate the garlic and ginger into a large roasting dish. Add the lentils, onions, cauliflower, turmeric and cumin seeds. Pour over 500ml boiling water and give everything a good mix. Rub the chicken thighs with the oil, curry powder and a pinch of salt and pepper. Nestle these into the lentils, then cook in the oven for 40 mins until the lentils and chicken are cooked through.

STEP 2

Add the spinach and tomatoes to the dish, remove the chicken and return to the oven briefly for a couple of mins until the spinach has wilted. Season to taste. Serve with the lemon wedges and yogurt.

Broccoli & pea soup with minty ricotta

Prep: 20 mins **Cook:** 20 mins - 25 mins

Serves 2

Ingredients

- 1 tbsp olive oil , plus extra for drizzling
- 1 onion , finely chopped
- 2 celery sticks, chopped
- 1 garlic clove , crushed
- 200g broccoli , broken into florets
- 150g fresh or frozen peas
- 500ml hot low-salt vegetable stock
- 1 lemon , zested and juiced
- 100g ricotta
- 1 tbsp finely chopped mint , plus a few whole leaves to serve
- 1 tbsp toasted pine nuts
- 2 slices bread , to serve (optional)

Method

STEP 1

Heat the oil in a flameproof casserole pot and fry the onion and celery for 10 mins. Add the garlic and fry for 1 min more.

STEP 2

Add the broccoli, peas and stock, bring to a simmer and cook, covered, for 10-15 mins, or until the broccoli is tender. Tip the mix into a blender and blitz until smooth, or use a hand blender. Season. Stir in half the lemon zest and juice, then taste, and add the rest, if you like.

STEP 3

Mix the ricotta with the mint and a pinch of salt. Ladle the soup into bowls, then top with the minty ricotta and the pine nuts. Drizzle over the extra olive oil and scatter with mint leaves, then serve with sliced bread, if you like.

Caponata with cheesy polenta

Prep: 15 mins **Cook:** 30 mins

Serves 2

Ingredients

- 1-2 tbsp olive oil
- 1 red onion , cut into thin wedges
- 1 courgette , cut into rounds
- 1 aubergine , cut into chunks
- 2 garlic cloves , crushed
- 2 tsp dried oregano
- ¼ tsp chilli flakes
- 400g can chopped tomatoes

- 30g pitted green olives, halved
- ½ tbsp capers, drained and rinsed
- ½ small bunch of basil, finely chopped, plus extra to serve
- 100g instant polenta
- a little milk, to loosen (optional)
- 40g parmesan or vegetarian Italian-style hard cheese, grated

Method

STEP 1

Heat the oil in a medium pan set over a medium heat, and fry the onion, courgette and aubergine for 5-10 mins, or until beginning to soften. Stir in the garlic, oregano and chilli flakes, followed by the tomatoes, olives and capers. Season to taste, then simmer, covered, for 20 mins, or until all the veg is soft and cooked through. Stir in the basil and taste for seasoning.

STEP 2

Meanwhile, cook the polenta following pack instructions – you may need to loosen with some water or milk if it's too thick. Mix with the parmesan, then spoon and spread over two plates. Top with the caponata and extra basil. Season.

Cauliflower & squash fritters with mint & feta dip

Prep:30 mins Cook:40 mins

Serves 4

Ingredients

- 100g gram (chickpea) flour
- 1 tsp turmeric
- 1 tsp ground cumin
- small bunch coriander, finely chopped (optional)
- oil, for shallow frying
- 150g natural yogurt
- 1 garlic clove, crushed
- 75g vegetarian feta, mashed
- 2 tbsp finely chopped mint
- pitta breads and salad, to serve

For the roast cauliflower & squash base

- 1 cauliflower, split into florets, the stalk cut into cubes
- ½ large butternut squash, cut into cubes

- 1 tbsp oil

Method

STEP 1

Heat oven to 180C/160C fan/gas 4. Toss the cauliflower and squash in oil and spread it out on a large oven tray. Roast for 25 mins, or until tender. If you're making the base ahead of time, you can leave it to cool at this stage then freeze in an airtight container for up to a month. (Defrost fully before using in the next step.)

STEP 2

Put the flour in a bowl and gradually stir in 125-150ml water to make a batter as thick as double cream. Stir in the turmeric and cumin and some seasoning. Break up the cauliflower and squash a little and mix it gently into the batter. Add the coriander, if using.

STEP 3

Heat a little oil in a frying pan and when it is hot, drop 2 heaped tbsps of the mixture into the pan, spaced apart. Fry until the fritters are dark golden, about 2-3 mins each side. Remove, keep warm and repeat with the remaining batter.

STEP 4

Mix the yogurt with the garlic, feta and mint. Serve the fritters with the mint & feta dip, some salad and pitta breads.

Lighter chicken cacciatore

Prep: 15 mins **Cook:** 50 mins

Serves 4

Ingredients

- 1 tbsp olive oil
- 3 slices prosciutto, fat removed, chopped
- 1 medium onion, chopped
- 2 garlic cloves, finely chopped
- 2 sage sprigs
- 2 rosemary sprigs
- 4 skinless chicken breasts (550g total weight), preferably organic
- 150ml dry white wine
- 400g can plum tomatoes in natural juice

- 1 tbsp tomato purée
- 225g chestnut mushrooms, quartered or halved if large
- small handful chopped flat-leaf parsley, to serve

Method

STEP 1

Heat the oil in a large non-stick frying pan. Tip in the prosciutto and fry for about 2 mins until crisp. Remove with a slotted spoon, letting any fat drain back into the pan, and set aside. Put the onion, garlic and herbs in the pan and fry for 3-4 mins.

STEP 2

Spread the onion out in the pan, then lay the chicken breasts on top. Season with pepper and fry for 5 mins over a medium heat, turning the chicken once, until starting to brown on both sides and the onion is caramelising on the bottom of the pan. Remove the chicken and set aside on a plate. Raise the heat, give it a quick stir and, when sizzling, pour in the wine and let it bubble for 2 mins to reduce slightly.

STEP 3

Lower the heat to medium, return the prosciutto to the pan, then stir in the tomatoes (breaking them up with your spoon), tomato purée and mushrooms. Spoon 4 tbsp of water into the empty tomato can, swirl it around, then pour it into the pan. Cover and simmer for 15-20 mins or until the sauce has thickened and reduced slightly, then return the chicken to the pan and cook, uncovered, for about 15 mins or until the chicken is cooked through. Season and scatter over the parsley to serve.

Red cabbage with apples

Prep: 10 mins **Cook:** 45 mins

Serves 8

Ingredients

- 1 red cabbage, finely shredded
- 2 bay leaves
- 5 star anise
- ½ tsp ground cinnamon
- 200ml vegetable stock or water
- 50g golden caster sugar
- 75ml cider vinegar
- 2 apples, cored and cut into wedges

Method

STEP 1

Place all the ingredients except for the apples in a large saucepan and season. Place over a medium heat, bring to the boil, then turn down the heat and simmer for 30 mins. Add the apples, then continue cooking for 15 mins until tender.

Indian bean, broccoli & carrot salad

Prep: 15 mins **Cook:** 15 mins

Serves 4

Ingredients

- 250g green bean , trimmed
- 1 head of broccoli , cut into florets
- 2 tsp vegetable oil
- 2 tsp black mustard seed
- ½ tsp dried chilli flakes

- 100g frozen pea (or use fresh)
- 3 large carrots , grated
- large bunch coriander , roughly chopped
- 3 tbsp sunflower seed

For the raita

- 200ml natural yogurt
- ½ cucumber , peeled and grated
- thumb-sized piece ginger , grated
- ½ tsp ground cumin

- juice and zest 1 lime
- 1 tbsp chopped mint leaves
- pitta bread , to serve (optional)

Method

STEP 1

Cook the green beans in a large pan of boiling salted water for 4-5 mins, adding the broccoli after the first 2 mins. Once all the vegetables are tender, drain well. Meanwhile, mix all the raita ingredients together, then set aside.

STEP 2

Heat the oil in a large frying pan and toast the mustard seeds and chilli flakes for a few mins until fragrant. Add the peas, green beans and broccoli, tossing until heated through. Turn off the heat and stir in the carrots and coriander.

STEP 3

Serve the salad warm (or cold for a working lunch) with a dollop of raita, sprinkled with sunflower seeds and some pitta bread, if you like.

Wild salmon veggie bowl

Prep: 10 mins no cook

Serves 2

Ingredients

- 2 carrots
- 1 large courgette
- 2 cooked beetroot, diced
- 2 tbsp balsamic vinegar
- ⅓ small pack dill, chopped, plus some extra fronts (optional)
- 1 small red onion, finely chopped
- 280g poached or canned wild salmon
- 2 tbsp capers in vinegar, rinsed

Method

STEP 1

Shred the carrots and courgette into long spaghetti strips with a julienne peeler or spiralizer, and pile onto two plates.

STEP 2

Stir the beetroot, balsamic vinegar, chopped dill and red onion together in a small bowl, then spoon on top of the veg. Flake over chunks of the salmon and scatter with the capers and extra dill, if you like.

Grilled salmon tacos with chipotle lime yogurt

Prep: 15 mins **Cook:** 10 mins

Serves 4

Ingredients

- 1 tsp garlic salt
- 2 tbsp smoked paprika
- good pinch of sugar
- 500g salmon fillet

To serve

- 8 small soft flour tortillas , warmed
- ¼ small green cabbage , finely shredded
- small bunch coriander , picked into sprigs
- 200ml fat-free yogurt
- 1 tbsp chipotle paste or hot chilli sauce
- juice 1 lime
- few pickled jalapeno chillies , sliced
- lime wedges, to serve
- hot chilli sauce to serve, (optional)

Method

STEP 1

Rub the garlic salt, paprika, sugar and some seasoning into the flesh of the salmon fillet. Heat grill to high.

STEP 2

Mix the yogurt, chipotle paste or hot sauce and lime juice together in a bowl with some seasoning, and set aside. Place the salmon on a baking tray lined with foil and grill, skin-side down, for 7-8 mins until cooked through. Remove from the grill and carefully peel off and discard the skin.

STEP 3

Flake the salmon into large chunks and serve with the warmed tortillas, chipotle yogurt, shredded cabbage, coriander, jalapeños and lime wedges. Add a shake of hot sauce, if you like it spicy.

Smoked paprika prawn skewers

Prep: 10 mins **Cook:** 10 mins plus marinating

Serves 6 - 8

Ingredients

- 12 large raw prawns
- ½ tbsp smoked Spanish paprika (sweet or hot, whichever you prefer)
- 2 large garlic cloves, finely chopped
- 1 tsp cumin seeds, toasted and ground
- couple of oregano sprigs, leaves finely chopped, or 1/2 tsp dried
- juice and zest of 1 large lemon
- 2 tbsp olive oil

You will also need:

- 12 mini wooden skewers

Method

STEP 1

Soak the skewers in a bowl of water for 10 mins. Meanwhile, peel the prawns, leaving the tails intact, and devein. To do this, run a sharp knife down the back, making a tiny incision just enough to remove the visible black vein. Wash the prawns and pat dry with kitchen paper.

STEP 2

In a medium-sized bowl, mix together the paprika, garlic, cumin, oregano, lemon zest and 1 tbsp olive oil. Add the prawns and leave to marinate for 15 mins at room temperature. Then skewer a prawn onto each stick.

STEP 3

Heat the remaining oil in a roomy frying pan and fry the prawns for 3-4 mins, turning halfway through until just cooked. You may need to do this in batches. Season, squeeze over some lemon juice and serve.

The ultimate makeover: Moussaka

Prep: 30 mins **Cook:** 2 hrs and 5 mins

Serves 6

Ingredients

- 2½ tbsp olive oil
- 1 onion, chopped
- 2 plump garlic cloves, finely chopped
- 2 large carrots (350g total weight), diced
- 450g 5% fat minced beef

- 100ml white wine
- 1 tsp ground cinnamon, plus extra
- ¼ tsp ground allspice
- 400g can plum tomatoes
- 2 tbsp tomato purée
- 1 heaped tbsp chopped oregano leaves
- 2 good handfuls chopped flat-leaf parsley, plus extra to garnish
- 3 aubergines (about 750g/1lb 10oz total weight), ends trimmed
- 1 tbsp lemon juice

For the topping

- 2 eggs
- 1 tbsp cornflour
- 300g 2% Greek yogurt
- 50g parmesan, grated

To serve

- halved cherry tomatoes and thinly sliced red onion and rocket salad

Method

STEP 1

Heat 1 tbsp oil in a large, wide sauté pan. Tip in the onion and garlic, then fry for 6-8 mins until turning golden. Add the carrots and fry for 2 mins more. Stir the meat into the pan, breaking it up as you stir. Cook and stir over a high heat until the meat is no longer pink. Pour in the wine and briefly cook until most of the liquid has evaporated. Stir in the cinnamon and allspice. Tip in the tomatoes, tomato purée and 1 tbsp water (mixed with any juices left in the can), then stir to break up the tomatoes. Season with some pepper, add all the oregano and half the parsley, cover, then simmer on a low heat for 50 mins, stirring occasionally. Season to taste. Mix in the remaining parsley. Can be done a day ahead and refrigerated overnight.

STEP 2

While the meat cooks (unless you are doing this a day ahead) prepare the aubergines. Heat oven to 200C/fan 180C/ gas 6. Brush a little of the remaining oil onto 2 large baking sheets. Mix the rest of the oil with the lemon juice. Slice the aubergines into 1cm thick lengthways slices, then lay them on the oiled baking sheets. Brush with the oil and lemon mix, then season with pepper. Bake for 20-25 mins until soft, then set aside. Lower oven to 180C/fan 160C/gas 4.

STEP 3

Spread 2 big spoonfuls of the meat mixture on the bottom of an ovenproof dish (about 28 x 20 x 6cm deep). Lay the aubergine slices on top, slightly overlapping. Spoon the rest of the meat mixture on top. Beat the eggs in a bowl. Slacken the cornflour with a little of the yogurt, stir in the rest of the yogurt, then mix this into the eggs with half the cheese. Season with pepper. Pour and spread this over the meat to cover it. Sprinkle with the rest of the cheese, a little cinnamon and a grating of pepper. Bake for 50 mins-1 hr until bubbling and golden.

STEP 4

Leave moussaka to settle for 8-10 mins, then scatter over some chopped parsley and cut into squares. Serve with a salad of tomato, red onion and rocket.

Cherry tomato, kale, ricotta & pesto pasta

Prep: 10 mins **Cook:** 15 mins

Serves 4

Ingredients

- 2 tbsp olive oil
- 3 garlic cloves , chopped
- 1 tsp crushed chilli flakes
- 2 x 400g cans cherry tomatoes
- 500g penne
- 200g kale , chopped
- 4 tbsp ricotta
- 4 tbsp fresh pesto
- parmesan or vegetarian alternative, to serve (optional)

Method

STEP 1

Heat the oil in a large saucepan, add the garlic and cook for 2 mins until golden. Add the chilli flakes and tomatoes, season well, and simmer for 15 mins until the sauce is thick and reduced.

STEP 2

While the sauce is cooking, cook the pasta following pack instructions – add the kale for the final 2 mins of cooking. Drain well and stir into the sauce, then divide between 4 bowls. Top each with a dollop of ricotta, a drizzle of pesto and shavings of Parmesan, if you like.

Cod with bacon, lettuce & peas

Prep: 8 mins **Cook:** 12 mins

Serves 2

Ingredients

- 2 tsp sunflower oil
- 2 rashers rindless smoked streaky bacon, cut into small pieces
- 1 long shallot or small onion, very finely sliced
- 1 garlic clove, crushed
- 2 x 140g/5oz thick skinless cod fillets
- 140g frozen pea
- 200ml chicken stock, fresh or made with ½ cube
- 2 Little Gem lettuces, thickly shredded
- 2 tbsp half-fat crème fraîche
- 2 thick slices crusty wholegrain bread, to serve

Method

STEP 1

Heat the sunflower oil in a medium non-stick frying pan. Add the bacon, shallot or onion, and garlic. Cook gently, stirring, for 2 mins, then push to one side of the pan.

STEP 2

Season the cod with ground black pepper. Fry in the pan for 2 mins, then turn over. Add the peas and stock, and bring to a simmer. Cook over a medium heat for a further 2 mins, then add the lettuce and crème fraîche. Cook for a couple mins more, stirring the vegetables occasionally, until the fish is just cooked and the lettuce has wilted. Serve with bread to mop up the broth.

Creamy veggie korma

Prep: 15 mins **Cook:** 30 mins

Serves 4

Ingredients

- 1 tbsp vegetable oil
- 1 onion, finely chopped
- 3 cardamom pods, bashed
- 2 tsp each ground cumin and coriander
- ½ tsp ground turmeric
- 1 green chilli, deseeded (if desired) and finely chopped
- 1 garlic clove, crushed
- thumb-size piece ginger, finely chopped
- 800g mixed vegetable, such as carrots, cauliflower, potato and courgette, chopped
- 300-500ml hot vegetable stock
- 200g frozen peas
- 200ml yogurt
- 2 tbsp ground almonds (optional)

Make it non-veggie

- ½ small raw chicken breast per portion

To serve

- toasted flaked almonds, chopped coriander, basmati rice or naan bread

Method

STEP 1

Heat the oil in a large pan. Cook onion with the dry spices over a low heat for 5-6 mins until the onion is light golden. Add the chilli, garlic and ginger and cook for 1 min, then throw in the mixed vegetables and cook for a further 5 mins.

STEP 2

Divide the mixture appropriately between two pans if serving vegetarians and meat eaters. Chop the chicken into small chunks and stir into one pan. Add the stock, dividing between the pans appropriately, and simmer for 10 mins (if only cooking the veggie version in one pan, use 300ml stock; if dividing between two pans, add 250ml to each). Divide the peas, if necessary, and add, cooking for 3 mins more until the veg are tender and the chicken is cooked through.

STEP 3

Remove from the heat and stir through the yogurt and ground almonds, if using. Serve sprinkled with the toasted almonds and coriander, with basmati rice or naan bread on the side.

Soy salmon & broccoli traybake

Prep:10 mins Cook:20 mins

Serves 4

Ingredients

- 4 skin-on salmon fillets
- 1 head broccoli , broken into florets
- juice ½ lemon , ½ lemon quartered
- small bunch spring onions , sliced
- 2 tbsp soy sauce

Method

STEP 1

Heat oven to 180C/160C fan/gas 4. Put the salmon in a large roasting tin, leaving space between each fillet.

STEP 2

Wash and drain the broccoli and, while still a little wet, arrange in the tray around the fillets. Pour the lemon juice over everything, then add the lemon quarters.

STEP 3

Top with half the spring onions, drizzle with a little olive oil and put in the oven for 14 mins. Remove from the oven, sprinkle everything with the soy, then return to the oven for 4 mins more until the salmon is cooked through. Sprinkle with the remaining spring onions just before serving.

BBQ chicken pizza

Prep:25 mins Cook:30 mins

Serves 4

Ingredients

For the base

- 250g wholemeal flour , plus a little for kneading if necessary
- 1 tsp instant yeast
- ¼ tsp salt

- 1 tbsp rapeseed oil, plus extra for greasing

For the topping

- pack of 3 peppers
- 1 large onion
- 1 tbsp rapeseed oil
- 1 tsp fennel seeds
- 2 tbsp barbecue sauce
- 2 tbsp tomato purée
- 1 large skinless chicken breast fillet (about 225g), diced
- 175g baby plum tomatoes, quartered
- 50g Applewood smoked cheese, grated

Method

STEP 1

Heat oven to 220C/200C fan/gas 7. Tip the flour into a mixer with a dough hook, or a bowl. Add the yeast, salt, oil and 200ml warm water then mix well to a very soft dough. Knead in the food mixer for about 5 mins, but if making this by hand, tip onto a work surface and knead for about 10 mins. The dough is sticky, but try not to add too much extra flour. Leave in the bowl and cover with a tea towel while you halve and slice the peppers and onions. There is no need to prove the dough for a specific time, just let it sit while you make the topping.

STEP 2

For the topping: toss the peppers and onions with the oil and fennel seeds then roast for 15 mins. Meanwhile mix the barbecue sauce and tomato purée with 5 tbsp water.

STEP 3

Take the dough from the bowl and press into the base and up the sides of an oiled 25x35cm Swiss roll tin. Don't knead the dough first otherwise it will be too elastic and will keep shrinking back. Spread with two thirds of the barbecue sauce mix then add the remainder to the chicken and toss well to coat it.

STEP 4

Take the roasted pepper mixture from the oven and spread on top of the pizza. Scatter over the tomatoes then evenly spoon on the barbecue chicken. Scatter with the cheese and bake for 15 mins. Serve with a salad or healthy coleslaw.

Prawn & lime noodles

Prep: 20 mins No cook

Serves 2

Ingredients

- 100g dried vermicelli rice noodle
- 2 tbsp each soy sauce , fish sauce and sesame oil
- juice 1 lime , plus wedges to serve
- ½ red chilli , deseeded and finely chopped
- 6 spring onions , finely shredded
- 2 large carrots , coarsely grated
- handful mint leaves, torn
- 150g pack ready-cooked king prawns
- 25g cashews or peanuts

Method

STEP 1

Put the noodles in a bowl, pour over boiled water from a kettle to cover and set aside for 5 mins. Drain and rinse under cold running water, then place in a large bowl.

STEP 2

Mix the soy, fish sauce, sesame oil, lime juice and chilli to make a dressing. Pour over the noodles and stir to coat. Add the spring onions, carrots, mint, prawns and nuts. Mix again and divide between 2 bowls to serve, with lime wedges on the side.

Simple roast radishes

Cook: 20 mins

Easy

Ingredients

- 450g radishes
- 2 tbsp olive oil

Method

STEP 1

Heat oven to 180C/160C fan/gas 4. Remove the leaves from the radishes and if they are nice and fresh, set aside. Halve the radishes and tip into a roasting tin with the olive oil.

STEP 2

Roast for 20 mins until shrivelled and softened, then remove from the oven. Season with salt, toss with some of the leaves to wilt and serve.

Moroccan tomato & chickpea soup with couscous

Prep: 20 mins **Cook:** 45 mins

Serves 4

Ingredients

- 75g couscous
- 3 tbsp olive oil
- 750ml low-sodium hot vegetable stock
- 1 large onion, finely chopped
- 1 carrot, chopped into small cubes
- 4 garlic cloves, crushed
- half a finger of ginger, peeled and finely chopped
- 1-2 tbsp ras-el-hanout
- 1 tbsp harissa paste, plus extra to serve
- 400g tin chopped tomato
- 400g tin chickpea
- juice ½ lemon
- roughly chopped coriander, to serve

Method

STEP 1

Tip the couscous into a bowl, season with salt and pepper and stir through 1 tbsp of the oil. Pour over enough hot stock just to cover and cover the bowl with cling film and set aside.

STEP 2

Heat the rest of the oil in a saucepan and cook the onion and carrot gently for 8 mins until softened. Add the garlic and ginger and cook for 2 mins more then stir in the ras el hanout and harissa and cook for another minute. Pour in the tomatoes and stock and give everything a good stir. Season, add the chickpeas and simmer everything gently for 20 mins until thickened slightly then squeeze over the lemon.

STEP 3

Uncover the couscous and fluff up with a fork. Spoon the soup into bowls, top each with a mound of couscous, scatter with coriander and serve with extra harissa for those who want it.

Salmon noodle soup

Prep: 15 mins **Cook:** 20 mins

Serves 4

Ingredients

- 1l low-salt chicken stock
- 2 tsp Thai red curry paste
- 100g flat rice noodle
- 150g pack shiitake mushroom , sliced
- 125g pack baby corn , sliced
- 2 skinless salmon fillets , sliced
- juice 2 limes
- 1 tbsp reduced-salt soy sauce
- pinch brown sugar
- small bunch coriander , chopped

Method

STEP 1

Pour the stock into a large pan, bring to the boil, then stir in the curry paste. Add the noodles and cook for 8 mins. Tip in the mushrooms and corn and cook for 2 mins more.

STEP 2

Add the salmon to the pan and cook for 3 mins or until cooked through. Remove from the heat and stir in the lime juice, soy sauce and a pinch of sugar. Ladle into 4 bowls and sprinkle over the coriander just before you serve.

Quinoa stew with squash, prunes & pomegranate

Prep: 15 mins **Cook:** 40 mins

Serves 4

Ingredients

- 1 small butternut squash, deseeded and cubed
- 2 tbsp olive oil
- 1 large onion, thinly sliced
- 1 garlic clove, chopped
- 1 tbsp finely chopped ginger
- 1 tsp ras-el-hanout or Middle Eastern spice mix
- 200g quinoa
- 5 prunes, roughly chopped
- juice 1 lemon
- 600ml vegetable stock
- seeds from 1 pomegranate
- small handful mint leaves

Method

STEP 1

Heat oven to 200C/180C fan/gas 6. Put the squash on a baking tray and toss with 1 tbsp of the oil. Season well and roast for 30-35 mins or until soft.

STEP 2

Meanwhile, heat the remaining oil in a big saucepan. Add the onion, garlic and ginger, season and cook for 10 mins. Add the spice and quinoa, and cook for another couple of mins. Add the prunes, lemon juice and stock, bring to the boil, then cover and simmer for 25 mins.

STEP 3

When everything is tender, stir the squash through the stew. Spoon into bowls and scatter with pomegranate seeds and mint to serve.

Greek salad omelette

Cook:20 mins **Serves 4 - 6**

Ingredients

- 10 eggs
- handful of parsley leaves, chopped (optional)
- 2 tbsp olive oil
- 1 large red onion, cut into wedges
- 3 tomatoes, chopped into large chunks
- large handful black olives, (pitted are easier to eat)
- 100g feta cheese, crumbled

Method

STEP 1

Heat the grill to high. Whisk the eggs in a large bowl with the chopped parsley, pepper and salt, if you want. Heat the oil in a large non-stick frying pan, then fry the onion wedges over a high heat for about 4 mins until they start to brown around the edges. Throw in the tomatoes and olives and cook for 1-2 mins until the tomatoes begin to soften.

STEP 2

Turn the heat down to medium and pour in the eggs. Cook the eggs in the pan, stirring them as they begin to set, until half cooked, but still runny in places – about 2 mins. Scatter over the feta, then place the pan under the grill for 5-6 mins until omelette is puffed up and golden. Cut into wedges and serve straight from the pan.

Pan-fried scallops with lime & coriander

Cook: 2 mins Ready in 10-15 mins

Serves 2 as a starter

Ingredients

- 6-8 scallops
- 1 tbsp olive oil
- 2 large chopped garlic cloves
- 1 tsp chopped fresh red chilli
- juice of half a lime
- roughly chopped coriander
- salt and pepper

Method

STEP 1

Fry the scallops in the olive oil for about 1 min until golden, then flip them over and sprinkle over the garlic cloves and chopped fresh red chilli into the pan. Cook for about 1 min more, then squeeze over the juice of the lime.

STEP 2

Finish off with roughly chopped coriander and salt and pepper. Serve straight away.

Baked potato with cheesy mince

Total time 1 hr Ready in around 1 hour

Serves 4

Ingredients

- 2 tbsp olive oil
- 1 finely chopped onion
- 1 crushed garlic clove
- 1 carrot , finely diced
- 1 celery stick
- 450g minced lamb
- 2 tbsp sun-dried tomato paste
- 1 tbsp Worcestershire sauce
- 300ml beef stock
- 2 tsp cornflour
- 2 tsp water
- baked potato with grated cheddar, to serve

Method

STEP 1

Heat the olive oil in a large pan and fry the onion, garlic, diced carrot and celery stick for 6-8 minutes. Stir in the minced lamb and cook for 3-4 minutes until browned, then add the sun-dried tomato paste and Worcestershire sauce. Stir in the beef stock and cover and simmer for 35-40 minutes until very tender. Season well. Mix the cornflour with cold water to a paste, stir in and cook for 1 minute. Serve over baked potatoes and top with grated cheddar.

Pea & mint soup with crispy prosciutto strips

Prep: 5 mins **Cook:** 15 mins

Serves 2

Ingredients

- 2 leeks , well washed and thinly sliced
- 200g potato (unpeeled), scrubbed and grated
- 500ml chicken or vegetable stock
- 200g frozen pea
- 150g pot 0% bio yogurt
- 2 tbsp chopped mint
- 2 slices prosciutto , all excess fat removed

Method

STEP 1

Put the leeks, potato and stock in a pan and bring to the boil. Cover and simmer for 8 mins.

STEP 2

Tip in the peas, cover and cook for 5 mins more. Take off the heat and blitz with a hand blender (or in a food processor) until smooth, then stir in the yogurt and mint.

STEP 3

Meanwhile, lay the slices of prosciutto in a large non-stick frying pan in a single layer and heat until crisp. Allow to cool a little, then tear into strips, ready to sprinkle over the soup with some ground black pepper. Will keep in the fridge for 2 days.

Red lentil & sweet potato pâté

Cook:30 mins Prep 10 mins plus chilling

Serves 4

Ingredients

- 1 tbsp olive oil , plus extra for drizzling
- ½ onion , finely chopped
- 1 tsp smoked paprika , plus a little extra
- 1 small sweet potato , peeled and diced
- 140g red lentil
- 3 thyme sprigs, leaves chopped, plus a little extra to decorate (optional)
- 500ml low-sodium vegetable stock (choose a vegan brand, if desired)
- 1 tsp red wine vinegar (choose a vegan brand, if desired)
- pitta bread and vegetable sticks, to serve

Method

STEP 1

Heat the oil in a large pan, add the onion and cook slowly until soft and golden. Tip in the paprika and cook for a further 2 mins, then add the sweet potato, lentils, thyme and stock. Bring to a simmer, then cook for 20 mins or until the potato and lentils are tender.

STEP 2

Add the vinegar and some seasoning, and roughly mash the mixture until you get a texture you like. Chill for 1 hr, then drizzle with olive oil, dust with the extra paprika and sprinkle with thyme sprigs, if you like. Serve with pitta bread and vegetable sticks.

Lemon cod with basil bean mash

Prep: 8 mins **Cook:** 18 mins

Serves 2

Ingredients

- 2 small bunches cherry tomatoes, on the vine
- 1 tbsp olive oil
- chunks skinless cod or other white fish fillet
- zest 1 lemon, plus juice of 0.5
- 240g pack frozen soya beans
- 1 garlic clove
- bunch basil, leaves and stalks separated
- 100ml low-sodium chicken or vegetable stock

Method

STEP 1

Heat oven to 200C/fan 180C/gas 6. Put the tomatoes onto a baking tray, rub with a little oil and some seasoning, then roast for 5 mins until the skins are starting to split. Add the fish to the tray, top with most of the lemon zest and some more seasoning, then drizzle with a little more oil. Roast for 8-10 mins until the fish flakes easily.

STEP 2

Meanwhile, cook the beans in a pan of boiling water for 3 mins until just tender. Drain, then tip into a food processor with the rest of the oil, garlic, basil stalks, lemon juice and stock, then pulse to a thick, slightly rough purée. Season to taste.

STEP 3

Divide the tomatoes and mash between two plates, top with the cod, then scatter with basil leaves and the remaining lemon zest to serve.

Spicy cauliflower pilau

Prep: 10 mins **Cook:** 5 mins

Serves 2

Ingredients

- 225g cauliflower florets (not the stalk)
- 3 cloves
- ½ cinnamon stick
- ½ tsp turmeric
- 6 curry leaves

Method

STEP 1

Put the cauliflower florets in a food processor and pulse to make grains the size of rice. Tip into a microwaveable bowl and stir in the cloves, cinnamon stick, turmeric and curry leaves.

STEP 2

Mix well, cover with cling film, pierce and microwave on High for 3 mins. Fluff up with a fork and serve.

Indian chickpea & vegetable soup

Prep: 10 mins **Cook:** 15 mins

Makes 4 lunches

Ingredients

- 1 tbsp vegetable oil
- 1 large onion , chopped
- 1 tsp finely grated fresh root ginger
- 1 garlic clove , chopped
- 1 tbsp garam masala
- 850ml vegetable stock
- 2 large carrots , quartered lengthways and chopped
- 400g can chickpea , drained
- 100g green bean , chopped

Method

STEP 1

Heat the oil in a medium saucepan, then add the onion, ginger and garlic. Fry for 2 mins, then add the garam masala, give it 1 min more, then add the stock and carrots. Simmer for 10 mins, then add the chickpeas. Use a stick blender to whizz the soup a little. Stir in the beans and simmer for 3 mins. Pack into a flask or, if you've got a microwave at work, chill and heat up for lunch. Great with naan bread.

Mixed bean goulash

Prep: 5 mins **Cook:** 20 mins Ready in 25 minutes

Serves 2

Ingredients

- 2 tbsp olive oil
- 1 large onion , finely chopped
- 1 tbsp smoked paprika
- 400g can chopped tomato with garlic
- 400g can mixed bean , drained and rinsed

Method

STEP 1

Heat the oil in a large saucepan, then fry the onion for 5 mins until beginning to soften. Add the paprika and cook for a further min, then stir in the tomatoes and 1/2 a can of water. Simmer gently for 10 mins until thickened and glossy.

STEP 2

Tip in the mixed beans and continue to cook for a further 2 mins to just heat through the beans. Spoon into warm bowls and serve with soured cream and toasted ciabatta slices, drizzled with olive oil.

Raid-the-cupboard tuna sweetcorn cakes

Prep: 15 mins **Cook:** 25 mins Plus chilling

Makes 4

Ingredients

- 450g potato , quartered
- 2 tbsp mayonnaise , plus extra to serve
- 2 x 185g cans tuna , drained
- 198g can sweetcorn , drained

- small bunch chives , snipped, or 1 tsp dried parsley
- 2 eggs , beaten
- 100g dried breadcrumb
- sunflower oil , for frying
- salad and your favourite dressing, to serve

Method

STEP 1

Cook the potatoes in boiling salted water until really tender. Drain and allow to steam-dry in a colander. Tip into a bowl, season and mash. Stir in the mayonnaise, tuna, sweetcorn and chives or parsley. Shape into 4 cakes and chill until cold and firm.

STEP 2

Dip each cake into the egg, letting the excess drip off, then coat in the breadcrumbs. Chill for 15 mins.

STEP 3

Heat a little of the oil in a pan and gently fry the cakes for 2-3 mins on each side until golden. You may need to do this in batches – keep warm in a low oven. Serve with extra mayonnaise and salad leaves.

Oven-baked fish & chips

Prep: 15 mins **Cook:** 40 mins

Serves 4

Ingredients

- 800g/ 1lb 12 oz floury potato , scrubbed and cut into chips
- 2 tbsp olive oil
- 50g fresh breadcrumb
- zest 1 lemon
- 2 tbsp chopped flat-leaf parsley
- 4 x 140g/5oz thick sustainable white fish fillets
- 200g/ 7oz cherry tomato

Method

STEP 1

Heat oven to 220C/200C fan/gas 7. Pat chips dry on kitchen paper, then lay in a single layer on a large baking tray. Drizzle with half the olive oil and season with salt. Cook for 40 mins, turning after 20 mins, so they cook evenly.

STEP 2

Mix the breadcrumbs with the lemon zest and parsley, then season well. Top the cod evenly with the breadcrumb mixture, then drizzle .0with the remaining oil. Put in a roasting tin with the cherry tomatoes, then bake in the oven for the final 10 mins of the chips' cooking time.

Kale & salmon kedgeree

Prep: 10 mins **Cook:** 30 mins

Serves 4

Ingredients

- 300g brown rice
- 2 salmon fillets (about 280g)
- 4 eggs
- 1 tbsp vegetable oil
- 1 onion , finely chopped
- 100g curly kale , stalks removed, roughly chopped
- 1 garlic clove , crushed
- 1 tbsp curry powder
- 1 tsp turmeric
- zest and juice 1 lemon

Method

STEP 1

Cook the rice following pack instructions. Meanwhile, season the salmon and steam over a pan of simmering water for 8 mins or until just cooked. Keep the pan of water on the heat, add the eggs and boil for 6 mins, then run under cold water.

STEP 2

Heat the oil in a large frying pan or wok, add the onion and cook for 5 mins. Throw in the kale and cook, stirring, for 5 mins. Add the garlic, curry powder, turmeric and rice, season and stir until heated through.

STEP 3

Peel and quarter the eggs. Flake the salmon and gently fold through the rice, then divide between plates and top with the eggs. Sprinkle over the lemon zest and squeeze over a little juice before serving.

Lemony prawn & chorizo rice pot

Prep: 15 mins **Cook:** 25 mins

Serves 4

Ingredients

- 1 tbsp olive oil
- 1 onion , sliced
- 2 small red peppers , deseeded and sliced
- 50g chorizo , thinly sliced
- 2 garlic cloves , crushed
- 1 red chilli (deseeded if you don't like it too hot)
- ½ tsp turmeric
- 250g long grain rice
- 200g raw peeled prawn , defrosted if frozen
- 100g frozen pea
- zest and juice 1 lemon , plus extra wedges to serve

Method

STEP 1

Boil the kettle. Heat the oil in a shallow pan with a lid, add the onion, peppers, chorizo, garlic and chilli, then fry over a high heat for 3 mins. Add the turmeric and rice, stirring to ensure the rice is coated. Pour in 500ml boiling water, cover, then cook for 12 mins.

STEP 2

Uncover, then stir – the rice should be almost tender. Stir in the prawns and peas, with a splash more water if the rice is looking dry, then cook for 1 min more until the prawns are just pink and the rice tender. Stir in the lemon zest and juice with seasoning and serve with extra lemon wedges on the side.

Lemon spaghetti with tuna & broccoli

Prep: 5 mins **Cook:** 10 mins

Serves 4

Ingredients

- 350g spaghetti
- 250g broccoli , cut into small florets
- 2 shallots , finely chopped
- 85g pitted green olive , halved
- 2 tbsp caper , drained
- 198g can tuna in oil
- zest and juice 1 lemon
- 1 tbsp olive oil , plus extra for drizzling

Method

STEP 1

Boil the spaghetti in salted water for 6 mins. Add the broccoli and boil for 4 mins more or until both are just tender.

STEP 2

Meanwhile, mix the shallots, olives, capers, tuna and lemon zest and juice in a roomy serving bowl. Drain the pasta and broccoli, add to the bowl and toss really well with the olive oil and lots of black pepper. Serve with a little extra olive oil drizzled over.

Pineapple, beef & ginger stir-fry

Prep: 15 mins **Cook:** 10 mins

Serves 2

Ingredients

- 400g rump steak, thinly sliced
- 3tbsp soy sauce
- 2tbsp soft brown sugar
- 1tbsp chilli sauce
- 1tbsp rice wine vinegar
- 2tsp vegetable oil
- thumb-sized piece ginger, cut into fine matchsticks
- 4 spring onions, cut into 3cm lengths
- 200g pineapple, cut into chunks
- handful coriander leaves, to serve
- rice and greens, to serve (optional)

Method

STEP 1

Mix the steak, soy sauce, sugar, chilli sauce and vinegar together, and set aside for 10 mins.

STEP 2

Heat a wok with 1 tsp of the oil. Lift the steak from the marinade and sear, in batches, then remove. Add a bit more oil and fry the ginger until golden. Add the spring onions and pineapple, and return the steak to the pan. Stir to heat through for 1 min, then add any remaining marinade. Keep stirring until the marinade becomes thick and everything is hot. Serve sprinkled with coriander, and with rice and greens, if you like.

Curry coconut fish parcels

Prep: 10 mins **Cook:** 10 mins - 15 mins

Serves 2

Ingredients

- 2 large tilapia fillets, about 125g/4½oz each
- 2 tsp yellow or red curry paste
- 2 tsp desiccated coconut
- zest and juice 1 lime, plus wedges to serve
- 1 tsp soy sauce
- 140g basmati rice
- 2 tbsp sweet chilli sauce
- 1 red chilli, sliced
- 200g cooked thin-stemmed broccoli, to serve

Method

STEP 1

Heat oven to 200C/180C fan/gas 6. Tear off 4 large pieces of foil, double them up, then place a fish fillet in the middle of each. Spread over the curry paste. Divide the coconut, lime zest and juice, and soy between each fillet. Bring up the sides of the foil, then scrunch the edges and sides together to make 2 sealed parcels.

STEP 2

Put the parcels on a baking tray and bake for 10-15 mins. Tip the rice into a pan with plenty of water, and boil for 12-15 mins or until cooked. Drain well. Serve the fish on the rice, drizzle over the chilli sauce and scatter with sliced chilli. Serve with broccoli and lime wedges.

Miso chicken & rice soup

Prep: 10 mins **Cook:** 10 mins

Serves 2

Ingredients

- 500ml chicken stock
- 2 skinless chicken breasts
- 50g long grain rice
- 8 Chanteney carrots, halved lengthways
- 2 tbsp miso paste
- 1 tbsp soy sauce
- 1 tbsp mirin
- 2 spring onions, sliced

Method

STEP 1

Bring the stock to a gentle boil in a medium saucepan. Add the chicken breasts and simmer for 8 mins until cooked through. Remove from the pan and shred the meat.

STEP 2

Add the rice and carrots to the hot stock. Bring back up to the boil, cover with a lid, then reduce the heat and cook for 10 mins until the rice is cooked and the carrots are tender.

STEP 3

Return the chicken to the pan and add the miso, soy and mirin. Scatter over the spring onions just before serving.

Roasted carrot, spelt, fennel & blood orange salad

Prep: 35 mins **Cook:** 25 mins

Serves 6

Ingredients

- 400g spelt
- 1 vegetable stock cube
- 4 tbsp extra virgin olive oil
- 400g baby carrots, scrubbed

- 3 blood oranges, 2 zested and 1 juiced
- 1 tbsp olive oil
- 2 tsp clear honey
- 2 fennel bulbs, thinly sliced
- 4 tbsp red wine vinegar
- 1 small red onion, finely chopped
- large bunch parsley, chopped
- 70g pack pitted, dry black olives or 85g couchillo (the very small black ones) or Kalamata olives
- small pack parsley, chopped (optional)

Method

STEP 1

Heat oven to 200C/180C fan/gas 6 and cook the spelt with the stock cube following pack instructions – don't overcook it, as it should still have a little nutty bite. When the spelt is done, drain it very well and toss on a platter with 1 tbsp of the extra virgin olive oil to stop it from sticking together too much.

STEP 2

Meanwhile, toss the carrots with the olive oil, blood orange zest and some seasoning in a roasting tin, then roast for 15 mins. Carefully stir through half the honey with the fennel. Continue roasting for another 10 mins, then cool for 5 mins. Cut away the pith and peel from the 2 zested oranges, then roughly chop or slice.

STEP 3

Whisk together the remaining extra virgin olive oil, 1 tsp honey, red wine vinegar and the blood orange juice with some seasoning. Scrape the roasted carrots and fennel plus any cooking juices on top of the spelt, along with the orange chunks, red onion, herbs and olives. Drizzle over the dressing and toss everything together well. The salad will happily hold at room temperature for a few hours, but the spelt will soak up the dressing – so if you're making it ahead, add half the dressing when assembling and stir through the rest just before you serve it. As you serve, stir through the parsley, if you like.

Sweet potato salad

Prep: 15 mins **Cook:** 35 mins

Serves 6

Ingredients

- 1.2kg sweet potato, peeled and cut into biggish chunks

- 1 tbsp olive oil

For the dressing

- 2 shallots (or half a small red onion), finely chopped
- 4 spring onions, finely sliced
- small bunch chives, snipped into quarters or use mini ones
- 5 tbsp sherry vinegar
- 2 tbsp extra-virgin olive oil
- 2 tbsp honey

Method

STEP 1

Heat oven to 200C/180C fan/gas 6. Toss the sweet potato chunks with the olive oil and some seasoning, and spread on a baking parchment-lined baking sheet. Roast for 30 - 35 mins until tender and golden. Cool at room temperature.

STEP 2

When just about cool whisk together all the dressing ingredients with a little more seasoning and gently toss through the potato chunks – use your hands to avoid breaking them up.

Superhealthy Singapore noodles

Prep: 20 mins **Cook:** 10 mins

Serves 4

Ingredients

- 3 nests medium egg noodles
- 2 tbsp sunflower oil
- 100g tenderstem broccoli, stems sliced at an angle
- 1 red pepper, deseeded, quartered then cut into strips
- 85g baby corn, quartered lenthways
- 2 garlic cloves, shredded
- 1 red chilli, deseeded and chopped
- thumb-sized piece fresh ginger, peeled and finely chopped
- 2 skinless chicken breasts, sliced
- 100g shelled raw king prawns
- 1 heaped tbsp Madras curry paste
- 2 tsp soy sauce
- 100g beansprouts
- 15g pack coriander, chopped
- 4 spring onions, shredded
- lime wedges, for squeezing

Method

STEP 1

Pour boiling water over the noodles and leave to soften. Meanwhile, heat half the oil in a large non-stick wok and stir-fry all the vegetables, except the beansprouts and onions, with the garlic, chilli and ginger until softened. If the broccoli won't soften, add a splash of water to the wok and cover to create some steam.

STEP 2

Tip the veg on to a plate, add the rest of the oil to the wok then briefly stir-fry the chicken and prawns until just cooked. Set aside with the vegetables and add the curry paste to the pan. Stir-fry for a few secs then add 150ml water and the soy sauce. Allow to bubble then add the drained, softened noodles and beansprouts, and toss together to coat.

STEP 3

Return the vegetables, chicken and prawns to the wok with the coriander and spring onions. Toss well over the heat and serve with lime wedges.

Blueberry & lemon pancakes

Prep: 10 mins **Cook:** 20 mins

Makes 14-16

Ingredients

- 200g plain flour
- 1 tsp cream of tartar
- ½ tsp bicarbonate of soda
- 1 tsp golden syrup
- 75g blueberry
- zest 1 lemon
- 200ml milk
- 1 large egg
- butter , for cooking

Method

STEP 1

First, put the flour, cream of tartar and bicarbonate of soda in the bowl. Mix them well with the fork. Drop the golden syrup into the dry ingredients along with the blueberries and lemon zest.

STEP 2

Pour the milk into a measuring jug. Now break in the egg and mix well with a fork. Pour most of the milk mixture into the bowl and mix well with a rubber spatula. Keep adding more milk until you get a smooth, thick, pouring batter.

STEP 3

Heat the frying pan and brush with a little butter. Then spoon in the batter, 1 tbsp at a time, in heaps. Bubbles will appear on top as the pancakes cook – turn them at this stage, using the metal spatula to help you. Cook until brown on the second side, then keep warm on a plate, covered with foil. Repeat until all the mixture is used up.

Moroccan lamb with apricots, almonds & mint

Prep: 2 hrs **Serves 4**

Ingredients

- 2 tbsp olive oil
- 550g lean lamb, cubed
- 1 onion, chopped
- 2 garlic cloves, crushed
- 700ml lamb or chicken stock
- grated zest and juice 1 orange
- 1 cinnamon stick
- 1 tsp clear honey
- 175g ready-to-eat dried apricots
- 3 tbsp chopped fresh mint
- 25g ground almonds
- 25g toasted flaked almonds
- steamed broccoli and couscous, to serve

Method

STEP 1

Heat the oil in a large flameproof casserole. Add the lamb and cook over a medium-high heat for 3-4 minutes until evenly browned, stirring often. Remove the lamb to a plate, using a slotted spoon.

STEP 2

Stir the onion and garlic into the casserole and cook gently for 5 minutes until softened. Return the lamb to the pot. Add the stock, zest and juice, cinnamon, honey and salt and pepper. Bring to the boil then reduce the heat, cover and cook gently for 1 hour.

STEP 3

Add the apricots and two-thirds of the mint and cook for 30 minutes until the lamb is tender. Stir in the ground almonds to thicken the sauce. Serve with the remaining mint and toasted almonds scattered over the top.

Charred spring onions

Prep: 5 mins **Cook:** 10 mins - 12 mins

Serves 6

Ingredients

- 2 bunches of spring onions (about 20)

Method

STEP 1

If your barbecue hasn't already been heated, light and heat until the ashes turn grey, or heat a griddle pan. Wash the spring onions and pat dry. Trim off the ends, then place the onions directly on the barbecue or in a hot griddle pan.

STEP 2

When the spring onions have softened and blackened, take off the heat and move to a hot spot on the barbecue top to keep warm before serving.

Chipotle black bean soup with lime-pickled onions

Prep: 10 mins **Cook:** 25 mins Plus pickling

Serves 2

Ingredients

- juice 2 limes
- 2 small red onions, thinly sliced
- ½ tbsp olive oil
- 2 garlic cloves, finely chopped
- ½ tbsp ground cumin
- ½ tbsp smoked paprika

- ½ tbsp chipotle paste , or Tabasco, to taste
- 400g can black bean , drained and rinsed
- 400ml vegetable stock
- half-fat soured cream , to serve
- coriander leaves, to serve
- crisp tortilla chips , to serve

Method

STEP 1

To make the lime-pickled onions, combine ½ the lime juice and ½ the onions in a small bowl, and season. Leave to pickle for 30 mins.

STEP 2

Meanwhile, heat the olive oil in a saucepan over a medium-high heat. Add the garlic and remaining onions, and season. Cook for 8 mins or until the onions are translucent. Add the spices and chipotle purée, cook for 1 min, then add the beans, stock and remaining lime juice. Simmer for 15 mins, then purée in a blender.

STEP 3

Pour the soup into a clean pan to reheat. Serve with a little of the drained pickled onions, topped with a small drizzle of soured cream and some coriander, and the tortillas on the side.

Courgette & quinoa-stuffed peppers

Prep: 10 mins **Cook:** 20 mins

Serves 4

Ingredients

- 4 red peppers
- 1 courgette , quartered lengthways and thinly sliced
- 2 x 250g packs ready-to-eat quinoa
- 85g feta cheese , finely crumbled
- handful parsley , roughly chopped

Method

STEP 1

Heat oven to 200C/180C fan/gas 6. Cut each pepper in half through the stem, and remove the seeds. Put the peppers, cut-side up, on a baking sheet, drizzle with 1 tbsp olive oil and season well. Roast for 15 mins.

STEP 2

Meanwhile, heat 1 tsp olive oil in a small frying pan, add the courgette and cook until soft. Remove from the heat, then stir through the quinoa, feta and parsley. Season with pepper.

STEP 3

Divide the quinoa mixture between the pepper halves, then return to the oven for 5 mins to heat through. Serve with a green salad, if you like.

Tangy trout

Prep: 10 mins **Cook:** 5 mins

Serves 4

Ingredients

- 4 trout fillets
- 50g breadcrumbs
- 1 tbsp butter , softened
- 1 small bunch parsley , chopped
- zest and juice of 1 lemon , plus lemon wedges to serve
- 25g pine nuts , toasted and half roughly chopped
- 1 tbsp olive oil

Method

STEP 1

Heat the grill to high. Lay the fillets, skin side down, on an oiled baking tray. Mix together the breadcrumbs, butter, parsley, lemon zest and juice, and half the pine nuts. Scatter the mixture in a thin layer over the fillets, drizzle with the oil and place under the grill for 5 mins. Sprinkle over the remaining pine nuts, then serve with the lemon wedges and a potato salad.

Vegetable & bean chilli

Prep: 10 mins **Cook:** 30 mins - 35 mins

Serves 4

Ingredients

- 1 tbsp olive oil
- 1 clove garlic , finely chopped
- thumb-sized piece ginger , finely chopped
- 1 large onion , chopped
- 2 courgettes , diced
- 1 red pepper , deseeded and chopped
- 1 yellow pepper , deseeded and chopped
- 1 tbsp chilli powder
- 100g red lentils , washed and drained
- 1 tbsp tomato purée
- x cans chopped tomatoes
- 195g can sweetcorn , drained
- 420g can butter beans , drained
- 400g can kidney beans in water, drained

Method

STEP 1

Heat the oil in a large pan. Cook the garlic, ginger, onion, courgettes and peppers for about 5 mins until starting to soften. Add the chilli powder and cook for 1 min more.

STEP 2

Stir in the lentils, tomato purée, tomatoes and 250ml water. Bring to the boil and cook for 15-20 mins.

STEP 3

Add the sweetcorn and beans, and cook for a further 10 mins.

Pea hummus

Prep: 10 mins No cook

Serves 4

Ingredients

- 200g cooked peas
- 1 garlic clove , crushed
- 1 tbsp tahini
- squeeze of lemon
- 1 tbsp cooked cannellini beans , from a can
- 2 tbsp olive oil
- strips of pitta bread , to serve
- raw vegetable sticks, to serve

Method

STEP 1

Blitz all the ingredients together using a hand blender or food processor. Add 1-2 tbsp water, then blitz again. Transfer a portion to a pot and add to a lunchbox with pitta bread strips and veg sticks. Keep the rest chilled for up to 3 days.

Beef & bean chilli bowl with chipotle yogurt

Prep: 5 mins **Cook:** 45 mins

Serves 4

Ingredients

- 1 tbsp olive oil
- 1 large onion , chopped
- 250g pack extra-lean minced beef
- 1 tbsp chipotle paste , plus a little extra to serve
- 1 tbsp Cajun seasoning mix
- 2 x 400g cans mixed bean salad, drained
- 400g can chopped tomato
- 1 low-sodium beef stock cube
- 2 squares 70% cocoa dark chocolate
- small pack coriander , chopped
- cooked brown rice and low-fat Greek yogurt, to serve

Method

STEP 1

Heat the oil in a frying pan and cook the onion on a medium heat until softened. Add the beef with some black pepper and a little salt, breaking up any lumps with a wooden spoon, and cook until browned. Add the chipotle and Cajun seasoning. Give it a good stir and cook for 1 min more.

STEP 2

Tip in the beans and tomatoes, then crumble over the stock cube. Add a can of water and simmer for about 20-30 mins, until thickened. Add the chocolate, and stir until melted, then add most of the coriander.

STEP 3

Serve the chilli in bowls on top of the rice sprinkled with the rest of the coriander, with a dollop of low-fat yogurt, and an extra drizzle of chipotle paste on top.

Courgette tortilla with toppings

Prep: 5 mins **Cook:** 6 mins

Serves 2

Ingredients

- 1 tbsp olive oil
- 1 large courgette, coarsely grated
- 1 tsp harissa
- 4 large eggs
- 3 tbsp reduced-fat hummus
- 1 large red pepper from a jar, torn into strips
- 3 pitted queen olives, quartered
- handful coriander

Method

STEP 1

Heat the oil in a 20cm non-stick frying pan, add the courgette and cook for a few mins, stirring occasionally, until softened. Meanwhile, beat the harissa with the eggs and pour into the pan. Cook gently, stirring, to allow the uncooked egg to flow onto the base of the pan. When it is two-thirds cooked, leave it untouched for 2 mins to set. Slide onto a plate, then return to the pan, uncooked-side down, to finish cooking.

STEP 2

To serve, tip onto a board and spread with the hummus. Scatter with the pepper, olives and coriander. Cut into quarters and eat warm or cold.

Spinach & sweet potato tortilla

Prep: 10 mins **Cook:** 1 hr

Serves 6 - 8

Ingredients

- 300g bag baby spinach leaves
- 8 tbsp light olive oil
- 2 large onions, thinly sliced

- 4 medium sweet potatoes (800g/ 1lb 12oz), peeled, cut into thin slices
- 2 garlic cloves, finely chopped
- 8 large eggs

Method

STEP 1

Put the spinach in a large colander and pour over a kettleful of boiling water. Drain well and, when cooled a little, squeeze dry, trying not to mush up the spinach too much.

STEP 2

Heat 3 tbsp oil in a 25cm non-stick pan with a lid, then sweat the onions for 15 mins until really soft but not coloured. Add another 3 tbsp oil and add the potatoes and garlic. Mix in with the onions, season well, cover and cook over a gentle heat for another 15 mins or so until the potatoes are very tender. Stir occasionally to stop them catching.

STEP 3

Whisk the eggs in a large bowl, tip in the cooked potato and onion, and mix together. Separate the spinach clumps, add to the mix and fold through, trying not to break up the potato too much.

STEP 4

Add 2 tbsp more oil to the pan and pour in the sweet potato and egg mix. Cover and cook over a low-medium heat for 20 mins until the base and sides are golden brown and the centre has mostly set. Run a palette knife around the sides to stop it from sticking. 5 To turn the tortilla over, put a plate face down onto the pan, then flip it over. Slide the tortilla back into the pan and cook for a further 5-10 mins until just set and golden all over. (Don't worry if it breaks up a little on the edges as you're turning it – it will look perfect when it's cooked through and set.) Continue cooking on the other side until just set and golden all over. Again use a palette knife to release the tortilla from the sides. Allow to rest for 5 mins, then tip onto a board before cutting into wedges.

Stuffed butternut squash with quinoa

Prep: 10 mins **Cook:** 1 hr

Serves 2 with filling leftover

Ingredients

- 1 medium butternut squash
- olive oil, for roasting
- pinch dried oregano
- 150g ready-to-eat quinoa (we used Merchant Gourmet Red and White Quinoa)
- 100g feta cheese
- 50g toasted pine nut
- 1 small carrot, grated (around 50g)
- small bunch chives, snipped
- juice half lemon
- 1 red pepper, chopped
- 50g pitted black olive
- 2 spring onions, chopped

Method

STEP 1

Heat the oven to 200C/fan 180C/gas 6. Halve the butternut squash, scoop out the seeds and score the flesh with a sharp knife.

STEP 2

Arrange the two halves on a baking tray, drizzle with a little olive oil, season with freshly ground black pepper and sea salt, sprinkle with dried oregano and cook for 40 minutes. Take out the oven, add the chopped peppers to the tray alongside the squash and cook for a further 10 minutes.

STEP 3

Meanwhile mix the rest of the ingredients. Take the tray out of the oven and carefully transfer the peppers to the stuffing mix. Stir together and spoon the filling onto the butternut squash. Return to the oven for 10 mins. Serve.

Quinoa, pea & avocado salad

Prep: 20 mins No cook

Serves 4

Ingredients

- 100g frozen peas
- juice 1 lemon
- 2 tbsp olive oil
- ½ small pack mint, leaves only, chopped
- ½ small pack chives, snipped
- 250g pack ready-to-eat red & white quinoa mix (we used Merchant Gourmet)

- 1 avocado, stoned, peeled and chopped into chunks
- 75g bag pea shoots

Method

STEP 1

Put the peas in a large heatproof bowl, pour over just-boiled water, then set aside.

STEP 2

Pour the lemon juice into a small bowl and whisk in some seasoning. Keep whisking as you slowly add the olive oil, followed by the mint and chives.

STEP 3

Drain the peas and tip into a large serving dish. Stir in the quinoa, breaking up any clumps. Pour over the dressing, then fold in the avocado and pea shoots. Serve immediately.

Chicken, edamame & ginger pilaf

Prep: 10 mins **Cook:** 17 mins

Serves 4

Ingredients

- 2 tbsp vegetable oil
- 1 onion, thinly sliced
- thumb-sized piece ginger, grated
- 1 red chilli, deseeded and finely sliced
- 3 skinless chicken breasts, cut into bite-sized pieces
- 250g basmati rice
- 600ml vegetable stock
- 100g frozen edamame / soya beans
- coriander leaves and fat-free Greek yoghurt (optional), to serve

Method

STEP 1

Heat the oil in a medium saucepan, then add the onion, ginger and chilli, along with some seasoning. Cook for 5 mins, then add the chicken and rice. Cook for 2 mins more, then add the stock and bring to the boil. Turn the heat to low, cover and cook for 8-10 mins until the rice is just cooked. During the final 3 mins of cooking, add the edamame beans. Sprinkle some coriander leaves on top and serve with a dollop of Greek yogurt, if you like.

Tomatillo salsa

Prep:5 mins **Cook:**5 mins plus cooling

Serves 4

Ingredients

- 400g tomatillos
- small pack coriander
- 1 white onion , chopped
- 2 green chillies , roughly chopped
- 1 garlic clove , roughly chopped
- 1 lime , juiced
- 1 avocado , cut into small cubes

Method

STEP 1

Put the tomatillos in a pan of boiling water, cook for 3 mins or until the skins split, remove with a slotted spoon and cool for 5-10 mins. Blitz in a food processor with the coriander, onion, chilli, garlic and lime. Tip into a bowl, stir in the avocado and season to taste.

Barley couscous & prawn tabbouleh

Prep:10 mins **Cook:**25 mins

Serves 2

Ingredients

- 125g barley couscous
- zest 1 lemon , juice of 0.5
- 1 tbsp extra virgin rapeseed oil
- ½ small pack dill , finely chopped
- good handful mint leaves , chopped
- ½ cucumber , chopped
- 2 nectarines , chopped
- 125g peeled prawns , or a handful of cashews or pecans for a vegetarian version.

Method

STEP 1

Tip the couscous into a bowl and pour over just enough boiling water to cover, following pack instructions. Leave for no more than 5 mins, drain thoroughly, then fluff up with a fork and tip into a bowl. Stir in the lemon zest and juice with the oil, dill and mint, then add the cucumber and nectarines.

STEP 2

Toss through the prawns or nuts and serve on plates or pack into lunch containers.

Turkey tortilla pie

Prep: 5 mins **Cook:** 25 mins

Serves 4

Ingredients

- 2 onions , finely chopped
- 1 tbsp olive oil , plus a little extra if needed
- 2 tsp ground cumin
- 500g pack turkey mince
- 1 ½ tbsp chipotle paste
- 400g can chopped tomato
- 400g can kidney bean , drained and rinsed
- 198g can sweetcorn , drained
- 2 corn tortillas , snipped into triangles
- small handful grated cheddar
- 2 spring onions , finely sliced

Method

STEP 1

In a deep flameproof casserole dish, cook the onions in the oil for 8 mins until soft. Add the cumin and cook for 1 min more. Stir in the mince and add a bit more oil, if needed. Turn up the heat and cook for 4-6 mins, stirring occasionally, until the mince is browned.

STEP 2

Stir in the chipotle paste, tomatoes and half a can of water, and simmer for 5 mins. Mix in the beans and sweetcorn, and cook for a few mins more until thick, piping hot and the mince is cooked.

STEP 3

Heat the grill. Take the pan off the heat and put the tortilla triangles randomly on top. Scatter over the cheese and grill for a few mins until the topping is crisp, taking care that it doesn't burn. Sprinkle with the spring onions and serve.

Feta-stuffed mushrooms with mustard slaw

Prep: 20 mins **Cook:** 35 mins

Serves 2

Ingredients

- 4 large Portobello mushrooms, each about 10cm across
- 1-2 tsp rapeseed oil
- 100g bulghar wheat
- 2 garlic cloves, finely grated
- 50g feta, crumbled
- 2 tsp finely chopped rosemary leaves
- 6 walnut halves, roughly broken
- 2 tbsp chopped parsley (optional)

For the slaw

- 2 carrots, coarsely grated
- 1 red onion, finely sliced
- 200g red cabbage, finely shredded
- 40g raisins
- 1 tbsp rapeseed oil
- 1 tbsp apple cider vinegar
- 1 tsp English mustard powder
- 4 tbsp four-seed mix (sesame, sunflower, golden linseed and pumpkin)

Method

STEP 1

Heat oven to 200C/180C fan/ gas 6 and snap the stalks from the mushrooms. Put the stalks in a large, shallow ovenproof dish along with the caps, turned upside down. Brush the caps with the oil and bake in the oven for 15 mins.

STEP 2

Meanwhile, boil the bulghar for 8 mins, then drain and toss with the garlic, feta, rosemary, walnuts and parsley (if using).

STEP 3

Take the mushrooms from the oven and turn the caps round the other way. Roughly chop the stalks, add to the bulghar mixture and pile it on top of the mushroom caps. Return to the oven for 10 mins while you make the slaw.

STEP 4

Put all the slaw ingredients in a bowl and toss well. Serve half with the mushrooms and chill the rest to serve for lunch with the Masala omelette muffins (see goes well with) another day.

Roast chicken thighs with brown rice & salsa verde

Prep: 10 mins **Cook:** 35 mins

Serves 2

Ingredients

- 3 skinless boneless chicken thighs, cut in half
- 2 tbsp rapeseed oil
- 2 garlic cloves, bashed
- ½ small pack coriander
- ½ small pack parsley
- 1 anchovy fillet
- ½ tbsp capers
- ½ lemon, zested and juiced
- 200g pouch cooked wholegrain rice
- 200g baby leaf spinach

Method

STEP 1

Heat oven to 200C/180C fan/gas 6. Season the chicken, rub with ½ tbsp oil, then put in a large roasting tin with the garlic and roast for 25-30 mins.

STEP 2

Meanwhile, blitz the herbs, anchovy, capers, lemon juice and remaining oil with some seasoning in a food processor until finely chopped. Set aside.

STEP 3

Once the chicken is cooked, remove the tin from the oven and squeeze the garlic out of their skins. Tip in the rice and use a wooden spoon to break it up, then add the spinach and lemon zest and toss. Return to the oven for 5 mins. Divide between bowls and dollop on the salsa verde.

Herby lamb fillet with caponata

Prep: 10 mins **Cook:** 25 mins

Serves 2

Ingredients

- 3 garlic cloves

For the caponata

- 2 tsp rapeseed oil
- 1 red onion, cut into wedges
- 1 aubergine, sliced and quartered
- 500g carton passata
- 1 green pepper, quartered, deseeded and sliced
- 6 pitted Kalamata olives, halved and rinsed
- 2 tsp capers, rinsed
- 1 tsp chopped rosemary
- 1 tsp balsamic vinegar

For the lamb & potatoes

- 4 baby new potatoes, halved
- 1 tsp chopped rosemary
- 1 tsp rapeseed oil
- 250g lean lamb loin fillet, all visible fat removed
- 240g bag baby spinach
- finely chopped parsley (optional)

Method

STEP 1

Slice 2 of the garlic cloves for the caponata, finely grate the other for the lamb and set aside. Heat the oil for the caponata in a wide pan, add the onion and fry for 5 mins to soften. Tip in the aubergine and cook, stirring, for 5 mins more. Add the passata and pepper with the olives, capers, rosemary and balsamic vinegar, then cover and cook for 15 mins, stirring frequently.

STEP 2

Meanwhile, heat oven to 190C/170C fan/ gas 5. Boil the potatoes for 10 mins, then drain. Mix the grated garlic with the rosemary and some black pepper, then rub all over the lamb. Toss the potatoes in the oil with some more black pepper, place in a small roasting tin with the lamb and roast for 15-20 mins. Meanwhile, wilt the spinach in the microwave or in a pan, and squeeze to drain any excess liquid.

STEP 3

Stir the garlic into the caponata and serve with the lamb, either whole or sliced, rolled in parsley if you like, with the potatoes and spinach.

Potato salad with anchovy & quail's eggs

Prep: 10 mins **Cook:** 20 mins

Serves 1

Ingredients

- 4 quail's eggs
- 100g green beans
- 100g new potatoes, halved or quartered if very large
- 1 anchovy, finely chopped
- 1 tbsp chopped parsley
- 1 tbsp chopped chives
- juice 0.5 lemon

Method

STEP 1

Bring a medium pan of water to a simmer. Lower the quail's eggs into the water and cook for 2 mins. Lift out the eggs with a slotted spoon and put into a bowl of cold water. Add the beans to the pan, simmer for 4 mins until tender, then remove from the pan with a slotted spoon and plunge into the bowl of cold water.

STEP 2

Put the potatoes in the pan and boil for 10-15 mins until tender. Drain the potatoes in a colander and leave them to cool. While the potatoes are cooling, peel the eggs and cut them in half. Toss the potatoes and beans with the chopped anchovy, herbs and lemon juice. Top with the quail's eggs to serve.

Chicken with mustard lentils

Prep: 15 mins **Cook:** 1 hr and 15 mins

Serves 4

Ingredients

- 1 tbsp vegetable oil
- pack of 4 chicken thighs and 4 chicken drumsticks
- 1 red onion, thinly sliced
- 2 garlic cloves, crushed
- 250g puy lentils
- 750ml hot chicken stock
- 2 tbsp crème fraîche
- zest and juice 1 lemon
- 1 tbsp Dijon mustard
- small bunch parsley, chopped
- green vegetables, to serve (optional)

Method

STEP 1

Heat the oil in a large flameproof casserole. Season the chicken pieces, then brown in the hot oil for 3 mins each side, until golden on all sides. Remove and set aside. Pour away all but 1 tbsp oil.

STEP 2

Add the onion to the pan and cook for 5 mins, then add the garlic and cook for 1 min more. Add the lentils and stock and stir well. Put the chicken on top, put the lid on and leave to simmer over a medium heat for 30 mins. Remove the lid and increase the heat. Bubble for another 20 mins until the lentils are tender, most of the stock has been absorbed, and the chicken is cooked through.

STEP 3

Stir in the crème fraîche, lemon zest and juice, mustard, parsley and seasoning. Serve with green veg, if you like.

Lighter lemon drizzle cake

Prep: 25 mins **Cook:** 40 mins

Cuts into 12 slices

Ingredients

- 75ml rapeseed oil, plus extra for the tin
- 175g self-raising flour
- 1 ½ tsp baking powder
- 50g ground almond
- 50g polenta
- finely grated zest 2 lemons

- 140g golden caster sugar
- 2 large eggs
- 225g natural yogurt

For the lemon syrup

- 85g caster sugar
- juice 2 lemon (about 5 tbsp)

Method

STEP 1

Heat oven to 180C/160C fan/gas 4. Lightly oil a 20cm round x 5cm deep cake tin and line the base with baking parchment. For the cake, put the flour, baking powder, ground almonds and polenta in a large mixing bowl. Stir in the lemon zest and sugar, then make a dip in the centre. Beat the eggs in a bowl, then stir in the yogurt. Tip this mixture along with the oil into the dip (see step-by-step number 1), then briefly and gently stir with a large metal spoon so everything is just combined, without overmixing.

STEP 2

Spoon the mixture into the tin and level the top (step 2). Bake for 40 mins or until a skewer inserted into the centre of the cake comes out clean. Cover loosely with foil for the final 5-10 mins if it starts to brown too quickly.

STEP 3

While the cake cooks, make the lemon syrup. Tip the caster sugar into a small saucepan with the lemon juice and 75ml water. Heat over a medium heat, stirring occasionally, until the sugar has dissolved. Raise the heat, boil for 4 mins until slightly reduced and syrupy, then remove from the heat.

STEP 4

Remove the cake from the oven and let it cool briefly in the tin. While it is still warm, turn it out of the tin, peel off the lining paper and sit the cake on a wire rack set over a baking tray or similar. Use a skewer to make lots of small holes all over the top of the cake (step 3). Slowly spoon over half the lemon syrup (step 4) and let it soak in. Spoon over the rest in the same way, brushing the edges and sides of the cake too with the last of the syrup.

Lemon pollock with sweet potato chips & broccoli mash

Prep: 15 mins **Cook:** 35 mins

Serves 2

Ingredients

- 2 garlic cloves
- For the chips
- 2 sweet potatoes (175g/6oz), scrubbed and cut into chips

For the fish & dressing

- 2 pollock fillets (about 100g/4oz each)
- ½ unwaxed lemon
- 2 tbsp extra virgin olive oil

For the broccoli mash

- 1 leek , chopped
- 4 broccoli spears (about 200g/7oz)
- 2 tsp rapeseed oil , plus extra for the fish
- ½ tsp smoked paprika
- 1 ½ tsp capers , rinsed and chopped
- 1 tbsp chopped dill
- 85g frozen peas
- handful mint

Method

STEP 1

Heat oven to 200C/180C fan/gas 6. Finely chop the garlic, put half in a bowl for the dressing and set the rest aside for the chips. Toss the sweet potatoes with the oil and spread out on a large baking sheet. Bake for 25 mins, turning halfway through.

STEP 2

Put the fish on a sheet of baking parchment on a baking sheet, brush with a little oil, then grate over the lemon zest and season with black pepper. Set aside.

STEP 3

Boil the leek for 5 mins, then add the broccoli and cook for 5 mins more. Tip in the peas for a further 2 mins. Drain, return to the pan and blitz with a stick blender to make a thick purée. Add the mint, then blitz again.

STEP 4

Meanwhile, toss the garlic and paprika with the chips and return to the oven with the fish for 10 mins. Add the olive oil to the garlic, with the capers and dill and 1 tbsp water. Serve everything together with the caper dressing spooned over the fish.

Chinese poached chicken & rice

Prep: 20 mins **Cook:** 40 mins

Serves 4

Ingredients

- large piece of ginger , 1 tbsp finely grated, the rest sliced
- 3 garlic cloves
- 1 tsp black peppercorns
- 1 tbsp soy sauce , plus 2-3 tsp (optional)
- 8 chicken legs
- 3 tbsp sesame oil
- 2 bunches spring onions , chopped
- 4 pak choi , halved
- cooked long-grain rice , to serve

Method

STEP 1

Put the sliced ginger, the garlic, peppercorns and half the soy in a large pan with the chicken legs. Add enough water to cover, and season with a little salt. Bring to the boil, then reduce to a low simmer, put on the lid and poach for 30 mins.

STEP 2

Meanwhile, heat a pan and add the sesame oil and spring onions. Soften for 1 min, then remove from the heat and stir in the grated ginger and remaining soy sauce to make a relish.

STEP 3

When the chicken is ready, remove from the pan, set aside 4 of the legs and chill for tomorrow. Add the pak choi to the poaching liquid and cook for 3-4 mins. Strain the poaching liquid to remove the ginger, garlic and peppercorns, reserving the liquid. Pull the skin from the remaining 4 chicken legs and discard. Tear the meat into thick pieces. Serve in bowls with rice, the pak choi, a ladle of the hot chicken broth, the spring onion relish and extra soy sauce, if you like.

Masala chicken pie

Prep: 15 mins - 20 mins **Cook:** 1 hr and 30 mins

Serves 6

Ingredients

- 2 tbsp vegetable oil
- 4 skinless chicken breasts
- 2 onions, chopped
- finger-length piece ginger, grated
- 3 garlic cloves, crushed
- 2 tbsp medium curry powder
- 2 tsp ground coriander
- 2 tsp ground cumin
- 2 tsp black or brown mustard seed
- 2 tsp white or red wine vinegar
- 2 tsp sugar (white or brown)
- 2 x 400g cans chopped tomatoes
- 150ml light coconut milk (buy a 400ml can- you'll need more for the topping)
- 1 large red pepper, deseeded and cut into large chunks
- 1 large green pepper, deseeded and cut into large chunks
- ½ a small bunch coriander, leaves roughly chopped, stalks reserved (see below)

For the topping

- 1 ½kg floury potato, cut into very large chunks
- 150ml light coconut milk
- 1 tsp turmeric
- juice 1 lemon
- 1 bunch spring onions, finely chopped
- stalks from ½ a small bunch coriander, finely chopped
- 1 tsp kalonji seeds (also known as nigella or onion seeds)
- naan bread, to serve (optional)

Method

STEP 1

Heat a deep frying pan or flameproof casserole dish and add 2 tsp of the oil. Brown the chicken breasts quickly but well on both sides, then remove to a plate. Turn down the heat and add the remaining oil, the onions, ginger and garlic. Fry gently until soft. Add the spices and cook for a few mins, stirring.

STEP 2

Stir in the vinegar, sugar, tomatoes and coconut milk. Bring to a simmer and bubble for 10 mins. Roughly chop the chicken breasts and stir into the pan with any chicken juices and the peppers. Simmer for another 20 mins until the chicken is cooked through and the sauce reduced a little. Take off the heat, stir in the coriander leaves and season to taste – it will need a good seasoning.

STEP 3

To make the topping, put the potatoes in a big pan of water, bring to the boil, then boil until cooked – 10-15 mins depending on how big your chunks are. Drain really well, then tip back into the pan and steam-dry for a few mins.

STEP 4

Add the coconut milk and turmeric to the pan, and mash really well. Season with the lemon juice and some salt, then stir through the spring onions and coriander stalks.

STEP 5

Spoon the chicken masala into a baking dish. Dollop on spoonfuls of mash to cover, then sprinkle over the kalonji seeds. Can be covered and chilled for up to 2 days (or frozen for up to a month).

STEP 6

Heat oven to 200C/180C fan/gas 6 and bake for 25-30 mins (or 45 mins from chilled) until hot through and crisping on top. Serve with naan bread, if you like.

Thai red duck with sticky pineapple rice

Prep: 20 mins **Cook:** 15 mins plus marinating and steaming

Serves 2

Ingredients

- 2 duck breasts , skin removed and discarded
- 1 tbsp Thai red curry paste
- zest and juice 1 lime , plus extra wedges to serve
- 140g jasmine rice
- 125ml light coconut milk , from a can
- 140g frozen peas
- 50g beansprouts
- ½ red onion , diced
- 100g fresh pineapple , cubed

- 1 red chilli, deseeded and finely chopped
- ¼ small pack coriander, stalks finely chopped, leaves roughly chopped

Method

STEP 1

Sit a duck breast between 2 sheets of cling film on a chopping board. Use a rolling pin to bash the duck until it is 0.5cm thick. Repeat with the other breast, then put them both in a dish. Mix the curry paste with the lime zest and juice, and rub all over the duck. Leave to marinate at room temperature for 20 mins.

STEP 2

Meanwhile, tip the rice into a small saucepan with some salt. Pour over the coconut milk with 150ml water. Bring to a simmer, then cover the pan, turn the heat down low and cook for 5 more mins. Stir in the peas, then cover, turn the heat off and leave for another 10 mins. Check the rice - all the liquid should be absorbed and the rice cooked through. Boil the kettle, put the beansprouts and red onion in a colander and pour over a kettleful of boiling water. Stir the beansprouts and onion into the rice with the pineapple, chilli and coriander stalks, and some more salt if it needs it, and put the lid back on to keep warm.

STEP 3

Heat a griddle pan and cook the duck for 1-2 mins each side or until cooked to your liking. Slice the duck, stir most of the coriander leaves through the rice with a fork to fluff up, and serve alongside the duck, scattered with the remaining coriander.

Zesty salmon with roasted beets & spinach

Prep: 10 mins **Cook:** 1 hr

Serves 2

Ingredients

- 4 small fresh beetroots, about 200g
- 1 ½ tbsp rapeseed oil
- 1 tsp coriander seeds, lightly crushed
- 2 skinless salmon or trout fillets
- 2 ½ small oranges, zest of 1 and juice of half
- 3 tbsp pumpkin seeds
- 1 garlic clove
- 1 red onion, finely chopped

- 4 handfuls baby spinach leaves
- 1 avocado, thickly sliced

Method

STEP 1

Heat oven to 180C, 160C fan, gas 4. Trim the stems of the beetroot and reserve any tender leaves that are suitable for eating in the salad. Cut the beetroots into quarters then toss with 1/2 tbsp oil, the coriander seeds, and some seasoning then pile into the centre of a large sheet of foil and wrap up like a parcel. Bake for 45 mins or until the beetroots are tender then top with the salmon, scatter over half the orange zest and return to the oven for 15 mins. If you want to toast the pumpkin seeds, put them in the oven for 10 mins.

STEP 2

Meanwhile cut the peel and pith from 2 oranges then cut out the segments with a sharp knife working over a bowl to catch the juices. Finely grate the garlic and leave for 10 mins to allow the enzymes to activate. Stir the garlic into the orange juice and remaining oil with seasoning to make a dressing.

STEP 3

Remove the parcel from the oven and carefully lift off the fish. Tip the beetroot into a bowl with the red onion, remaining orange zest, pumpkin seeds and spinach leaves and toss well. Gently toss through the orange segments and avocado with any beet leaves then pile onto plates and top with the warm salmon. Drizzle over the dressing and serve while still warm.

Masala omelette muffins

Prep: 10 mins **Cook:** 20 mins - 25 mins

makes 4

Ingredients

- rapeseed oil, for greasing
- 2 medium courgettes, coarsely grated
- 6 large eggs
- 2 large or 4 small garlic cloves, finely grated
- 1 red chilli, deseeded and finely chopped
- 1 tsp chilli powder
- 1 tsp ground cumin
- 1 tsp ground coriander
- handful fresh coriander, chopped

- 125g frozen peas
- 40g feta

Method

STEP 1

Heat oven to 220C/200C fan/ gas 7 and lightly oil four 200ml ramekins. Grate the courgettes and squeeze really well, removing as much liquid as possible. Put all the ingredients except the feta in a large jug and mix really well.

STEP 2

Pour into the ramekins, scatter with the feta and bake on a baking sheet for 20-25 mins until risen and set. You can serve the muffins hot or cold with salad, slaw or cooked vegetables.

Easy ratatouille

Prep: 25 mins **Cook:** 40 mins

Serves 4

Ingredients

- 2 aubergines
- 3 medium courgettes
- 2 red peppers
- 2 tbsp olive oil
- 1 large onion , finely diced
- 3 garlic cloves , crushed
- 2 x 400g cans chopped tomatoes
- 1 tsp dried oregano , basil or Italian mixed herbs
- small bunch basil , chopped, plus a few leaves to serve
- 1 tbsp red wine vinegar
- 1-2 tbsp sugar

Method

STEP 1

Dice the aubergine, courgette and pepper into 3cm chunks. Heat the olive oil in a large casserole or deep frying pan over a medium heat. Fry the onion for 10 mins until soft and translucent. Add the chopped veg, turn the heat to high and fry for another 10 mins until softened.

STEP 2

Stir the garlic into the pan, and toss everything together, frying for 1 min more. Tip in the chopped tomatoes, plus half a can of water (200ml), the dried herbs and the chopped basil. Simmer for 20 minutes on a medium heat, stirring occasionally, until the veg is tender and the tomatoes are thick and coating the veg. Season and add the vinegar and sugar to balance the sweet and acidity of the tomatoes. Scatter with the basil leaves, and serve with rustic bread, or pasta.

Lemon & garlic roast chicken with charred broccoli & sweet potato mash

Prep: 10 mins **Cook:** 1 hr - 1 hr and 15 mins

Serves 2

Ingredients

- 1 small free-range chicken (about 1kg)
- 2 garlic cloves
- 1 tsp rapeseed oil
- small bunch thyme
- 1 lemon, halved
- 1 small head broccoli (about 200g), cut into small florets
- 200g sweet potato, peeled and cubed (cook 100g extra if you are using for Chicken wrap with sticky sweet potato, see 'goes well with')
- 1 tbsp low-fat cream cheese

Method

STEP 1

Heat oven to 200C/180C fan/gas 6 and put the chicken in a large non-stick roasting tin. Halve 1 garlic clove and rub it over the chicken. Drizzle with oil, rub in with your fingers, then stuff the cavity with the thyme, 1 lemon half and the garlic you just used.

STEP 2

Cut the other lemon half into quarters and scatter around the chicken with the other garlic clove, halved.

STEP 3

Cover the tin with foil and bake for 40 mins, then remove the foil and spoon over the hot juices. Arrange the broccoli around the chicken, turning well in the juices, and return the tin to the oven for another 20-30 mins. To check that it is cooked through, pierce between the leg and thigh – if the juices run clear, the chicken is ready. Re-cover with foil and set aside while you prepare the sweet potatoes.

STEP 4

Put the sweet potatoes in a pan of boiling water, return to the boil, then simmer for 7-10 mins until tender. Drain well, then mash. Set aside 100g of sweet potato mash if using for Chicken wrap with sticky sweet potato, see 'goes well with', then add the cream cheese to the rest and stir well.

STEP 5

Remove the broccoli from the roasting tin and divide between 2 plates. Put the chicken on a serving plate, discard the lemon and garlic from the tin and remove as much of the fat from the juices as possible. Pour the remaining juices into a serving jug.

STEP 6

Carve the chicken and serve about 100g (1-2 slices) per person (keep the rest of the chicken for Chicken wrap with sticky sweet potato if making, see 'goes well with'). Serve with the broccoli and mashed sweet potatoes, and a drizzle of the lemony-garlic juices on top.

Tropical overnight oats

Prep: 10 mins No cook

Serves 1

Ingredients

- 50g rolled porridge oats
- 20g coconut yogurt
- 2 sliced kiwis
- 1 passion fruit
- ½ tsp toasted mixed seeds

Method

STEP 1

Soak the oats in 150ml water with a pinch of salt, then cover and chill in the fridge overnight.

STEP 2

The next day spoon half the oats into a bowl. Layer with the coconut yogurt, sliced kiwis, the pulp of the passion fruit and the rest of the oats, then top with the toasted mixed seeds.

Summer vegetable curry

Prep: 10 mins **Cook:** 35 mins

Serves 4

Ingredients

- 1-2 tbsp red Thai curry paste (depending on taste)
- 500ml low-sodium vegetable stock
- 2 onions, chopped
- 1 aubergine, diced
- 75g red lentil
- 200ml can reduced-fat coconut milk
- 2 red or yellow peppers, deseeded and cut into wedges
- 140g frozen pea
- 100g bag baby spinach, roughly chopped
- brown basmati rice and mango chutney, to serve

Method

STEP 1

Heat the curry paste in a large non-stick saucepan with a splash of the stock. Add the onions and fry for 5 mins until starting to soften. Stir in the aubergine and cook for a further 5 mins – add a little more stock if starting to stick.

STEP 2

Add the lentils, coconut milk and the rest of the stock, and simmer for 15 mins or until the lentils are tender. Add the peppers and cook for 5-10 mins more. Stir through the peas and spinach and cook until spinach has just wilted. Serve the curry with rice and mango chutney.

Prawn & tomato stew with gremolata topping

Prep: 10 mins **Cook:** 35 mins

Serves 4

Ingredients

- 500g new potato
- 2 tbsp olive oil
- 1 large onion, sliced
- 4 celery sticks, cut into pieces
- 2 garlic cloves, chopped
- 2 anchovy fillets, chopped
- pinch chilli flakes
- 400g can chopped tomato
- 250ml white wine
- 200ml vegetable stock
- 400g raw king prawn, peeled
- zest and juice 1 lemon
- 1 tsp salted baby caper, rinsed
- large handful parsley, chopped
- toasted bread, to serve

Method

STEP 1

Put the potatoes in a saucepan of cold salted water and bring to the boil. Reduce the heat to medium and simmer for 15-20 mins or until cooked but still firm. Drain and, when cool enough to handle, thickly slice.

STEP 2

Meanwhile, heat the oil in a large saucepan over a low-medium heat. Add the onion, celery, garlic, anchovy and chilli, season and cook for 8 mins or until softened. Increase the heat to medium-high, add the tomatoes, wine and stock, and cook for 15 mins. Add the prawns, lemon juice, capers and potatoes. Cook for 5 mins more, or until the prawns turn pink and are just cooked. Mix together the parsley and lemon zest, then scatter over the stew, then serve with toasted bread, for dunking.

Tomato & courgette stew

Prep: 10 mins **Cook:** 1 hr

Serves 4

Ingredients

- 1 tbsp olive oil
- 1 onion, chopped
- 2 garlic cloves, crushed
- 3 courgettes, quartered lengthways and cut into chunks
- 2 x 400g cans chopped tomatoes
- small bunch basil, torn
- 25g parmesan (or vegetarian alternative), finely grated

Method

STEP 1

Heat the oil in a large frying pan over a medium heat. Add the onion and cook for about 10 mins until softened and starting to go golden brown. Add the garlic and cook for 5 mins more.

STEP 2

Add the courgettes and cook for about 5 mins until starting to soften. Tip in the tomatoes and give everything a good stir. Simmer for 35-40 mins or until tomatoes are reduced and courgettes soft, then stir in the basil and Parmesan.

Turkey & coriander burgers with guacamole

Prep: 15 mins **Cook:** 15 mins

Serves 4

Ingredients

- 400g turkey mince
- 1 tsp Worcestershire sauce
- 85g fresh breadcrumb
- 1 tbsp chopped coriander
- 1 red onion , finely chopped
- 1 large ripe avocado , or 2 small
- 1 chilli , deseeded and finely chopped
- juice 1 lime
- 4 ciabatta rolls, cut in half
- 1 tsp sunflower oil
- 8 hot peppadew peppers, roughly chopped

Method

STEP 1

Mix the mince, Worcestershire sauce, breadcrumbs, half each of the coriander and onion, and some seasoning until combined. Form into 4 burgers, then chill until ready to cook.

STEP 2

To make the guacamole, mash the avocado with the remaining coriander and onion, the chilli and lime juice, and season.

STEP 3

Heat a griddle pan or barbecue until hot. Griddle the rolls, cut-side down, for 1 min, then keep warm. Brush the burgers with the oil to keep them from sticking. Cook for 7-8 mins on each side until charred and cooked through. Fill the rolls with the burgers, guacamole and peppadews.

Courgette & couscous salad with tahini dressing

Prep: 10 mins no cook

Serves 4

Ingredients

- 200g couscous
- zest and juice 1 lemon
- 2 tbsp olive oil
- 2 tbsp tahini paste
- 1 garlic clove , crushed
- griddled courgettes
- 4 tomatoes , roughly chopped
- 200g pack feta cheese , crumbled
- small pack mint , leaves picked
- small pack parsley , leaves picked
- 1 red chilli , deseeded and sliced

Method

STEP 1

Put the couscous in a heatproof bowl and pour over boiling water to just cover. Cover with cling film and leave to stand for 5 mins.

STEP 2

Mix the lemon zest and juice, oil, tahini and garlic, and season to taste. Fluff the prepared couscous and season. Spoon onto a large serving platter and scatter over the courgettes, tomatoes, feta, herbs and chilli. Drizzle over the dressing.

Quinoa, squash & broccoli salad

Prep: 10 mins **Cook:** 10 mins

Serves 2

Ingredients

- 2 tsp rapeseed oil
- 1 red onion , halved and sliced
- 2 garlic cloves , sliced
- 175g frozen butternut squash chunks
- 140g broccoli , stalks sliced, top cut into small florets

- 1 tbsp fresh thyme leaf
- 250g pack ready-to-eat red & white quinoa
- 2 tbsp chopped parsley
- 25g dried cranberries
- handful pumpkin seeds (optional)
- 1 tbsp balsamic vinegar
- 50g feta cheese , crumbled

Method

STEP 1

Heat the oil in a wok with a lid, add the onion and garlic, and fry for 5 mins until softened, then lift from the wok with a slotted spoon. Add the squash, stir round the wok until it starts to colour, then add the broccoli. Sprinkle in 3 tbsp water and the thyme, cover the pan and steam for about 5 mins until the veg is tender.

STEP 2

Meanwhile, tip quinoa into a bowl and fluff it up. Add the parsley, cranberries, seeds (if using), cooked onion and garlic, and balsamic vinegar, and mix well. Toss through the vegetables with the feta. Will keep in the fridge for 2 days.

Wild garlic & nettle soup

Prep: 15 mins **Cook:** 35 mins

Serves 4 - 6

Ingredients

- 1 tbsp rapeseed oil , plus extra for drizzling
- 25g butter
- 1 onion , finely diced
- 1 leek , finely diced
- 2 celery sticks, thinly sliced
- 1 carrot , finely diced
- 1 small potato , peeled and diced
- 1.2l good-quality vegetable stock
- 300g young nettle leaves
- 200g wild garlic leaves (keep any flowers if you have them)
- 3 tbsp milk

Method

STEP 1

Heat the oil and butter in a large saucepan. Add the onion, leek, celery, carrot, potato and a good pinch of salt, and stir until everything is well coated. Cover and sweat gently for 15-20 mins, stirring every so often to make sure that the vegetables don't catch on the bottom of the pan.

STEP 2

Pour in the stock and simmer for 10 mins. Add the nettles in several batches, stirring, then add the wild garlic leaves and simmer for 2 mins.

STEP 3

Remove from the heat and blend using a stick blender or tip into a blender. Return to the heat and stir through the milk, then taste for seasoning. Ladle into bowls and drizzle over a little extra oil, then top with a few wild garlic flowers, if you have them.

Pastry-less pork pie

Prep: 55 mins **Cook:** 1 hr and 15 mins plus cooling

Serves 6 - 8

Ingredients

- 4-5 large courgettes
- 1 tbsp olive or rapeseed oil , plus a drizzle
- 50g dried breadcrumbs , plus 2 tbsp
- 1 red onion , finely chopped
- 2 garlic cloves , crushed
- 290g jar red peppers , drained and chopped
- small bunch parsley , chopped
- zest 1 lemon
- 1 large egg
- 500g minced pork
- 2 tsp chilli flakes
- 2 tsp fennel seeds

Method

STEP 1

Cut the courgettes lengthways into thin slices (use a mandolin if you have one), stopping when you reach the seedy middle (set this aside). Heat a griddle pan. Toss the courgettes in a little oil to coat, then cook in batches until soft and marked with griddle lines. Drizzle a little oil into an 18cm springform tin and brush all over the base and sides. Line the base with a circle of baking parchment. Use the courgettes to line the tin, overlapping them across the base, up the sides and over the edge – you need enough overhang to cover the top and the filling, so you may need to double up on slices up the sides. Scatter 2 tbsp breadcrumbs over the base.

STEP 2

Heat the oil in a large frying pan. Add the onion and cook for 5 mins until softened a little. Meanwhile, finely chop the centre pieces of courgette and add to the pan with the garlic. Cook for about 5 mins until the courgette has softened, then set aside to cool.

STEP 3

Heat oven to 180C/160C fan/gas 4. Mix the cooled veg, the peppers, parsley, lemon zest, breadcrumbs, egg, pork, chilli, fennel seeds and plenty of seasoning in a bowl. Pack the mixture into the courgette-lined tin, pressing it firmly into the edges and flattening the top – try not to move the courgette slices too much. Fold over the overhanging courgettes to cover the top of the pie and press down firmly.

STEP 4

Place the tin on a baking tray – some juice may leak out of the tin so you will need the tray to catch this. Bake for 1 hr 15 mins – if you have a meat thermometer, the temperature should read at least 70C. Cool in the tin for 10 mins.

STEP 5

Remove the pie from the tin, pouring away any juices, and flip over so that the neater side is facing up. Remove the baking parchment and leave to cool completely, then store in the fridge. Transport in a cooler bag and serve in wedges.

Courgette & tomato soup

Prep: 10 mins **Cook:** 35 mins

Serves 8

Ingredients

- 1 tbsp butter
- 2 onions , chopped
- 1kg courgette , sliced
- 1kg tomato , chopped

- 2 tbsp plain flour
- ½ tsp turmeric
- 2l low-sodium chicken or vegetable stock from cubes
- crusty bread, to serve (optional)

Method

STEP 1

Melt the butter in a large pan, add the onions and courgettes, and cook for 5 mins on a medium heat, stirring occasionally.

STEP 2

Add the tomatoes and flour. Cook for a couple of mins, stirring around to stop the flour from becoming lumpy. Add the turmeric and stock, cover and simmer for 30 mins.

STEP 3

Purée with a stick blender, then sieve if you want a really smooth texture. Serve hot with crusty bread, if you like, or chill, then freeze for up to 2 months.

Instant berry banana slush

Prep: 5 mins no cook

Serves 2

Ingredients

- 2 ripe bananas
- 200g frozen berry mix (blackberries, raspberries and currants)

Method

STEP 1

Slice the bananas into a bowl and add the frozen berry mix. Blitz with a stick blender to make a slushy ice and serve straight away in two glasses with spoons.

Sesame chicken salad

Prep: 10 mins **Cook:** 10 mins

Serves 2

Ingredients

- 2 skinless chicken breasts
- 85g frozen soya bean
- 1 large carrot , finely cut into thin matchsticks
- 4 spring onions , finely sliced
- 140g cherry tomato , halved
- small bunch coriander , chopped
- small handful Thai or ordinary basil leaves , chopped if large
- 85g herb or baby salad leaves
- 1 tsp toasted sesame seeds

For the dressing

- grated zest and juice 1 small lime
- 1 tsp fish sauce
- 1 tsp sesame oil
- 2 tsp sweet chilli sauce

Method

STEP 1

Put the chicken in a pan and pour over cold water to cover. Tip the soya beans into a steamer. Bring the pan to a gentle simmer, then cook the chicken for 8 mins with the beans above.

STEP 2

Meanwhile, mix the dressing ingredients in a large bowl. When the chicken is cooked, slice and toss in the dressing along with the beans, carrot, onions, tomatoes, coriander and basil. Mix really well, pile onto the salad leaves and sprinkle with the sesame seeds.

Fruit & nut breakfast bowl

Prep: 5 mins **Cook:** 5 mins - 10 mins

Serves 2

Ingredients

- 6 tbsp porridge oats
- 2 oranges
- just under ½ x 200ml tub 0% fat Greek-style yogurt
- 60g pot raisins , nuts, goji berries and seeds

Method

STEP 1

Put the oats in a non-stick pan with 400ml water and cook over the heat, stirring occasionally for about 4 mins until thickened.

STEP 2

Meanwhile, cut the peel and pith from the oranges then slice them in half, cutting down either side, as closely as you can, to where the stalk would be as this will remove quite a tough section of the membrane. Now just chop the oranges.

STEP 3

Pour the porridge into bowls, spoon on the yogurt then pile on the oranges and the fruit, nut and seed mixture.

Strawberry & banana almond smoothie

Prep: 5 mins No cook

Serves 1

Ingredients

- 1 small banana
- 7 strawberries , hulled
- 3 tbsp 0% bio-yogurt
- 3 tbsp skimmed milk
- 2 tbsp ground almond

Method

STEP 1

Slice the banana into the bowl of a food processor, or a jug if using a hand blender. Add the strawberries, yogurt, milk and ground almonds, and blitz until completely smooth. Pour into a glass and enjoy.

Sticky baked meatloaf with avocado & black bean salsa

Prep: 25 mins **Cook:** 1 hr

Serves 4

Ingredients

For the meatloaf

- 1 tbsp rapeseed oil , plus a little for greasing
- 2 large onions , halved and thinly sliced
- 4 large garlic cloves , grated
- 1 tsp allspice or mixed spice
- 1 ½ tsp fennel seeds
- 2 tbsp smoked paprika
- 2 tbsp tomato purée
- 50g quinoa
- 160g grated carrot
- 1 tsp dried oregano
- ½ tsp ground cumin
- 400g pack turkey leg and breast mince
- 1 large egg
- 1 tsp black treacle

For the salsa

- 400g black beans , drained
- 1 small red onion , finely chopped
- 1 avocado , finely chopped
- 2 tomatoes , finely chopped
- ½ small pack fresh coriander , chopped
- 1 red chilli deseeded and finely chopped (optional)
- juice 1 lime

Method

STEP 1

Heat oven to 180C/160C fan/gas 4. Grease and line a deep 500g loaf tin with baking parchment. Heat the oil in a large, non-stick frying pan. Add the onions and fry for 10 mins, stirring occasionally until golden. Stir in the garlic and spices, toast over the heat for 3 mins, then add the purée. Scrape half into a small bowl for the topping.

STEP 2

Stir the quinoa and 4 tbsp water into the frying pan and cook for 2 mins. Tip into a bowl, leave to cool for 5 mins, then add the carrot, oregano, cumin, turkey mince and egg. Season with black pepper and mix well. Pack into the greased tin and bake, uncovered, for 35 mins until firm.

STEP 3

Meanwhile, mix all the salsa ingredients in a serving bowl, and add 3 tbsp water to the remaining onion mixture with the black treacle.

STEP 4

When the meatloaf is cooked, carefully turn it out of the tin onto a shallow ovenproof dish and spread the onion mixture over the top. Return to the oven, bake for 10 mins more, then slice and serve with the salsa.

Raspberry coconut porridge

Prep: 10 mins **Cook:** 10 mins plus overnight soaking

Serves 4

Ingredients

- 100g rolled porridge oats (not instant)
- 25g creamed coconut , chopped
- 200g frozen raspberries
- 125g pot coconut yogurt (we used COYO)
- a few mint leaves , to serve (optional)

Method

STEP 1

Tip the oats and creamed coconut into a large bowl, pour on 800ml cold water, cover and leave to soak overnight.

STEP 2

The next day, tip the contents of the bowl into a saucepan and cook over a medium heat, stirring frequently, for 5 -10 mins until the oats are cooked. Add the raspberries to the pan with the yogurt and allow to thaw and melt into the oats off the heat. Reserve half for the next day and spoon the remainder into bowls. Top each portion with mint leaves, if you like.

Speedy soy spinach

Prep: 5 mins **Cook:** 5 mins

Serves 4 as a side dish

Ingredients

- 1 tbsp vegetable oil
- 1 garlic clove
- 200g bag spinach
- 2 tbsp soy sauce

- 1 tbsp toasted sesame seeds

Method

STEP 1

Heat the oil in a pan and cook the garlic for a few secs. Tip in the spinach and cook for 2 mins, stirring often until just beginning to wilt. Drizzle over the soy sauce, toss through and scatter with sesame seeds. Great served with chicken or grills.

Mumsy's vegetable soup

Prep: 10 mins **Cook:** 30 mins

Serves 4

Ingredients

- 200g sourdough bread, cut into croutons
- 1 tbsp caraway seeds
- 3 tbsp olive oil
- 1 garlic clove, chopped
- 1 carrot, chopped
- 1 potato, chopped
- 600ml vegetable stock (we use bouillon)
- 100g cherry tomatoes, halved
- 400g can chopped tomatoes
- pinch of golden caster sugar
- 1 bouquet garni (2 bay leaves, 1 rosemary sprig and 2 thyme sprigs tied together with string)
- 1 celery stick, chopped
- 200g cauliflower, cut into florets
- 150g white cabbage, shredded
- 1 tsp Worcestershire sauce
- 2 tsp mushroom ketchup

Method

STEP 1

Heat oven to 180C/160C fan/gas 4. Put the bread on a baking tray with the caraway seeds, half the oil and some sea salt, and bake for 10-15 mins or until golden and crisp. Set aside.

STEP 2

Meanwhile, heat the remaining oil in a large saucepan over a medium heat. Add the garlic, carrot and potato and cook for 5 mins, stirring frequently, until a little softened.

STEP 3

Add the stock, tomatoes, sugar, bouquet garni, celery and seasoning and bring to a rolling boil. Reduce the heat, simmer for 10 mins, then add the cauliflower and cabbage. Cook for 15 mins until the veg is tender.

STEP 4

Stir in the Worcestershire sauce and mushroom ketchup. Remove the bouquet garni and serve the soup in bowls with the caraway croutons.

Asparagus & lentil salad with cranberries & crumbled feta

Prep: 10 mins **Cook:** 20 mins

Serves 2

Ingredients

- 1 garlic clove
- 125g puy lentils
- 100g pack fine asparagus tips
- 3 spring onions, finely sliced
- 25g dried cranberries
- 1 tbsp extra virgin rapeseed oil, plus a little extra (optional)
- 2 tsp organic apple cider vinegar
- 140g cherry tomatoes, halved
- 50g feta (read back of pack for vegetarian option)

Method

STEP 1

Finely grate the garlic and put in a bowl. Boil the lentils for 25 mins, and put the asparagus in a steamer over them for the last 5 mins until just tender.

STEP 2

Meanwhile, put the onions, cranberries, oil and vinegar in the bowl with the garlic and stir well. When the lentils are ready, drain and toss them into the dressing with the tomatoes. Tip into plastic containers (for a packed lunch), or onto plates, then top with the asparagus and crumble over the feta. Drizzle with a little extra oil, if you like.

Spicy mushroom & broccoli noodles

Prep:10 mins **Cook:**10 mins

Serves 2

Ingredients

- 1 low-salt vegetable stock cube
- 2 nests medium egg noodles
- 1 small head broccoli, broken into florets
- 1 tbsp sesame oil, plus extra to serve
- 250g pack shiitake or chestnut mushroom, thickly sliced
- 1 fat garlic clove, finely chopped
- ½ tsp chilli flakes, or crumble one dried chilli into pieces
- 4 spring onions, thinly sliced
- 2 tbsp hoisin sauce
- handful roasted cashew nuts

Method

STEP 1

Put the stock cube into a pan of water, then bring to the boil. Add the noodles, bring the stock back to the boil and cook for 2 mins. Add the broccoli and boil for 2 mins more. Reserve a cup of the stock, then drain the noodles and veg.

STEP 2

Heat a frying pan or wok, add the sesame oil and stir-fry the mushrooms for 2 mins until turning golden. Add the garlic, chilli flakes and most of the spring onions, cook 1 min more, then tip in the noodles and broccoli. Splash in 3 tbsp of the stock and the hoisin sauce, then toss together for 1 min using a pair of tongs or 2 wooden spoons. Serve the noodles scattered with the cashew nuts and remaining spring onions. Add a dash more sesame oil to taste, if you like.

Roasted summer vegetable casserole

Prep:15 mins **Cook:**1 hr

Serves 2 - 3

Ingredients

- 3 tbsp olive oil
- 1 garlic bulb , halved through the middle
- 2 large courgettes , thickly sliced
- 1 large red onion , sliced

- 1 aubergine, halved and sliced on the diagonal
- 2 large tomatoes, quartered
- 200g new potatoes, scrubbed and halved
- 1 red pepper, deseeded and cut into chunky pieces
- 400g can chopped tomatoes
- 0.5 small pack parsley, chopped

Method

STEP 1

Heat oven to 200C/180C fan/gas 6 and put the oil in a roasting tin. Tip in the garlic and all the fresh veg, then toss with your hands to coat in the oil. Season well and roast for 45 mins.

STEP 2

Remove the garlic from the roasting tin and squeeze out the softened cloves all over the veg, stirring to evenly distribute. In a medium pan, simmer the chopped tomatoes until bubbling, season well and stir through the roasted veg in the tin. Scatter over the parsley and serve.

Beetroot & lentil tabbouleh

Prep: 15 mins No cook

Serves 4

Ingredients

- 1 small pack flat-leaf parsley, plus extra leaves to serve (optional)
- 1 small pack mint
- 1 small pack chives
- 200g radishes
- 2 beetroot, peeled and quartered
- 1 red apple, cored, quartered and sliced
- 1 tsp ground cumin
- 4 tbsp olive oil
- 250g pack cooked quinoa
- 400g can chickpeas, drained and rinsed
- 400g can green lentils, drained
- 2 lemons, juiced

Method

STEP 1

Put the herbs, radishes and beetroot in a food processor and blitz until chopped into small pieces. Stir in the rest of the ingredients, adding the lemon juice a bit at a time to taste – you may not need all of it. Season, then place on a large platter topped with a few parsley leaves, if you like, and serve straight away.

Sweet mustard potato salad

Prep: 10 mins **Cook:** 10 mins

Serves 10

Ingredients

- 1.2kg waxy potatoes , such as Charlotte, cut into small chunks
- 400g good-quality mayonnaise
- 2 tbsp American mustard
- 2 tbsp cider vinegar
- 2 tbsp honey
- hard-boiled eggs , finely chopped
- 8 spring onions , sliced

Method

STEP 1

Put the potatoes in a pan of salted water, bring to the boil, then cover and simmer for 8-10 mins or until cooked through – a cutlery knife should easily pierce them. Drain and leave to cool in a colander.

STEP 2

Combine the mayo, mustard, vinegar, honey and eggs, then season well. Stir through the potatoes and half the spring onions, transfer to a serving dish and scatter over the remaining onions. Chill until you're ready to serve. Can be made 1 day ahead.

Burnt leeks on toast with romesco

Prep: 20 mins **Cook:** 25 mins

Serves 6

Ingredients

- 50g whole blanched almonds
- 100g cooked red peppers from a jar, drained
- 1 large ciabatta loaf, sliced
- ½ tbsp olive oil , plus 2 tsp
- 1 tsp sherry vinegar
- 1 red chilli , deseeded
- ¼ tsp smoked paprika
- 1 garlic clove , crushed
- 3 leeks , each cut into 4 pieces

Method

STEP 1

Toast the almonds in a dry pan until golden. Put the almonds, peppers, 1 small ciabatta slice (about 10g – an end piece is ideal), 1/ 2 tbsp olive oil, the vinegar, chilli, paprika , garlic and some seasoning in a food processor (or use a stick blender). Blend until smooth, then transfer to a bowl and chill in the fridge until needed. Can be done a day in advance.

STEP 2

Put the leeks in a saucepan and cover with water. Bring to the boil and cook for 5 mins. Drain on kitchen paper until needed.

STEP 3

When you're ready to serve, heat grill to high. Put the cooked leeks on a baking tray, season and drizzle with 2 tsp olive oil. Grill the leeks until starting to blacken, about 8-10 mins, turning once during cooking.

STEP 4

Toast the remaining ciabatta slices and spread with a little of the romesco. Gently pull the leeks into ribbons and pile them on top. Season well and serve immediately.

Corn cups with prawns, mango & chillies

Prep: 15 mins **Cook:** 10 mins

Makes 24

Ingredients

- 8-10 corn tortillas
- 3 tbsp vegetable oil
- 100g small shelled prawns
- juice 1 lime
- ½ mango , peeled, deseeded and finely diced
- 2 tbsp finely diced red onion
- 1 red chilli , finely diced
- handful coriander , finely chopped and some whole leaves reserved

Method

STEP 1

Heat oven to 200C/180C fan/gas 6. Using a 6cm pastry cutter, cut out circles from the tortillas. Heat the tortilla circles from the tortillas. Heat the tortilla circles for 5 secs in a microwave, then press into a mini muffin tin. Brush with the oil and bake for 8-10 mins until golden and crisp. Remove and leave to cool completely.

STEP 2

Chop the prawns into small pieces and marinate in the lime juice for 5 mins. Put the prawns and lime juice in a bowl with the mango, red onion, chilli and coriander. Season, mix together and use to fill the corn cups just before serving. Top with coriander leaves.

Poor man's vongole rosso

Prep: 10 mins **Cook:** 25 mins

Serves 4

Ingredients

- 2 tbsp olive oil
- 3 garlic cloves , thinly sliced
- 400g can cherry tomatoes
- glass of white wine
- small pinch of golden caster sugar
- 750g cockles , rinsed
- 400g linguine
- 1 tbsp good-quality extra virgin olive oil

Method

STEP 1

Heat the olive oil in a large saucepan with a lid. Add the garlic and sizzle for 1 min, then tip in the tomatoes. Use the white wine to swirl round and rinse out the tomato can, then tip it into the pan, sprinkle over the sugar and turn up the heat. Simmer until everything becomes thick, making sure you stir occasionally so it doesn't burn on the bottom of the pan – this will take 15-20 mins.

STEP 2

Once the tomatoes have had about 10 mins, cook the pasta in a big pan of salted water until just cooked – this will take about 10 mins – then drain. When the tomatoes and wine have reduced to a thick sauce, throw the cockles into the pan, stir once, cover with a lid and turn the heat up to max. Cook for 3-4 mins until all the cockles have opened, then stir again. Turn off the heat and stir through the pasta with the extra virgin olive oil until everything is coated. Try a strand of pasta and season with salt to taste. Bring the pan to the table with a separate bowl for the shells, and serve straight from the pan.

Butternut squash & sage soup

Prep: 20 mins **Cook:** 40 mins

Serves 8

Ingredients

- 1 tbsp olive oil
- 1 tbsp butter
- 3 onions , chopped
- 2 tbsp chopped sage
- 1.4kg peeled, deseeded butternut squash - buy whole squash and prepare, or buy bags of ready-prepared
- 1 tbsp clear honey
- 1 ½l vegetable stock
- bunch chives , snipped, and cracked black pepper, to serve

Method

STEP 1

Melt the oil and butter in a large saucepan or flameproof casserole. Add the onions and sage, and gently cook until really soft – about 15 mins. Tip in the squash and cook for 5 mins, stirring. Add the honey and stock, bring to a simmer and cook until the squash is tender.

STEP 2

Let the soup cool a bit so you don't burn yourself, then whizz until really smooth with a hand blender, or in batches in a blender. Season to taste, adding a drop more stock or water if the soup is too thick. Reheat before serving, sprinkled with chives and cracked black pepper.

Sushi burrito

Prep: 45 mins **Cook:** 10 mins

Serves 4

Ingredients

- 150g sushi rice
- 2 tsp rice wine vinegar
- ½ cucumber, cut into matchsticks
- 1 carrot, cut into matchsticks
- 1 tbsp soy sauce
- 4 nori sheets
- 2 tsp wasabi paste
- 50g pickled ginger, finely chopped
- 1 lime, juiced
- 2 very ripe avocados, halved, stoned, peeled and sliced
- 200g sushi grade tuna steak, sliced
- small pack coriander, leaves picked

Method

STEP 1

Put the rice in a bowl, cover with cold water and massage to remove the starch. Drain and repeat until the water runs clear. Put the rice in a small saucepan, cover with 2.5cm of water and put on a tight-fitting lid. Simmer on a medium heat for 10 mins, then take off the heat (leaving the lid on) and steam for a further 15 mins. Stir in the vinegar, then cool completely.

STEP 2

Toss the cucumber and carrot matchsticks in the soy and leave to marinate.

STEP 3

Lay out a sushi mat and put a nori sheet, shiny-side down, on top of it. Spread a quarter of the rice over the nori, leaving a 1cm border at the top. Mix the wasabi, ginger and lime juice.

STEP 4

Layer with the avocado, cucumber and carrot, and tuna. Top with the wasabi mix and coriander. Dampen the top border with a little water, fold in both sides of the nori sheet, then use the sushi mat to help roll. Wrap in foil, slice in half and serve.

Seared tuna & anchovy runner beans

Prep: 5 mins **Cook:** 10 mins

Serves 2

Ingredients

- 3 tbsp snipped chives
- 12 basil leaves
- 2 tbsp chopped mint , plus a few small leaves, for serving
- zest and juice 1 small lemon
- 2 tbsp extra virgin olive oil
- 1 tbsp Dijon mustard
- 1 tbsp small capers
- 6 anchovies (smoked or unsmoked), chopped
- 300g runner beans , sliced diagonally
- 2 tuna steaks
- small handful flat-leaf parsley
- 2 tbsp toasted flaked almonds

Method

STEP 1

Put the chives, basil and mint in a small food processor with the lemon zest and juice, oil and mustard. Blitz to a purée. Take out 2 tbsp to use as a coating for the fish, then stir the capers and anchovies into the rest.

STEP 2

Cook the runner beans in boiling salted water or steam for 5 mins until tender but still with a little bite.

STEP 3

Brush the tuna with the reserved herby mixture and griddle for 2-3 mins each side until cooked but still a little pink in the centre. Toss half the caper dressing through the warm beans with the parsley and pile onto plates. Top with the tuna, spoon over the remaining dressing and scatter with the almonds and mint leaves.

Green breakfast smoothie

Prep: 10 mins No cook

Serves 2

Ingredients

- 1 handful spinach (about 50g/2oz), roughly chopped
- 100g broccoli florets, roughly chopped
- 2 celery sticks
- 4 tbsp desiccated coconut
- 1 banana
- 300ml rice milk (good dairy alternative - we used one from Rude Health)
- ¼ tsp spirulina or 1 scoop of greens powder or vegan protein powder (optional)

Method

STEP 1

Whizz 300ml water and the ingredients in a blender until smooth.

Courgette, pea & pesto soup

Prep: 10 mins **Cook:** 15 mins

Serves 4

Ingredients

- 1 tbsp olive oil
- 1 garlic clove, sliced
- 500g courgettes, quartered lengthways and chopped
- 200g frozen peas
- 400g can cannellini beans, drained and rinsed
- 1l hot vegetable stock
- 2 tbsp basil pesto, or vegetarian alternative

Method

STEP 1

Heat the oil in a large saucepan. Cook the garlic for a few seconds, then add the courgettes and cook for 3 mins until they start to soften. Stir in the peas and cannellini beans, pour on the hot stock and cook for a further 3 mins.

STEP 2

Stir the pesto through the soup with some seasoning, then ladle into bowls and serve with crusty brown bread, if you like. Or pop in a flask to take to work.

Baba ganoush & crudités

Prep: 15 mins **Cook:** 30 mins plus draining

Serves 6

Ingredients

For the baba ganoush

- 4 large aubergines (about 1.2kg), pricked all over with a fork
- zest and juice of 1 lemon
- 2 fat garlic cloves, chopped
- 3 tbsp tahini
- 4 tbsp extra virgin olive oil, plus a little extra for drizzling

For the crudités (optional)

- 4 large carrots, ends trimmed and spiralized into thick noodles
- 1 large cucumber, ends trimmed, spiralized into thick ribbons and patted dry to remove excess water
- 1 large courgette (about 145g), ends trimmed and spiralized into thick noodles
- 150g pack mixed radishes, cut into random shapes

Method

STEP 1

Cover the hob in tin foil for ease of cleaning then put each aubergine on a single gas hob and cook, turning occasionally with tongs until the aubergines are completely charred and collapsed, this will take 10–15 mins. Alternatively, heat the grill to its highest setting, lay the aubergines on a baking tray and cook, turning occasionally, for 30 mins to achieve the same effect. While the aubergine is cooking, prep the vegetables if using.

STEP 2

Allow the aubergines to cool slightly then scoop out the soft flesh into a colander. Leave to drain for 30 mins to remove any excess water then blitz the aubergine along with the other baba ganoush ingredients and some seasoning in a food processor to however smooth or chunky you like.

STEP 3

Spoon the dip into a bowl and serve in the centre of the vegetable crudités.

Smoky paprika seafood rice

Prep: 15 mins **Cook:** 35 mins

Serves 4

Ingredients

- 1.3l fish or chicken stock
- large pinch of saffron (optional, see tip)
- 4 tbsp olive oil
- 4 garlic cloves, 1 left whole, 3 finely chopped
- 12 large prawns, shells on
- 4 baby squid (about 250g), cleaned and sliced
- 1 onion, very finely chopped
- 2 celery sticks, very finely chopped
- 1 tsp fennel seeds, lightly crushed
- 2 tbsp tomato purée
- 1 tsp smoked paprika (hot or sweet)
- 300g paella rice
- 250ml fino sherry or dry white wine
- 300g fresh mussels, cleaned (discard any that are open)
- large handful parsley, roughly chopped
- 1 lemon, cut into wedges, to serve

Method

STEP 1

Heat the stock in a large saucepan. Add the saffron to infuse, if you like. Take off the heat and set aside. In a large deep-sided frying pan or paella pan, heat 1 tbsp of the oil. Smash the whole garlic clove and add to the oil. Throw in the prawns and cook for 2 mins until just turning pink but not cooked through. Push to one side of the pan and add the squid to the garlicky oil for 1 min or so, again just to colour. Remove the seafood to a plate.

STEP 2

Add the remaining oil to the pan, and cook the onion and celery slowly for 15 mins until very soft and beginning to caramelise. Add the finely chopped garlic, the fennel seeds, tomato purée and paprika, and cook for 5 mins more. Meanwhile, bring the stock to a simmer. Add the rice to the pan with the onion mixture, give everything a good stir, then add the sherry and 1 litre of the hot stock. Bring to the boil and simmer gently for 15 mins, shaking the pan from time to time.

STEP 3

When the rice is almost cooked but still has a little bite, dot over the prawns, squid and the mussels. Add the cooking juices and the rest of the stock. Cover and cook for 5 mins until the seafood is cooked through, the mussels have opened and the rice is just tender. (You may have to add a splash more water if the rice looks dry.) Discard any mussels that haven't opened. Sprinkle over some chopped parsley and serve with lemon wedges to squeeze over.

Three-grain porridge

Prep: 5 mins **Cook:** 5 mins

Serves 18

Ingredients

- 300g oatmeal
- 300g spelt flakes
- 300g barley flakes
- agave nectar and sliced strawberries, to serve (optional)

Method

STEP 1

Working in batches, toast the oatmeal, spelt flakes and barley in a large, dry frying pan for 5 mins until golden, then leave to cool and store in an airtight container.

STEP 2

When you want to eat it, simply combine 50g of the porridge mixture in a saucepan with 300ml milk or water. Cook for 5 mins, stirring occasionally, then top with a drizzle of honey and strawberries, if you like (optional). Will keep for 6 months.

Sardines & tomatoes on toast

Prep: 10 mins no cook

Serves 1

Ingredients

- 2 slices sourdough bread, toasted
- 1 large garlic clove , halved

- 135g can sardines in olive oil
- 130g cherry tomatoes , halved
- handful watercress
- 1 tbsp parsley , roughly chopped
- 1/2 lemon , to serve (optional)

Method

STEP 1

Rub each piece of toast with the garlic. In a small bowl, mix the sardines and their oil with the tomatoes and the watercress, then season. Sit half the mixture on each slice of toast, piled high. Scatter over the parsley and squeeze over the lemon, if you like.

Printed in Great Britain
by Amazon